Defeat from the Jaws of Victory

Defeat from the Jaws of Victory

Inside Kinnock's Labour Party

RICHARD HEFFERNAN
and
MIKE MARQUSEE

V

VERSO
London · New York

First published by Verso 1992
© Verso 1992
All rights reserved

Verso
UK: 6 Meard Street, London W1V 3HR
USA: 29 West 35th Street, New York, NY 10001-2291

Verso is the imprint of New Left Books

ISBN 0-86091-351-1
ISBN 0-86091-561-1 (pbk)

British Library Cataloging in Publication Data
A Catalogue record for this book is available from the British Library

Library of Congress Cataloging-in-Publication Data
A Catalogue record for this book is available from the Library of Congress

Typeset by York House Typographic Ltd, London
Printed in Great Britain by Biddles Ltd, Guildford and Kings Lynn

Contents

Acknowledgements

In the course of researching this book we interviewed scores of Party members – Labour MPs, trades unionists, Party employees, as well as numerous constituency activists – who all gave us fascinating insights and information. Though much of what they told us has not been referred to here directly, all of it helped to inform our understanding of what happened in the Labour Party during the past decade and more. We also read a huge volume of material from newspapers of all kinds, as well as official and unofficial Party documents.

Access to Tony Benn's remarkable personal archives was invaluable; we could not have written the book without it. In a party where memories are notoriously and conveniently short, the existence of the Benn archives is a safeguard for all our futures. Like Tony, we do not believe that Labour should make decisions behind closed doors. A great deal of our research has been devoted to finding ways to throw the doors open.

We would like to acknowledge the generous help given by the following: John Nicholson, Jane Ashworth, Jeremy Corbyn MP, Joan Maynard, Dennis Skinner MP, Ken Livingstone MP, Lol Duffy, Liz Williams, Tony Benn MP, Kathy Ludbrook, Ruth Winstone, John Wilton, Pauline Purnell, Reg Race, Mandy Moore, Alice Mahon MP, Dave Nellist, Kevin Flack, Bryn Griffiths, Steve King, Graham Bash, Helen Barry, Liz Davies, Tommy Coyle, Peter Hain MP, Mike Craven, Steve Taylor, Vladimir Derer, Vera Derer, Pete Willsman, Danny Nicol, Jim Mortimer, Dorothy Macedo, Liz Phillipson, Pete Firmin, Hilda Kean, Paul Gosling, Sarah Roelofs, Mark Hill, the late Eric Heffer, Greg Tucker, Joan Twelves, Steve French, Martha Osamor, Dave Lewney, Jean Calder, Rod Fitch, Gary Kent, Paul Davies, Paddy Reynolds, Keith Hackett, Lesley Mahmood, Sarah Norman, Sam Semoff, Guy Daly, Len Mason, Barry Robinson, Elsie Robinson, Tony Jennings, Mandy Mudd, Andy Winter, Percy Lea, Garth Frankland, Keith Nathan, Richard Hanford, Karl Statton, Mark Cole, Dave Palmer, Peter Doble, Dave Osler, Ron Huzzard, Geoff Sheridan,

James Curran, Fiona Winders, Mick Gosling and Colin Robinson. We also received assistance from many other Labour Party members who preferred to remain nameless. We hope that in future years no one in the Labour Party will be afraid to speak his or her mind in public. We also wish to acknowledge the assistance we received from staff at the Newspaper Library of the British Library, Colindale, the Labour Party Library, the British Library of Political and Economic Science and *Tribune*.

Of course, none of the above is in the least responsible for what follows. That burden belongs to the authors alone.

INTRODUCTION
Grinding an Axe

On an occasion of this kind, it becomes more than a moral duty to
speak one's mind. It becomes a pleasure.

Oscar Wilde

Few commentators were prepared to address Labour's real problems in
the wake of its fourth successive general election defeat. Here was the
principal party of opposition in a country bogged down in economic
crisis, in a society riven by social inequalities, unable even to secure its
core vote among youth, pensioners, manual workers, the poor or the
unemployed. Labour woke up on the morning of 10 April 1992 to find
itself bereft of policies and ideology, financially bankrupt and stripped of
one third of its membership. Without roots in the working class or in the
communities it claimed to represent, the Party was infected with a
culture of careerism that combined, in unhealthy measure, forelock-
touching and back-stabbing.

This was Neil Kinnock's legacy to the Party, but it was not his alone.
Kinnock's grip on the Party was made possible only by the support he
received at crucial moments from others – including many of those who
still remain at the top of the Party ladder. This book is the story of how
Labour came to this pass and the people responsible for it.

Of course, Labour's failure at the ballot box on the 9th of April was in
part symptomatic of a worldwide crisis of socialism, which would have
caused serious difficulties for Labour under any leadership. It was the
result also of a string of industrial defeats stretching back over a decade,
and reflected the prolonged shrinkage in trade union membership and
influence. Britain's continuing economic decline had removed the material basis for Labour's previous achievements in office. Within the
framework of a market-dominated economy, it had become harder
and harder to offer a convincing progressive alternative.

But Labour's crisis was not simply the result of objective political
forces. It was also the result of errors and failures of leadership, of

political mistakes and organizational blunders that could have been avoided. The task we have set ourselves in this book is to examine the political record of the Labour leadership over the past ten years. We recount the decisions taken at crucial junctures and expose the machinations behind them. We believe that Labour must face up to its recent history because without such a reckoning there can be no accountability and no renewal. We cannot avoid the mistakes of the past unless we know exactly what they were, when and how they occurred and who made them and why. It is easy enough to ridicule the left's alleged obsession with betrayal, but there is an assumption underlying that facile jibe that we cannot accept: that political failure does not matter as long as you get away with it.

Our concern to document the double talk, hypocrisy and opportunism of the Party hierarchy stems from our conviction that Labour, if it is to be effective in representing and ultimately empowering the people who support it, must be able to hold to account all those who speak in its name, all those who enjoy privilege, prestige and power at its expense. We have researched and written this book in an openly partisan spirit. We have an indictment to make and we make no apologies for pursuing it single-mindedly.

In the following pages we examine in detail the roles played by Neil Kinnock, leading Labour MPs, officials at Labour Party headquarters at Walworth Road, the shadow cabinet and the national executive committee (NEC). We chronicle Labour's general election campaigns of 1983, 1987 and 1992 and examine the policies and tactics that led to defeat.

By going behind Labour's closed doors we have sought to lay bare the reality of the Kinnock leadership and to detail the ways in which it managed the Party. We look at the myths surrounding the rise of the Labour left in the 1970s and the early 1980s and the backlash against it which has fuelled so many of the changes in the Party since 1983. We argue that these changes were imposed from the top down through bullying, bureaucratic manipulation and patronage. To prove our point, we present case studies of the Party's U-turn on unilateralism and its collusion in the Gulf War.

Kinnock's transformation of the Party could not have happened, however, without the acquiescence of a sizable chunk of the rank and file, whose demoralization and disorientation in the wake of successive defeats was skilfully exploited by the Party leadership. A key layer of activists, those former supporters of the "Bennite" insurgency who came to be known as the "soft left", proved themselves ready, willing and able to make any compromise and abandon any principle as and when it suited the interdependent requirements of the leadership and their own personal interests.

This is not a book about the Labour left (such a volume would need to be three times as long as this one!). It is about the Labour right. It is a portrait of the Labour establishment and its contending and shifting components. We make no claim that this is a comprehensive history; we have been deliberately selective. We have not been able to deal with Scotland or Wales, with the inner-Party debates about proportional representation, constitutional reform or Europe, with the stormy and at times baffling history of the Party in Liverpool, with the decline of the Party in rural areas, with Labour's internal conflicts over local government and the Poll Tax, with racism and the struggle for black self-organization in the Party, with the struggle by women in the Party for equal representation and power, with the Party's response to lesbian and gay rights, abortion and Ireland, with the Party's financial and organizational mess. These are vital concerns and we hope someone else comes along to record just how the Kinnock leadership failed the Party and the country on all these counts.

We believe that socialism remains essential for the future of the human race. Its remedies for the injustices of existing society are more pertinent than ever. As long-standing opponents of Stalinism, we have not seen any reason to abandon our democratic, pluralist and anti-authoritarian conception of socialism because of the collapse of the Soviet Union and its satellites. At root, modern society remains divided into two classes with irreconcilable economic and social interests. The mission of the Labour Party is to represent and serve one of those classes and challenge the sway of the other. To abandon that mission, to sever Labour's remaining links with the working class and the trade union movement, would be to abandon any chance of an opposition party in this country ever mounting a serious challenge to the status quo.

For us, the ideals of public ownership, of a planned economy whose managers are accountable to the majority of the population, of a democratic system of government rigorously controlled from the bottom up, remain irreplaceable. They must be renewed and revitalized.Without the political ambitions articulated by Clause Four of the Party constitution, Labour is rudderless, an organization bereft of principle or purpose.

Our partisanship is born of long, bitter and exhausting experience as grassroots Labour Party activists. We have done all the routine Party jobs; we have delivered leaflets and run street stalls; we have campaigned full-time in local and general elections, often for candidates with whom we had profound political disagreements; we have been embroiled in the inner-Party battle, more often than not on the losing side. But our bitterness stems from the fact that in the end it was Labour as a whole that was on the losing side – and that fate could have been avoided.

Nevertheless we are more committed than ever to our involvement in the Labour Party, which we believe is still the only vehicle for positive social change available to working people in this country. That is the reason for our strong opposition to attempts to change the Party's identity or to abandon its historical mission. This book is intended as part of that opposition. So, yes, we have an axe to grind. In this we are no different from all the other commentators on the Labour Party, whether they find space for their views in the *Guardian* or in the *Daily Mail*. The difference is that we are explicit about it; too many of the others pursue hidden agendas under the guise of allegedly objective reporting. They too played a part in Labour's defeat in 1992, and their role is chronicled in the pages that follow.

It will be said: all this is very well but what do socialist principles profit Labour if they lose elections? We do not underestimate for one minute the vital importance of winning elections. But we do not believe that electoral success – even less, the single-minded pursuit of electoral success – justifies all. We do believe that principles matter in politics and must matter to the Labour Party if it is to serve the people whose votes it solicits. If Labour politicians can do nothing but accommodate themselves to the prevailing political winds, then what is the point of having a Labour Party? If people are not prepared to take risks in the pursuit of political principles, the result will be endless reruns of the general election defeats of 1979, 1983, 1987 and 1992.

Our argument is not that all Labour has to do to solve its problems and win the next election is to adopt left-wing policies and to elect Tony Benn as leader, although these would be a start. Nor do we claim that the left itself has not made many mistakes. Indeed, both the Party's left and its right have had to learn over the past thirteen years that there are no short-cuts to political success. But we do argue that given time, resources and a united commitment from the leadership and the rank and file, Labour can win the next election on a socialist programme. In any case, that is the only way the Party can both win and then go on to exercise power in the interests of the people who vote for it. For those people, for the working class in all its diversity, there is no alternative to the Labour Party. They will sink or swim with it. We agree with Neil Kinnock's statement that "the people of this country deserve far better than they got on April 9th 1992". By analysing the errors of the past we hope to make some contribution to the vital task of refounding the Labour Party, of re-equipping it ideologically and organizationally, so that it is ready to win the next general election.

Prelude

I can never get to sleep with that fellow behind me.
Jim Callaghan, 1980 Labour Party Conference,
referring to Tony Benn

1

The Fall and Rise
of the Labour Right

"Never again"

On Monday morning, September 29th, 1980, top trade union official
Derek Gladwin, chair of the powerful conference arrangements committee (CAC), addressed the annual Labour Party conference in Blackpool.
Gladwin reported the proposed order of debate with his usual air of
authority, only to find himself immediately confronted with the first of a
succession of challenges from the floor.

To fervent applause, Ted Knight, then leader of Lambeth Council,
attacked the platform's attempt to obstruct debate on the local government cuts just announced by Environment Secretary Michael Heseltine.
Knight was followed to the rostrum by one Patricia Hewitt, delegate from
the St Pancras North constituency, who stepped up the attack on
Gladwin and demanded a "strategy against the Tory government cuts
around which we can unite and fight".[1]

Within a few years Hewitt was to become one of Neil Kinnock's closest
advisers, an architect of much of what passed for Labour's strategy
between the Party conference of 1983 and the general election of 1992.
Ted Knight, in contrast, was in 1986 to suffer surcharge and a five-year
disqualification from local government office – for pursuing precisely the
"unite and fight" strategy demanded by Hewitt in 1980. Strangely, it was
Knight and not Hewitt who was to be condemned for "gesture politics".
With his fellow ex-councillors he paid off his surcharge and served out
his disqualification only to find his return to Lambeth Council blocked
not by the Tory government or even the local electors but by the Labour
National Executive Committee (NEC), which in 1991 refused to allow his
name to go forward to the local Party for possible selection as a Labour
council candidate.

Read more than a decade after the event, the official report of the
proceedings of the 1980 conference is full of ironies. Not the least of them
is the fact that it is no longer possible to read the proceedings of

Party conferences at all, since Kinnock's NEC junked verbatim reports in 1990 – ostensibly on financial grounds, though the alleged savings of £20,000 hardly made a dent in the Party's ever-swelling overdraft.

That week in Blackpool saw the climax of a battle not simply between left and right, but between the bulk of the labour movement – the trade unions and the constituency parties in rare alliance – and the traditional right-wing establishment of Labour MPs within the Parliamentary Labour Party (PLP), personified by the leaders of the discredited Labour government of 1974–79. At the time, it seemed to many that the latter were in permanent retreat. Conference passed resolutions on economic policy, Europe, defence and local government that effectively repudiated the course taken by the last Labour government. It also endorsed the mandatory reselection of Labour MPs and the principle that the leader and deputy leader of the Party should be chosen no longer by MPs alone but by a wider electoral college including the constituency parties and the trade unions.

Looking back, it is startling to find how pervasive within the Party the arguments and aspirations of the left had become. In the wake of the economic, industrial, social and finally electoral collapse of the Callaghan government, no one could get far in the labour movement unless they dissociated themselves from its abysmal record.

In the course of the conference, Labour's education spokesperson, Neil Kinnock, denounced private schools and called for "an end to the division of our education system by chequebook and by class privilege".[2] Kinnock now stood second only to Tony Benn in the ballot to elect the seven NEC members chosen by constituency parties. In a bid to outflank the NEC from the left, he told delegates that its call for a return to pre-Tory levels of state funding for education was not going to be enough. Labour's "quarrel with the private school", Kinnock said, was about "the structure of power, about the perpetuation of privilege. . . . Do not let us just get rid of [then Tory ministers] Carlyle and Boyson. Do not let us just exchange with the Tories. Let us declare war on the system that breeds their attitude, that sustains their attitude, that benefits from their endowment and then we will create a system of education that for the first time in the history of this country makes its objective the elevation, the emancipation, the real liberty, the liberation of the British people."[3]

At first sight it might seem that the only continuity between Kinnock model 1980 and Kinnock model 1992 was verbosity, vagueness and an addiction to alliteration. However, as many of those present were well aware, Kinnock's speech was an attempt to make up ground that he had lost among the left in the constituencies because of his refusal in Parliament to commit a future Labour government to restoring education spending to pre-Tory levels. It is a measure of the political weather of the conference that Kinnock, the barometer, felt he had to set his course to the left. Nothing else would be acceptable to the grass roots of the movement, embittered by years of retreat and betrayal, and determined to change the policies and structure of the Party so that these could never be repeated.

"Never again" was, indeed, the watchword of the hour. Many commentators have sought to portray the Kinnock reforms of the late 1980s as efforts to break the Party from the stale traditions and bad habits of decades. In fact, the real attempt to break from the past, in particular from the past practice of failed Labour governments, was the Bennite rebellion of the late 1970s and early 1980s, which reached its apogee in Blackpool in 1980.

Of course, had Neil Kinnock and his supporters presented their much-acclaimed reforms as simply a return to the bad old days of the 1964–70 and 1974–79 Labour governments, there would have been few takers. Cannily, the leadership chose a different course. It claimed to be offering a radical transformation, a "modernization" of the Party and its policies. In order to pull off this big lie, the leadership needed to misrepresent the Bennite rebellion as backward-looking and "fundamentalist", appealing only to the shibboleths of the 1940s rather than facing the future of the 1990s.

But the last thing on the minds of the delegates gathered in Blackpool in the autumn of 1980 was a return to the labour movement's "old ways". Margaret Thatcher's first-term scorched earth policy brought British manufacturing industry to its knees as half a million workers joined the dole queue in her first twelve months in office. The government was implementing the biggest cuts seen in the public sector in a generation.

Labour's grass roots were outraged and impatient; they wanted immediate action to stop the rot. They wanted the Party to commit itself to take the measures needed not only to undo Thatcher's damage, but to ensure that it could not happen again. Thatcher's 1979 success – and all that had followed from it – was blamed on the failure of the Callaghan government. Anyone who had willingly supported the policies of that government therefore had to appear before the 1980 Labour conference in sackcloth and ashes.

In the economic debate, former Chancellor of the Exchequer Denis Healey pledged his support to the radical economic policy being proposed by the TUC–Labour Party Liaison Committee, backed by the left-wing NEC. The fact that this policy was largely the one that Healey had refused to implement as Chancellor was not lost on delegates. He was followed at the rostrum by an angry constituency representative who was loudly applauded for denouncing Healey's "crocodile tears". Earlier, Michael Foot, then deputy leader of the Party, had made a half-hearted attempt to exonerate the previous Labour government. But even he felt

compelled to reassure delegates that "when we get power in the future
. . . it is impossible for anyone to imagine that you can solve a crisis of
that scale and that nature with the economics of the market and a free
competitive society". Foot also acknowledged the dynamism of the new
forces pushing the Party to the left when he referred to the power of "the
labour movement of this country, reawakened and reinvigorated".[4]

The main economic resolution, moved by that master of the middle of
the road General and Municipal Workers Union (GMWU) general secretary David Basnett, would not have made it as far as the conference
agenda a decade later. It demanded restrictions on the flight of capital, an
"extension of public ownership with industrial democracy", "reflation of
public sector service spending", "a substantial cut in arms expenditure",
a "wealth tax", import controls, a 35-hour week with no loss of pay, and
recognition that "Britain's economic and social problems can only be
resolved by socialist planning".[5] In commending these "practical policies" to the conference, Basnett went out of his way to assure delegates
that a return to incomes policy, which had been pursued with such
disastrous consequences by the last Labour government, was out of the
question. Not one person spoke against the GMWU composite, which
was carried as Labour policy by a huge majority on a show of hands.

Contrary to the myths subsequently purveyed by the Labour right and
its friends in the media, the policies outlined in the GMWU resolution
were not traditional Labour Party fare. It was clear to everyone who
attended the 1980 conference, including the journalists who reported it,
that this was a new Labour Party rejecting its post-1945 heritage of
consensus and welfare-state paternalism. Replying to the economic
debate for the NEC, Tony Benn, in the first of his nearly daily conference
interventions, won a huge ovation when he called for "self-management
as an alternative to market forces or the hideous bureaucracy of some of
our nationalized industries . . . "[6] Benn singled out the necessity to
address the specific economic concerns of women and black people; he
talked about the challenges of new technology, the need for local and
regionally based economic strategies, the role of workers' co-operatives
and alternative industrial plans produced by workers themselves. "We
do not want all the policies to be determined on a centralized basis in
London," he said. Finally, he asked, "What does all this really mean from
the point of view of those whose support we shall seek in an election?
They are entitled to know." Benn then spelled it out. Three major pieces
of legislation would have to be passed within the first month of a new
Labour government: an Industry Bill to implement the GMWU resolution; a bill to transfer the powers needed to do that from the European
Economic Community (EEC) to the House of Commons; and a third bill
to abolish the House of Lords and thereby prevent the Tory-dominated
second chamber from sabotaging the first two bills. If necessary, he said,

Labour would have to create a "thousand peers" to vote the Lords into oblivion.[7]

The next day the newspapers lashed out at Benn and the Labour Party, but none of them was under the illusion that Benn's radical demands amounted to a return to the policies of 1945, as Basnett's successor as GMB general secretary, John Edmonds, was to put it some years later. On the contrary, the right-wing media saw Benn, the left programme and its supporters as a menace to the status quo that had to be crushed by any means necessary. One of those means was to give support to any Labour politician who was prepared to tackle Benn and who was capable of making inroads into his base of support within the Labour Party and the unions.

So wide was this base at the time that nearly everyone in the Party hierarchy had to pay lip service to its convictions. On behalf of the NEC Sam McCluskie denounced Tory privatization and called for "renationalization without compensation". He argued that the next Labour government should go beyond merely taking back into public ownership the firms privatized by the Tories and "should be looking at the profitable sections of private enterprise" for further nationalization.[8] Patrick Seyd, the delegate from Sheffield Hallam CLP, warned against ever again giving the Parliamentary Labour Party the whip hand; within a few years Seyd was one of the leading theorists of the great "realignment" of 1985 which did precisely that. When the NEC recommended that the next Labour government withdraw from the EEC, the only person to speak against the motion was David Owen.

In the defence debate a succession of constituency party speakers passionately backed unilateral nuclear disarmament and cuts in arms spending; only the defence spokesperson Bill Rodgers, later to join the Social Democratic Party (SDP), and the EETPU leaders spoke openly against the NEC recommendation. Even they had to proceed with caution, couching their arguments in the rhetoric of the peace movement and making plain their respect for venerable anti-militarists like Philip Noel Baker and Fenner Brockway, both of whom also spoke in the debate. They were joined by MP Robin Cook, who said, "I will not bandy words with Bill Rodgers as to whether his position or my position will be the better electoral asset. I cannot think of a more frivolous position on which to make up our mind on the central issue facing mankind. . . . I do not believe we have a hope of convincing people in the streets, in the factories, in the pubs so long as they see us hedging and fudging our opposition to nuclear arms . . ."[9]

From the platform, Joan Lestor promised the NEC's full support for unilateralism and opposition to any repeat of the old Labour backsliding on nuclear weapons: "There must be no more secret deals under a Labour government . . . it is morally wrong to build up arsenals for destruction." When the result of the vote embracing a non-nuclear defence policy was announced, it was greeted with a great display of joy by Neil Kinnock sitting on the conference platform.

In the local government and housing debate, Clive Betts, then a delegate from Sheffield Brightside Constituency Labour Party (CLP), later leader of Sheffield City Council and elected MP for Sheffield Hillsborough in 1992, moved a resolution committing the Party to reverse the Tory "right to buy" policy on council housing. When asked by the NEC to remit the resolution, Betts refused, declaring, "This party must be just as determined to put its political principles into practice as the Tories."[10] Gerald Kaufman, then shadow environment spokesperson, backed the Sheffield Brightside motion and promised delegates "a socialist housing policy, a policy based on need, not on the market".[11]

Perhaps the most revealing moment in the week came on Tuesday morning when Jim Callaghan, erstwhile Labour prime minister and still leader of the Party, addressed the delegates. He started with a wry, self-mocking reference to the polite – but merely polite – applause he received on taking the rostrum. It was the first of many defensive notes he was to strike during his speech. It was a much more informal, conversational performance than the contrived addresses to the television cameras in which Neil Kinnock was to specialize at later conferences. "I can never get to sleep with that fellow behind me," Callaghan said, indicating Tony Benn seated on the platform. When his reference to Clement Attlee was met with applause, he wryly observed, "There may come a time when even I shall be cheered by the constituency parties."

Like other right-wing speakers faced with that year's overwhelmingly left-wing audience, Callaghan made both the ritual appeal for unity and the safe, standard attack on the "centre parties" then being mooted in the press (at the time, future defectors David Owen, Bill Rodgers and NEC member Shirley Williams were still within the Labour fold). "Of course," Callaghan confessed, speaking of the last Labour government, "I know we got a lot of things wrong. . . We have all learned lessons from what has happened over the last two or three years. I do not exempt myself from that." It was an extraordinary admission of error from a national leader under pressure neither from the media nor from the opposition but solely from his own rank and file. "I have never seen so much talent as there is burgeoning in the Labour Party at the present time," Callaghan acknowledged. This time the applause was more than polite.[12]

The delegates were not going to be satisfied with crumbs from the leader's table. They wanted constitutional changes that would profoundly alter the distribution of power within the Party. Delegates referred repeatedly to the need to make these changes if Labour was ever again to have any credibility with its working-class electorate; they insisted that all the resolutions were useless unless the Parliamentary

Labour Party could be forced to implement them. The delegate from Hampstead CLP, a then little-known Ken Livingstone, announced that a Labour Greater London Council (GLC) would slash fares on London transport by 25 per cent, but added that unless there were changes in "the way in which the manifesto is drawn up, the way in which the leader of the Party is elected and [the] automatic reselection of MPs", all the good intentions on transport, housing and so forth would be "just talking" because the next Labour government would be no different from the last.[13]

This drive for constitutional change was embraced by nearly the entire extra-parliamentary Labour Party. Introducing the report of the commission of inquiry into the Party's structure and organization, David Basnett pointed out that the commission had received 2,460 pieces of written evidence from Party bodies and affiliates. Fifty separate resolutions had been submitted to conference on the question of the leadership election alone. Unlike the constitutional changes passed by the Kinnock leadership a decade later, which were imposed upon the Party from above, these reforms were entirely the product of rank-and-file opinion. No one was fully in control. Hence the confusion when the conference finally approved the principle of an electoral college for the leadership and deputy leadership elections but could not agree on its composition. A special conference had to be scheduled in January 1981 to decide on the final form such a college would take.

In the debate over the procedure for drawing up the Party's election manifesto, Patricia Hewitt again came to the rostrum. "Many of us at this conference are . . . angry about much of what the last Labour government did and a great deal of what the last Labour government failed to do. And we have a right to be angry and to do something about our anger . . . what we need and what we have a right to demand is a guarantee that the next Labour government will implement the policies which this Labour Party decided on and not the policies of a handful of Cabinet ministers and . . . civil servants."[14]

Once again, in this debate, it fell to Tony Benn to reply for the NEC. It was his most powerful speech of the week and one of the most incandescent indictments of the traditional, autocratic style of Labour leadership ever delivered at a Party conference. "We are talking about the lifeblood of democracy and we are not engaged in arid constitutional wrangles," he said, arguing the case against the PLP's veto over the contents of the manifesto: "if you have a veto, those who oppose policies do not bother to argue with conference, because they wait till the Clause Five meeting and kill it secretly, privately, without debate." This was a reference to the joint meetings of the shadow cabinet and NEC that decide Labour Party manifestos. Benn cited Callaghan's refusal to allow Party policy on abolition of the House of Lords into the 1979 manifesto.

"They let the conference pass it and it was vetoed secretly, late, quietly, before the Party could discover what had happened. That is wrong and it is out of that that mistrust in our Party grows."[15] In the course of his brief speech (brief in comparison with the 45-minute, carefully scripted – and press-released – platform perorations that became *de rigueur* for NEC members ten years later) he was interrupted for loud applause nine times.

Despite Benn's performance, the NEC's recommendation and the nearly unanimous support of delegates from the constituencies, the proposal was narrowly defeated. As so often, the GMWU swung the vote. It opposed the NEC recommendation on the grounds that there should be trust between the PLP and the NEC. But left-wingers were not unduly demoralized by what seemed at the time a merely temporary setback; they had won on nearly everything else, and they expected only to grow stronger in the coming years.

Looking back, however, it is clear that 1980 was the high-water mark for the left, at least on the national Labour Party stage. In the NEC elections left candidates, including Neil Kinnock, swept all seven places in the constituency section with handsome majorities. In those days there were as many as thirty-four candidates from across the political spectrum standing for the NEC constituency parties section; ten years later there were only fifteen. The left could also count on substantial support in the women's and trade union sections of the NEC. Its candidate for treasurer, Tribunite MP Norman Atkinson, easily beat former industry minister Eric Varley, a result that was to be reversed a year later when the Labour right began its long climb back into the driving seat.

Although after 1980 the left was in retreat on the NEC, for some years it continued to grow at the grass roots. Indeed it was the new spirit visible at the 1980 conference that attracted tens of thousands into the Party in the years that followed. There was an obvious incentive to join a Labour Party in which local activists seemed to have such a powerful voice. To the media and the Labour right, the conference may have seemed a shambles, but to many others it offered, for the first time in their lives, the prospect of a Labour Party that would take seriously its historical mandate to change society, that would respond to grassroots pressure, that was open, argumentative and democratic and determined to become more than simply one of the two pillars of the hidebound British establishment.

The 1980 conference revealed to Labour's traditional right wing just how little support it enjoyed in the Party outside its parliamentary enclave. It was appalled at the policies that had been passed and deeply shocked at the notion that the parliamentary elite should be held accountable to the rank and file. But it was divided in its response to this crisis.

One faction despaired of the Labour Party, and the 1980 conference clinched its decision to make a break. These were the self-styled "social democrats" who had supported Roy Jenkins before he had departed the House of Commons and Labour politics for the European Commission in 1977. In their own way they were as scathing about Callaghan as was the left. In their eyes, he had utterly failed to maintain control over the Party and had become far too indebted to the trade union leaders. In the face of the advance of a left that revolutionized the entire practice of the Party, this old Jenkinsite faction, now led by the media-styled "gang of three" (David Owen, Bill Rodgers and Shirley Williams), came to the conclusion that the Labour Party was no longer a suitable political vehicle for their ambitions. Suddenly they discovered moral objections to the way the Labour Party operated – especially to constituency general committees (which had elevated the three to the House of Commons in the first place) and trade union block votes (5 million of which had, in 1980, placed Shirley Williams on the NEC for the tenth year running). Having failed to persuade the Labour Party of the merits of their political case, they cried foul and set up a new political party.

The real visionaries of 1980 proved to be not David Owen and his gang but those right-wingers who resisted the siren song of a centre party and insisted on remaining within the structures of the labour movement. Many of these were MPs who had preferred Jim Callaghan over Roy Jenkins in the leadership election of 1976, which followed Harold Wilson's resignation. In 1980 Roy Hattersley, Gerald Kaufman, Jack Cunningham, Giles Radice and others were able to see one fact to which so many others – in the media and especially on the left of the Party – were blind: that the tide could and would turn, that the left gains were by no means entrenched, that it would take far more than a few conference victories to change the nature of the Labour Party.

However, it is doubtful whether even they saw that their most powerful allies in arresting and ultimately reversing the left onslaught would be some of the very people against whom they were so bitterly ranged in 1980, people who had risen to prominence as a result of the rank-and-file rebellion, including some of the stellar performers at the Blackpool conference.

The media ridiculed the Party's divisions and the occasional chaos of the proceedings in Blackpool. But many of the speakers insisted that what the media found so amusing was nothing less than democracy in action: a freewheeling, unscripted, bottom-up democracy more precious to the Party than any other political asset. There were 179 contributions from the conference floor during that week in 1980 – including 113 from constituency delegates.

A decade later it became commonplace to make jokes about the conferences of the early 1980s and to deride the unseemly spectacle of front-bench Labour MPs having to queue up for their turn at the rostrum. For many media pundits the ascendancy of the rank and file was an affront to their conception of politics as a game played out within the precincts of Westminster and a handful of television studios, a game in which they controlled the rules and kept the score. They loathed the 1980 Labour conference above all because they could not control its agenda, because it allowed to be placed before masses of people arguments – about alternative economic policies, about democracy, about workers' rights, about the horror of nuclear weapons – which they had spent much of their careers excluding from public view.

On the Friday morning, during the last session of the conference, the Party's general secretary, Ron Hayward, tried to make a virtue of the fierce debates and unpredictable votes. "Have a look at the Tory conference," he advised delegates, then joked, "We are going to do it to you next year. I will select the resolutions; you will darned well see no other resolutions will come on. We shall make sure the standing ovations are done at the right time. You cannot really get much life in a cemetery, can you?"[16] Ten years later, Ron Hayward could have been talking about Labour's own conferences, purged of dissent, calculated and controlled to the last detail. What he had meant as a joke was, under the leadership of Neil Kinnock, to become a reality.

The Abstainer

At the 1980 Labour conference, many union leaders, notably David Basnett, had urged Jim Callaghan to remain in post until the Party had agreed a formula for its new electoral college at the special conference scheduled for the following January. But soon after his return to London, Callaghan declared his intention of resigning as Party leader. His game plan was obvious: to ensure that his successor was elected not under the wider franchise of the new electoral college but under the old rules, which restricted the vote to Labour MPs. It was a pre-emptive strike against the rank and file designed, above all, to prevent Tony Benn from becoming leader of the Labour Party.

In the ballot of Labour MPs that followed, Michael Foot beat Denis Healey, who was then elected unopposed as deputy leader. Foot's victory owed a great deal to a realization amongst numerous MPs that at this moment only a leader from the left could carry the Party with him.

The special conference held at Wembley in January 1981 decided that in the electoral college that would choose Labour's next leader 40 per cent of the vote would be cast by affiliated trade unions, 30 per cent by the constituency Labour parties and and 30 per cent by Labour MPs. For the "gang of three", David Owen, Bill Rodgers and Shirley Williams, this was the excuse for a final break from Labour. They announced the formation of a new centre party, to be known as the Social Democratic Party (SDP).

To many in the Parliamentary Labour Party, the Foot–Healey combination represented a political balance, but to the new left in the constituencies it seemed distinctly unbalanced. At recent conferences, they had pushed policy sharply to the left and won breathtaking democratic reforms to the Party's constitution. The obvious next step was to use those reforms to elect a leadership prepared to advocate that policy. A direct challenge to Michael Foot was ruled out. After all, he was a long-time champion of the Party's new non-nuclear defence policy. Denis Healey, who did not support and was not prepared to campaign in favour of conference policies, was the obvious target. With one of their own at Foot's side as deputy leader, the left reasoned, the Party could be prised at last from the dead hand of the old parliamentary right.

Following intensive discussions across the left, on 3 April Tony Benn declared that he would stand for election as deputy leader at the next Party conference. To the left, Tony Benn, articulate, experienced and full of conviction, was an automatic standard-bearer. To the Labour right, he was a standing affront. Former Labour cabinet ministers, backed by the Tory press and the Labour-supporting *Daily Mirror*, queued up to condemn Benn for daring to use the Party's new democratic machinery. Few politicians have had to endure the abuse dished out to Benn during the months that followed. Fighting on an unambiguous political platform, he took his campaign to the grass roots of the Labour Party and the trade unions. In every major city in the country he addressed public meetings the size and like of which had not been seen in the labour movement for years. In those months Benn appeared to be everywhere, speaking to audiences big and small, groups of Party and union activists, peace campaigners, striking workers, unemployment marchers. Wherever he went he received an enthusiastic response not only from Party members but also from a substantial swathe of the public which felt bitterly betrayed by the last Labour government.

Benn sought the deputy leadership not as an individual politician offering himself for high office but as the chosen representative of a groundswell of left opinion among Labour's rank and file. It was because his message found a ready echo at the grass roots that Benn's campaign took the labour movement by storm throughout the spring and summer of 1981. Indeed, even though the candidate himself was hospitalized for much of the campaign, it continued unabated, belying the claim that this was simply a one-man band.

The energy and success of the Benn campaign and the possibility that he would win the election at the Labour conference in October shook the establishment – and not only the Labour establishment – profoundly. At this time Labour was ahead of the Tories in the opinion polls; the prospect of a Labour government under left leadership taking office in the near future seemed a real one to newspaper proprietors, television pundits, City bankers, industrialists, military men and other pillars of the status quo.

For the Labour right, the threat from Benn on the left was compounded by the threat from the newly founded SDP on the right. It was vital for them that Denis Healey won. But Healey and his supporters fought a wretchedly defensive campaign, evading the arguments and relying heavily on media hostility to their opponent. Healey knew that he had no base of support within the constituency parties and hoped that the trade unions and the payroll vote of Labour MPs would save him. Yet the strength of the Labour left was such that he felt obliged to respond to its political demands. He declared himself in favour of a Labour government that would "carry through a planned socialist programme". Its first objective would be to "restore full employment" and implement an "alternative economic strategy", which would require "real increases in public expenditure". As a supporter of what he called "genuine disarmament", Healey called for "the cancellation of Trident" and for a Labour government to "reduce the level of defence expenditure". This arch-European even said that he supported "restoring the sovereignty of Britain from control by the Common Market".[17] Such a political platform would have had the old right-wing warhorse branded a dangerous and expellable leftist in the Labour Party that Neil Kinnock was to lead into the 1992 general election.

When it did not echo Benn's rhetoric, the Healey camp was resorting to personal denunciations of him and his supporters. Unwilling to accept that their own failures had spurred the spontaneous growth of a new grassroots left wing, Labour's parliamentary leaders painted the Benn forces as an alien conspiracy which had to be extirpated from the Party. In July 1981, shadow Chancellor Peter Shore denounced Benn's supporters as people "who have joined our ranks not to further the democratic socialist cause but to subvert it . . . they should be strongly dealt with because there is no room for infiltrators, conspirators and wreckers in the Labour Party".[18]

One London Labour MP, Arthur Lewis, denounced his local constituency party as "100 per cent Trotskyist, Militant Tendency, Communist and IRA supporters".[19] Lewis was soon deselected by the constituency he detested so much. He then showed his loyalty to Labour by standing against it as an independent in the 1983 general election. He fared poorly. But his was only an extreme example of the mentality that gripped many in the Labour and trade union hierarchy. They were all too prepared to break the electoral back of their own party rather than see the left triumph. Their public attacks on Benn increasingly became attacks on the

Party's membership, and endless grist to the Tory media's mill. Labour was to pay an electoral price for this for years to come.

Michael Foot, who saw his function as keeping the warring factions from tearing the Party apart, came under intense pressure from members of his shadow cabinet to protect Healey and repudiate the Benn challenge. After some hesitation he publicly called on Benn to stand against him, and not Healey, if he disagreed with the direction in which he and Healey were taking the Party. Benn maintained that as the only candidate for the deputy leadership who had voted for Foot in both ballots in the 1980 leadership election, it would be strange if he now chose to stand against him rather than Healey, the deputy who had never supported Foot. The left was disgusted by Foot's attack. Asked to choose between the Party in the country and the Party in Parliament, Foot decided to back the latter, with a vengeance.

The trade union bureaucracy was also terrified by the Benn campaign, but for other reasons. In steering their unions in 1979–81 to support constitutional reform as well as left policies on the economy and defence, union bureaucrats were reacting against the debacle of the Wilson–Callaghan government. Many were under severe rank-and-file pressure, especially from shop stewards disgusted by the Labour leadership and determined to avoid any repeat of the anti-union policies of the last Labour government. But as early as 1980 Tony Benn observed in his diary that the ageing, mainly ex-Communist trade union left were "afraid that if you stir it up they will be defeated either by an angry right-wing backlash or by a new real left".[20]

This prophecy proved all too correct. The Benn campaign of 1981 addressed the trade union rank and file in a way never before seen in the Party, thus displeasing the union bureaucracy, which has always discouraged direct links between their own grass roots and the Labour left. During the frenzied months of the deputy leadership contest, the usually dormant and highly bureaucratized link between Labour and the trade unions flared briefly into life. Left demands for Party democracy naturally spilled over into demands for union democracy. Union leaders moved quickly to stamp out the flames.

Tom Jackson of the Union of Communication Workers (UCW) wrote to Labour's general secretary, Ron Hayward, demanding that he ban a planned appearance by Benn at a 1981 UCW conference fringe meeting. Hayward pointed out that such action was entirely outside his powers. Benn spoke to a gathering of over six hundred UCW delegates. The next day one third of the conference voted for Tony Benn, a strong showing in a union without a nationally organized left faction.

For the media the possibility of a strong Benn showing in the unions was further proof that the link between the Labour Party and the trade unions was a menace to society. They filled column after column with tales of undemocratic left-wing union bosses fixing votes for Benn against the wishes of the silent majority of "ordinary" union members who, it was assumed, were devoted to the Healey cause. The reality was not so simple.

The steelworkers' leader Bill Sirs cast his union's block vote for Healey without consulting his members, his executive or the union's delegation at the Labour conference. Clive Jenkins of the Association of Scientific, Technical and Managerial Staffs (ASTMS), who liked to see himself as Labour's kingmaker, was a vociferous opponent of the deputy leadership contest and had personally warned Benn not to stand. At Jenkins's urging the ASTMS executive recommended a vote for Healey. However, when Benn addressed a fringe meeting at the 1981 ASTMS conference, half the delegates turned up. The next day the conference voted narrowly to support him, against the executive's wishes.

The National Union of Public Employees executive, contrary to media expectations, did not advise its members to back Benn, though his campaign was closely associated with many causes close to NUPE's heart. Bernard Dix, its deputy general secretary, who had played a key role in turning NUPE towards the left, was in hospital throughout the summer. In his absence there was no national campaign for Benn within the union. On general secretary Alan Fisher's advice, the NUPE executive made no recommendation and a branch consultation backed Healey by 60 per cent to 40 per cent. The NUPE delegation at the Labour conference cast its vote accordingly.

The General and Municipal Workers Union (GMWU) executive, assuming that its own clearcut support for Healey would be easily ratified by the rank and file, consulted branches over the deputy leadership choice. It found widespread discontent with both candidates; in the end Healey won six regions and Benn three. In the EETPU, despite general secretary Frank Chapple's self-proclaimed championship of democracy, secret ballots and "one man one vote", when it came to casting the union's block vote for Labour's deputy leader there was no ballot and no consultation, just a unanimous decision by the executive council to back Healey.

The confusion within the Transport and General Workers' Union (TGWU) over the deputy leadership provided handy ammunition for the media campaign against the left. The TGWU executive, split down the middle, decided to consult. Consultation revealed a preference in the regions for Healey over either Benn or the third candidate, John Silkin, a TGWU-sponsored MP. This was not an expression of right-wing sentiment among TGWU members but simply an indicator of the balance of forces at this time among full-time officials in the regions. In the end, the union's delegation to the 1981 Labour Party conference was left to decide for itself how to cast its vote. It supported Silkin on the first ballot and, after a series of heated delegation meetings, cast its huge block vote for Benn in the second. As Benn stood for all the policies democratically determined by the TGWU biannual delegate conference, the union's supreme governing body, and Healey opposed most of of them, the delegation acted perfectly honourably, although Fleet Street leader-writers and the Labour right were up in arms.

By mid 1981 the union bureaucracies had had enough of constitutional reform; the spectre of left-wing power in the Party and of left-wing movement among their own rank and file frightened them. The apparent success of the SDP and Labour's collapse in the opinion polls under-mined their facile assumption that Thatcher was a temporary phenome-non and that the Labour Party would return to government at the first electoral opportunity. Panic seized the top echelons of nearly all the unions and the word went out: apply the brakes and silence the left.

But neither the trade union bureaucracy nor the old parliamentary right could have succeeded in stopping Benn without the crucial inter-vention of a small coterie of Labour MPs associated with the ostensibly left-wing Tribune Group. By 1981 sections of the group had become closely linked with the Labour leadership. Michael Foot himself was a long-standing member, as were Albert Booth and John Silkin, both members of the shadow cabinet. They had played no role in the upsurge of the new, extra-parliamentary Labour left after 1979 and looked upon it as a foreign, unappealing phenomenon. They were hostile to Benn, who had joined the group only briefly and belatedly, in early 1981. Some Tribune MPs, including Dennis Skinner, Eric Heffer, Joan Maynard, Frank Allaun and Reg Race, urged the group to make links with the left outside the House of Commons, but their arguments were always rejected by other leading Tribunite MPs such as Jack Straw, Oonagh McDonald and Neil Kinnock, who systematically opposed any sugges-tion that Tribune should broaden its base outside Parliament – on the grounds that such a step would narrow its base inside Parliament.

The strains within the Tribune Group came to a head with Benn's bid for the deputy leadership. Several Tribune MPs, among them Robin Cook, attempted to persuade Benn not to stand. But it was impossible for them to support Denis Healey and retain any credibility at the base of the Party. They began to look for a third candidate. Eric Heffer and Joan Lestor were approached but declined to stand. Neil Kinnock, although not involved in the initial attempts to derail the Benn campaign, was also mentioned as a candidate but he too refused nomination.

Eventually John Silkin, the Labour MP for Deptford in south London, accepted the challenge. Silkin's candidacy, stripped of its rhetoric, was from first to last nothing more than a "stop Benn" campaign promoted by Labour MPs unwilling or unable openly to support Denis Healey. In Silkin's posthumously published autobiography he entitled the chapter dealing with the deputy leadership contest "Belling Benn".[21] Though considered mildly left-wing and known as an opponent of the EEC, Silkin had held office in both the past two Labour governments and in reality had been a paid-up member of the Labour establishment for well over a generation.

Although Silkin had harboured leadership ambitions for some time, even he knew that he had no chance of winning. The best he could hope for was a decent showing in the first ballot before he was forced out and the electoral college was left, once again, with a clear choice between Healey and Benn. This was precisely the choice that many in the Tribune Group did not want to make. The Silkin candidacy gave them cover in the run-up to the conference, but would still leave them naked in the second ballot. At this crucial juncture a lead was needed and it was given by Neil Kinnock.

Elected to Parliament in 1970, at the age of twenty-eight, for the safe south Wales seat of Bedwellty, Kinnock had immediately joined the Tribune Group. Proclaiming Aneurin Bevan as his hero, he placed himself self-consciously on the far left of the Parliamentary Labour Party and set about building a reputation as a radical firebrand. In speeches delivered to constituency Labour parties, trades councils, Fabian societies, Co-op parties and local Tribune groups up and down the country, Kinnock demanded "an irreversible shift of wealth and power in favour of working people and their families", a phrase coined by Tony Benn and reproduced in Labour's 1973 programme. In a speech in the House of Commons in July 1972 Kinnock advocated the "100% nationalization of all the production and distribution industries".[22] Two years later, in an article in *Labour Monthly*, a magazine closely associated with the Communist Party, Kinnock wrote that there was no need "to be apologetic about the extension of public ownership or the establishment of workers' control" because "they are now prerequisites of the economic survival of Britain".[23] In 1975 Kinnock advocated the total confiscation of all incomes over £10,000 a year (£46,000 in 1992 prices).[24]

His tub-thumping speeches at conferences and rallies and his bonhomie won him friends in many quarters of the labour movement. But from early on he also acquired a reputation among parliamentary colleagues as a shameless self-publicist, prepared to play court jester to the Tribune Group in order to get himself a place on its public platforms. Eric Heffer recalled the Kinnock of those days as an "ultra-left" posturer who would say anything to attract attention. Tony Benn observed as early as 1976 that Kinnock was really just "a media figure".[25]

Kinnock had joined the Campaign for Nuclear Disarmament (CND) in 1961, at the age of nineteen; he opposed the Vietnam War and repeatedly vilified the US State Department and all its works. In the 1970s he made a name for himself as a critic of the Royal Family. He voted against a

Labour government-proposed increase in the Queen's allowance in February 1975 and in 1977 he joined Dennis Skinner in boycotting the Queen's Speech in the House of Lords. After a brief stint as Michael Foot's parliamentary private secretary in 1974, Kinnock spurned Callaghan's offers of junior ministerial office and became instead a persistent and public critic of the Labour government. As a result, he was elected in 1978 to the constituency parties section of the NEC, along with Dennis Skinner.

As a member of the Campaign for Labour Party Democracy Kinnock had supported the left's crusade to democratize the Party. At the NEC in June 1979 he backed both mandatory reselection and proposals to widen the franchise for the election of the Party leader.[26] In July 1979 he seconded a proposal by Eric Heffer that the manifesto should be controlled by the NEC and not decided by the cabinet, the shadow cabinet or the Party leader.[27] In September 1979 he proposed "that all levels of the Party leadership and all aspects of the work of the Party are fully accountable and responsive to the wishes of the membership".[28]

Following Labour's 1979 defeat, Callaghan appointed Kinnock education spokesperson, though he had no previous ministerial experience and had not won a place in the shadow cabinet. In early 1980, the *Sunday Times* reported that Kinnock was part of a group of left-wingers on the NEC who were seeking to detach themselves from Tony Benn and what it termed the "hard left". At the time, Kinnock vehemently denied the charge, but the storm aroused by Benn's deputy leadership bid changed his tune.

In an article published in *Tribune* in September 1981, Kinnock declared that he had decided not to vote for Tony Benn and would abstain in the second round of the ballot to be held at the Brighton conference in October. Whilst Healey was insupportable because of his past record, Kinnock argued, Benn was equally insupportable because of the divisions he was creating in the Party. In reality, Kinnock had decided that at all costs – including a Healey victory – Benn must not win the election. But he knew that the only way to achieve this was by setting up a third camp between Healey and Benn, a refuge for beleaguered careerists of both left and right. Thus the "soft left" was born, not in the spirit of ideological innovation as so many of its acolytes later claimed, but in a fit of old-fashioned political expediency.

For Kinnock, it was a calculated risk. It could have been his undoing but was, in the end, his making. Until this time he had given no indication that he would not support Benn. His *Tribune* article made headlines in Fleet Street. A startling break from the left by one of its parliamentary stars was a major development in Labour's ongoing civil war, with which the media were fascinated. Kinnock's manoeuvre helped to take Healey and the discredited right wing out of the firing line.

The crying need for radical change at the top of the Party was now subordinated to a confusing debate about "divisive" tactics in which the goalposts were constantly moved at the convenience of a small parliamentary elite.

At that October's conference, as the ballots were cast and counted on the Sunday evening in the conference hall, both left and right knew that the future of the Labour Party was at stake. Rumours multiplied. Which way would NUPE go? What price the TGWU? The result was bound to be close; the hopes and fears of left and right rose and fell minute by minute. Healey's final margin of victory in the second ballot was desperately narrow: 50.426 per cent to Benn's 49.574 per cent.[29] The deputy leadership of the Labour Party, and much more besides, had been decided by less than 1 per cent of the total vote cast in the electoral college.

Benn had humiliated Healey in the constituencies, winning 78 per cent in the first ballot to 17 per cent for Healey – a clear indication that Benn was the overwhelming choice of Party members. In the trade union section Healey was the clear victor, but his margin of 3,969,000 to 2,383,000 was much too close for comfort for the right wing. In fact, it was a remarkable showing for Benn, given the usual political composition of the delegations of affiliated unions, and their traditional role as leadership loyalists.[30]

In the end, the result was decided by members of the Parliamentary Labour Party. In the first ballot Healey won the support of 124 MPs, Benn 55 and Silkin 65. In the second ballot Healey collected 137 MPs to Benn's 71. And 35 MPs who had voted for Silkin in the first ballot abstained on the second, including Neil Kinnock, Norman Buchan, John Evans, Doug Hoyle, Robert Kilroy-Silk, Joan Lestor, Alf Morris, Martin O'Neill, Stan Orme, Jeff Rooker and John Silkin himself. If only 10 of these had voted for Benn, the left would have won. Indeed, 16 MPs, including Frank Dobson, Alf Dubs, Judith Hart, Jack Straw and Robin Cook, did vote for Silkin in the first ballot and Benn in the second while 13, including Frank Field, voted for Silkin in the first ballot and switched to Healey in the second.[31] Over half the MPs who voted for Healey represented constituencies that backed Benn. In addition, a dozen Labour MPs voted for Healey and then departed for the SDP, most within days of the end of the conference.

Healey's narrow victory was the prelude for a right-wing backlash which steadily gathered strength in the succeeding years. It began at the 1981 conference with the removal of five left-wingers from the NEC by a right-wing trade union cabal organized by Roy Grantham of APEX. Charlie Kelly of the Union of Construction, Allied Trades and Technicians (UCATT) and Bernard Dix of NUPE were replaced by Roy Evans of the Steelworkers and David Williams of the healthworkers' union COHSE. In the Women's Section, Margaret Beckett and Renee Short lost their places to Betty Boothroyd and Gwyneth Dunwoody, and treasurer Norman Atkinson was defeated by Eric Varley. This was the first move in the construction of the solid right-wing bloc that was later to enable Kinnock as leader to win vote after vote on the NEC. But for the moment, the balance was still very fine; the right had secured a majority thanks to the manipulation of a handful of trade union block votes, not through any change in political alignments at the base of the Party.

Because of his well-publicized intention to abstain in the deputy leadership vote, Kinnock's vote in the constituency section of the NEC fell by 61,000 while Benn's vote increased by 64,000. But Kinnock had the satisfaction of seeing the tide beginning to turn away from Benn and the left. More important, he had the quiet gratitude of the trade union bureaucracy, now clearly moving decisively to the right, as well as that of the Party leader, deputy leader and other key figures in the shadow cabinet. By breaking with the Labour left he had proved his credentials with the media and the establishment; when push came to shove, they now knew, Neil Kinnock could be counted on to serve their interests.

Who Lost the 1983 General Election?

Within the Labour Party, long before June 1983, the right were determined that the left should take the blame for the impending defeat at the ballot box. This did not mean that they actually surrendered control of the election campaign to the left. On the contrary, as polling day approached they took an ever firmer grip on the Party, organizationally and politically.

Immediately after the election, Gerald Kaufman dubbed the manifesto "the longest suicide note in history". As a shadow cabinet and campaign committee member Kaufman was in fact intimately involved in drawing up and presenting the manifesto, but he had made it abundantly clear that he did not support key parts of it and indeed refused to campaign on it in his own constituency. His quip stuck. Labour's 1983 manifesto has become an object of scorn among thousands who have never laid eyes on it. Whatever its faults, the manifesto was the product of the most extensive and democratic consultations ever undertaken by the Labour Party. The NEC co-opted Party members with direct experience – on the shop floor, in local community campaigns or in well-established pressure groups – onto working parties which drew up the preliminary plans for the manifesto. Their input gave the document the kind of concrete detail so rarely seen in election propaganda. Much of the fresh policy impetus came from new members attracted into the Party by the recent democratic reforms and by the dynamism of Benn's deputy leadership challenge.

After the general election, this new input was derided as the "capturing" of the Party by "special interest" groups. In fact, it was nothing other than a momentary broadening out of policy-making beyond the "special interests" of the shadow cabinet.

The 1983 manifesto was drawn from the 279 pages of *Labour's Programme 1982*, which itself was the result of ten years of sharp debate and bitter experience within the Party and the unions. The programme was clearly a left-leaning document, with unequivocal and detailed commitments to economic planning, public ownership, redistribution of wealth, women's rights (a major innovation), nuclear disarmament and withdrawal from the EEC. Some commentators have described the 1982 programme as a Bennite credo, but they miss two key points. First, plenty of left-wing policies (on NATO, Ireland, private schools, nationalization and nuclear power) never made it to the final draft. The programme had been hammered out within both the NEC and the TUC General Council over a long period of time and reflected the delicate political balance on both those bodies. Second, the key commitments – to planning, public ownership, restoration of trade union rights, EEC withdrawal and nuclear disarmament – were not the exclusive property of the left wing but were supported by the vast bulk of the CLPs and trade unions and even a sizable number of Labour MPs.

But once the 1982 conference passed the programme, which was supposed to provide the basis for the manifesto, control of Labour's policies – and above all of their presentation – came to be increasingly in the grip of the rump of right-wing MPs most hostile to them. Even before the 1982 conference, members of the shadow cabinet were anonymously quoted in the press describing the programme as "absurd" and "an affront".[32] Denis Healey, at that time the Party's foreign affairs spokesperson, made a series of well-publicized moves to get the NEC to delete any commitment to unilateral nuclear disarmament, but could win support only from the hardest members of the NEC right wing such as John Golding, Gwyneth Dunwoody and Eric Varley. As for Party leader Michael Foot, he cancelled the press conference scheduled to launch *Labour's Programme 1982* because he preferred to attend the Commons to support Thatcher's motion congratulating the Queen on the birth of Prince William.[33]

The programme was endorsed by the 1982 Labour conference by 6,420,000 votes to 224,000, an illustration of the breadth of support it commanded within the Party. Then the horse-trading over the shape of the final manifesto at the joint NEC and shadow cabinet Clause Five meetings began. Benn had already been threatened by Foot with exclusion from these meetings for supposedly leaking their discussions to *Tribune*. But when, in a single week in November 1982, Callaghan, Healey, Hattersley and Shore all made well-publicized attacks on key aspects of Party policy (including nuclear disarmament, trade union rights, EEC withdrawal and import controls), Foot said not a word.

In April 1983 the NEC home policy sub-committee approved Labour's interim manifesto, *New Hope for Britain*. Healey succeeded in getting the commitment to scrap Polaris replaced by a promise to include the submarines "in nuclear disarmament negotiations in which Britain must take part".[34] In the days before the meeting of the home policy committee that agreed the draft, the press reported unnamed shadow cabinet members describing this watered-down version of *Labour's Programme 1982* as merely a background document; they dropped clear hints that Labour in office would not feel bound by any of these commitments.

During the election campaign, the manifesto sold 85,000 copies and was one of the few items in the Walworth Road catalogue in which the public showed any interest.[35] The real problem with the manifesto was not its length but the fact that it was left to dangle in a political vacuum. As Tony Benn put it in the post-election issue of *New Socialist*:

> The Conference was strongly behind the manifesto policies; the main centre of opposition was the PLP . . . in the years leading up to the election there was no proper parliamentary advocacy of those policies. The case for a non-nuclear defence strategy, for the closure of US bases, for British withdrawal from the Common Market; for the full alternative economic strategy was simply not put in the Commons.[36]

The right had a ready reply: it was no good blaming the shadow cabinet; the voters did not support these policies. But while it is true that the bulk of traditional Labour voters may not have been straining at the leash for radical socialist policies, the data does not support the casual but widespread assumption that Labour's policies in the 1983 election were intrinsically unpopular. In the months leading up to the general election, opinion polls showed that 61 per cent of the public favoured a redistribution of income and wealth towards ordinary people and 51 per cent favoured withdrawal from the EEC.[37] The most exhaustive academic work on the subject, *How Britain Votes*, concluded that if detailed policy statements were decisive, "Labour would not in fact have gone down to defeat at all." On unemployment and inflation, taxation and government spending, Labour's policies were preferred to those of the Tories. Even on defence, by the end of 1982 58 per cent opposed cruise missiles and 56 per cent opposed Trident; 47 per cent wanted removal of US nuclear bases and though only 35 per cent were in favour of getting rid of the "British deterrent", even this was a good 7 per cent more than voted Labour a few months later.[38]

In the end the right wing's real objection to the manifesto was that there were things in it with which they disagreed; in this they were no different from the left. But where the left, contrary to popular mythology, was prepared to close ranks behind the manifesto and make a stab at winning the election, the right had already written it off as lost and were preparing for the aftermath.

In later years the 1983 campaign came to be synonymous with all that was inept, boring, embarrassing and "old-fashioned" about Labour under Michael Foot's leadership. The chief criticisms were that the campaign was badly organized and its media strategy non-existent. These failings were later used by the Kinnock leadership to justify changes in Party organization, policy-making and campaigning methods. They became a stick with which to beat the left, and an excuse for excluding the rank and file from all real influence.

There can be no doubt that the 1983 election campaign at a national level was a fiasco. But was the left really responsible? Formal responsibility rested with the "campaign committee" established in late 1982, which was dominated by trade union leaders and members of the shadow cabinet. Of the forty members at least half could be considered firmly on the right – including chief whip Michael Cocks, Gwyneth Dunwoody, John Golding, Denis Healey, Roy Hattersley, Gerald Kaufman and John Smith – and another sixteen in the centre – including Foot, Kinnock, John Silkin, Stan Orme, David Basnett and the Party's future general secretary, Larry Whitty. Only a handful were on the left – Eric Heffer, Arthur Scargill and Judith Hart. Among NEC members excluded from the campaign committee were Tony Benn, Joan Maynard, Jo Richardson and Dennis Skinner.

Midway through the campaign, the committee appointed a much smaller "action group" composed of Golding, Hattersley, general secretary Jim Mortimer and the Walworth Road department heads; its aim was to try to focus the campaign on "jobs and social services, including the NHS and pensions" but, according to Mortimer, "it was no more successful than the campaign committee in avoiding unexpected diversions".[39]

The campaign was run from Party headquarters at Walworth Road (serving for the first time as an election base) by Joyce Gould, who had been promoted from assistant national agent and national women's officer to campaign organizer. The fact that Gould later escaped blame for the campaign debacle while Mortimer was heaped with it suggests that political alignments were more important to the post-1983 leadership than any genuine assessment of what really went wrong. Though Gould was responsible for some of the most inept elements in the campaign, including the allocation of full-time staff, the distribution of literature and the co-ordination of campaigns in marginal constituencies, she was promoted to director of organization in the shake-up of Party headquarters in 1985.

The right-wing majority on the NEC inaugurated the campaign by imposing sitting MP Reg Freeson as parliamentary candidate on a reluctant Brent East CLP, which preferred GLC leader Ken Livingstone. Livingstone was effectively barred from Labour's headquarters in Walworth Road throughout the election campaign, even though his personal standing in the opinion polls exceeded that of Michael Foot. Indeed, support for Labour in London was growing while in the rest of the country it was on the slide. When Thatcher decided to include abolition of the GLC in her manifesto, Gerald Kaufman, at that time Labour's environment spokesperson, equivocated on Labour's response when quizzed about it on television. Within a year, opposition to the GLC's abolition would command overwhelming support among Londoners.

Throughout the three-week campaign, John Golding, the right's number one political fixer, was ever-present at Walworth Road. Shadow cabinet members toured the country according to whim and their own personal agendas, making statements without co-ordination or approval from head office. Neil Kinnock hardly set foot in Labour's headquarters, barnstorming the country as one of Labour's most visible campaigners, arranging his own engagements and issuing his own statements to the press. Peter Shore led off at every one of the first week's daily press conferences, pressing his own economic hobbyhorses regardless of whatever else the media were covering. Michael Foot and Denis Healey spoke at well over one hundred engagements each during the campaign, but the schedules of both were arranged exclusively by their own parliamentary offices, without reference to Jim Mortimer or Walworth Road. "Speeches by leading public figures appeared often to be uncoordinated," Mortimer wrote, generously, in his NEC report on the election.[40] He also pointed out that the Labour campaign was hampered by the lack of a national membership list and the fact that "some of the office equipment is out-dated and the existing computer breaks down frequently".[41] Again, after the election, these faults were attributed to the left, when in fact they were the result of many years of tenacious right-wing control over an apparatus whose main purpose was always seen as controlling, not serving, the Party membership.

By common consent Labour's campaign literature was of poor quality. The posters and leaflets produced by the central campaign team were dull and confusing and the manifesto did not include a single visual illustration. There was no printed campaign handbook, as there had been in previous years, allegedly because of lack of cash, and policy briefings and other materials for local campaigns were delayed because the research department had been engaged in ironing out policy confusions, notably on defence and the economy, up to the very moment the election was called. Only forty-three constituencies enjoyed the services of a full-time agent during the campaign and the rest were run entirely on a voluntary basis.[42] The Tories, by contrast, had full-time officials operating in well over two hundred constituencies.

Labour's general election fund was heavily dependent on the trade unions: £2,171,000 out of Labour's total £2,236,000 national general election income came from Trade Unionists for a Labour Victory. As usual, the TGWU was the single biggest donor, weighing in with £508,000; the next-largest was the GMBATU, as the GMB then was, with £306,000. The left-leaning NUPE contributed £220,000 but the right-wing Amalgamated Engineering Union (AEU), then with over 750,000 members, gave only £150,000, while the Scargill-led National Union of Mineworkers (NUM), with fewer than one third as many members, donated £234,000.[43]

Labour's media strategy in the campaign was widely and deservedly pilloried, and was later used by the Kinnock regime as a convenient point of contrast. But a quick review of it is revealing. Nick Grant, a member of Labour Solidarity, a right-wing pressure group, had taken over as press and publicity director in January 1983. At the outset of the campaign he had only one press officer in post out of an establishment of three; seven others had to be drafted in during the campaign. Not surprisingly, given the ad hoc nature of the team, the NEC report later complained of "poorly co-ordinated" poster and advertising initiatives. But why was the right-wing majority on the NEC (and the trade union bureaucracy, which was footing the bill) so late in acting on such an obvious campaign requirement? Clearly, for those running Labour's campaign there were more pressing priorities.

The daily press conferences at TUC headquarters at Transport House rapidly became bear gardens in which the press baited Jim Mortimer and the various shadow cabinet members who appeared with him. Though planning for these encounters with the media was the top item at every meeting of the campaign committee, at no time was Labour able to set the media agenda. The political timidity and staggering lack of imagination in the presentation of Labour policies was a reflection of the huge gulf between those who had created the policies, the Party's rank and file, and those responsible for presenting them, the shadow cabinet.

Grant's first publicity initiative had been a ten-day advertising blitz for the May 1983 local elections. According to the official report, "research had indicated opposition to slanging between political parties and a strong sense of hopelessness and helplessness among the public".[44] Grant, advised by advertising agents Wright and Partners, decided an appropriate theme would be "Think Positive, Vote Labour". The campaign committee decided that, having already invested £200,000 in this slogan, it should be adapted for the general election as "Think Positive, Act Positive, Vote Labour". Apart from the grammatical solecism involved, the slogan left people all over the country bewildered. At the NEC, Frank Allaun tried at the last moment to get it changed to "Peace,

Jobs, and Freedom", a slogan that tied in with Labour's chief manifesto themes and had been used at the previous year's conference. The right-wing NEC majority, advised by Nick Grant, stuck to the "Think Positive" slogan.

During the last week of the campaign Grant and the "action group" came up with a new theme: "Are you going to vote for no tomorrow?" This was reinforced by a decision to focus on six "positive" Labour policies agreed by the campaign committee including jobs, rents, pensions, prices, child benefit and the NHS. Clearly this was a desperate bid to focus on issues perceived to be helpful to Labour, but it was already too late; the shopping-list approach, later condemned by the Kinnock leadership as a "left-wing fetish", further strained the Party's credibility.

The first four televised party election broadcasts starred Foot, Kinnock, Shore, John Smith, David Basnett, Roy Hattersley, Denzil Davies, Denis Healey and Joan Lestor. The final production, entitled "The Team", aimed to reassure the public by displaying Labour's competent, sensible, collective leadership; it featured Foot, Healey, Shore, Hattersley, Kinnock, John Smith, Lestor and Ann Taylor (the last two about to lose their parliamentary seats). As the majority of the personnel involved were former ministers in the Wilson and Callaghan governments they may well have contributed to a reawakening among the electorate of what the official NEC report described as "the memory of the disagreements and strife of the closing days of the last Labour government".[45]

Although defence policy was virtually excluded from the Labour campaign, it was the issue that filled the most newspaper column inches; it also accounted for a high proportion of the phone calls from the public to Walworth Road. Of fifteen separate leaflets issued by Party headquarters during the campaign only one, a confusing little piece headed "End the Arms Race", was directly concerned with nuclear disarmament. Only one other, "Defence and Jobs", even referred to the issue. Of all the information papers and research notes issued by Walworth Road only one, curiously entitled "Towards a Real Zero Option", dealt with the election's most vexed issue.

Midway through the campaign, former Prime Minister Jim Callaghan delivered a carefully timed denunciation of Party defence policy at a public meeting at a school in his Cardiff constituency. Thanks to advance notice from Callaghan's office, the national media, including television cameras, were all at hand. This intervention caused mayhem in the Labour camp and demoralized Party workers, who had to cope with increasingly sceptical responses on the doorstep. Yet it took three days before the Party's daily briefing for Labour candidates responded. Michael Foot's own confusions about whether or not Labour would really get rid of all nuclear weapons in the lifetime of a single Parliament also made headlines. A spreading cloud of political double talk obscured the basic humanistic message about nuclear disarmament which, opinion polls had shown, was capable of commanding substantial public support.

Even on unemployment, which the campaign committee declared to be the Party's leading election issue, the right's hatred of the left paralysed Labour's campaign. One illustration is the leadership's quandaries about the second People's March for Jobs, which made its way from Glasgow to London during the campaign. Initially, the proposal for the march was resisted by Party and union leaders. Party officials claimed it would detract from other necessary activities. Under pressure from trades councils and some large affiliates, the TUC was forced to back the People's March, but the Labour leadership stayed away. In contrast to the enormous demonstration in Trafalgar Square that had welcomed the first People's March two years before, there were hardly any Labour Party banners and few leading Party speakers to greet the second march when it entered central London on June 5th, days before the general election. The first march had united the labour movement and impressed on a broad public that an alternative existed to Tory cynicism and despair. For several weeks it had ensured that unemployment surfaced as the number one issue of public concern in the opinion polls. In 1983 an ideal opportunity to reawaken that concern and identify Labour with it was thrown away – simply because the priority of the Labour right was to deny the left any platform during the general election.

Michael Foot toured Britain tirelessly but his speeches were windy, vague and unsuitable for televised soundbites. In the preceding years he had expended huge energy in his struggle to contain the left, hold the Parliamentary Labour Party together and maintain some semblance of order in the Party ranks. His aim through it all was undoubtedly the election of a Labour government. But when the time came to take on the Tories he was woefully inadequate. The problem was not just that he was old or that he walked with a stick or that he had white hair or dressed shabbily or spoke in long meandering sentences. All these things became damaging only because they seemed to confirm the general impression of a dithering and divided Labour Party.

From late 1982 onwards there had been a well-publicized whispering campaign against Foot in the shadow cabinet. The "Foot must go" drive undermined the Party's public image and disorientated the rank and file. It should be remembered that not one constituency party, trade union or other labour movement body passed a resolution calling for Foot's resignation; the demand originated within the shadow cabinet and was then taken up by the media, including the pro-Labour *Daily Mirror*. This whispering campaign reached its height in the wake of the disastrous defeat in the Bermondsey by-election, which had followed eighteen months of attacks on the Labour candidate, Peter Tatchell, by the Party leadership. It ceased only when Labour held Darlington in a subsequent by-election.

The nadir for Foot (and for Labour) was the leader's appearance on *Panorama* on June 6th, three days before the election. When Robin Day accused Foot of "appeasing the extreme left", Foot answered, "I repudiate all suggestions that I have appeased the extreme left. . . . I am the first leader of the Labour Party that has taken action against the Militant Tendency." He thus confirmed to millions of viewers that the Party he led was indeed, as the press claimed, an organization riddled with alien subversives. When asked by Day if in Bradford North he would back Ben Ford, the deselected Labour MP, now standing in the election as a so-called "moderate Labour" candidate, or the officially endorsed Labour standard-bearer, Pat Wall, a Militant supporter, Foot replied, "I'm not going to answer in that way."[46] Pressed by Day, Foot struggled vainly with basic questions about Labour policy. Every fudge and contradiction he himself had negotiated in recent years came back to haunt him: on Polaris, on unilateral and multilateral disarmament, inflation, pay policy, public spending and trade unionism. Quotes from Peter Shore and Jim Callaghan criticizing Party policy were thrown at him. Finally, in the wake of outbursts by Healey and Kinnock over the Tories' exploitation of the "Falklands factor", Day asked Foot if he thought "it fair or relevant that the sinking of the Belgrano should be an issue in this campaign in any way?" Foot replied that he did not think that it should be an issue; instead, he averred that the campaign should concentrate on what he called "the great issues".[47]

Labour's campaign was at its strongest in constituencies where the new membership and zeal born of the Bennite upsurge found expression. Here the manifesto was not forgotten; in constituencies dotted around the country unilateralism, EEC withdrawal, public ownership and planning all featured extensively in local literature. Election meetings were held in constituencies which had not seen a Labour public meeting in decades, and Party membership grew across the country as Labour recruited people attracted to the ideals outlined in the manifesto. Even Walworth Road had to acknowledge that in marginal seats "there was a high turnout of Party workers".[48] But on top of the endless attacks in the press, the poor campaign and the stream of own-goals from the leadership combined to give the Party no chance to stem the political tide that swept Labour away on polling day.

The sheer scale of the Labour defeat on June 9th traumatized the Party. A 3.8 per cent swing to the Tories left Labour with only 28.3 per cent of the vote (compared with 36.9 per cent in 1979), its lowest share since 1918. The Party now had fewer MPs than at any time since the 1930s. It lost a record number of deposits (112 compared to 22 in 1979), and came third or worse in 292 constituencies.

The flight of the skilled working class away from Labour, particularly in the West Midlands and the south, which had begun in 1979, continued apace. Less than 40 per cent of all trade unionists voted Labour. In the southern region outside London, Labour could not manage to win a single one of the seventy-seven seats. In the south-west it won only one and in the eastern region only two. The only areas in the country where Labour received more than 50 per cent of the vote were the hard-core inner cities and the old coalfields. Not surprisingly, these constituencies were to become the sites of the two great battles against Thatcher during the coming Parliament.

After the 1979 defeat the Party leadership had insisted, "No inquests". Again in 1983 there was no Walworth Road investigation and no formal NEC or shadow cabinet analysis. Instead, shadow cabinet members, rightward-moving activists and a supporting troop of pundits and academics rushed into print to explain why and how Labour had lost the election. For the most part, the aim of these outpourings was simply to scapegoat the left. Eric Hobsbawm, for one, blamed the left for "engaging in a civil war rather than fighting the right" but offered not a word of criticism of the civil war waged by Callaghan, Healey, Golding, Shore and Hattersley – entirely outside the Party's rules and structures and largely through the pro-Tory press.[49] Members of the rightward-moving Labour Co-ordinating Committee (LCC), hitherto one of the major components of the Bennite bloc, took up the theme and claimed the left/right split had immobilized the Party; mass politics, they argued, was the way forward. They were happy to ignore two truths: first, the Labour right with which they were seeking an accommodation would always oppose "mass politics" of any kind; second, "mass politics" was already being practised by some of the most solidly Bennite constituency parties – and with good electoral results.

A more convincing postmortem was delivered by Jim Mortimer at the 1983 conference. He concluded that the cause of Labour's defeat was "primarily political and not organizational".[50] While acknowledging some of the failings of the campaign as run by Walworth Road and the shadow cabinet, Mortimer pointed out that Labour's private polls had shown clearly that there was widespread discontent about unemployment but no faith in Labour's ability to reduce it; a majority of the electorate believed a Conservative government would provide more effective economic management. Many people also believed that Labour was making promises it could not fulfil. The polls also showed how profoundly Labour had been damaged by its "reputation for disunity and internal strife"[51] – a reputation that owed not a little to the readiness of leading members of the shadow cabinet to engage in denunciations of the left, personal attacks on leading Labour MPs and criticisms of agreed Party policy.

THE FALL AND RISE OF THE LABOUR RIGHT

The academic study *How Britain Votes* subsequently pointed out that it was not programme or policies that lost the 1983 election but lack of coherence and purpose, reflected in the Foot leadership. Dismissing the common claim that Labour's class base had shrunk so much as to make it forever unelectable, it pointed out that it was precisely among Labour's traditional "natural supporters" that its vote had been crucially weakened. According to its detailed survey, between 1966 and 1983 there had been a 1 per cent decline in Labour's "ideological heartland" as a proportion of the total electorate, while in the same period there was a 10 per cent decline in the Labour vote. The implication was that, as in 1979, Labour lost the 1983 election because of its failure to mobilize voters in its traditional class base.[52]

In the mid 1980s the citing of demographic trends became a substitute for analysis and a cover for the restoration of the politics favoured by the Labour establishment. The decline of the manual working class and deindustrialization, the rise in home and car ownership, the flight to suburbia and various cultural developments eroding traditional class loyalties were all adduced not only as reasons why Labour lost in 1983 but why it had to shift to the right if it wanted ever to win again. That Labour's share of the vote had been declining since the mid 1960s and that Labour had failed to receive more than 40 per cent of the vote in a general election since its losing performance in 1970 might have suggested that the reasons and remedies were otherwise. Indeed, the statistics suggested that electoral failure might just have something to do with the poor performance of successive Labour governments and leaderships. After all, according to Gallup the Tories were ahead of Labour for only fifteen of the forty-eight months of the 1979–83 Parliament. Popular discontent with the Thatcher government over unemployment, the NHS, pensions and even defence policy was there to be exploited. Labour failed to rally people around these issues, leaving the Conservatives free to fight and win the election on their own uncompromisingly ideological agenda.

Contrary to myth, the Labour left was utterly dismayed by the outcome of the election. *London Labour Briefing* called it "a historic defeat, almost comparable in its own way to the electoral disaster of 1931. We ended up with almost the worst possible combination which could have been imagined: a programme which broke with the old consensus politics, spoken for by a leadership which clung to that consensus like grim death."[53]

But while the left was aghast, others in the Party began to bring long-laid plans to fruition. Back in February 1983, Hugh Macpherson, *Tribune*'s parliamentary correspondent, had observed "a distressed little picket of MPs . . . gloomily looking beyond defeat at the next general election and saying that Master Kinnock was just the right material to build up for the election beyond the next".[54] For the Labour right, the 1983 defeat was, in time, to prove a godsend. Certainly it was to be the making of Neil Kinnock.

The Dream Ticket

In the days following the 1983 defeat, a number of trade union leaders, among them Clive Jenkins of ASTMS, Alan Tuffin of the UCW and, more privately, Moss Evans of the TGWU, began touting the 41-year-old Neil Kinnock as a successor to Michael Foot, whose unhappy tenure of the Party leadership had obviously come to an end. Later, supporters of other would-be Party leaders such as Peter Shore complained that the outcome of the contest had been decided even before it had begun. The deal to make Kinnock leader was struck, it was alleged, by a clique of trade union general secretaries, led by Jenkins, at a private meeting during a barbecue held at the residence of the American Ambassador shortly after the June election.[55]

Kinnock's prospects were assiduously advanced by the media, which suggested that he had been one of Labour's few public performers to emerge with credit from the election disaster. This made him appealing to the union bureaucrats, who were desperately in search of media approbation. Even more important, Kinnock was widely perceived as a strong supporter of Labour's current, left-wing political programme, and notably of unilateral nuclear disarmament. Despite his actions during the deputy leadership campaign of 1981, he could still count on substantial support from the constituency parties and left-leaning trade unions. And because of those actions, he could also count on a surprising degree of support from Labour's centre and right.

Some of the more far-sighted members of the centre-right, particularly within the trade unions, saw in Kinnock a "unity candidate" who could be relied on to protect the interests of the Labour establishment and "stand up" to the left when it really counted. They realized that precisely because of his left background and political base, Kinnock was better placed to shift the Party back to the right than was his openly right-wing rival, Roy Hattersley.

The trade union bosses who set the Kinnock bandwagon moving in June 1983 had the measure of the mood in the Labour Party. *Tribune*, then under the editorship of Chris Mullin, a firm friend of the Bennite left, reported, "Because the Party is in deep trouble, some members are allowing themselves to be panicked into looking for quick and easy solutions." A case in point, Mullin noted, was the "dream ticket" of Kinnock and Hattersley, promoted by some union leaders as an instant "solution" to the Party's problems.[56]

Kinnock's flying start in the campaign to succeed Foot gave him a huge advantage. Indeed, the trade union kingmakers had decreed their support for him even before the outgoing leader had announced his intention to resign. Because of its close connections to Foot, the Kinnock camp knew that the incumbent would not complain if they jumped the gun. This enabled Kinnock to emerge almost immediately as the frontrunner, which proved crucial to his eventual success. Without consulting their members or in some cases even their executives, a number of trade union leaders pledged their block votes to Kinnock, thus foreclosing any other options for large sections of the labour movement. Even before his campaign had officially been announced, Kinnock was assured of the support of ASTMS (thanks to the personal endorsement of Clive Jenkins), the traditionally right-wing UCW, SOGAT 82 and the TGWU, whose executive committee declared it would support Kinnock should Foot not wish to stand for re-election at the Party conference in October.

The right-wingers who declared their candidatures only after Foot announced his resignation, Hattersley and Peter Shore, whose seniority within the Parliamentary Labour Party would normally have given them the edge, were left at the starting post. David Basnett, whose GMBATU had become the crucial swing union within the Labour Party, declared that his union did not mind whether Kinnock or Hattersley became leader of the Party provided that the unsuccessful candidate became the deputy leader, thus ensuring that "unity" would prevail. This was the seal of approval on the "dream ticket".

The ultra-right EETPU had declared that it would refuse to cast a vote in the leadership ballot because it was opposed to the principle of the electoral college. Two years before, no such qualms were evident when the union cast its 228,000 block votes for Denis Healey in the deputy leadership contest. The EETPU had set aside its professed scruples at that time simply because the choice was so crucial and the result too close to call. The choice between Kinnock and Hattersley was an entirely different matter. Revealingly, Kinnock received a personal endorsement from the EETPU general secretary Frank Chapple, who said that he would personally vote for Kinnock, whom he considered to be on the "balls wing of the Party". Within a year Chapple was sitting on the SDP benches in the House of Lords.

The decision of the EETPU not to cast its vote in the electoral college was a setback for Hattersley, as was the snowballing union support for Kinnock. But he was determined to run for the leadership regardless of the eventual result. As the standard-bearer of the old parliamentary right wing he knew that he would not be humiliated. In contrast, the candidacy of Peter Shore, lacking any base of support in the Party either in Parliament or in the country, squeezed from both left and right, was dead from the start.

Neil Kinnock counted on strong support from the constituency parties, not least because he expected a clear run on the left in the absence of the natural candidate, Tony Benn, who was ineligible to stand because he had lost his parliamentary seat in the general election. Benn had refused on principle to seek a safe Labour seat elsewhere when the Bristol South East constituency he had represented for over thirty years was abolished as a result of boundary changes. Denied the nomination for the safe seat of Bristol South by right-wing trade union delegations skilfully organized by John Golding, he had chosen to fight the marginal seat of Bristol East and had been narrowly defeated. His absence from the contest made it easier for Kinnock's campaign team to argue that a vote for their man was a vote to protect the constitutional and policy changes that had been won by the left since 1979.

Opposing Kinnock from the left, Eric Heffer based his campaign on policy. He issued a variety of statements and manifestos, which, had they been put directly to the vote among constituency members in 1983, would have won overwhelming approval. But in the wake of the Party's humiliating defeat in the June general election, members were wary of voting on the basis of policy. They accepted the Kinnock camp's arguments about the need for improved "presentation" and its claims that only Kinnock could "sell" the Party's policies to the electorate. In addition, many left activists felt they had to "stop Hattersley" at all costs and reluctantly concluded that Kinnock was the candidate best placed to do this.

In the wake of the general election defeat, political commentators, most of them hostile to the Party, questioned whether Labour had a future at all as a party of government. At the grass roots, many members were gripped by fear. Could it be true, as the pundits insisted, that three-party politics were here to stay, that left-wing Labour could never win? After all, the SDP–Liberal Alliance had only narrowly failed to beat Labour into third place in share of the popular vote.

Well aware of this crisis of confidence, Kinnock's advisers were determined to present their man as the new face of a forward-looking Labour Party. His relative youth, his energy and informality, his ease with television were constantly emphasized by his supporters as necessary attributes for any modern political leader. They sold his image and style as the perfect antidote to Michael Foot, while at the same time they claimed Foot's political mantle.

During the campaign, Kinnock emerged unscathed from a serious car crash on the M4 and declared that "somebody up there" liked him. Truly, in 1983 he was the right man in the right place at the right time. A few years before or a few years later, Kinnock would not have been seen as even a likely contender for the Labour leadership, much less as a frontrunner. His record on the front bench and his political inexperience would have ruled him out; the delicate political balance inside the Party would have been tipped against him.

Of the four candidates for the leadership only Hattersley and Heffer offered the membership distinctive political programmes. Kinnock, in contrast, sought to avoid political controversy of any kind. He offered himself as the candidate around whom all strands of opinion within the Party and all sections of it – constituencies, trade unions and Labour MPs – could rally. On defence he presented himself as all things to all people. "We have to explain and reassert our non-nuclear defence policy," he insisted, then added, "The Labour Party is irretrievably committed to securing strong and secure defences." While he refused to rule out future action against left-wingers, he declared, "I hope that there will be no need for expulsions" because "we must not be a Party which has got a system of political policing."[57] Although Kinnock did argue that "withdrawal from the EEC was not an option for the late 1980s", he made a point of associating himself with the Party's existing economic policy, including its commitment to strong trade union rights, extended public ownership and increased public expenditure.[58] Kinnock assured Party members repeatedly that he "had no quarrel with the policies of the last election" and that his prime objective as leader would be to "put those policies over to the electorate more persuasively".[59] In his view, Labour had to find ways to change public perceptions of it but it "did not have to shift its ground or dilute its democratic socialist commitment".[60]

In interviews and speeches, Kinnock emphasized the personal contribution he could make to restoring Labour's electoral fortunes. In a *Tribune* interview in July, Kinnock's message, despite the tortured syntax, was clear:

> I can do the job that the Labour Party requires, of the presentation of a policy with conviction and a clarity that is understood and appeals to the general public. . . . I have got the temperament and the strong desire to bind the Party together and to secure the fraternity which is a precondition of our success.[61]

In other words: vote for me and I will resolve the Party's long-standing problems of poor communications and public disunity.

In the course of promoting this argument, the staple of his three-month campaign for the leadership, Kinnock adopted an increasingly authoritarian tone. On the eve of his victory he warned, in the *Mail on Sunday*:

> Left, right and centre of the Party have only to observe one discipline, the self-discipline of the will to win. To those who won't realise this, who insist on short term squabbles, who'd rather fight ally than enemy, I'll give no quarter.[62]

Hattersley, in contrast, was happy to set out his political stall. In an interview with *Tribune* editor Chris Mullin, a man he clearly loathed,

Hattersley argued that "expulsions must continue whenever and wherever necessary". He came out in support of "one member one vote" in conference decision-making and a trigger mechanism for MPs' reselection; he also gave his support to the keeping of US nuclear bases in Britain and to multilateral rather than unilateral nuclear disarmament.[63] But despite warnings from the left, few would have believed in 1983 that a Labour Party that voted for Kinnock would end up with Hattersley's policies.

Nor did Party members expect that they would end up not with the livewire, the media darling, the populist communicator whom they were told would boost the Party at the ballot box, but with the dour, mistrustful and remote figure whom the public roundly rejected in both 1987 and 1992. Whatever Kinnock's achievements as leader might have been, ease with the media, fluency in explaining policy and a positive impact on the public were not among them. Yet these were the very virtues for which he was originally elected.

Towards the end of July, the TGWU biannual delegate conference voted, on the advice of Moss Evans and Alex Kitson, to back Kinnock and not to hold a membership ballot on the issue. After that, Hattersley knew he was beaten. From the right came the usual demands for union leaders to ballot their members; Kinnock, later such a champion of this cause, said not a word about it throughout the entire leadership contest.

With the outcome of the contest stitched up in Kinnock's favour, public attention turned to the race for the deputy leadership. Several candidates, Gerald Kaufman, Michael Meacher, Denzil Davies and Gwyneth Dunwoody, who formed a joint ticket with Peter Shore, had declared themselves as soon as Denis Healey announced he was following Michael Foot into retirement. Both Kinnock and Hattersley got themselves nominated for deputy as well as for leader. As early as the second week of the contest there seems to have been an agreement between their respective camps that if either won the leadership the other would become deputy. With Kinnock the clear favourite for the leadership, the Hattersley camp was determined to ensure that their man would be elected deputy. Gerald Kaufman quickly withdrew to give Hattersley a clear run. Kinnock and his advisers saw supporting Hattersley for deputy as a means to win the political confidence of the parliamentary right and, even more important, block the election of Michael Meacher, the candidate of the Bennite left.

Many on the left who had already conceded the leadership contest to Kinnock believed Meacher's deputy leadership bid had a real chance of success. In the light of Kinnock's behaviour during the 1981 deputy leadership contest, they saw a Kinnock–Meacher leadership as the real, balanced ticket and believed that as deputy Meacher would be the logical representative of the constituency left from which Hattersley remained deeply alienated.

In private, Kinnock was a strong supporter of Hattersley. His advisers formed a "stop Meacher" alliance with Hattersley's people, pooling media contacts and trade union influence. Throughout August and September, when it appeared that Meacher had a good chance of beating Hattersley, stories appeared in the press clearly designed to damage the Meacher candidacy. It was reported in the *Guardian* that Hattersley, Healey and other "senior former ministers were unprepared to serve in a Kinnock–Meacher shadow administration".[64] It was also rumoured that a number of unnamed Labour MPs would leave the Party if Hattersley were not elected deputy.

Spurned by Kinnock, with whom he had hoped to negotiate a deal, and desperate to challenge the "dream ticket" juggernaut, Meacher wrote a series of articles critical of Hattersley. In the *Guardian*, he asked:

> Does the Party want to jettison policies that have been fought for for years? Does it want to reverse the constitutional changes that provide for greater democratisation within the Party? Does it want to have a clear-out of the Party and a head on collision with Conference?[65]

He argued that Labour did not need leaders who would repudiate policies debated and agreed by a majority vote at conference. (It got just such a leader in Neil Kinnock, the candidate whom Meacher eventually decided to vote for.)

Meacher's flagging campaign was revived in September when he won the backing of the TGWU executive council. In opposition to Evans and Kitson, both strong supporters of the "dream ticket", the executive voted by nineteen votes to seventeen with two abstentions to direct the union's delegation to the Labour Party conference to cast its huge block vote for Meacher. Hattersley supporters moved rapidly to discredit the narrow executive vote. They informed the press that four members of the TGWU executive were also members of the Communist Party. This attempt to redbait the Meacher campaign backfired when it became known that although one Communist executive member had indeed supported Meacher, two others had voted for Hattersley while the fourth had been absent.[66]

A week later the *Mail on Sunday* published an interview with Kinnock. He was quoted describing Michael Meacher as being "as weak as hell" and Tony Benn as someone "unable to knock the skin off of a rice pudding".[67] Although Kinnock claimed he had been quoted out of context, his comments signalled his attitude to the deputy leadership contest and his intention of excluding Bennites of any stripe from his future regime. It was also a foretaste of the macho insults with which he was to greet all inner-Party criticism in the coming years.

At the conference in October, Kinnock was easily elected leader of the Party, winning over 70 per cent of the votes cast in the electoral college. Roy Hattersley came a poor second. The size of Kinnock's success in a four-horse race was underlined by his showing in each division. He won 29 per cent of the 40 per cent allocated to trade unions, and he only narrowly failed to win an outright majority – 14.7 per cent out of 30 per cent – among Labour MPs, who by now knew just which way the wind was blowing. In the constituency section Kinnock took 27 per cent of the allocated 30 per cent.

Even more gratifying to the Kinnock camp was the success of the "dream ticket" propaganda, with Hattersley securing victory over Michael Meacher by a larger majority than anyone had predicted. Despite Meacher's long-standing association with the fight against low pay, the NUPE leadership ensured that the union backed Hattersley for deputy. Similarly, Moss Evans had promised Kinnock he would deliver the TGWU block vote for Hattersley, despite the executive's recommendation for Meacher. After numerous meetings and extraordinary pressure from full-time officials, the TGWU delegation voted by twenty-seven to eighteen to overturn its executive and back Hattersley. Hattersley also scored a surprise success in the constituency section. Only two years before it had cast 79 per cent of its votes for Tony Benn; now it chose Hattersley over Meacher.

The NEC elections held at the same time revealed that although the Party wanted a new start following the general election, it had no wish to jettison agreed policies or backtrack on its constitutional reforms. The constituency section once again returned a full slate of left-wingers. Tony Benn, Eric Heffer and Dennis Skinner topped the poll. They were joined by Audrey Wise, Jo Richardson and, for the first time, Meacher himself. David Blunkett, the leader of Sheffield City Council, was also elected, very much as a standard-bearer of Labour's new local government left. The conference reaffirmed a wide range of the very policy commitments that Kinnock was eventually to tell the Party had cost it the general election.

In an article published in the *New Statesman* shortly after his victory, Kinnock spoke about "my socialism". Quoting Marx, Trotsky, Engels and Gramsci (twice), he defended "democratic socialism, deeply rooted in the history of Labour and Parliamentary democracy". Railing against the SDP defectors, he smirked:

> Those of less intellectual honesty and stature . . . find it difficult to admit their mistakes especially if their political careers are at stake. When rational argument prevails, they seek refuge inside a new bastion; a party based on expediency, opportunism, nostalgia and self-importance and living on the new elixir of proportional representation.[68]

In the article Kinnock used the word "socialism" no fewer than thirty-nine times; in the 1992 Labour Manifesto drawn up under his aegis the word was not used once.

Kinnock's big majority in the electoral college conferred upon him an almost unparalleled authority. As the first leader to be elected under the wider franchise, Kinnock could claim to represent the entire Labour Party, not just Labour MPs. At the outset, he could count on a greater repository of loyalty and good will than almost any Labour leader in living memory. In the coming years he was to use this authority and this loyalty for purposes very different from those which the members had in mind when they voted him into office.

Laying the Foundations

In the early years of Neil Kinnock's leadership, the "soft left" liked to portray him as a prisoner of the right. On that basis it explained away his failure to fulfil the aspirations of the Party members who had elected him in 1983. But the reality was that before 1985 he was a prisoner of the left. His room for manoeuvre was circumscribed by the continuing influence of the left and by the abiding commitment of the Party as a whole to left policies.

Kinnock did not become leader with a comprehensive and conscious strategy for turning the Party to the right. What came to be known as "Kinnockism" emerged, haltingly, out of a confluence of pressures and counter-pressures. But its driving force from the beginning was Kinnock's ambition to be seen as a strong leader. He was determined never to repeat the unhappy experience of Michael Foot, who had been unable to command his own party. Because of that ambition Kinnock not only repeatedly set himself up against the rank and file, which won him friends in the traditionally right-wing PLP, but also gradually concentrated all power in his own office, which by the end of his regime had supplanted the authority of virtually every other Party body, including the PLP itself.

This could not have happened without the defeat of all alternative, independent poles of attraction within the labour movement. The process began in 1981 with Benn's defeat in the deputy leadership contest, and continued with the defeat of both the miners and the ratecapping campaigns in 1985 and the subsequent defection of the "soft left" to the leader's camp. It was accompanied by the steady march of New Realism within the labour movement as a whole. The New Realists in the unions argued not only that confrontation with the Thatcher regime was futile but also that it positively damaged Labour's electoral fortunes. Increasingly, any direct challenge to Thatcher was seen as a challenge to the Labour leadership itself.

As each year passed more Labour members came to say, "We must defer to Neil's wishes. We cannot rock the boat and run the risk of letting the Tories in again. There is no alternative." Kinnock's constant refrain was that the only concession Labour could make to Thatcherism was to let it win again. He insisted that unity, meaning conformity with his wishes, was the essential precondition for electoral success. To argue against him, to flout his wishes, was to undermine that unity and compromise the prospects for success. A Labour Party hungry for victory proved to be highly vulnerable to this argument.

Kinnock's election as leader was a curious by-product of both the success and the failure of the Bennite rebellion. Unlike his immediate predecessors Kinnock could rely upon a considerable base of political support within the Party outside Parliament. He took command at a moment when the right had regained the offensive but long before the left had exhausted itself. He was therefore able for a long period to command the support both of the parliamentary right (which looked to him to hold the left in check) and of much, though not all, of the constituency left, which looked to him to protect left policies from the right. Circumstances thus provided him with a unique base from which to impose his will on the Party.

Yet this position of apparent strength concealed considerable vulnerability. The political balance within the Party that had produced the "dream ticket" was still far from stable. Kinnock's huge majority in the electoral college was a product of that balance and the narrow options open to all concerned. He enjoyed no deep personal support in either the Parliamentary Labour Party or the unions and his famous base in the constituencies was unreliable. The success of the Thatcher government itself was by no means, at this stage, a foregone conclusion. A rise in mass resistance to it would have altered the balance within the Party and subjected any Labour leader to enormous conflicting pressures.

Added to this was Kinnock's own sense of inadequacy and chronic insecurity. It was vital to him to construct a core of followers, centred in his own office, whose first loyalty would always be to him and him alone. Kinnock knew from his own experience that the left would never offer the kind of loyalty he required. He knew, in particular, that it would bitterly oppose any attempt to undo the advances of 1979–83 and to steer the Party back to the right. To Kinnock, the Labour left was an enemy – the enemy – which he would have to defeat if he was to impose his authority on the Party. From the beginning, therefore, he set out to deal with left opposition by excluding it whenever possible. This was in sharp contrast to the strategy pursued by previous Labour leaders of seeking to tame the left by incorporating it.

In the previous period the NEC had been the central fulcrum of power within the Labour Party. It had been constantly at odds with Jim

Callaghan and often with Foot as well. Though in 1981 and 1982 the right had gained a tenuous majority on the NEC, the left's presence remained substantial. An additional problem was that the independent authority of the NEC posed a potential threat to any parliamentary leadership. Kinnock therefore set out not only to isolate the left on the NEC but to undermine the power of the NEC as a whole.

During Kinnock's leadership campaign, the Labour Co-ordinating Committee (LCC) had published a paper, largely drafted by Patricia Hewitt, calling for the establishment of a "campaign and strategy committee". This would be more than another NEC sub-committee: it would be a "leader's committee" incorporating members of the shadow cabinet and the NEC, senior full-time officials and outside experts, as well as what it called a "full-time campaign organizer" (who was to emerge two years later in the figure of Peter Mandelson). Hewitt's proposals corresponded to the widespread hunger in the Labour Party for greater co-ordination at the top and a more efficient technical service to hard-pressed members. Contrary to myth, at this juncture there was little disagreement within the Party about the need for more vigorous and imaginative campaigning and a more effective use of the media (though there was, however, suspicion that this rhetoric would be used to cover a shift to the right).

Immediately after his election as leader, Kinnock appointed Hewitt as his press secretary. A proposal for a revamped campaign committee to include Labour MPs and trade union representatives as well as members of the NEC, originally advanced in July 1983 by Party officers, now re-emerged, backed by the authority of the new leader armed with the Hewitt/LCC paper.

At Kinnock's first NEC meeting as leader, shortly after the 1983 Party conference, he formally proposed the creation of a "campaign strategy committee". Under the terms of reference endorsed by the NEC, the CSC was to "advise the NEC" on "the overall strategy for the Party's work until the general election" and to co-ordinate "all the Party's campaign work and all the national campaigns of the Party".[69] Crucially, it was also empowered, when considering resolutions from Party conference, to "establish priorities and to work to a clear and consistent programme of activity".[70] From now on the full NEC, though technically supreme, was no longer responsible for Labour Party campaigns or communications.

In the wake of the disastrous election campaign, in which divisions between the Parliamentary Labour Party and the Party in the country, between Walworth Road and the shadow cabinet, were an obvious handicap, the campaign strategy committee seemed to many a sensible innovation. But all it really ever achieved was the institutionalization of a new relationship between the parliamentary leadership and the trade union bureaucracy. It enabled Kinnock and his advisers to secure support for their initiatives from the Party's two key non-accountable power bases – the PLP and the trade union bureaucracy – before seeking the formal approval of the Party's democratically elected NEC. Crucial campaigning decisions – on the production and content of party political broadcasts, on priorities for full-time officials at Walworth Road, on advertising schemes and on opinion polling – all went through the campaign strategy committee and bypassed the NEC, until Kinnock had an NEC more to his liking.

Later, when he achieved his rubberstamp NEC, Kinnock no longer needed the campaign strategy committee. The leadership and its advisers worked out what they wanted and submitted it to the relevant bodies for automatic endorsement. Ultimately, the campaign strategy committee was wound down; by the end of the 1980s it had ceased to play any meaningful role.

Back in 1983, Kinnock felt himself very much a captive of the NEC and its seesaw political balance. One of his key backers, John Golding, was removed from the NEC at the 1983 conference when the New Left majority on his trade union executive refused to renominate him. This left the influential position of chair of the NEC's home policy committee vacant. Only one year before Tony Benn had been ousted from this position by a narrow right-wing NEC majority engineered by Golding himself. Now, in the first of many off-the-record unattributed press briefings, Kinnock let it be known that he did not wish to see Benn regain the home policy chair, which for eight years he had used to revolutionize the work of the NEC, building it up as a powerful policy-making body independent of the parliamentary leadership. At the same October 1983 NEC that saw the establishment of the campaign strategy committee, a list of members proposed for the various NEC sub-committees was circulated. In the absence of Jim Mortimer, the general secretary, the list had been compiled by Kinnock's advisers with help from David Hughes, the right-wing national agent.

The membership of each committee was carefully chosen to ensure that Kinnock's will would prevail. Doug Hoyle, an influential "soft left" NEC member, was named chair of home policy. Benn declined to stand against him, knowing he would be defeated and reluctant to be accused of rocking the boat so soon after the election of a new leader.

It was suggested by figures close to the leadership that existing specialist policy groups operating under the control of the NEC sub-committees should be replaced by joint policy committees (JPCs) composed of NEC and shadow cabinet members. This proposal was submitted to the NEC in December 1983. Although the initiative had originated in Kinnock's office, the paper outlining the new system was presented by the head of research, Geoff Bish. It proposed that the new joint policy committees would each be made up of six members of the NEC, six members of the shadow cabinet and selected trade union leaders.[71] The left was able to ensure that these committees would report to the NEC through the home policy sub-committee, but in an ominous clause it was also stipulated that their remit was to "develop policies which could be jointly agreed between the NEC and the shadow cabinet".[72]

At the meeting Kinnock criticized the existing system of policy formation. "The blunderbuss approach to policy has been tried and has failed and the activists have been confused by a mass of documents. . . . We cannot have a policy so broad as to be incomprehensible." The existing "over large and fluctuating" committees were, he said, "unrepresentative" and "remote".[73]

For the traditional parliamentary right, the new committees were a chance to regain control over a policy-making process that had veered sharply to the left over the previous decade. At this stage it was still not possible to make any fundamental changes to existing policies, given the broad support they enjoyed within the Party. The most the right could hope for was to weaken and undermine them, to repackage them according to its own priorities. Not surprisingly, therefore, of the joint policy committees established in 1983–84 only one, the Jobs and Industry group, was really active, and that was solely because it was linked to Kinnock's first big public relations exercise (see Chapter 8).

On becoming leader in 1983 Kinnock had inherited the remnants of the shadow cabinet presided over by Michael Foot. New members such as Michael Meacher, John Prescott and Robin Cook came from the Tribune Group but on balance it remained, as before, a preserve of the right, dominated by members of Solidarity, the right-wing pro-Washington, pro-EC pressure group that had been set up by the Labour right after the SDP defections.

The Labour shadow cabinet is elected in a secret ballot of Party MPs and therefore its overall composition does not always conform to the desires of the leader. But the allocation of portfolios within it is at the leader's discretion and very much reflects his political and personal biases. Kinnock knew the power of the old parliamentary right and wanted its support. He had watched these people undermine and ultimately destroy Michael Foot. He was determined to take them on board. This was more than merely expedient alliance-building. Instinctively, Kinnock sensed that people who knew exactly what they wanted and how to get it would be more useful to him than the vacillating Tribunites.

Thus, although the new leader had been elected with the strong support of members of the Tribune Group in Parliament, Tribune MPs who thought that their ship had come in were in for a rude awakening. Traditional right-wingers who had voted for Roy Hattersley were given virtually all the major shadow portfolios. In accordance with the deal struck during the private negotiations through which the "dream ticket" had been constructed, Kinnock made Hattersley shadow Chancellor. Denis Healey was appointed shadow foreign secretary and Gerald Kaufman became shadow home secretary. John Cunningham, a right-wing newcomer to the shadow cabinet elected on the Solidarity slate, was appointed environment spokesperson, a position much coveted by Tribunite MPs, who reckoned that they were closer in spirit than Cunningham to Labour's new echelon of local government leaders.

While Peter Shore was made shadow Leader of the House as well as spokesperson on trade and industry, Eric Heffer, an elected member of the NEC who had finished ahead of Shore in the leadership contest, was forced to accept the minor post of spokesperson on housing and construction. Another Solidarity supporter and Hattersley backer, John Smith, took over the employment brief.

Kinnock's major battles in the early years were fought not in the Parliamentary Labour Party but at the NEC, where the left was still powerful enough to impose some restraints on him. His big shifts to the right would come only after he had constructed a solid and steadfast NEC majority. As long as he had to rely on the faceless NEC trade union representatives and was opposed by nearly all the left-wing constituency section he was hamstrung. After all, the left-wing constituencies had made him; they could still break him. An indication of the delicate balance in the Party in the first year of Kinnock's leadership can be found in an official Party leaflet produced for the European elections of June 1984. Its headline, "Working Together for a Labour Victory", was juxtaposed with pictures of both Hattersley and Benn. Within a year, following the defeat of the miners' strike and the local government campaign against ratecapping, it was inconceivable that Benn's image would appear on anything produced by Walworth Road for public distribution.

Lions, Donkeys and Jackals

The miners' strike of 1984–85 was not only the key British industrial dispute of the 1980s but also a moment of truth for the labour movement and the Labour Party in particular. A union celebrated for its militancy, for its tradition of solidarity and for its central role in the TUC and the Labour Party faced a Tory government whose whole economic, social and political strategy required its defeat.

For a full year the miners waged a titanic struggle against the government, which spent billions to crush its "enemy within". In the face of the sequestration of nearly all their union's assets, slow starvation at the hands of the benefit system and credit companies, a media united in vilifying their aims, tactics and leaders, and tens of thousands of police determined to break the strike using everything from roadblocks in Kent to savage physical attacks at Orgreave and elsewhere, the miners doggedly defended their industry, their union and the integrity of their communities.

In its response to the miners' strike the Labour Party was split by a chasm, not between left and right (although many of the arguments about the meaning and consequences of the strike divided along these lines), but between the entire base of the movement on the one hand and a small leadership clique on the other. From day one of the strike, support for the miners among grassroots Party members, left, right and centre, was broad, determined and generous. Party branches, general committees, Labour groups on local authorities, women's sections and Young Socialists branches all threw themselves into fundraising and other support activities. Party members turned out again and again at local meetings and rallies, stood week in week out on high streets collecting money and food, sometimes facing police harassment and arrest for their pains. The Party was united in a genuine determination to provide maximum material aid to the hard-pressed strikers. Some Labour councils, including the GLC and other London bodies, gave the miners high-profile political support. Others, like Leeds, took another route: right-wing council leader George Mudie funnelled tens of thousands of pounds to miners in his area. There was less publicity, but the desire to give support was just as real. This reflected a consensus at the base of the Party: the miners were involved in a struggle so fundamental that it had to be won.

Jim Mortimer, Labour's general secretary from 1982 to 1985, threw himself into the fray, touring the country, using NEC resolutions supporting the NUM (passed every month during the dispute) as his mandate. Everywhere he went he made it clear that he was speaking on behalf of the whole Labour Party. Mortimer later observed: "The only time I can recall the Party being as united behind a single cause as it was during the miners' dispute was in the late 1930s when it gave such tremendous backing to Republican Spain." Despite Mortimer's efforts, aided by that year's Party chair, Eric Heffer, and the groundswell of support at the Party base, Labour's Walworth Road headquarters failed to issue a single leaflet explaining or backing the miners' case, and regional and national organizers played no role in the strike support groups. Only the Party newspaper, *Labour Weekly*, gave real support, publishing a stream of stories about the strike, highlighting police abuses, outlining court actions against the union and publicizing the political use of the Department of Health and Social Security (DHSS), all matters misreported or simply ignored by Fleet Street.

From the beginning, the Labour leadership viewed the miners' strike with horror. Given the strength of feeling at the base of the Party, the

leadership's room for manoeuvre was restricted, especially at the outset
when no one could predict with certainty how the strike would be
resolved. Even before he had become leader, Kinnock had come to
believe that industrial action of any kind was damaging to the Party's
electoral fortunes. By the spring of 1984, in keeping with previous Labour
leaders, he had come to perceive it as a threat to his own authority within
the labour movement.

The strike provided Labour with numerous opportunities to attack the
Tories on their weak points – mass unemployment, a wasteful, short-
term energy policy, a disregard for civil liberties, the destruction of long-
established communities and the pouring of taxpayers' money into a
political vendetta – but Kinnock and his supporters declined to exploit
these. Instead, they adopted a damage limitation approach which
allowed the Tories to attack both Labour and the miners on *their* weak
points – particularly the divisions over tactics and leadership.

In March 1984, at the first meeting of the NEC following the outbreak of
the dispute, the leadership presented a cautious emergency resolution
opposing pit closures. An amendment from the left had to be added to
include explicit support for the strikers and condemnation of the government's handling of the dispute. The amendment was accepted by the
leadership and the motion as a whole was passed without opposition.[74]

The balance of forces on the NEC in this period was delicate. Kinnock
had always to reckon with the sensitivities of the centre-left trade union
members and the then united bloc of left-wing CLP representatives.
Nearly all members of the NEC were under heavy pressure from their
various constituencies to extend strong support to the NUM. In those
days of recorded and well-publicized NEC votes, anything that could be
interpreted as a vote against the miners' struggle would spell trouble for
the perpetrator.

Although they did not enjoy a close working relationship, Kinnock and
Hattersley instinctively coalesced against the miners. Unwilling to act
openly, they allowed others on the NEC to speak for them. The right-
wing duo of Ken Cure and Gwyneth Dunwoody, dubbed the "terrible
twins" by Dennis Skinner, always sat and voted together and made plain
their hostility to the miners' cause from the beginning. Although the
NEC voted unanimously throughout the strike to give unequivocal
support to the miners, the NEC left believed that the real struggle was to
make that support concrete and force the leadership to address the
political issues raised by the strike. Jim Mortimer ensured that all NEC
decisions on the miners were recorded in the NEC annual report to the
1984 Party conference – not least because he was concerned to demonstrate that in stumping the country for the miners he, at least, had been
acting in line with official Party policy.

At a Parliamentary Labour Party meeting held after the March NEC, Bassetlaw MP Joe Ashton argued that the opposition debate on education scheduled for the following week should be changed to an emergency debate on the miners. Like many Labour MPs, Ashton had been inundated with stories about horrific police behaviour on picket lines and felt the matter needed to be aired urgently in the House of Commons. He was backed not only by left MPs but significantly by such unlikely figures as former cabinet ministers Merlyn Rees and John Morris. Desperate to keep the miners' strike in the background and off Labour's agenda, a furious Kinnock protested, "I'm for leadership and we shouldn't lead with our chins. You're asking me to jump out of the window. This would be a gesture."[75] Chief whip Michael Cocks (running the meeting in the absence of the regular PLP chair) refused to take any vote and Ashton's proposal fell.

Over the next few weeks pressure built up both inside and outside the PLP for a Commons debate on what was, after all, the number one issue in the country. After his initial outburst at the PLP meeting, Kinnock learned to keep his thoughts on the miners more to himself, at least for the time being. Unable to question the strike in public, the Labour leader chose to remain silent, but his silence was eloquent, especially as interpreted by the NUM-hating press.

Those who wished to see the miners defeated hammered away at the union's refusal to hold a national ballot to authorize industrial action. This provided an excuse for several trade union leaders and Labour MPs reluctant to support the strike. The NUM executive ruled out a ballot as unnecessary because successive NUM conferences and local ballots had provided a mandate for strike action. Immediately following the NUM executive's decision, Kinnock, in one of his rare prompt responses to any event connected with the strike, issued a public call to the NUM to hold a ballot, thus joining forces with the media lobby that was trying to paint the strike as a conspiracy hatched by unrepresentative NUM leaders.

The April meeting of the NEC agreed that constituency parties should organize a 50p weekly levy of all members for the miners. This left initiative was passed unanimously, with no objections from Kinnock, despite mutterings from Ken Cure. Apart from informing all CLP secretaries of the NEC decision, Walworth Road offered no practical assistance in implementing it. None the less, by the end of the strike, the money raised from the levy and from a plethora of other fundraising activities organized by Party members was estimated to total millions of pounds.

At a meeting of the PLP in May, Bradford West MP Max Madden proposed a £5 a week levy for the miners on all Labour MPs. His motion was opposed by NUM-sponsored MP Michael McGuire, who attacked Arthur Scargill for wanting to impose "totalitarianism" on Britain. McGuire was later deselected by his constituency party. In his speech

Kinnock felt obliged to emphasize that he wanted the miners to win and that he recognized the "massive sacrifices" being made in the coalfields. "The movement is trying to help," he said, "but the levy gives the impression that there is a reluctance to subscribe and if the levy fell below its official sum, there would be a propaganda point given to our enemies." In response to this manoeuvre, Madden dropped the reference to a "levy" and successfully proposed that a £5 per week contribution be sought from all Labour MPs. Kinnock had no alternative but to accept the proposal.[76]

For months the shadow cabinet dithered on the strike. Because of its refusal to raise the matter in the House of Commons during opposition time, backbench Labour MPs were forced to use private notice questions and other parliamentary devices to confront the government on its handling of the dispute. When Labour MPs tried to chide the Tories for refusing to discuss the strike in Parliament, ministers were quick to reply that it was up to Labour to schedule a debate on the miners in official opposition time. The Speaker, Bernard Wetherall, made the same point in refusing applications from backbenchers for emergency debates.

As a substitute for action, the leadership promoted the activities of Stan Orme, the shadow energy spokesperson. He embarked on a long, over-publicized and completely ineffectual attempt to act as a conciliator between the two sides. While the government fought to defeat the strike, the Labour opposition merely sued for peace. When questioned about the strike, the leadership praised Orme's efforts and castigated the government for failing to respond to his pleas for renewed negotiations. Pressed behind the scenes by MPs and Party officers anxious about the lack of public support for the NUM, Kinnock's staff replied with the constant refrain, "Stan Orme will sort it out."

In June a resolution on the miners' strike was finally tabled in the House of Commons in the Opposition's name. Proposed by Orme, it condemned the government's handling of the dispute and called for a negotiated settlement. It specifically avoided any mention of support for the NUM. On the same day 20,000 miners and supporters marched through Fleet Street to Jubilee Gardens beside the GLC headquarters. The march was led by NUM national officials and Jim Mortimer and Eric Heffer representing the Labour Party. Kinnock did not attend. He did not participate in the debate in the House or even appear on the front bench during it.

The June NEC had agreed to consult with NUM leaders about launching a joint campaign to publicize the miners' case. This was precisely the sort of action that Party members at the grass roots had long demanded. It never materialized. Once again Kinnock had allowed a motion to pass through the NEC only to kill it behind closed doors. The consultations with the NUM, which had to involve the Labour leader if they were to have any meaning, were postponed repeatedly.

In the early months of the strike, support for the government fell away in the opinion polls. In June, July and August 1984, Labour was fractionally ahead for the first time since 1981. Significantly, public satisfaction with the government's record plummeted and by January 1985 it was down to 31 per cent. However, Labour's support also fell away in the winter of 1984–85. According to Gallup, Kinnock's personal rating declined from 47 per cent in March 1984 to 37 per cent in August 1984 and 31 per cent in February 1985. Whatever the public may have thought about the Tories' handling of the miners' strike, they were clearly not very impressed with the way in which Neil Kinnock had handled it either.

In a further attempt to weaken the strike, opponents of the NUM turned their attention to alleged picket-line violence. The events at Orgreave in the summer of 1984, in which mounted police charged down pickets in a pre-planned attack, became the focus of debate. Years after the conclusion of the strike, it was proved in court that the police attack on the miners had been unprovoked and premeditated. Hundreds of miners arrested at the scene were acquitted of offences and many were paid compensation for injuries suffered at the hands of the police. But at the time the BBC televised edited footage of the fracas that reversed the real sequence of events, implying that police had reacted to violence by miners, rather than the opposite, which was the case. Though the Labour leadership was apprised of the nature of the police attacks at Orgreave and elsewhere, condemnations of "picket-line violence" became a Kinnock staple for the rest of the strike.

After much behind-the-scenes negotiation, Kinnock agreed to speak at the Durham Miners' Gala held in July. It was attended by 100,000 miners and their families, who gave a warm response to Arthur Scargill and Dennis Skinner. Though it was a long-standing tradition for the leader of the Labour Party to address this event, one of Britain's premier working-class celebrations, when Kinnock began his speech three of the famous brass bands struck up and began to march slowly off the field. Kinnock spoke in generalities about the government's perfidy, but offered the miners nothing in the way of concrete support. By the end of his speech three-quarters of the crowd had vanished, a remarkable snub from an audience usually noted for its deference to Labour leaders.

That same month, Kinnock at last delivered a speech in the House of Commons on the miners' strike. It was the only time he would do so. Much of it was taken up with recitation of statistics about the price of coal and the cost of the dispute. He hardly mentioned the miners, the NUM or the strike itself. Margaret Thatcher responded with a vigorous, political speech, which tore into the NUM and denounced picket-line violence and trade union brutality. The debate was wound up for the government by Chancellor Nigel Lawson, who boasted that the £400 million spent by the government to defeat the miners was a "worthwhile investment". The outcome of the Commons debate was a media triumph for Thatcher and another debacle for Kinnock. Caught sitting on the fence, the Labour leadership was unable and unwilling to rebut the arguments of the Tories.

No further formal debate on the miners' strike was held in Parliament until December 1984. Throughout the months that formed the make-or-break heart of the miners' struggle, the Labour leadership conspired to keep the issue out of the country's foremost debating chamber. In contrast, the 1984 Labour conference in Blackpool was dominated by the strike, much to Kinnock's annoyance. Resolutions poured in from constituency parties around Britain demanding Labour support for the miners. The NUM leadership was well organized and everything it wanted found its way onto the conference agenda.

The conference debate on the strike was scheduled for the session on energy policy on Monday afternoon. Jim Mortimer, by this time deeply alienated from Kinnock's leadership, proposed that Tony Benn reply to the debate on behalf of the NEC. Kinnock suggested Doug Hoyle as an alternative but Hoyle declined the offer. The hard right, in the form of Charles Turnock of the NUR and Gwyneth Dunwoody, then proposed Dennis Skinner. Skinner saw through the ruse and supported Benn, who after all had been Labour's last Secretary of State for Energy.

A large number of resolutions on the police role in the strike, which had particularly disturbed rank-and-file activists, were due to be debated in the "law and order" session on Monday afternoon, following the main debate on energy policy. Kinnock proposed that Roy Hattersley reply for the NEC, but on the casting vote of Eric Heffer in the chair, Jo Richardson was given the task. At the final meeting of the NEC on the Sunday afternoon before the start of conference, Gwyneth Dunwoody railed against Composite 66, which criticized the police role in the strike. She was supported by Kinnock, who asked the NEC to consider the impact on the electorate and successfully moved that the NEC ask for the composite to be remitted.

On the Monday afternoon, Arthur Scargill led off the main debate. He denounced "state violence against miners" and argued that the miners were entitled to Labour support because they were "fighting against the whole concept of this government's economic policy which is designed to destroy jobs and wreak havoc amongst the British Labour and trade union movement".[77] His speech was repeatedly interrupted by cheers and at its end he received a prolonged standing ovation. In the debate that followed, Ron Todd of the TGWU and Ray Buckton of the rail-workers' union ASLEF pledged their support, though the fighting tenor of their rhetoric was not matched by specific proposals for action. David

Basnett, more circumspect, urged support for "the TUC strategy" which was to "keep this dispute where it should be, as an industrial dispute to be settled by negotiation between the NUM and NCB". He asked that conference "not serve this government's purpose by ourselves over-politicizing this conflict". Referring to alleged picket-line violence, he stated that "the TUC condemns violence, whoever commits it, whoever causes it". Directly addressing Scargill, he concluded, "Arthur, it would help those who are striving to help you if your members do not let themselves be provoked."[78]

Speeches from the floor were fiery; the miners were backed and the government, the police and the media were pilloried. The lone public dissent came from Eric Hammond of the EETPU. He condemned the NEC statement for lacking any "demand for the violence and the hooliganism on the picket line to be stopped" and lashed out at "the cult of personality and the cult of violence". He claimed that the strike was undermining Neil Kinnock and wound up by comparing Benn, Skinner and Scargill to Oswald Mosley. His speech was interrupted by jeers at several points and Eric Heffer in the chair had to intervene to calm delegates.[79] As so often, however, Hammond was only saying aloud what most of the TUC General Council and certainly the Labour leadership actually thought.

The NEC statement on the dispute, which called for full support for the miners and condemned "organized violence against miners, their picket lines and their communities" by the police, was carried overwhelmingly on a show of hands, as was the NUM-backed composite.

The debate on the policing of the strike was opened by Paul Whetton, a striking miner representing Newark CLP, who began his speech by bringing fraternal greetings from "the police state of Nottingham". Other delegates from Hull, Barnsley, Durham and Wakefield spoke angrily of their personal experiences at the hands of the police. Even shadow home secretary Gerald Kaufman felt obliged to join the attack. Jo Richardson, summing up for the NEC, began by placing on the rostrum, in full view of the television cameras, a large photograph showing a woman being batoned by a mounted policeman. This had been banned from the Fleet Street press but had featured as a *Labour Weekly* front page. Richardson lashed out at police handling of the dispute, then dutifully announced that the NEC would not support either Composite 66, because it stated that police should play no role in industrial disputes, or Composite 68, because it called for "day to day" accountability of the police. The movers refused to remit and the conference, in defiance of the leadership, passed both composites by substantial majorities.

The next day Neil Kinnock rose to deliver his first full leader's speech to a Labour Party conference. He attacked Thatcher's handling of the dispute and recited his usual litany of statistics proving what he liked to call the "case for coal", a substitute for the case for the miners and the NUM. But the key passage, delivered with passion and repeated over and over again on television, was: "I condemn violence, I abominate violence, I damn violence – all violence. All violence, without fear or favour. That's what I do . . . the only side I'm prepared to take when it comes to violence is to oppose it."[80] This was the denunciation the media had been demanding and Kinnock gave it to them from the Labour Party's premier public platform. He also made a more oblique attack on the NUM by arguing that "the people who need the support and safeguard of trade unionism and of public services cannot afford to be part of any Charge of the Light Brigade . . ."[81]

The applause that followed his speech was tepid and dutiful. But that did not matter to Kinnock. His remarks were addressed not to the delegates but to the media. He could afford to lose the odd conference vote – but not the confidence of the British establishment.

The miners' funds were sequestrated in early October, an unprecedented step in British industrial relations and a transparent attempt to break the strike by bankrupting the union. The Parliamentary Labour Party, meeting for the first time since July, failed to respond after the chair ruled out all motions on the subject. The NEC agreed to hold a formal meeting with the NUM to discuss further Party assistance to the miners. The meeting – officially a meeting between representatives of the Labour NEC and the NUM executive – was held in the shadow cabinet room in Westminster in early November. The NUM national officers urged members of the NEC and shadow cabinet to attend the picket lines and see for themselves what was going on. They also wanted to pursue the joint NUM and Labour Party campaign called for by the NEC. Kinnock prevaricated, saying that the detail would have to be discussed at the NEC. At the conclusion of the meeting Kinnock's staffers set to work briefing the parliamentary lobby. The next day the press was full of stories to the effect that Kinnock had "told off" the miners' leaders. When the matter was raised at the December NEC, Jim Mortimer insisted that no Party officer had given any briefing to the press. Kinnock then announced casually that Patricia Hewitt had given the briefing.

From the beginning of the strike, Kinnock had been asked repeatedly by rank-and-file miners and Party members to join one of the scores of picket lines being maintained daily by the NUM. For months he refused to respond to any of these requests, and only turned up, sheepishly, at a carefully selected picket line in south Wales towards the very end of the strike. Even then he made sure he was not photographed standing close to placards with militant slogans. Having earlier declined all invitations to attend NUM rallies because his diary was "full", Kinnock finally spoke at a miners' meeting in November. It was a ticket-only affair in Stoke-on-

Trent organized by the Labour Party through the leader's office. Strenuous efforts were made to screen out angry rank-and-file miners and members of the women's support groups. Jim Mortimer declined to speak.

At the December NEC, Eric Clarke of the NUM proposed that the Party hold a national demonstration in support of the miners before the end of the year. Tom Sawyer and John Evans said it was "unrealistic" because there was "not enough time" to organize it properly. Kinnock argued that the NUM should have given the Party "longer notice". The outcome was a decision to "consult" with the TUC and the NUM over the timing of a "mass rally".[82] The rally was eventually held in February, without support from the Labour leadership, the front bench or the NEC.

Frances Curran, the Young Socialists representative on the NEC, proposed that a future Labour government should reimburse fines incurred by striking miners both under the Tory anti-union laws and under the common law. Kinnock vehemently opposed this as "an incitement and after all we want the law enforced". Others, such as Alan Hadden of the GMB, Sid Tierney of USDAW and Michael Meacher, realizing that the defeat of this motion by the NEC would do severe damage to the movement's morale, urged that the motion be referred back to the home policy committee. Benn was angry. He said any failure to support reimbursement would be "a betrayal of the miners who need it now". Kinnock snapped back: "Anyone who says this is a stab in the back for the miners will have to answer to me."[83] Finally, the motion was referred back to the committee by the narrow margin of 15 votes to 13.[84]

In December, the government cut social security benefits for the families of striking miners. The shadow cabinet refused repeated requests from backbench Labour MPs to raise the issue. As a result, the Campaign Group of left-wing Labour MPs decided to stage a symbolic protest in the Commons. At an agreed time a small band of left MPs led by Eric Heffer stood quietly in front of the Mace and refused to leave. Amidst chaos, the Speaker had no alternative but to adjourn the House. Kinnock was furious at this breach of Commons decorum. At the next meeting of the Parliamentary Labour Party, held in early January 1985, right-wing MPs launched a fierce attack on the left, which found itself defended by some unlikely allies, including Dale Campbell-Savours. Kinnock rounded on the left and criticized the NUM. "It's a miracle the miners' battle hasn't overwhelmed us already," he shouted. "We want to minimize the damage and think about tactics . . . the root of that damage is that there is no unity . . . the pickets don't want public meetings – they want an end to the strike." He went on to condemn "Pharisees who fight to the last drop of everyone else's blood. We could have a debate but would the real issues be discussed? No. . . . I can tell you this," he concluded, "this is the last miners' strike that we will see in our lifetime."

All this was delivered with much fist-shaking, table-thumping and shouting.[85] The gist of it, shorn of the intemperate language, was immediately leaked to the press by Kinnock's office.

As the strike entered its agonizing last months, it became clear that the government was suffering in the opinion polls because of its attacks on the miners. In March 1985, Labour led the Tories by 39.5 per cent to 33 per cent in the opinion polls. Party membership rose throughout the strike and the year-end membership figure for 1984 of 330,000 stands as an all-time high for the Labour Party since it began keeping meaningful records in 1979. Around Britain Party activity was intense and attendance at meetings was consistently high.

As hardship in the coalfields and the drift back to work increased, the enemies of the miners within the TUC and Labour hierarchies grew bolder. From the beginning, the real danger for these people was that the miners might win. If that had happened – and no one was sure at the beginning of the strike who would come out on top – New Realism would have been strangled at birth. Pressure from below would have increased on all union leaders and Kinnock's authority would have been weakened. His intense dislike of Arthur Scargill was at least partly based on his intuitive sense that the man was a dangerous rival, not for the Labour leadership, but for the heart and soul of the Party. Kinnock's politics, his style of leadership and his ambitions for office were all predicated on a defeated, passive Labour Party and a defeated, passive trade union movement. Without doubt, had the miners won, Neil Kinnock's leadership would have been undermined.

Labour's January 1985 NEC had passed yet another resolution outlining the relevance of the strike to the problem of fuel poverty, especially among the elderly, and calling on "all members of the Parliamentary Labour Party to devote their energies to promoting" these arguments. In response to demands from the left and the NUM, the NEC also included a phrase in the resolution urging "all Labour members to avoid actions or pronouncements which suggest less than wholehearted commitment to the cause of the striking miners" and adding that "with unity of purpose and presentation, government policy can be exposed". Kinnock voted for these phrases without comment.[86]

A month later, as the strike was about to end, Kinnock voted once again for an NEC resolution calling on Party members "to redouble their efforts in support of the NUM".[87] When supporters of the miners were later accused of "gesture politics", it seemed strange to many that this charge was not levelled against those who had endorsed such resolutions month after month at the NEC, while at the same time refusing to lift a finger to see them implemented.

In March 1985 the NUM was forced to concede defeat and its members returned to work. 11,000 miners had been arrested during the course of the dispute and 7,000 had been injured in clashes with the police. Over the next few years, Arthur Scargill's pit closure predictions were proved to be conservative.

Kinnock moved quickly to quash the legacy of the strike. In June 1985 the Campaign Group published a Miners' Amnesty Bill drafted by Tony Benn. It called for an amnesty for miners arrested or convicted in the course of the strike, for sacked miners to be reinstated by the National Coal Board and for the NUM to be compensated for losses incurred through fines and sequestration. This proposal was immediately attacked by Kinnock, who declared that it was impossible to take such a proposal seriously. The leadership even tried to blame those who had promoted the bill, particularly Benn, for Labour's failure to win the Brecon and Radnor by-election that summer, in which the Conservatives were beaten by the SDP–Liberal Alliance.

At the TUC in September, unions voted by a narrow 64,000 majority to call on the next Labour government to reinstate sacked miners and reimburse the NUM for sequestration and fines. The motion was passed against the recommendation of the General Council, evidence that despite attitudes at the top, among union activists loyalty to the miners' cause and anger at Tory anti-union laws remained intense.

A large number of resolutions favouring reinstatement and reimbursement had already been submitted to the Labour conference and the NUM was pushing hard for conference support. The media urged Kinnock to fight these demands and he was happy to oblige. Throughout September, in the run-up to the conference, Kinnock's office placed one story after another in the broadsheet press to the effect that Kinnock would never permit Labour to adopt a policy of compensating the NUM for monies lost during the strike. Senior shadow cabinet members swung into action to convince key unions not to support the NUM demands. They registered one success when the ASTMS executive voted to reverse its earlier support for reimbursement.

None the less, given the trade union support already promised to the NUM, it must have been clear to Kinnock and his supporters that the composite would be easily carried. Why then did they insist on opposing it? As so often, their primary audience was the Tory media, which had made it clear that they would crucify Kinnock if he did not oppose his party on this issue. The leadership's aim was to use the 1985 conference to slay the ghost of the miners' strike in the most public fashion possible.

At the NEC meeting prior to the conference, the NEC backed Kinnock after a tense debate and rejected the NUM composite by fifteen votes to fourteen.[88] With several trade union representatives unable to support Kinnock because of mandates from their unions, the crucial swing vote was cast by Michael Meacher, one of the key figures, along with Tom Sawyer and David Blunkett, of the newly "realigned" left. As Meacher declared his vote, Kinnock shouted across the table, "You won't lose by this, Michael." Given his treatment at Kinnock's hands in later years, Meacher may well have come to rue this moment.

The scene was thus set for battle at Bournemouth. This time, Kinnock organized the conference session his way. He convinced the NEC that he himself should reply to the debate on the NUM composite. Interviewed on BBC television on the night before the debate, Kinnock proclaimed that "there was not a cat in hell's chance" that the NUM demands would be included in Labour's election manifesto. According to the *Guardian*, he assured the press that he and he alone would have the last word on the manifesto: "It is not a question of vetoing. There is a process of argument that goes on. I will win that argument as it is already very, very clear from all of those likely to be involved in that discussion about what we put in the manifesto."[89] In other words, Kinnock was fully confident that he controlled the NEC and the shadow cabinet, whatever the conference might decide.

Proposing the NUM composite, Arthur Scargill reminded delegates that the 1982 conference had agreed, by 6,000,000 votes to 66,000 that a future Labour government would reimburse trade unions for fines incurred breaking Tory anti-union laws. The NUM, he argued, should not be punished for carrying out the policy of the TUC and the Labour Party. The conference chair was Alan Hadden, a right-wing union bureaucrat of the old school, formerly of the Boilermakers, now of the merged GMB. After the composite had been moved, he called Eric Hammond, general secretary of the EETPU, who poured vitriol on the NUM. The miners' financial plight was of their own making, Hammond insisted, and went on to chide the newly realigned "soft left" for supporting the miners at Blackpool the previous year. He concluded by excoriating the NUM leaders, whom he famously compared to World War One generals. The miners, he said, were "lions led by donkeys".[90]

Hammond was followed by an anti-NUM constituency delegate, then by Gavin Laird, general secretary of the AEU, who denounced Scargill as a "Marxist" and argued that the NUM should pay its own fines and not come "running to the Labour Party".[91] David Basnett in his last conference appearance argued that Labour would lose the next general election if it passed motions of this kind and said that the Party should not give the miners "a blank cheque". Having called two CLP delegates supporting the resolution and two opposing it, along with three trade union general secretaries opposing it, Hadden moved to finish the debate. He was prevented by howls of protest from the floor, which finally forced him to back down and call Ron Todd for a last contribution.

Todd's speech was impromptu and somewhat incoherent. He referred to the pressure that had been put on the TGWU because of its support for the NUM resolution: "People tell me, 'You can't rock the boat . . . ' I ask you what will I do when they come and tell me they do not like my union's policy on incomes? What will I do if they tell me they do not like unilateral nuclear disarmament? Will I change it?" To enormous applause, he went on: "I will not betray the National Union of Mine-workers. . . . I have heard reference this morning to lions led by donkeys. Well, I am an animal lover and I tell you something. I prefer donkeys to jackals."[92]

Kinnock then rose to reply and took sixteen minutes to do it. The overall balance of speakers' time during the debate was more than two to one against the NUM composite, despite the fact that it had the support of the overwhelming majority of CLP delegates and about half the trade unions. In his speech, Kinnock advanced various reasons for opposing the composite, including a number of technical and legal objections to particular details. As "the strike wore on, the violence built up", Kinnock argued, his voice rising with calculated indignation, "the court actions came and as a consequence of their attitude to the court actions the NUM leadership ensured that they would face crippling damages. . . . It is a fact that if we were ever to endorse the idea of retrospective reimburse-ment we would harm our chances because people would be very confused about our attitude towards the rule of law."[93]

It was a strained, sarcastic, aggressive performance by a man who had set himself up to lose. The TGWU delegation voted for the NUM motion, in accordance with TGWU policy and despite vigorous attempts by Alex Kitson to swing the delegation behind Kinnock. As a result it was carried on a card vote by 3,542,000 to 2,912,000. But the decisive political intervention was the leader's televised denunciation of the strike, subse-quently repeated in broadcast after broadcast.

The miners' strike was the key political event in Britain in the 1980s, a watershed for the trade unions, the Labour left, Kinnock and the Thatcher regime. Both Scargill and Kinnock, like Thatcher, understood that the stakes were high. The stronger the miners and their leadership might become, the weaker Kinnock and the parliamentary right would be. Conversely, as the strike progressed and the miners became weaker, Kinnock and the parliamentary right became stronger. The NUM's ultimate defeat led to a loss of confidence at all levels of the labour movement. It left the base of the Labour Party increasingly reliant on the leadership to win elections for it, thereby consolidating Kinnock's origi-nal 1983 claim that he and he alone could bring victory over the Tories. The left in the CLPs and the unions was severely weakened. The traditional division of functions between trade union leaders and the parliamentary leadership was reinforced, leaving both freer than ever to address themselves to the media and ignore the rank and file. The defeat of the miners was a disaster for the labour movement, but a victory for Neil Kinnock.

Realignment in Retrospect

Within the Labour Party, the miners' defeat sparked off a fierce debate. Many members were profoundly disorientated, their hopes of seeing off the government sooner rather than later dashed. If the miners, with all their determination and industrial clout, could not shift the government, people asked, then who could?

In this fertile ground opportunism and double talk of all kinds flourished. The "soft left" Labour Co-ordinating Committee (LCC) promptly issued a position paper entitled *After the Strike*. It said "no blame" should be attached either to Scargill or Kinnock, to the "ultra-left" or to the right. It referred gently to the "leadership distance" from the strike, a distance bizarrely dismissed as "overcompensation for emotional identification". It also insisted that the LCC, for all its criticisms of Scargill's tactics, was still strongly in favour of "extra-parliamentary activity" because "centre politics and new realism are not adequate weapons to take on Thatcherism".[94] None the less, the LCC became the fulcrum for the realignment of the left that was to take place in the Labour Party over the following months, a realignment whose sole effect was to institutionalize so-called centre politics in the Labour Party.

What had seemed the inexorable rise of New Realism after 1983 had been held in check for a year by the miners' strike and the campaign against ratecapping waged by Labour councils. At the base of the Party, the "soft left" had formally backed both these extra-parliamentary struggles. Peter Hain, then vice-chair of the LCC, called on Labour to support Liverpool, Lambeth and the miners "regardless of any argument over illegality".[95] Increasingly, however, Hain's colleagues on the LCC executive did not share his views. In the LCC office in London's Soho, cynical contempt for the miners' struggle appeared to be the order of the day; Arthur Scargill and Peter Heathfield were favourite targets for criticism. Similarly, although "soft left" councillors around the country agreed in meeting after meeting to support the strategy of non-compliance with ratecapping, most had little intention of pursuing it to its ultimate conclusion, which could have meant surcharge and disqualification from office. None the less, they played their part in the high-profile public campaign; they never argued for any alternative to the agreed Labour Party line of not setting a rate. When the campaign collapsed, they turned on their erstwhile left allies and sought to scapegoat them for the debacle.

The emergent "soft left" knew that if either the miners' or the ratecapping struggle had succeeded, the whole balance of forces within the labour movement – and between that movement and the government – would have been transformed. For most of 1984–85 the "soft left" hung fire out of a fear of finding themselves on the losing side. When both the miners' and the ratecapping struggles ended in defeat, the "soft left" emerged in a blaze of publicity as fierce critics of the "hard left" and champions of a new *rapprochement* with the Party and trade union leaderships.

For many years, the "soft left" and the LCC had enjoyed friendly relations with the Communist Party of Great Britain. Much of what passed for the intellectual groundwork of realignment had already been laid by the Communist Party and its publicity organ, *Marxism Today*. In *The Politics of Thatcherism*, published in 1982, Stuart Hall and Martin Jacques had argued that the new Tory right had created "a political and ideological repertoire which permitted Thatcher to outflank Labour and appeal directly to working class support", thus undermining Labour's electoral base. By combining the old Tory chauvinist appeal to "nation, family, duty, authority, standards and traditionalism" with the new right politics espousing "the aggressive themes of a revived neo-liberalism, self-interest, competitive individualism, and anti-statism", Thatcher, they claimed, had created a "reactionary common sense" which had struck a chord with sections of Labour's working-class base.[96]

Despite a surfeit of survey data to the contrary, *Marxism Today* and later the "realigned" Labour left insisted that working people had succumbed to Tory ideology and that to expect mass action by them against the government was absurd. Hence, they argued, the miners' and ratecapping struggles were wrong-headed, because they arrogantly assumed that working people could be rallied to defend a discredited collectivist ethic. Left out of the account was any assessment of the responsibility of the Labour and trade union leaderships, ostensibly guiding and speaking on behalf of a movement of millions. The bitterly disappointing performances of previous Labour governments, in particular the attempt to make working people pay the price of the mid-1970s recession, were simply ignored.

This refusal to examine the role played by the Labour and trade union leaderships was in sharp contrast to the focus placed on the alleged misdemeanours of the left – the NUM leadership, the Campaign Group of Labour MPs in Parliament, Ted Knight and other surcharged councillors in Lambeth and Liverpool – who were blamed for the failure of the ratecapping and miners' struggles. The "soft left" spent much time counterposing their own commitment to the "new social movements", notably those involving women and black people, to what they alleged was the Bennite left's narrow loyalty to a white-male-dominated "class politics". In fact, it was the Bennite left (although certainly not the supporters of Militant) who had been responsible for placing the varied questions of race and gender, democracy and ecology, internationalism and decentralization on the agenda of the Labour Party in the first place. But the "soft left" apologists, like their allies in the Communist Party, were never over-troubled by such details of history.

The Eurocommunists and the "soft left" claimed that the electoral defeats of 1979 and 1983 were part of a profound crisis for the whole labour movement rooted in Britain's declining proportion of manual workers, the slow death of the traditional working class, and Labour's concomitant failure to reach out to new sectors of the population. They concluded that what was required was an abandonment of Labour's traditional socialist aims and class base. Eric Hobsbawm, widely touted at this time as "Kinnock's favourite Marxist", argued that "we can no longer rely on an absolute majority of proletarian Britain to sweep a Labour government in single-handed".[97]

For the Eurocommunists, this implied a "broad democratic alliance" for "limited purposes" against "Thatcherism" – an alliance that reached well to the right of the Labour Party. In effect, they were calling for a re-run of the Communist Party's "popular front" strategy of the 1930s. But for Labour's "soft left", bound by the iron chains of Labour loyalism, the Eurocommunist analysis had a different function. It was an excuse to jettison the radical aspirations that had sparked the left rebellion in the Party and to forge a "historic compromise" with the Labour right. The arguments of Eric Hobsbawm and Stuart Hall were simply a means to an end: the justification for a "realignment" behind the Party leadership.

In 1990, the former editor of *Marxism Today*, Martin Jacques, surveying the demise of Stalinism and the wreckage of his own Communist Party, boasted that its great achievement in recent times had been to make "much of the intellectual running for Labour's Kinnockite revolution":

> The CP in the eighties acted like the Labour revisionists of the fifties . . . it was the main centre of opposition to the Scargill strategy in the miners' strike. It has been the ideological protagonist against the hard left.[98]

What all this meant in practice within the Labour Party began to become clear even before the miners' strike was over. Just prior to Christmas 1984, newspapers reported that Michael Meacher, Tom Sawyer and David Blunkett would offer Kinnock a centre–left bloc on the NEC as a counter-weight to the centre–right bloc on which, it was alleged, he was forced to rely in the face of continuing intransigence from the "hard left". Within six months this new bloc was a reality, giving Kinnock the unassailable majority on the NEC that he enjoyed until his resignation in 1992.

The loudest starting pistol for the rush to the right that was dignified with the name of "realignment" was the publication in *Tribune*, in January 1985, of a leading article by the newspaper's new editor, Nigel Williamson. Entitled "Working to Win", the article was significant because it was written by an erstwhile Benn supporter and prominent member of the "hard left". Indeed, Williamson had begun his political/ journalistic career penning diatribes in *London Labour Briefing* attacking, among others, Neil Kinnock. Under the editorship of Williamson's predecessor, Chris Mullin, *Tribune* had moved to the left and become a hard-hitting critic of first the Foot and then the Kinnock leadership. Williamson's editorial was a renunciation of "Bennism" and a signal that *Tribune* wanted to return to the leadership fold.

Before publishing the article, Williamson had consulted prominent "soft lefts" and had won the support of the majority of the *Tribune* board, including chair Michael Meacher, for the change of political direction. Throughout this period he was in close contact with Kinnock's office through Patricia Hewitt. Williamson also spent a great deal of time on the telephone briefing the media on his volte-face. Not surprisingly, the parliamentary lobby took considerable interest in what they interpreted as the break-up of the left coalition that had taken Labour by storm in the early 1980s.

In return for *Tribune*'s support, Williamson suggested that Kinnock should abandon both his drive to force "one member, one vote" onto the Labour Party and the proposed extension of the Militant purge. The leader and his office were delighted with their new champion but they paid no heed whatsoever to his advice.

The May 1985 edition of *New Socialist* carried a lengthy article entitled "Bennism Without Benn". Long before the magazine actually appeared on the newsstands, the contents of the article had received extensive publicity. Extracts were published in the *Guardian*, and the *Times* headline on 6 April ran: "Benn isolated as allies work to build up Kinnock". The *Observer* followed suit on 21 April. Suddenly the break-up of the Benn bloc and "the realignment of the left" were everywhere. Much of the coverage was orchestrated from Kinnock's office by Patricia Hewitt, who knew in advance about the *New Socialist* article.

"Bennism Without Benn" was published under the name of Patrick Seyd, an academic at the University of Sheffield, with additional research credited to journalist Christian Wolmar. In fact, the article was heavily influenced by the new editor of *New Socialist*, Stuart Weir, who rewrote some of it without Seyd's permission. In effect the article had been drawn up by a "committee" which included, among others, Nigel Williamson and Frances Morrell, then leader of the Inner London Education Authority (ILEA) and Benn's erstwhile political adviser. From the beginning it was conceived – certainly by Weir – as an attempt to transform the internal balance of Labour Party politics.

The article called for a "new left", which would create room for a "popular and realistic democratic socialist politics, for a third force independent of the right and the ultra left".[99] Seyd argued that the Labour Party was now united behind a limited but well-defined set of left-wing policies, including nuclear disarmament, and that the priority now was to win the next general election in order to give the leadership a real chance of implementing them. Kinnock should be offered support in order to "detach him from the embrace of the parliamentary right".[100] The "ultra-left" Dennis Skinner was cast as a villain of the piece, exercising a demonic influence on Tony Benn and the Campaign Group of Labour MPs, and alienating key figures like Tom Sawyer with his "abrasive" style.

The key to "realignment", the article argued, lay within the constituency parties, where there was a strong desire for unity around the existing policies and leadership. This was also reflected in Parliament, where "key Bennites in the PLP, like Meacher and [Stuart] Holland, have decided to work constructively for left policies with the leadership".[101]

For Kinnock and his office, the spate of realignment publicity was a welcome means of encouraging hesitant "soft lefts", particularly the Meacher, Blunkett, Sawyer triumvirate on the NEC, to take the final plunge and back the leader. By the summer of 1985, this had been accomplished; thanks to their defection from the left, Kinnock now enjoyed a reliable majority. Although by the end of the decade he was taking the support of "soft left" NEC members for granted, between 1985 and 1987 Kinnock rarely attempted anything controversial on the NEC without first assuring himself of their acquiescence, usually by approaching them in private before crucial meetings. In return, the "soft left" expected greater influence and a check on the leadership's movement to the right, but all they got was more demands for loyalty. The argument had been that Kinnock was a "prisoner" of the right and the "soft left" would liberate him; the reality was that the "soft left" became prisoners of Kinnock. The only people in the Party who were liberated by realignment were the old-guard hard right.

The LCC found itself in the difficult position of trying to reconcile its support for Kinnock with its claims to radical socialist ideology. In an attempt to square this circle, its apologists devised the spurious thesis that the "oppositionalism" of the Labour left had driven a reluctant Kinnock into the arms of the parliamentary right. But as early as January 1985, *Tribune* itself explained that "Kinnock advisers were reported to be sceptical about the proposal of the realigners."[102] Although Kinnock's people recognized that in *Tribune* he had gained a "valuable and unexpected ally", the idea that the new inner-Party line-up would "require a move to the left on the part of Kinnock was strongly rejected".[103] Indeed, Kinnock himself refuted the "soft left" thesis in a rare pre-conference interview in *Tribune* in September 1985. "I'm not a prisoner of the right," he insisted, "I lead the Party in the way I want to lead it and I am under obligation to no faction, grouping or wedge in the Party."[104]

Upwardly mobile Party members now realized that they could no longer progress through Labour's power structure by continuing to mouth the slogans of the left, as they had done in the previous period.

Their problem was that they could not simply change their tune overnight; the hard right was prepared to treat with them only because of their base of support in the left-leaning constituencies, the base that had elevated "soft left" MPs to their present eminence. What was therefore required was a rationale for their turn to the right that would enable them to retain a significant proportion of that still mostly left-wing base.

At the end of May 1985 rival slates for the forthcoming elections to the NEC's constituency section were in circulation. The LCC withheld its support from Tony Benn, Dennis Skinner and Eric Heffer while the Campaign Group backed all the sitting members except David Blunkett. Much was made by the "soft left" of what was described as the "sectarian" decision of the Campaign Group to drop Blunkett, but somehow the LCC decision to turn against Benn, Heffer, and Skinner – because they voted against the leadership on the NEC and not because of any policy disagreements – was in a different category. Constituency members re-elected Benn, Skinner and Heffer with hefty majorities; they also backed Blunkett, who for the first time topped the poll with both left- and right-wing constituencies voting for him.

Realignment gave Kinnock the chance he had awaited to construct a new, dominant coalition on the NEC that would support his leadership without question. These "soft lefts" were often described by the press as powerbrokers on the NEC, as arbiters within the Party between left and right. In reality, all they had achieved was to change the existing political balance on the NEC without changing its personnel. The "soft left" had made a gift of its much-vaunted independence to a leadership that had no use for independence of any kind. Their determination to offer the leadership "constructive" and "critical" support enabled that leadership, in the coming years, to transform the NEC into a rubber stamp and strip it of most of its traditional functions.

At the base of the Party, it was clear that realignment enjoyed real but limited support. A frustrated membership desperately wanted a way out of the impasse of electoral and industrial failure and internecine strife. The arguments of the realigners carried particular weight with members only casually involved in Party affairs and therefore reliant on the mainstream media for information about the inner-Party debate. The masterminds of realignment in the Parliamentary Labour Party and the LCC were well aware of this current of feeling and exploited it with ruthless cynicism, repeatedly promising that left policies backed by the membership could be protected by a right-wing leadership.

The real key to realignment for many among the Party elite – the parliamentarians, councillors, Party and trade union officials, and especially the LCC cadre – was the pursuit of personal preferment. All the ideological hand-wringing, the carefully planted articles and unattributed quotations, the sober strategic reassessments were nothing more for most of those involved than a cynical camouflage. The proof? Within five years all the strategic perspectives used to justify realignment and all the residual left principles avowed by the leading realigners had been discarded without ceremony.

Memories in the Labour Party have become conveniently short in recent years, so it is worth emphasizing how much of the "realignment" was accompanied by radical socialist rhetoric. In 1985 the LCC stated that its aim was "to bring the vital dimension of extra-parliamentary politics to the Labour left".[105] It claimed that "Parliament and local government are central vehicles for change" but that extra-parliamentary strategies would be needed to "build the mass base from below through struggle and campaigning". The Labour Party needed to turn outwards to create "the kind of power base necessary to make the implementation of socialist policies feasible".[106] In practice, however, the LCC opposed each and every extra-parliamentary struggle that arose over the next five years.

Similarly, a "*Tribune* relaunch statement" entitled "Democratic Socialism", ostensibly written by Tribune Group MPs and published in *Tribune* before the 1985 Party conference, argued for "economic power to be made publicly accountable through an extension of social ownership, planning and industrial democracy"; it also declared that "a determination to disengage immediately from the nuclear arms race . . . must form the basis of our international approach. We believe a Britain not aligned to any major power is best placed to advance these policies." Finally, it called for a Labour Party which "clearly puts socialism on the political agenda; is open and outward-looking in the expression of its values; campaigns in a way which clearly links our policies with the underlying socialist principles which must shape them; and that encourages the presentation of ideas and debate in a spirit which recognizes the legitimacy of minority views".[107] The final point seems today a startling expression of a bygone libertarianism. The signatories included most of the leading lights of realignment, including Blunkett, Meacher, Sawyer, Kevin Barron, Derek Fatchett, Joan Lestor, Glyn Ford and David Martin (the last two of whom were later to become leading Kinnock supporters in the European Parliamentary Labour Party), Gordon Brown, Harriet Harman, Bill Gilby (then chair of the LCC and now, as NUPE political officer, Tom Sawyer's fixer-in-chief), Bryan Gould, Robin Cook, Martin O'Neill, Jack Dromey of the TGWU, Margaret Beckett, and Paul Convery (then LCC secretary, now Margaret Hodge's hard right adjutant on Islington Council).[108]

Within a few years all of these individuals were to turn their backs, without a word of explanation or self-justification, on virtually every element in the *Tribune* statement, a fact that *Tribune* itself declined to note as it continued its forlorn search for a "political space" between the leadership and the "oppositionalist left".

The immediate upshot of realignment was not a halt to the leadership's slide to the right but a renewed attack on the left, most vividly in Kinnock's denunciation of Liverpool Council at the 1985 conference in Bournemouth. The day before his main address, the LCC in its daily conference bulletin urged Kinnock to avoid dividing the Party and warned against a "Rambo"-style speech. But the following day's bulletin praised the leader for saying "publicly what many of us had been saying privately".[109]

Kinnock's attack on Liverpool Council marked the start of a new purge of the left which continued to the end of his regime. It was precisely this sort of attack that the "soft left" had claimed it could prevent by "realigning" behind Kinnock. Significantly, at the height of the press uproar over realignment in May 1985, the NUPE conference voted to back a purge of *Militant* supporters. Tom Sawyer had delivered for Kinnock; NUPE had joined the GMB as a bulwark of the group of centre trade unions on which Kinnock would rely in years to come. The conference resolution had been moved by Jane Kennedy of NUPE's Liverpool branch, an LCC supporter and long-time opponent of the Militant Tendency; she was later to become a NUPE official and eventually the Labour MP for Liverpool Broadgreen following the expulsion of the sitting MP, Terry Fields.

By the autumn of 1986 some of the leading "soft lefts" were already admitting that realignment had failed in nearly all its ostensible aims. Writing in *Tribune*, Nigel Williamson confessed as follows:

> . . . those involved in this realignment have not achieved what they set out to create, namely a centre–left coalition around Neil Kinnock in the Shadow Cabinet and on the NEC instead of the centre–right forces which predominated then and still do . . . the realigners made it clear at the time that they were not interested in one-way streets and were very much looking for a two-way traffic with the Labour leadership. That it hasn't really turned out like that is partly because Neil Kinnock calculated that although it was a useful tool against the hard left, the soft left did not really wield any power within the party.[110]

In other words, Kinnock had called the "soft left" bluff. On the economy, on nuclear power, on nuclear weapons, on mass campaigning, Kinnock had spurned them. "The realigned left . . . is heavily locked into a strategy of supporting Kinnock . . . and its criticism of the direction of the party and its policies are tempered by this."[111] As a result, Williamson said, the "soft left" had become the "least coherent" group in the Party.[112] Within a year, Williamson had given up completely on *Tribune* and "realignment" and chosen instead to become the most abject of leadership loyalists as editor of the Walworth Road in-house journal, *Labour Party News*.

If the claims made by the "realigners" in 1985 are taken at face value and measured against the reality of Labour politics after the general election defeat of 1987, their project must be judged an abysmal failure. It led directly to the abandonment of the very policies that the "realigners" claimed to be defending. For the clearest verdict, one has only to return to the "new style" *Tribune* of 24 May 1985. In a set-piece exchange between ex-editor Chris Mullin and successor Nigel Williamson, Mullin commented thus:

> I believe that there is a simple explanation for what is happening. It is that many of the upwardly mobile young men and women in the foothills of the Labour Party power structure scent power – and they want to be part of the winning faction by the time the music stops. . . . Their definiton of victory is when they get the jobs. My definition of victory is when something changes for the better.[113]

In reply, Williamson derided the notion that Kinnock was irretrievably lost to the left and insisted that it was not "impossible to wean him away from the old-style machine politicians". It was absurd, Williamson argued, for Mullin to compare Neil Kinnock to Harold Wilson. "Do you honestly believe", he asked, "that a government led by Neil Kinnock would support American military global adventures as Wilson did in Vietnam?"[114] Less than six years later, Kinnock was backing the US-led war in the Gulf.

The single most important achievement of "realignment" was to give Neil Kinnock decisive authority within the NEC and a free hand in the Parliamentary Labour Party. In time this authority allowed him to do with the Labour Party as he and his advisers pleased. Above all, the changed balance of forces at the top of the Party enabled Kinnock and friends to exploit the despair that engulfed the rank and file following the defeat of 1987.

Who Lost the 1987 General Election?

From the last months of the miners' strike in 1985, Labour ran the Tories close in the opinion polls. It pulled ahead of the government in the summer of 1985 and established a clear lead in early 1986 following the Westland affair, in which the scandal surrounding the collapse of a helicopter manufacturer had led to accusations of a high-level government cover-up. The bombing of Libya by US jets based in Britain and the nuclear accident at Chernobyl strengthened Labour's case for a non-nuclear defence policy independent of the United States, as did the soaring popularity of Gorbachev and the widespread distrust of Reagan.

The legacy of the campaigns against ratecapping and the abolition of the GLC was positive and Labour did well in the local elections in the spring. The Party had hopes of success in the coming general election, but in retrospect 1986, like 1990 and 1991, was to prove a false dawn.

At the 1986 Conservative Party conference, the government unveiled a new package of deeply reactionary proposals on education, housing and other social issues, backed by an attack on Labour's record on defence and local government. Ultimately, this attack wrought havoc in Labour's ranks, but for many months it made no impression on the opinion polls. Although by the end of the year the Tories had managed to pull back Labour's lead, this reflected a rise in the Tory vote at the expense of the SDP–Liberal Alliance rather than a fall in Labour support, which held steady. The Tories did finally pull ahead, but only slightly, in the first weeks of 1987, thanks to the beginning of Chancellor Nigel Lawson's economic upswing.

In contrast to the relatively stable support enjoyed by the Labour Party as a whole, the public standing of its leader was falling rapidly. In October 1986 Kinnock had stood neck and neck with Thatcher, but by February 1987 he had slipped more than ten points behind. None the less, at this stage most Labour leaders were hopeful of victory. Even as late as mid February 1987, the general election was considered too close to call. It was only at the end of that month, after the Greenwich by-election, that Labour entered a slump which continued up to and through the general election campaign. This slump and Labour's defeat at the polls in June gave the Labour right another chance to scapegoat the left, now known as the "loony left", for the third defeat in a row.

The by-election in the marginal seat of Greenwich in inner London, which followed the death of Labour MP Guy Barnett, was fought at a time when the Tory attack on Labour's record in local government was at last beginning to bite. The modest measures taken by a handful of Labour councils to tackle racism and sexism, and especially their tentative initiatives on lesbian and gay rights, sparked off a media reaction of unprecedented ferocity. Later, the "soft left" accused these councils of making errors in the pace and presentation of these minimal reforms. But there can be little doubt that, in an election year, even the most low-key attempts to redress the grievances around race, gender and sexuality held by many long-time Labour supporters would have been used by the Tories and the press to whip up a backlash. The choice was either not to raise the issues at all or to campaign openly on them, isolate opponents as small-minded bigots and seek to persuade voters that everyone would benefit from a more equal and tolerant society. Where this approach was tried, for example in Haringey, it produced positive results. Elsewhere Labour panicked. The damage done by media and Tory attacks was compounded. Labour seemed divided and dissembling.

There was an outcry when Labour-controlled Brent Council in London brought in a team of race advisers to work in local schools. Originally the Tories on the council had voted for the appointment of the advisers, whose posts were funded by central government under Section 11 of the Race Relations Act. But following the McGoldrick affair – in which a local head teacher was accused of racism – the national media whipped up a backlash against Brent in particular and local authority anti-racist strategies in general. Thanks to the tabloid press, bizarre fabrications – among them tales that Labour councils had banned as racist the use of black rubbish bags and the nursery rhyme "Ba Ba Black Sheep" – entered popular folklore. The Tories, with Norman Tebbit in the lead, exploited the confusion to their own advantage, but they were assisted in this by the refusal of the Labour front bench to nail the tabloid lies or to defend the practical, long-overdue measures being taken by Labour councils to ensure a fair deal for black citizens and other victims of discrimination. Roy Hattersley publicly disavowed the Brent initiative. "I do not deny the existence of unacceptable behaviour in some local education authorities," he said. "I want to eliminate it."[115]

A draft leaflet prepared by Labour's Walworth Road headquarters staff for the May local elections revealed the defensive mentality gripping the leadership. It was in question and answer format. One question read: "But if I vote Labour won't I get a loony left council like those in London?" The answer: "Left councils are exceptions, Neil Kinnock has told them to mend their ways and he is in full charge of the Labour Party".[116]

Although this attack helped the Tories to edge ahead of Labour in the national polls, early polls in Greenwich showed Labour set for a big win, with a 17 per cent swing from the Tories. Greenwich, after all, was an inner-city area in which government policies had wrought havoc. In the 1986 local elections Labour had won nine out of the ten wards. The Tories had come second with the SDP a poor third.

Then came the controversy over the selection of Deirdre Wood as Labour's candidate, a controversy almost entirely the product of machinations and press briefings by the Labour leadership. There were fifty-one applicants for the Labour nomination in Greenwich but Wood, a long-time member of the local Labour Party and for some years a mildly left-wing member of the GLC and ILEA, was the overwhelming local favourite. In the *Guardian* journalist Martin Linton, who was well connected to the Labour establishment, reported that the by-election would be dominated by the "loony left" issue. Labour Party strategists were planning to counterattack by promoting Greenwich as a "caring council". However, he warned, "the success of this campaign will depend crucially on the candidate chosen by the CLP".[117] In the course of the selection process in Greenwich, seven hundred individual Labour Party members attended nominating meetings and two thirds of them voted for Deirdre Wood. Nearly all the delegates at the local selection conference had consulted the organizations they represented before voting. Walworth Road attempts to promote other candidates, notably Kinnock-loyalist Glenys Thornton, were rebuffed.

Shortly after the selection the Tory candidate alleged that Deirdre Wood was not popular with the Labour Party's national leadership and that her views were not those of traditional Labour voters. Vincent Hanna later reported that the smear campaign against Deirdre Wood had been started by elements at Walworth Road keen to prevent her being selected.[118] To the Tory media Deirdre Wood was just another obscure local Labour politician until she had been targeted for attack by the leadership of her own party.

During the course of the by-election campaign, the press, with help from Conservative Central Office, ran story after story purporting to expose the depravity of Labour in local government, with which Deirdre Wood was personally linked by all manner of journalistic sleight of hand. Coupled with an open and ugly appeal to every prejudice in the book was an attack on the alleged wastefulness and inefficiency of Labour local authorities. Though the Labour leadership realized that a defeat in Greenwich in the run-up to the general election would be a major setback for the Party, its attempts to contain the damage only made things worse. It decided, first, that the contentious issues of race, gender and sexuality were to be kept out of the campaign. This meant that the bigotry whipped up by the Tory press was left unanswered. Voters were left with the impression that Labour really did have policies it was ashamed of and wanted to hide.

Second, Walworth Road decided to strip the by-election campaign of all local influences and neuter the candidate. The polling date was imposed against the advice of local activists, who wanted a delay. Local Labour councillors were ordered not to canvass in their own wards. Instead of making a virtue of Wood's long-standing involvement with a wide range of local campaigns and voluntary bodies, Walworth Road tried to disguise it. The attempt to sanitize Deirdre Wood backfired; she looked suspect and dissembling.

The Tory media, well aware that the Tories could not win in Greenwich, promoted the SDP as the main challenger to Labour. A stream of opinion polls and daily hype in the press and on television mobilized the anti-Labour vote behind SDP candidate Rosie Barnes, whose sole appeal to voters seemed to be that she was not Deirdre Wood.

Although Labour boasted that it was sending in its "top strategists" and a team of fifty "mainstream" Labour MPs, it failed to mount any direct resistance to the rising SDP challenge until two days before the by-election. Polls showed the Labour lead slipping away. Wood came under increasing pressure from the tabloids, who made abusive references to her age and her figure. When intrusive stories about her family were published, she broke down in tears at a press conference. On polling day the SDP won the by-election with 52 per cent of the vote. The Tories slumped to 11 per cent in a seat where they had formerly garnered 35 per cent. For them it was a sacrifice well worth making. They had succeeded in inflicting severe damage on Labour's credibility with large sections of the working-class electorate. They had cast doubts on the Party as a serious contestant for parliamentary power. But even more damaging to Labour than the by-election result itself was the leadership's reaction to it in the days and weeks that followed.

The Sunday after the by-election, Bristol South MP Michael Cocks, a former Labour chief whip, informed *Sunday Times* readers that the "London left" was obsessed with "irrelevant minorities". He was only one of a number of right-wingers who suggested that, in future, by-election candidates should be selected by the NEC and not the local Party. In a speech to the Parliamentary Labour Party Kinnock declared, "We make it categorically clear that the people at the fringe of our movement have no influence and will get no influence." At the same time he condemned the "political illiterates" who indulged in "slack and idle talk of the leadership imposing candidates".[119] Within a year he was to steer a constitutional amendment through Party conference providing for precisely that.

On 4 March the front-page headline of the *Sun* read "Gays put Kinnock in a panic – secret letter lashes loonies". A letter from Patricia Hewitt, Kinnock's strategist-in-chief, written on the day after the Greenwich defeat to Labour MP Frank Dobson, who had supervised the Greenwich campaign, had been leaked to the press:

> It is obvious from our own polling, as well as from the doorstep, that the "London effect" is now very noticeable. The "Loony Labour Left" is now taking its toll; the gays and lesbians issue is costing us dear amongst the pensioners and fear of extremism and higher taxes/rates is particularly prominent in the GLC area.

Hewitt defended her letter, saying that "nothing in it contradicts what Neil Kinnock said after the Greenwich by-election in his speech to the Parliamentary Labour Party".[120] At a stroke, the entire Tory and media campaign against local Labour councils' equal opportunities initiatives was vindicated – by the Labour leadership itself.

The Association of London Authorities, a body bringing together all Labour councils in the capital, sought a meeting with the leader to clarify the issues but was rebuffed. Kinnock also chose to cancel a previously scheduled meeting with London MPs and parliamentary candidates after 150 invitations had been issued. The first post-Greenwich poll put

Labour 4 per cent behind the Tories, their biggest lead in two and a half years.

Seeing their chance, a clique of traditionalist right-wing London Party members, including Brian Nicholson of the TGWU, Roger Godsiff of APEX, John Spellar of the EETPU, Roy Shaw of Camden Council and Diane Hayter of the Fabian Society, formed the short-lived "Londoners for Labour", which, they boasted to the press, would reclaim Labour in London from "the loonies". It had no presence in the Party on the ground but gave the media yet another excuse to attack the London left and Labour as a whole.

Following Kinnock's disastrous visit to Washington, where he was slighted by Ronald Reagan, Labour continued its slide down the opinion poll ratings. The Party's crisis was compounded by a row over Labour Party Black Sections and the parliamentary candidate for Nottingham East, Sharon Atkin. Founded in 1983 by black Labour activists dismayed by the discrepancy between the Party's reliance on black votes and its long-term failure to address black issues or promote black candidates, Black Sections had mounted a sustained campaign for the right of black self-organization within the Labour Party. In the face of stubborn resistance from the leadership, the campaign had succeeded each year in attracting more and more support at Party conference. A priority for Black Sections was the selection of black candidates in winnable parliamentary seats. That implied a challenge to white domination of local parties in areas with large black populations, and a threat to a number of sitting Labour MPs. Through intensive effort a handful of black sections supporters had succeeded in being selected in 1985 and 1986, one of whom was Atkin, a left-wing Lambeth councillor chosen to contest the highly marginal seat of Nottingham East.

At a national conference held in Nottingham in March 1987, Black Sections adopted a radical manifesto designed to highlight issues of concern to black people that the Labour Party hierarchy was ignoring. At Kinnock's urging, the March NEC condemned the statements attributed to the Black Sections conference "that implied separatist organizations and caucuses in a way that is both divisive and contrary to the central principles of the Party". With only the left dissenting, the NEC warned that "any decisions to undertake selective support for candidates, separate campaigns, statements or manifestos will result in action being taken under the Party constitution against any Party members endorsing or acting upon such decisions".[121]

Kinnock and his supporters admitted that they had not received any direct reports on the proceedings of the Nottingham conference and that their motion was based purely on the media version of the event. Precipitate and ill-informed, their intervention was none the less a

calculated attack on the bogey of black militancy, an attack intended for
public consumption.

On April 3rd five Birmingham Labour MPs – Roy Hattersley, Denis
Howell, Jeff Rooker, Terry Davis and Robin Corbett – wrote to Sharon
Atkin, Bernie Grant (then Labour leader of Haringey Council and prospective parliamentary candidate for Tottenham) and Linda Bellos (then
Lambeth Council leader), demanding that they cancel their scheduled
appearances at a Birmingham Labour Party Black Sections public meeting booked for April 7th. The tone of the letter, copies of which were sent
by the signatories to the national press, was one of deliberate abuse. In
effect, it proclaimed Birmingham a no-go area for Labour's most prominent black activists.

Despite the threats, the Birmingham meeting went ahead and Atkin
and Bellos, joined by local black Labour activists, addressed a mainly
black audience of over 250 people. During the course of Atkin's speech
she was heckled by black nationalists who were hostile to the Labour
Party. They claimed that she and the other speakers were colluding with
the racism of the Labour leadership and selling out black people. "You
don't give a damn for black people," one of them said, "you are only
interested in a parliamentary seat and when you are elected you will
forget all about black people. You are a puppet of Neil Kinnock and a
racist Labour Party." Outraged, Atkin replied: "I was told not to come to
this meeting tonight if I want to keep my parliamentary seat. But I didn't
want a parliamentary seat if I can't represent black people . . . so I don't
give a damn about Neil Kinnock and the racist Labour Party."

Her remarks were picked up by the media, which were present
because of the publicity given to the meeting by the five Birmingham
Labour MPs. Kinnock instructed Larry Whitty, the Labour Party's
general secretary, to prepare a report on Atkin for the April meeting of
the NEC. Patricia Hewitt then advised lobby correspondents that at this
meeting Kinnock would have Atkin removed as a parliamentary candidate. For Kinnock, this was not only a test of strength between him and
the Black Sections; more important, it was a chance to reassure the
electorate that he was prepared to take a stand against the "loony left".

Whitty reported to the NEC that because of illness Atkin would not be
able to attend the April meeting or produce a written submission to it. A
letter from Atkin reiterating her preparedness to abide by the rules was
circulated to all members. Dennis Skinner proposed that no action be
taken against Atkin but was supported only by five other left-wingers.
The NEC then proceeded to try Atkin in her absence. Keva Coombes, her
solicitor, appeared on her behalf and made it clear that Atkin had no
intention of issuing a separate election manifesto and that she was
prepared to apologize for any offence she had unintentionally given.
Coombes also pointed out that in view of the medical evidence there was

no court or disciplinary tribunal in the land that would not have granted a delay.

Kinnock, chairing the meeting in the absence of Syd Tierney, an official of the shopworkers' union USDAW, told the NEC to disregard these arguments. The only evidence Whitty had produced to support the charge of a "sustained course of conduct prejudicial to the Party" was a transcript of a BBC recording of Atkin's remarks to the Birmingham meeting. Whitty claimed complaints about Atkin's behaviour had been made on the telephone and in writing but refused to say who had made them. He did not refer to over one hundred letters of support for Atkin that Walworth Road was known to have received.

Kinnock himself moved that Atkin was in breach of the constitution and must therefore be reported to the National Constitutional Committee (NCC) for disciplinary action. He also moved that since the committee would not meet until after the general election Atkin would have to be suspended as a parliamentary candidate. His motion, which violated all codes of natural justice and due process, was carried by eighteen votes to six. Immediately Kinnock moved another resolution: that, in place of Atkin, Mohammed Aslam be imposed as the parliamentary candidate in Nottingham East. Again this was agreed, as were the previous resolutions, with the support of all the members of the "soft left", including Michael Meacher, David Blunkett and Tom Sawyer.

Kinnock's behaviour throughout the meeting was aggressive in the extreme. An angry Tony Benn told the NEC that "the leader of the Party, acting today as the Chairman of the Party, acting as the prosecutor, acting as the judge, was acting as the jury and coming up with an alternative candidate . . . I've heard of one member, one vote but I did not know that it meant that the leader was the one member and his was the only vote."[122]

The Labour Party's director of campaigns and communications, Peter Mandelson, told the waiting press that Aslam had been chosen by the NEC because he had been runner-up to Atkin in the original selection contest. In fact, Aslam had failed even to make the final shortlist from which Atkin had been chosen. Ironically, four years later Aslam himself was charged with disciplinary offences by the NEC.

The same NEC meeting that removed Atkin was asked to deal with statements made by Frank Field. The Labour MP for Birkenhead had advised voters to back the SDP–Liberal Alliance in seats where it was placed second to the Tories. Benn moved that Field be asked to issue a statement calling on electors to vote Labour in all constituencies. This was opposed by Kinnock on the grounds that Field might refuse to do so. With the energetic support of David Blunkett, who attacked Benn for being divisive, a motion was carried that Benn's proposal not be put to the NEC.

Field's conduct was far more obviously in defiance of the March NEC threat of action against anyone attempting to "undertake selective support for candidates" than anything Atkin had done, but his treatment at the hands of the leadership was markedly different. Field, of course, was a favourite of the right-wing press, whereas Atkin was a hate figure. But if the leadership had thought that any positive publicity would come out of its attack on Atkin it was mistaken. As with the Greenwich affair, the leadership's desire to defuse the political dynamite of race and sex led it to denounce sections of its own party to the general public, with negative effects on the opinion poll standing of the Party as a whole. On polling day, Labour in Nottingham East failed to overturn the sitting Tory MP's slim 1983 majority of 1,464. A marginal seat had been thrown away by the leadership in another vain attempt to appease the media.

In his report on the general election to Party conference in October, campaign director Peter Mandelson painted a bizarre picture of this period. "Events distracted attention from the Party's economic campaigning priorities. In part, the defeat of the candidate at the Greenwich by-election and its aftermath, together with widespread unfavourable publicity concerning defence policy and black sections, severely hampered our campaign efforts for a crucial period."[123] In fact, in each and every one of these cases it was decisions made by the Labour leadership that initiated the chain of events that led to disaster. Moreover, the negative impact of all these controversies on Labour's general election hopes would possibly have been contained had it not been for the hollowness of the Party's economic strategy, the core of its appeal to voters.

In early January 1987, at a weekend general election strategy session held by the shadow cabinet at the ASTMS retreat at Bishop's Stortford, it was agreed that plans to combat unemployment would be at the centre of the Party's manifesto. On the advice of campaign strategists, it was also agreed that spending plans would not be detailed until after the election was called. Bryan Gould, newly elected to the shadow cabinet, had been appointed campaign organizer without even a formal reference to the NEC. At Bishop's Stortford he was also given overall responsibility for Labour's "programme for national renewal" and was asked to arbitrate between shadow Chancellor Roy Hattersley and employment spokesperson John Prescott on the costing of Labour's job creation plan. A number of members of the shadow cabinet informed the media that they regarded the principal achievement of the Bishop's Stortford gathering to be the effective removal of Prescott from command of the Party's employment strategy, its general election centrepiece.[124]

In February, Peter Mandelson presented his campaign strategy to the NEC. Labour, he explained, would highlight the contrast between what people felt about the "declining quality of life under the Tories" and what

Labour offered as an alternative. He devised a series of stock phrases –
"we are not paying our way", "the real economy is in decline" and "the
Tories are cutting our real defences" – to be reiterated throughout the
campaign.[125] Kinnock recited them to a special joint meeting of the NEC
and the shadow cabinet held in the boardroom at Transport House a
week later. At this meeting, members of the Shadow Communications
Agency (SCA), the team of public relations consultants recruited by
Mandelson, informed the Party's elected representatives of the strategy
to be followed in the coming campaign. They identified Labour's weaknesses as taxation, defence and the London left but offered no measures
to deal with them. Their grand design, shorn of jargon, seemed to boil
down to a hope that the SDP–Liberal Alliance would eat into the Tory
vote. This was in the midst of the Greenwich by-election, in which
precisely that happened – but not to Labour's advantage.

A paper submitted to the meeting by Tony Benn was ignored and its
existence was not even mentioned in the official minutes. Like Peter
Mandelson, Benn insisted that the Party's "main problem" was one of
"credibility". In this assertion he was backed up by a Marplan survey
which showed that only 48 per cent of Labour supporters thought the
Party would "keep its promises". In contrast to Mandelson, however,
Benn urged the Party to "address our arguments directly to our natural
constituency, which must include those millions who never vote"; he
asked the leadership to refrain from "damaging" disciplinary proceedings and asked all present to "refuse to comment on all internal matters
in the Party from now to polling day". Benn's plea fell on deaf ears.
Internal attacks on the left had become the very stuff of Kinnock's appeal
to the voters.

As the election approached, the contradictions and ambiguities in
Labour's programme were exposed; once again, under media scrutiny,
all the fudges in Labour's policies – intended by the right as insurance
against excessively radical commitments – came unstuck. The Tories
costed Labour's programme at an outrageous £34 billion; it did not matter
whether this was accurate or not, the fact that Labour could not reply
with a precise and convincing counter-claim made the attack stick. Day
after day, the Party announced new jobs, training, investment initiatives,
but all the buzzwords melted away in the glare of a single question: how
much will it cost? The disarray on this among front-benchers was all too
visible.

Hattersley denounced Lawson's tax cuts as a boon "for the rich"
although it was obvious that many working-class people gained from
them; he promised to reverse them when in office. Worse yet, he said the
extra revenue gained would be used not to fund extra spending on social
needs but to reduce public borrowing. Of course, Hattersley and his
front-bench associates were trying to portray Labour as a party of fiscal

responsibility, but for many voters, their statements confirmed what the tabloids said: a Labour government would tax them to the hilt to help the poorest of the poor. The decision to switch Labour's campaigning emphasis from economic to social issues only compounded the problem. Many people became even more convinced that Labour intended to make them bear the burden of improvements to health, education and transport. In that context, it is perhaps no wonder the "loony left" stories struck home.

A report by the Party's pollsters MORI to the April meeting of the campaign strategy committee made grim reading. Labour was fast sliding out of contention and faced certain defeat in the impending election. Public attitudes towards the Party were much worse since the defeat in Greenwich. An increasing proportion of the electorate considered the Party too extreme and did not trust it to handle the economy. What the meeting was not told was that Kinnock's own standing was plummeting fast. From February to March he sank from a 26 per cent to a 22 per cent approval rating. A Gallup poll in April capped it all off: 63 per cent of those polled thought Kinnock was doing "badly" as leader of the Labour Party, a negative rating exceeded only by Michael Foot in his worst months of 1983. None the less, Labour's strategists proceeded with their plans to focus the campaign on the alleged "popular appeal" of the Labour leader. On the advice of the Shadow Communications Agency, it was decided that the coming Labour campaign would showcase Kinnock, Hattersley, Denis Healey, John Smith, Gerald Kaufman and Jack Cunningham as its top television performers.

A small campaign management team, comprising Bryan Gould, Walworth Road officials Larry Whitty, Geoff Bish, Joyce Gould and Mandelson, plus Charles Clarke and Patricia Hewitt from the leader's office, was set up, with a mandate to report directly to Kinnock. The leader's office boasted to the press of its new, streamlined campaign command structure. It wanted to make clear that, unlike Michael Foot in 1983, Neil Kinnock would be running a tight electoral ship with a loyal crew. Just before the election date was announced, decisions about campaigning strategy were handed to an even smaller group, made up of Bryan Gould, members of Kinnock's personal staff and representatives of the Shadow Communications Agency. Walworth Road officials were left to deal with the technical end of the campaign.

When Margaret Thatcher called the election for June 11th, the NEC, the shadow cabinet and even the campaign strategy committee ceased to matter. All power was effectively in the hands of Neil Kinnock, Bryan Gould, Peter Mandelson, Patricia Hewitt and Charles Clarke, the leader's aide-de-camp. They ran Labour's campaign with military-style discipline but proved unable to respond creatively to the unpredictable pressures inevitably produced by the heat of electioneering. Locked entirely into its own rhythms and wedded to a game plan determined months before, Labour's 1987 campaign was unable to vary its course or break out into fresh ground.

The manifesto was drafted by Geoff Bish and rewritten by Charles Clarke, who removed all of Bish's references to previous Party policy statements. It was rubberstamped by a joint meeting of the NEC and shadow cabinet. The shortest and least revealing of all the major parties' manifestos, it was published under the title *Britain Will Win*. Its seventeen sparse pages, each set in large, bold type, were launched with great fanfare at the Queen Elizabeth II Conference Hall in London. To the accompaniment of soft lights and Brahms's Anthem in D, Kinnock and Hattersley entered the room and walked down the aisle almost arm in arm. It was clear to all that Labour had opted to promote the messengers rather than the message.

Where the Tory manifesto was crammed with eyecatching and firmly political proposals on such issues as housing, education, local government and taxation, Labour's lacked any single similarly bold commitment. Although there was no reference to abolishing the House of Lords, withdrawing from the EEC, closing down US bases, stopping council house sales or extensive nationalization, this manifesto gave as many hostages to fortune as the much-derided "suicide note" of 1983. Its sheer lack of substance was taken as evidence that there was an "iceberg" manifesto of radical left-wing Labour commitments only barely submerged beneath the anodyne pleasantries of cuddly Kinnockism.

Kinnock replied to this accusation in the only way he knew: by attacking his own left wing. In answer to Thatcher's "iceberg" jibe, he said: "People who have a separate manifesto . . . it will be impossible for them to remain in the Party."[126] Kinnock's object in making these statements was undoubtedly to reassure voters that they could trust him, but all he managed to achieve was to assure voters that they certainly could not trust his party.

The first week of Labour's campaign got a tremendous reception in the media. Labour's publicity machine was referred to in awestruck tones. A revivalist atmosphere took hold, a belief that it was quite easy to win an election once you knew what you were doing and were allowed to get on with it without the nasty distractions of conference policy or Party democracy.

But Roy Hattersley's poor performance as shadow Chancellor and Labour's lack of a coherent economic policy soon allowed the otherwise lacklustre Tory campaign to score telling points on taxation and public spending. When the Chief Secretary to the Treasury, John MacGregor, claimed that Labour would need huge tax increases to pay for its social programme, the response was confused. Bryan Gould and Hattersley dithered for a day before claiming that Labour's tax increases would not hurt anyone earning less than £500 a week. Shortly after, in a separate interview, Kinnock implied that the tax increases *might* affect some people earning below that amount.

Labour's strategists remained transfixed by the notion of a "presidential style" campaign. Before the election, they had agreed on a draft script for a party political broadcast promoting the leader's virtues. Hugh Hudson, director of *Chariots of Fire*, volunteered to make it, along with *Chariots of Fire* scriptwriter Colin Welland. The model Hudson was asked to work from was a broadcast entitled "What Manner of Man?", produced for Walter Mondale's uninspired and unsuccessful 1984 US presidential campaign. The film, Labour's first election broadcast of the campaign and its tone-setter, was transmitted on May 21st and was an overnight sensation, attracting more media comment than any other political broadcast in the genre's history.

In *Labour Rebuilt*, the account by Wintour and Hughes of Kinnock's new model party, Peter Mandelson is given credit for the broadcast. This is not surprising, as Mandelson himself was the main source for the book. In fact, Mandelson had nothing to do with the making of the film, though it was an excellent illustration of the Mandelson strategy. Welland and Hudson, following advice from members of the Shadow Communications Agency, highlighted Kinnock's wholesomeness and inserted testimonies from his uncle and aunt and references to his parents, his patriotism and the strength of his marriage, symbolized by the famous cliffside walk with Glenys. But the single most important element in the broadcast was a display of Kinnock's command over his wayward party. It was Patricia Hewitt who insisted that a clip from Kinnock's 1985 Bournemouth conference speech denouncing the Liverpool Party, Militant and Derek Hatton be included in the film.

Staff at Labour's Walworth Road headquarters were aghast at the way Hudson had chosen to underscore the Kinnock tirade with an ominous musical background worthy of the climactic killing spree in *The Godfather*. Hudson also startled them by ending his film with KINNOCK spelt out in bold letters across the screen instead of the traditional VOTE LABOUR. There was some concern about whether the whole thing was over the top, but it was too late to change it.

The portrait of Kinnock as a tough-minded Party boss, ready, willing and able to take on the sinister miscreants within his own ranks, fitted perfectly with the long-term strategy of building up the leader at the expense of the Party. But to thousands of Party members at that very moment campaigning in the streets, it gave deep offence. And in the minds of floating voters it simply confirmed yet again that Labour, in spite of its leader, was a party unworthy of trust.

In the wake of the Hudson broadcast, the "Kinnock weepie", as it came to be known, Kinnock's personal rating increased by 10 per cent, a notable achievement for any piece of film-making. It is clear, however, that whatever it did for Kinnock, the broadcast did nothing for the Labour Party, whose standing in the polls failed to mirror the rave reviews from the media.

The next two broadcasts dealt with education and the NHS, two areas in which Labour's sharp attack on the Tories was blunted by the Party's failure to say how it would fund the urgently needed improvements. The fourth and final broadcast was supposed to be about unemployment, the issue identified by Bryan Gould as the Party's number one campaigning focus. It was cancelled and a rerun of the "Kinnock weepie" took its place. This time there was only a small, fleeting "Kinnock blip" in the opinion polls; retrospectively, most of Labour's strategists admitted the rerun was a waste of precious air time.

One fourth of all the election addresses sent out by Labour candidates included a photo of Kinnock. In contrast, only 4 per cent of Tory addresses had a photo of Margaret Thatcher, demonstrating that the Tories had a shrewder grasp of their own party's strengths and weaknesses than did Labour. By polling day, opinion polls revealed that 43 per cent agreed that Kinnock had fought the best campaign but only 28 per cent thought he would make the best leader.[127]

On the two issues which most exercised voters' minds at the height of the campaign, Kinnock was unable to offer any lead. In the penultimate week the Tories turned on Labour's defence policy. In reply, the Labour leadership blustered and fudged. Then came the long-awaited onslaught on tax. The Tories deluged the media with claims that a disaster would befall voters' take-home pay if Labour were to win the election. Throughout the last week of the campaign, the headlines of all the daily papers were dominated by this issue. But by now all Labour's spokespersons on the economy had been stripped of credibility and the Party had little response to make.

The slogan devised by the Shadow Communications Agency and repeated on every possible occasion was "The country's crying out for change". This was altered in the last week to a more hopeful "The country's crying out for Labour". The negative appeal, whose message was simply "We are not the Tories", was accompanied by visual imagery evoking a dark, Dickensian Britain of poverty and decay. During the election postmortem the advocates of what became the Policy Review made great play of what they argued was a damaging tendency of Labour to identify itself with the past, with the welfare state, with a dying working class, with a fading industrial culture, with all that was dreary and depressing about class-riven, strife-torn, failing, feeble Britain. Long before the campaign had started, however, Patricia Hewitt had warned against this sort of approach; that was why Birmingham and not Scotland had been preferred for Kinnock's campaign launch. The people who decided to run these advertisements, Mandelson, Philip Gould, Charles Clarke and Hewitt herself, were the very people who later tried to put the blame for them and associated failures on the "fundamentalist", "backward-looking" left and the Party's trade-union-based traditions.

If looking backwards was such a huge error, why did not these people do something about it during the 1987 campaign, over which they had total control? Could it be that they had no real strategy at all, that all practical decisions regarding campaign strategy were taken ad hoc and only subsequently backed up with convenient political rationales? Could it be that in the absence of any clear policy alternatives Labour had only one thing to say: Thatcher is bad and Britain will get worse under her? In fact, apart from promoting Kinnock personally, the rest of Labour's campaign consisted entirely of knocking copy.

Labour's campaign strategy had been based on hopes of a strong finish following a major breakthrough in the opinion polls in the last week. The breakthrough failed to materialize. From the final weekend on, Labour's strategists were floundering. Hermetically sealed in their Walworth Road redoubt from the reality of impending disaster, they ran themselves ragged but produced little.

Their final "Come home to Labour" plea was unconvincing. After all the hi-tech hoopla and the bluster about "modernizing" the Party's image, the final message was nothing but a blatant appeal to traditional loyalties. Clearly, part of the point of the slogan was a subliminal message that Labour was "safe" again, that the left had been routed. But in the absence of any serious and sustained riposte to the Tories' highly effective "loony left" campaign, the promise contained in the slogan was empty. The slogan was also, of course, an appeal to the residual loyalty of working-class voters to the welfare state. As Butler and Kavanagh observed in their study of the election, Labour's "modern" campaign relied overwhelmingly on the ideology and achievements of the labour-ism of the 1940s.[128]

This ultimate focus on welfarism was not part of the original campaign plan. It emerged in Kinnock's speeches and infected all aspects of the Party's appeal to the electorate because, in the end, when confronted with the Tory onslaught, Labour had nothing else to offer. In a positive sense, it was an assertion, virtually involuntary, of the Party's class identity. As such, it undoubtedly touched a chord with substantial numbers of voters. In a negative sense, it was an admission of the bankruptcy of the Labour leadership, its inability to come up with anything other than emotive slogans which committed it to nothing.

A large eve-of-poll rally was held in Islington in north London. Billed as the "Comin' up Roses" rally, it was designed to provide an attractive environment for Kinnock's final television peroration. Under Margaret Hodge, the London borough of Islington was now considered relatively "safe". The new Business Design Centre which had risen within the skeleton of the old Agricultural Hall seemed an appropriate showcase for Labour's new image. The rally was advertised by Walworth Road as a "family day". The audience was ticket-only and was made up entirely of hand-picked Labour activists, many of them drafted in from north London constituencies. Any visible left-wing presence was carefully screened out as Walworth Road stewards searched everyone at the doors for compromising propaganda; one unwary punter had his copy of the *New Statesman* confiscated. Streamers were laid out on the tables accompanied by instructions on when to throw them. The local MP for Islington South and Finsbury, Chris Smith, a member of the Tribune Group, was invited to speak but the equally local Islington North MP Jeremy Corbyn, a member of the Campaign Group, was kept as far from the cameras as possible.

The atmosphere was one of fervent self-congratulation. This was meant to be a victory rally. There was no sign of self-doubt, no hint among any of the participants that all was for nought, though the polls by now had made it clear that Labour would lose. Self-congratulation had become the Party's only theme, the hollow core of its general election message. Even in the face of defeat it kept piping out the same tune, oblivious to the fact that the public had stopped listening some time before.

On polling day, Labour captured only 32 per cent of the popular vote. The extra millions spent on advertising and the extra £275,000 paid to MORI for polling services, the well-reviewed political broadcasts, the leadership focus, the media-friendly daily campaign schedule all produced only a meagre 1.6 per cent national swing from Conservative to Labour. Even this was distributed unevenly throughout the country. In Scotland the Tories were wiped out and Labour made major gains. But in the south, outside of London, the Tories gained five seats and Labour gained one. In the West Midlands, Labour gained one and lost one. In the East Midlands, Labour gained three. In the north it gained seven seats but failed to win key target marginals.

For the Labour leadership, however, the election defeat was a triumph. Once more Neil Kinnock sought personal comfort from political adversity. Peter Mandelson now claimed there had never been any real hope of winning from the low base of the 1983 election result. The real aim, he insisted, had been to establish Labour in a solid second place and despatch the SDP–LiberalAlliance as a serious contender. That aim had been achieved. Therefore, Labour's campaign had been a success. This thesis was repeated in numerous interviews and in the NEC report to the 1987 Labour conference. It has become the authorized version of the 1987 general election. But is it true?

First, no such aims were ever mentioned in any known memorandum, private or public, by any member of the campaign team in the months running up to the election. It was never mentioned at any meetings of the NEC or the campaign strategy committee. Second, Labour had had a lead in the opinion polls and the local and by-election results to back them up for most of 1986. During this period there were reasonable grounds to believe a Labour victory was a possibility, and Labour's leadership expressed this belief both privately and publicly. Third, Labour made no effort to target the Alliance either in its public campaign or in its organizational priorities. Indeed, it had placed its hopes on an increased Alliance vote to stop the Tories.

Finally, there is the little matter of an order placed by Peter Mandelson for several thousand commemorative mugs bearing the inscription "Winner 1987 General Election" over a picture of Neil Kinnock superimposed on a Union Jack. Labour's director of campaigns and communications ordered the mugs during the campaign. All but a few were secretly destroyed following defeat.

For members of the Kinnock circle the commemorative mug may have been more appropriate than they cared to admit. Their campaign might have been a defeat for the Labour Party as a whole, but it was a victory for Kinnock in his war against the Party. With some skill and not a little luck, Kinnock and his supporters were to turn Labour's loss into their gain. Once again, they were able to scapegoat the left and the policies with which it was associated as the cause of defeat at the polls – even though strategy and tactics during the campaign and the run-up to it had been entirely in the hands of the right-wing leadership.

As in 1983, this scapegoating necessitated a revision of history. The price of this revision was paid five years later, in the general election of 1992, when the leadership used more or less the same political approach as it had in 1987 with only slightly improved results, despite the far more favourable economic circumstances. For five years, with the help of a compliant media, it had done everything in its power to suppress the truth about the 1987 election campaign and distort the debate about its implications. The errors of the past were thus repeated, not least because the individuals who made them were still in charge of the Labour Party.

Notes

1. *Labour Party Annual Conference Report* 1980.
2. ibid.
3. ibid.
4. ibid.
5. ibid.
6. ibid.
7. ibid.
8. ibid.

9. ibid.
10. ibid.
11. ibid.
12. ibid.
13. ibid.
14. ibid.
15. ibid.
16. ibid.
17. Denis Healey, campaign statement for the deputy leadership, May 1981.
18. *Tribune* 10 June 1981.
19. ibid.
20. Benn diaries, 1 May 1980.
21. John Silkin, *Changing Battlefields*, London 1988.
22. *Sunday Times* 23 February 1992.
23. *Labour Monthly* December 1974.
24. *Sunday Times* 23 February 1992.
25. Benn diaries, 28 September 1976.
26. NEC minutes June 1979.
27. NEC minutes July 1979.
28. NEC Organization Sub-Committee minutes September 1979.
29. *Labour Party Annual Conference Report* 1981.
30. ibid.
31. ibid.
32. *Tribune* 28 May 1982.
33. *Tribune* 9 July 1982.
34. NEC Home Policy Committee minutes April 1983.
35. NEC Report to Annual Conference 1983.
36. *New Socialist* September–October 1983.
37. *Tribune* 19 November 1982.
38. John Curtice *et al.*, *How Britain Votes*, London 1985.
39. NEC Report to Annual Conference 1983.
40. ibid.
41. ibid.
42. ibid.
43. ibid.
44. ibid.
45. ibid.
46. Michael Foot, *Another Heart and Other Pulses*, London 1984.
47. ibid.
48. NEC Report to Annual Conference 1983.
49. *Marxism Today* October 1983.
50. NEC Report to Annual Conference 1983.
51. ibid.
52. Curtice *et al.*, *How Britain Votes*.
53. *London Labour Briefing*, No. 31, July 1983.
54. *Tribune* 25 February 1983.
55. *Guardian* 20 June 1983.
56. *Tribune* 24 May 1983.
57. *Tribune* 1 July 1983.
58. ibid.
59. Neil Kinnock, Manifesto for the Labour leadership, published on 18 July 1983.
60. ibid.
61. *Tribune* 15 July 1983.
62. *Mail on Sunday* 30 September 1983.
63. *Tribune* 22 July 1983.
64. *Guardian* 13 September 1983.
65. *Guardian* 15 July 1983.
66. *Guardian* 20 September 1983.

67. *Mail on Sunday* 30 September 1983.
68. Neil Kinnock, "My Socialism", *New Statesman*, 7 October 1983.
69. NEC Report to Annual Conference 1984.
70. ibid.
71. ibid.
72. ibid.
73. Benn diaries 7 November 1983.
74. NEC minutes March 1984.
75. Benn diaries, 4 April 1984.
76. Benn diaries, 16 May 1984.
77. *Labour Party Annual Conference Report* 1984.
78. ibid.
79. ibid.
80. ibid.
81. ibid.
82. Benn diaries, 12 December 1984.
83. ibid.
84. NEC minutes December 1984.
85. Benn diaries, 17 January 1985.
86. NEC minutes January 1985.
87. NEC minutes February 1985.
88. NEC minutes September 1985.
89. *Guardian* 30 September 1985.
90. *Labour Party Annual Conference Report* 1985.
91. ibid.
92. ibid.
93. ibid.
94. LCC paper "After the Strike", April 1985.
95. *Socialist Action* 11 May 1984.
96. Stuart Hall and Martin Jacques (eds), *The Politics of Thatcherism*, London 1982.
97. *Marxism Today* April 1985.
98. *The Times* 13 September 1990.
99. "Bennism Without Benn", *New Socialist*, May 1985.
100. ibid.
101. ibid.
102. *Tribune* 18 January 1985.
103. ibid.
104. *Tribune* 20 September 1985.
105. LCC recruitment leaflet, spring 1985.
106. ibid.
107. *Tribune* 20 September 1991.
108. ibid.
109. *Labour Activist conference bulletin* October 1985.
110. *Tribune* 26 September 1986.
111. ibid.
112. ibid.
113. *Tribune* 24 May 1985.
114. ibid.
115. *Guardian* 9 January 1987.
116. *Tribune* 16 January 1987.
117. *Guardian* 26 January 1987.
118. *Guardian* 3 March 1987.
119. *Guardian* 5 March 1987.
120. *Guardian* 5 March 1987.
121. NEC minutes March 1987.
122. Benn diaries, 29 April 1987.
123. NEC Report to Annual Conference 1987.

124. *Guardian* 13 February 1987.
125. NEC minutes February 1987.
126. *Guardian* 24 May 1987.
127. David Butler and Dennis Kavanagh, *The General Election of 1987*, London 1987.
128. ibid.

Kinnock in Command

═══════════════════ 2 ═══════════════════

Repudiations and Recriminations: the Aftermath of the 1987 Defeat

> We need to develop radical policies which are not only true to our
> socialist values but also appeal to the self-interest of those
> whose votes we need.
>
> *Bryan Gould, July 1987*

At the first meeting of the Parliamentary Labour Party following the 1987 general election defeat, Neil Kinnock thanked the Walworth Road staff responsible for what he called "the most successful campaign in the history of the Party, recognized as such by Labour's opponents and the media". He proceeded to deliver a long, meandering lecture that betrayed an astonishing self-satisfaction in a leader who had just been roundly rejected by the electorate. He did, however, note the Party's failure to win in the south, and argued that Labour must deal with "the changes that have occurred in society". Above all, he demanded "practical policies" and "self-discipline" to ensure that Labour would win next time.

By any logic Kinnock and his supporters should have borne overall responsibility for the failure of 1987. After all, Kinnock had become leader nearly four years before by promising the Party that he could win. But the presidential style of the campaign that Labour had fought and the media response to it shielded Kinnock from the usual consequences of political failure. He and his entourage emerged from the election stronger than ever. There was at that time no possibility of a challenge to him from the Labour right, which needed his support to continue the attack on the left. The "soft left", which following the 1987 election believed itself to be in what Robin Cook called the "driving seat" of the Party, was heavily reliant on his patronage and hardly likely to upset a balance of forces that it believed was moving in its favour. The left, which had never had any illusions about either Kinnock's politics or his ability to beat the Tories at the ballot box, was too weakened by defections and defeats to represent a threat to his leadership.

Precisely because Labour's 1987 campaign was deemed such a success in comparison to 1983, the poor result was bitterly disappointing to the rank and file. While there had been widespread scepticism about Kinnock's leadership before the campaign, hopes had risen during it. The 1987 effort may not have been as radical and innovatory on the ground as it had been in some places in 1983, but it did at least involve large numbers of Party members, certainly far more than were involved in the campaign of 1992. The usually dormant supporters who paid their subscriptions once a year but never attended meetings turned out in force, eager to make a personal contribution to the ousting of the Tories. When that effort proved futile, defeatism set in.

The professionalism of the Labour campaign, backed by a chorus of praise from the press, simply accentuated the despair. Literally tens of thousands of Party members across the country abandoned any personal involvement with politics. This left the activist left high and dry and painfully vulnerable to attacks from the activist right, whose position had been strengthened by the way in which the election had been fought and the way that blame for defeat was parcelled out.

Many Labour Party members previously on the left now decided to throw their lot in with the right. This time there was nothing wrong with the campaign or the organization, they reasoned, so it must be something else: the left, the policies, the unions, perhaps the membership itself. We redesigned the product but still nobody bought it; perhaps it is time, they concluded, we found ourselves a new product to sell.

EETPU official John Spellar, assuming no responsibility for his second successive failure to win the marginal seat of Birmingham Northfield, used the pages of the post-election edition of *New Socialist* to launch a fierce attack on the left:

> The dominant issue raised by the Tories was fear, not just fear of a defenceless Britain but fear of extremism, of economic uncertainty, of crime, of their children being corrupted in schools, of minority groups, of the unknown. These fears had been steadily built up over the previous years and the impact was steady, insidious, and often unfair. We have to accept, however, that the behaviour of some sections of the party had given a degree of credibility to those fears. In this context the party in London, particularly elements around *Labour Briefing* and other self-indulgent journals, have a lot to answer for.

Left-wing CLPs, he argued, should face "clear alternatives, conformity or closure".[1]

Spellar's case against the left was at least cogent and straightforward. The same could not be said for Bryan Gould, who advanced, in the same issue of *New Socialist*, a more sophisticated, ultimately far more influential, but deeply dishonest argument for blaming the left and upping the tempo of the Party's move to the right. The Tories, he said, had been able to use North Sea oil to create enough prosperity in the Midlands and the south to protect themselves from the electoral consequences of their other policies. Labour had to find ways to appeal to these relatively prosperous voters who had, not without reason, "marked us down on two major grounds: competence and trustworthiness". The lesson he drew was couched in unobjectionable, anodyne terminology: "We must first learn to give new and more welcoming signals to the electorate", "talk in a more modern language", "present ourselves as a modern and democratic party" and "sharpen up the process of policy formulation".[2]

This election postmortem issue of *New Socialist* was produced under the acting editorship of former *Tribune* editor Nigel Williamson, then moving to the right at the speed of light. Williamson argued that "Labour needs to attract votes from the better off majority if it is to have a real chance of power" which, in his view, would require "not so much a change in ideology as a change in style . . . making Labour once again the party of progress, a modern party which promises a more efficient tomorrow and not merely a better yesterday". Similar themes were taken up by Paul Thompson of the Labour Co-ordinating Committee: "policies structured around the defence of collective provision were necessary but not enough. In isolation they confirmed the image that Labour was the party of the past."[3]

Having played the Labour loyalty card and come up a loser in the election, the Party establishment decided that far from being an asset this card was actually a serious liability. In a display of crude economism, the leadership and its apologists on the "soft left" accepted that the Lawson economic boom was a permanent feature and that the "success" of the Thatcher government had enabled the Prime Minister to implant her values within a significant section of the working class. These values could not therefore be contested by the labour movement. There was no more mileage to be gained by talking about poverty and public services or the welfare state. The arithmetic of electoral success demanded that Labour repudiate anything in its programme, practice or presentation that might not appeal to the newly discovered stratum of "affluent" voters.

The general outline of the case was not novel. The Gaitskellite revisionists had advanced similar arguments – with rather sturdier analytical and material foundations – in the 1950s. Indeed, responses to Labour's 1987 defeat bore a striking resemblance to responses to its equally devastating 1959 defeat. In both 1987 and 1959, siren voices both inside and outside the Party proclaimed that Labour was out of touch, out of date and condemned in perpetuity to opposition status. Once again academics, pollsters and psephologists cited the gradual disappearance of the industrial working class and the shrinking of Labour's traditional electoral base to claim that society had changed so much that Labour could not expect to win in the foreseeable future unless it drastically "modernized" its appeal. These arguments, already secondhand and frayed at the edges in 1987, were to be reiterated by many of the same people in the aftermath of Labour's defeat in 1992, as if they were new discoveries, as if they had not provided the basis for all that had gone wrong in the Party in the years between 1987 and 1992.

The arguments were based on fear. Time and again, Kinnock and his supporters threatened that if their proposals to modernize policy and structure were not implemented, Labour would not only lose yet another election but also cease to exist as a viable political party. Like Thatcher before him, Kinnock declared "There is no alternative". This argument was a reflection within the labour movement of Thatcher's success. In the coming years, Kinnock's counsel of defeat and retreat was to echo with dreary familiarity from the top to the bottom of the Labour Party, resulting in a precipitate decline in Party membership, finance and activity.

In response, the left argued that the biggest obstacles to winning back alienated working-class voters in the south and the Midlands were Labour's poor record in government (economic instability, public spending cuts, wage restraint, inflation) and the confused policies on taxation and public spending with which it had fought the general election. A cursory examination of recent history would have shown that it was the Party's right wing that had saddled it with these albatrosses, but in the despair and intellectual confusion gripping the Party in the wake of the 1987 defeat, real self-examination was impossible. It was much easier to conclude that what was alienating affluent workers was not the Party's unchallengeable leadership but its rank and file, its socialist traditions, its links with the trade unions and oppressed minorities. In short, it was much easier to challenge everything associated with the Party's demonized left wing than to question the wisdom of the media, the pollsters, the academics and the vast majority of Labour MPs.

The "soft left" played a crucial role in selling these arguments to the Party. The likes of John Spellar could never be as effective as, for example, the emollient Labour MP for Islington South and Finsbury, Chris Smith, who argued that Labour "must make our altruism relevant to those who at present are simply not responding to the call to have a conscience".[4] Tom Sawyer took up the theme: "We failed to appreciate fully the appeal of 'people's capitalism' . . . we have to face the decline in our traditional working-class vote."[5]

But Bryan Gould, ubiquitous in the summer of 1987, was the chief proponent of the new double talk. At an LCC conference entitled "Labour's Renewal – The Next Step" Gould urged the Party to change both its image and its policies to appeal directly to voters in the south. "We need to develop radical policies which are not only true to our socialist values but also appeal to the self-interest of those whose votes we need."[6]

Ignoring the rhetoric, the *Independent* reported that "both the right and soft left . . . want a rolling programme of rule changes to purge the 'illegitimate left' and expect the Party to accept the importance of market capitalism as a generator of wealth more enthusiastically".[7] That the real agenda of the Party establishment, including its "soft left" component, was simply an old-fashioned purge of left personnel and policies was revealed not only by off-the-record briefings but by an increasingly explicit clamour from trade union leaders and LCC spokespersons for an end to "gesture politics". Party treasurer Sam McCluskie of the National Union of Seamen (NUS) urged the Party to change its rules to block the "hijack of constituency parties by factions unrepresentative of the broad mass of Labour supporters" at the same time that he called on Labour councils to stop "espousing the cause of minority interests".[8]

In July 1987 Peter Mandelson sent a private memorandum to Kinnock's office entitled "Moving Ahead". Outlining a "communications strategy" for the coming years, it stressed that Labour should present itself as a "listening, innovating, forward-looking Party". The three building blocks of Party renewal would be "democratic constitutional change, policy renewal and leadership enhancement". The "policy modernization" that would be "the key to Labour's election image" would require "moving from a policy committee based process to a communications based exercise. . . . This activity is the core of campaign 90 – the longest-running general election campaign, which runs for four years."

Mandelson also argued that "Neil's role in implementation is crucial – it is his means of further enhancement. He needs to instigate, participate, guide and finally present to the nation."[9] It was a call for a top–down Labour Party in which the leader and his office set the pace and everyone else did nothing but follow. Of course, Kinnock's supporters at this time took extreme care not to allow this reality to become too apparent. If their intentions had become known to a wider Party membership, they would have confirmed all the suspicions voiced by the left and made it much more difficult for the leadership to win the Party over to its proposals for change.

A pseudo-scientific underpinning for the move to the right was provided by a survey entitled "Labour and Britain in the 1990s" commissioned from the Shadow Communications Agency by Kinnock's office. It was unveiled to a joint meeting of the shadow cabinet and the NEC in November 1987, where it was presented as "a programme of political, demographic and opinion research . . . to map out the problems and opportunities facing the Party".[10] The survey argued that social and economic changes (the rise of an affluent, home- and car-owning working class, the growth of service industries, etcetera) had led to shifts in

"values" to which Labour must address itself. "Individualism", "consumerism", choice, security, all counted for more now than the old
class-based values of collective action and provision. Labour was too
associated with the unions, the poor, the disadvantaged. Its greatest
handicaps were its perceived "extremism" and "disunity".[11] If the Party
was to succeed it would have to break its links with the past and create
itself anew.

Although presented as being the work of outside experts, the report
bore the heavy imprint of the leader's office. Kinnock himself was the
only politician to have sight of it before the joint meeting. Its findings
were based on "qualitative" research carried out with a sample of only
eighty people. In assembling this "national" sample, no account had
been taken of regional differences in Party support.

Within less than two years, all the social assumptions upon which
"Labour and Britain in the 1990s" was based had been proved incorrect.
The real world of the 1990s was a world of recession, of high interest rates
and a stagnant property market, of mass unemployment in the south and
the Midlands as well as the north, of rising racism at home and endemic
warfare abroad. It had little to do with the world as forecast by the experts
of the Shadow Communications Agency. In the years that followed, the
new "consumerism" was quickly forgotten as Labour once again sought
to portray itself as the party of production and investment.

Another survey was conducted in the much-discussed Battersea constituency in south London, where a previously safe Labour seat had been
lost to the Tories, even though it had been defended by a popular "soft
left" MP, Alf Dubs. The Greater London Labour Party commissioned a
survey to determine why voters in the constituency had abandoned
Labour. Full-time official John Braggins summarized the findings: "People will vote Labour again – as the report indicates – when we get our act
together, when they are convinced that we share the aspirations and
fears of ordinary people. These are people who want to own their own
home, people who have reasonably well-paid jobs, people who put the
well-being of their family above all else."[12] The discovery that most
voters wanted a better standard of living for themselves and the people
they cared for was hardly the revelation Braggins seemed to think.
Moreover, these sweeping generalizations about Labour's lost voters
were made entirely on the basis of an opinion survey of white, skilled
working-class council tenants who had not voted Labour in 1987 but
claimed they had in the past. Everyone else was excluded.

At a Fabian Society day conference entitled "Socialism in the 1990s",
Peter Mandelson used the Battersea survey to argue that ordinary people
were afraid of a Labour Party which they believed was no longer for them
but "for blacks or for gays or for losers".[13] Glenys Thornton argued that
Labour in London had deteriorated into "something unattractive"

because it was perceived as being dominated by "57 varieties of ultra-leftist". The findings of the Battersea survey had been horrifying, she argued, because they demonstrated that most people thought that "Labour wasn't interested in them but in women, blacks, the Irish, whatever; but not in them and their families".[14]

Some weeks earlier Kinnock, in his 1987 Labour Party conference speech, made great play of a £400-a-week docker with a holiday home in Marbella. The leader affected a stage-cockney accent when quoting a trade union official asking rhetorically how Labour could possibly address this affluent docker with a promise to "take you out of your misery, brother". Even as Kinnock mounted the rostrum in Brighton the facts of wage-earning life were these: the top 10 per cent of all male workers were earning an average of £350 per week and the top 10 per cent of male manual workers were earning £261. The mythical £400-a-week docker provided the leadership with a bogus sociological justification for a comprehensive re-examination of Labour's traditional commitments. Accordingly, the 1987 conference endorsed the idea of a leadership-led Policy Review, which would "reassess", "re-examine" and "review" Labour's entire programme.

Within the Labour Party, the defeat of 1987 popularized the so-called lessons of 1983. Whereas before 1987, the left remained a power in the constituencies and could still command a clear majority on a wide range of issues, after 1987 the Party in the constituencies was consumed by fear, caution and conservatism. The effects of the 1987 defeat on the Labour Party's grass roots were more profound than in 1983, even though the actual result was not as bad, because the Party and the wider movement now appeared utterly helpless against the ideological and material onslaught of the Tories. Defeatism and despair replaced the passion that had fired the Party in the early 1980s and during the miners' strike. In the years that followed, they allowed the leadership to impose a top–down, authoritarian rule the like of which the Party had not seen in decades. Confusion and pessimism at the grass roots provided the ideal foundations for the cardboard edifice of the Policy Review, the "mass membership campaign", "one member one vote", and all the other paraphernalia of the Kinnock regime.

Notes

1. *New Socialist* summer 1987.
2. ibid.
3. ibid.
4. *Tribune* 19 June 1987.
5. *Tribune* 21 August 1987.
6. *Tribune* 10 July 1987.
7. *Independent* 19 June 1987.
8. *Tribune* 7 August 1987.

9. Colin Hughes and Patrick Wintour, *Labour Rebuilt*, London 1990.
10. "Labour and Britain in the 1990s", NEC paper November 1990.
11. ibid.
12. *Tribune* 8 January 1988.
13. *Guardian* 7 December 1987.
14. ibid.

3

The Leader in His Bunker

I'm in to win. That's my attitude to life and politics.
Neil Kinnock, Panorama, *BBC1, December 1989*

In early 1988 there was pressure from the "soft left" for a statement of the "aims and values" of the Labour Party to be drawn up. A previous attempt to draw up such a document had foundered in early 1985 when the leader lost interest. This time Kinnock and his advisers recognized the value of such a statement for assuaging fears that the impending Policy Review would involve an abandonment of ideology.

The leadership decided, without reference to the NEC, to prepare a statement. Roy Hattersley drafted a paper entitled "Aims and Values" on behalf of Kinnock, who was neither willing nor equipped to undertake the task. Hattersley's paper was essentially a résumé of his 1987 book *Choose Freedom,* but it also included, at Kinnock's request, a number of key passages emphasizing the importance of the free market. This was intended to signal an end to the economic approach with which Labour was traditionally associated. Excluding health care, education, social security and other public services, the draft of "Aims and Values" argued, "in the case of the allocation of most other goods and services, the operation of demand and supply and the price mechanism is a generally satisfactory means of determining provision and consumption".[1] This was a very different argument from that pursued by Neil Kinnock throughout the 1970s when he railed against the "religion of price" and the inherent injustice of the free market.

Members of both the NEC and the shadow cabinet greeted the Kinnock–Hattersley paper without enthusiasm. Robin Cook, John Smith and others expressed reservations about the stress on the efficacy of markets. The initial shocked reaction of the leadership to this show of dissent turned to anger when details of the joint meeting and its half-hearted response to the document were leaked to the press. The leader's office entered the fray, telling journalists that unnamed shadow cabinet members who had offered criticism of the document "failed to understand it". Robin Cook in particular was singled out.

Kinnock's office then lobbied hard to persuade key shadow cabinet members to drop their objections. A slightly modified version of the paper was presented to the NEC on 23 March, when members who had not been consulted were given only twelve minutes to read the twenty-page document. The NEC majority rejected a proposal that the document should be circulated and discussed throughout the Party before any agreement was reached. The document was then agreed by the NEC without amendment by twenty-two votes to four with only the left members, Tony Benn, Ken Livingstone, Dennis Skinner and the Young Socialists representative, Linda Douglas, voting against. [2]

At the Labour Party's Blackpool conference that autumn, "Aims and Values" was endorsed with virtually no debate at all. It had been offered to the delegates as unamendable. This was a typical Kinnock ploy: take it or leave it, back me or sack me. By raising the stakes at every turn he made open debate impossible. The useful life of "Aims and Values" was in effect ended when it was adopted by conference. The paper was of no interest to the voting public and indeed was never issued or even excerpted in any form designed for mass consumption. Nor was it ever disseminated among Party members. Its real audience was the elite corps of "opinion formers" in the media, who duly reported that Kinnock was surreptitiously dropping Clause Four socialism in favour of a new consumerism. This was a far cry from the kind of ideological confrontation Hugh Gaitskell had courted when he sought to have Clause Four removed from the Party constitution in 1959–60.

When the left-wing Campaign Group of Labour MPs announced in March 1988 that it would stand candidates for leader and deputy leader, everyone in the Party was aware that this was a political statement by the left of its discontent, not a realistic threat to Kinnock's authority. Tony Benn and Eric Heffer were standing for the leadership because they wished to lodge a protest against the direction in which Kinnock was taking the Party; they knew perfectly well they had no hope of winning or even running Kinnock and Roy Hattersley close. None the less, Kinnock was enraged. He denounced the use of the Party's democratic machinery by Benn and Heffer as an "outrageous distraction" which would "not be forgiven". [3]

Through Kinnock's office, maximum pressure was brought to bear on every Labour MP to support the Kinnock–Hattersley ticket. Any erstwhile critic who abandoned the Campaign Group to back the leader was rewarded by elevation to or within the front-bench team. Anyone who hesitated or who toyed with an abstention or a vote for John Prescott (the "soft left" member of the shadow cabinet who was standing for deputy leader) was threatened with demotion or removal from the front bench. This was the ultimate loyalty test and anyone who failed to pass it with flying colours could expect short shrift from the leadership. It was not enough for Kinnock to win or even to win well. Victory had to be crushing.

The extraordinary thing was how even this token challenge from the left, ridiculed in the media and easily brushed off with the help of a solid phalanx of trade union block votes, made Kinnock so uneasy that he stumbled into a series of major blunders over defence policy. Part of Kinnock's unease during this period stemmed from the discrepancy between his apparent command of the Party apparatus and his real standing with its members and supporters. A MORI poll conducted in April 1988 showed that only 61 per cent of Labour's own supporters were satisfied with Kinnock as leader while only 37 per cent of trade unionists were satisfied with his performance and 49 per cent were positively dissatisfied. A straw poll conducted by the *Sunday Times* revealed in June 1988 that eight out of ten Labour MPs believed he lacked authority and four out of ten did not want him to lead the Party into the next general election.[4]

In the early summer Kinnock forced a compliant NEC to accept a rule change that would require all candidates for leader or deputy leader to secure the nominations of 20 per cent of the PLP before they could get their names on the ballot form. The aim was to bar all future challenges from the left. David Blunkett proposed a compromise of 10 per cent, but this was rejected by the leader when it was realized that the Campaign Group membership just exceeded this figure.

In the end, Neil Kinnock's majority in the electoral college at that autumn's annual conference was overwhelming. But there was to be no grace in victory. He declared that the result had given him a "mandate" to lead the Party as he wished. That year Kinnock served as chair of the Party, in which capacity he presided over every meeting of the NEC and the annual conference, at which he also gave opening and closing addresses in addition to the traditional leader's speech. No previous conference had been so dominated by a Party leader. But while his power within the Party seemed unchallengeable, his personal standing in the country remained as low as ever.

In the aftermath of the 1988 conference, despite all the favourable publicity surrounding the first stage of the Policy Review, the opinion polls showed no sign of moving in Labour's favour. In November, the Party was humiliated in the Glasgow Govan by-election, in which a safe Labour seat was lost to the Scottish National Party (SNP) in an unprecedented mid-term swing against an opposition party. The Poll Tax dominated the by-election, which had been called after Kinnock had nominated the sitting Labour MP, Bruce Millan, as an EEC commissioner. On the ground, the dramatic SNP success in overturning a 19,500 Labour majority was seen as a negative verdict on Labour's rejection of the movement that was to campaign successfully for widespread non-payment of the Poll Tax. The successful SNP candidate, former Labour MP Jim Sillars, was able to present himself with some conviction as the candidate most likely to threaten the Thatcher government. The "Tartan Tory" tag which Labour usually tried to pin on the SNP would not stick; instead, Kinnock's party was forced to rebut the SNP charge of advocating a "watered-down Thatcherism".

Immediately after the Govan defeat, the Party establishment – which had managed the campaign from start to finish – mounted a concerted effort to scapegoat the defeated Labour candidate Bob Gillespie. The leadership spread the word that the candidate had been ineffective because he did not represent the "modern" Labour Party; he was an "old-fashioned" trade union activist with tattoos on his arms. The electorate was more clear where the blame for Labour's defeat should lie. In December 1988 Kinnock's personal approval rating in a MORI poll dropped to an all-time low of 18 per cent, at a time when Margaret Thatcher was still riding high with 45 per cent. The government had engineered a boom by means of tax cuts, cheap credit and privatization receipts; this seemed set to go on and on, and the chances of Labour winning the next election appeared to recede as each day passed. Kinnock's closest supporters feared that he would resign during the Christmas recess but the leader fought back in the only way he knew: by attacking the left within his own party. In his New Year message for 1989, Kinnock blamed Labour's electoral difficulties on "division" within the Party, despite his triumph in the electoral college and the Party's acquiescence in the Policy Review. On 2 January 1989, the latest MORI poll put Labour trailing ten points behind the Conservatives.

Kinnock's luck was to change dramatically over the next few months as a result of circumstances not of his own making. Beyond the hothouse confines of his private office, dramatic changes in the real political world rapidly transformed Labour's standing in the opinion polls. In the course of 1989 the Poll Tax emerged as a major focus for anti-Tory sentiment. The economy slipped into recession in the wake of the inflationary Lawson boom; interest rates rose and industrial militancy grew. With the parties of the former SDP–Liberal Alliance in disarray, Labour was the unchallenged beneficiary of the Tories' electoral decline. At last, the Party overtook the Tories in the opinion polls, defeated them in the 1989 European elections and even began to take seats from them in by-elections. But while Margaret Thatcher's approval ratings fell substantially during 1989, they still remained ahead of Kinnock's.

Buoyed by the long-awaited scent of electoral success, the leadership pressed ahead with its "modernization" of the Party. At the 1989 Labour conference, the major stage of the Policy Review was endorsed by the Labour conference. Unilateralism was abandoned and the government's laws against trade unions were embraced. So successful was the leadership in getting its way that year that many of Kinnock's advisers publicly regretted not having used the occasion to press home even more "radical" changes in Labour's programme and constitution.

In retrospect, 1989 was Kinnock's *annus mirabilis*. His mastery of the Labour Party seemed complete. All its component bodies were under his personal command. The Party itself seemed poised, at last, for victory at the next general election. Unfortunately, Labour's rise in the opinion polls was a reflection of Tory government failure and popular movement against it; Labour's bedrock problems of ideology, policy, organization, membership and finance remained unresolved. Neil Kinnock had triumphed over nothing but his opponents within the Party. The Tory dragon was not dead and would live to fight another day.

Despite the praise lavished on him by camp-followers, the stage-managed adulation, the calculated gravitas of the sober suits and straight-to-camera addresses to the nation, Kinnock remained, to the end, strikingly apprehensive of the stab in the back. He was the classic example of the king in a medieval court: an insecure leader, ever fearful of potential rivals, intolerant of criticism and protected from all contact with reality by a small circle of cynical courtiers. Anyone with an independent mind or any vestigial commitment to one of the many principles that the leader himself had abandoned over the years was ruthlessly weeded out.

The ease with which Neil Kinnock changed his mind on virtually every major political question of the last quarter of a century became legendary. What annoyed many critics within the Party was not simply that he changed his mind but that he expected everyone else to do so at the same time. Anyone who failed to follow his various Damascene conversions was singled out for attack. Worse yet, he would then rewrite history to belittle the importance of the opinions he had once held. In an interview in the September 1991 issue of the *Director*, Kinnock denied that Labour had ever really subscribed to common ownership as stipulated in Clause Four of the Party constitution. "They were tunes of glory that were coming out," he explained. "Well, we've stopped that nonsense."[5]

Kinnock's lack of government experience was never the problem some commentators made it out to be. After all, the public quickly accepted John Major, whose career on the government front bench had been relatively brief and hardly noteworthy. No, the real problem for Kinnock was the public perception – disastrously confirmed by the 1992 Sheffield rally – of limited personal ability allied to unlimited arrogance. Like every vainglorious leader, Kinnock believed far too much of his own propaganda. This made him prone to tactical blunders and, even worse, unable to acknowledge or correct mistakes.

Kinnock's notoriously prolix oratory reflected this combination of insecurity and arrogance. The confusing welter of clauses and sub-clauses, the pointless litanies and profuse alliteration were all an attempt to disguise a hollow core in an elaborate container. At meetings of the NEC or PLP he would announce his intention to speak for only three or four or five minutes – only to go on for ten or twenty or sometimes thirty. Logic and fact would be lost as the sentences snaked on and the adjectives and adverbs piled up. Of course, his staff were well aware of his reputation for windbaggery. But no matter how they coached and cajoled him, no matter how many times they would edit and hone his speeches, Kinnock would always reinsert his repetitions and above all his favourite alliterations.

Throughout, he demonstrated a remarkable capacity for hatred, espe-cially of anyone who challenged him from the left. In contrast, his response to those who challenged him from the right – including the Tories – was always one of fear and indecision. He was transparently intimidated by those more powerful or better connected than he. His "tough guy" routine with the Labour left – the "enemy within" – was in stark contrast to his unwillingness to challenge any institutions or representatives of the establishment. This one-time scathing critic of the royal family had become, by the end of his term as Labour leader, a loyal courtier whose praise for the monarchy embarrassed even some of his closest supporters. In December 1986 he called the tax-avoiding royal family "extremely productive" and "a bargain for Britain" and pledged that Labour would spend just as much money on the Civil List as the Conservatives. On the Queen Mother's ninetieth birthday he declared in the House of Commons that she has "the attributes of someone who has greatness". In April 1991 he informed the House that he had enjoyed the "enormous honour" of spending the night with the royal family at Windsor Castle.

This extremely thin-skinned man found criticism, even of the most comradely variety, unbearable. He never forgot or forgave a slight, real or imagined. In the upper echelons of the Party, his vindictiveness became legendary. It reached new heights in his long-running vendetta against Arthur Scargill and the NUM, whose offence was to have dared to offer the labour movement an alternative to New Realism (and to Kinnock's leadership) in the 1984–85 strike. At the 1991 annual British Press Awards dinner, Kinnock presented "Reporter of the Year" awards to the *Mirror* journalists who, at the behest of Robert Maxwell, had spent months attacking Scargill and NUM general secretary Peter Heathfield. Kinnock made no effort to disguise his very personal delight in rewarding these journalists for their efforts, though by that time most of their allegations had been disproved and their witnesses discredited. Within a few months, the proprietor who had paid for it all was revealed to the world as a thief and con-man on an epic scale.

At that year's annual NUM conference, Yorkshire Area vice-president Ken Capstick moved a resolution expressing "profound disgust" with the Labour leader for associating himself with the *Daily Mirror*'s "disgraceful smear campaign against NUM officials". The conference passed Capstick's resolution unanimously. Three months later the leader took his revenge. The death of NUM-sponsored MP George Buckley prompted a by-election in the safe Labour seat of Hemsworth, Yorkshire. Capstick, born and bred in the constituency, was the obvious local favourite and would have walked away with the local nomination on the first ballot had not Kinnock's NEC intervened. After interviewing the nominees, a panel led by Roy Hattersley decided to strike Capstick off the list.

Kinnock enjoyed a strange love–hate relation with the media. They had made him and they could break him. He needed them to wage his inner-Party battles but he also feared them. Journalists found direct access to Kinnock restricted by his private office, which tried to control every bit of news relating to either the Party or the leader and regarded any story that they themselves had not planted as a threat. For a leader of the Opposition, who should have been hungry to broadcast his views wherever and whenever possible, he gave very few interviews, and those few were given only to members of the press willing to adhere to a prearranged agenda. For some years he simply refused to appear on Brian Walden's *Weekend World* television interview programme. Every morning he would peruse a selection of press clippings prepared by his private office. Unfavourable coverage would make him explode. Kinnock found it hard enough taking a hammering from the Tory press; he simply could not abide attacks from his own side. When he took over as Party leader in 1983, Labour could boast two regular publications, *Labour Weekly* and *New Socialist,* which both, in their different ways, offered serious, well-researched and original journalism, attracted independent freelance contributors and commanded a genuine, if modest, readership. When he resigned nearly nine years later, the Party was left with *Labour Party News.*

Labour Weekly had been shut down ostensibly because it was losing money, but *Labour Party News* ended up a far greater drain on the Party's scarce resources, accounting for £169,000 of the Party's £289,000 deficit for 1990. Between 1986 and 1990, the magazine cost Party members nearly £750,000, not counting the substantial income from advertising, merchandising and fundraising that it generated and immediately consumed.[6] Kinnock and his advisers thought nothing of this expense because, from the beginning, the magazine had been conceived of as a vehicle for the aggrandizement of the leadership. In the first issue after the 1987 election, Kinnock explained in the course of an interview that "*Labour Party News* is vital because it gives us, for the first time in the history of the Labour Party, a direct means of contact between the individual member of the Labour Party and the leadership."[7] But this contact was strictly a one-way affair; *Labour Party News* was an exercise in vanity publishing from whose pages all criticism of the leader was banished. In the January–February 1992 issue, Party members gearing up for the general election were treated to five separate pictures of the leader, supplemented by pictures of no fewer than twenty-eight other front-bench Labour MPs. Aptly described by one Labour MP as the "in-flight" magazine of the Labour Party, *Labour Party News*, whose readership was nominal, was a mirror in which the leadership preened itself – at considerable expense to the members.

When the Party elected Kinnock as leader in 1983 it did so because of what it took to be his positive image, his skills as a communicator and his ability to perform on television. But as time wore on it became apparent that while he could display these attributes as a backbencher or as a spokesperson in the shadow cabinet he found it impossible to retain them as leader of the Party and putative Prime Minister. Kinnock abandoned the duffle coat, the checked shirts and the trade union ties. One of the last times he wore his TGWU tie in public was on the day of his election as leader in 1983. In their place came regimental ties, dark, expensive suits and white shirts. Increasingly he appeared a cantankerous martinet, perpetually uncomfortable in the role he had chosen to play. Kinnock was consumed by a fear of appearing out of place and a desire to conform to accepted practice. The search for respectability, as defined by an establishment whose real workings he little understood (unlike Jim Callaghan, who understood them all too well), became the be-all and end-all.

In his early years in the Commons Kinnock was seen as highly approachable, "clubbable" and warm. As leader he became ever more watchful and wary, a loner intimate only with the very few whose political destinies were wedded to his own. One old-time university friend, Tom Davies, observed that Kinnock "is now too afraid of the possible pain of betrayal to have any real close friends".[8] Those who were not for him were always considered to be against him. To most of his parliamentary colleagues he was a remote, inaccessible figure, rarely seen in the Commons other than when casting a vote, discharging his duties at Prime Minister's Question Time or attending major parliamentary set-pieces. Immured in his private office he no longer appeared at the various Commons bars, cafeterias and tearooms that he had frequented prior to 1983. This inaccessibility led to a build-up of frustration across the political spectrum of Labour MPs. In the last years of his regime Kinnock would proceed through the Commons lobby surrounded by a praetorian guard led by his parliamentary private secretary

Adam Ingram, who would positively discourage MPs from approaching their leader.

Despite careful preparation, Kinnock persistently botched his set-piece confrontations with both Margaret Thatcher and John Major. He failed to make a favourable impression on the Commons either in Prime Minister's Question Time or in debate. His performances on major Commons occasions, such as the debates on the Westland affair in January 1986 and on the motion expressing "no confidence" in Thatcher's government in November 1990, were often greeted with horror by Labour MPs.

The Leader of the Opposition is a paid minister of the Crown, a member of the Privy Council and by tradition an influential politician in his own right. His or her comments on almost any political or social topic make headline news. In his nine years in this privileged post, Kinnock travelled extensively, dined with heads of state and enjoyed private discussions with the likes of François Mitterrand, George Bush and Mikhail Gorbachev. Yet he was more than willing to spend the whole of one day every month at a meeting of Labour's NEC investigating the activity of Militant Tendency supporters in Liverpool, proscribing the small left-wing group Socialist Organiser, suspending a score of non-aligned socialists in Brighton or Lambeth, or intervening in the selection of parliamentary and local council candidates in constituencies up and down Britain. Most observers felt that his zeal in these latter endeavours far outstripped anything he displayed in tackling the Tories over the despatch box in the House of Commons.

Kinnock spent more time and energy on internal Party management than any other Labour leader. He was forever preoccupied with preparations for the monthly meetings of the NEC and its sub-committees, drafting motions, arranging majorities and browbeating individuals and unions to ensure they would back him on the NEC or in the shadow cabinet. For Kinnock, triumph in the internal faction fight was always the *sine qua non* of leadership. It was not enough to have majority support on the NEC or the shadow cabinet; anything less than an overwhelming majority would be a threat. To this end he set out, behind closed doors, to impose his authority over every component of the Party, to reconstruct its policies and to change its constitution to ensure that the leader's status would never again come under the kind of threat it suffered during the late 1970s and early 1980s.

In his pursuit of personal domination over the Party, Kinnock constructed a private office larger and more powerful than that of any of his predecessors. Fourteen members of the office were listed in the 1991 House of Commons telephone book. In addition to these, his personal staff was swelled by a number of other unpaid or informal advisers from Walworth Road or the media or the City or academia. What they all shared in common was an overriding loyalty not to the cause of Labour but to the career of Neil Kinnock. In assessing any policy shift or inner-Party controversy, the one question they seemed to ask was: what course of action would best enhance Neil's status? In assessing any individual, they appeared to adopt Margaret Thatcher's famous litmus test: was he or she "one of us"? At times of crisis, it became Kinnock and his private staffers against the world.

In order to protect his always shaky pre-eminence, Kinnock and his office regularly used off-the-record briefings to journalists in order to undermine Party colleagues who posed either a real or an imagined threat. This practice was nothing new in Westminster and had been favoured by both Harold Wilson and Margaret Thatcher. Where Wilson relied upon Joe Haines and Thatcher upon Bernard Ingham, Kinnock variously used Patricia Hewitt, Charles Clarke and Peter Mandelson. Leadership favourites such as Gordon Brown, Tony Blair and Margaret Beckett were ceaselessly promoted while others, including at various times John Prescott, Michael Meacher, Bryan Gould and even on occasion Jack Cunningham or John Smith, found themselves on the receiving end of unattributable abuse.

Of course, the private office of any politician naturally works to further the interests of its employer. What made Kinnock's office something special was the influence it came to exercise over the whole of the Labour Party. Indeed, some would say that in the end it came virtually to replace the Party itself. Certainly in the final years of the Kinnock regime it exercised more real power than the NEC, the shadow cabinet or the annual conference. Votes and debates at all these bodies became mere rubber stamps of approval for decisions previously taken in private by Kinnock and his advisers.

Just how Kinnock funded such a large private office was always something of a mystery. It was reported that he used as much as half the "Short money" (an allocation of funds from the Exchequer for the use of opposition parties) on his own staff. This would imply that in 1991 some £400,000 was spent to pay the wages and meet the expenses of his entourage.

The office became a fortress within the Palace of Westminster, derisively referred to by several shadow cabinet colleagues as "the bunker". Patricia Hewitt, Kinnock's first press secretary, was dubbed "Checkpoint Pat" because Labour MPs wishing to speak to their leader had first to negotiate an appointment through her. Some well-wishers in the Parliamentary Labour Party urged Kinnock to make a greater effort to improve his nonexistent lines of communication with alienated backbenchers. They suggested he should set up meetings with Labour backbenchers or drop by the Commons tearooms, but Kinnock always rejected their advice; communicating via unelected, appointed intermediaries was much more to his taste.

Charles Clarke, often described as Kinnock's "political adviser", acted in fact as the equivalent of a White House chief of staff in a US presidential administration. Clarke was Kinnock's chief henchman, political fixer and general minder. In the words of one member of the shadow cabinet, he was "Kinnock's eyes and ears". He ran the leader's private office and dominated its internal life. More than anyone else, he was Kinnock's one indispensable confidant. When he spoke to Kinnock, the leader listened; when he spoke to anyone else, they too listened – because they assumed they were hearing his master's voice.

Educated at public school and Oxford, Clarke was elected president of the National Union of Students in 1975 on the Communist Party-dominated Broad Left ticket. Interviewed in *Labour Weekly* after his election, he listed as political heroes the former Chilean president Salvador Allende and the US Communist Angela Davies as well as the Labour MPs Tony Benn and Judith Hart. Clarke described himself as an unashamed Marxist, "if by that you mean the classical definition of a Marxist as someone who looks at society in class terms and who believes that the ruling class can be overturned by revolutionary change".[9]

Clarke's career in the student movement included a stint as chair of the World Youth Council, a body with well-documented CIA connections. For Clarke, it was no problem blending this involvement with his association with the Communist Party. Clarke began working for Kinnock in 1980 as a part-time adviser. His salary was paid out of a grant from the Rowntree Trust, which Kinnock received in his capacity as shadow education spokesperson. That same year, Clarke was elected a Labour councillor for the London borough of Hackney and in 1982 he became chair of the housing committee under an unreconstructed right-wing local government regime. His performance there was unimpressive and appears to have marked the end of his ambitions for elected office. On Kinnock's accession to the Labour Party leadership in 1983, Clarke resigned as Hackney's chair of Housing, pleading the pressure of his new work commitment. He remained on the council, however, and in spring 1985 he joined other right-wing rebels in breaking the Labour whip and overturning the local campaign against ratecapping.

Clarke's eminence within Kinnock's private office was constructed slowly over a period of years. Originally, Kinnock had appointed Dick Clements, former editor of *Tribune* and adviser to Michael Foot, to take charge of his private office. Clarke, then aged thirty-three, was made a "personal assistant" to Kinnock and was clearly second in rank to Clements, who was much more experienced and enjoyed extensive personal connections throughout the Party. But Clarke's personal influence with Kinnock was already obvious to anyone permitted access to the inner sanctum. Julia Langdon, then of the *Guardian*, aptly described him in 1983 as "never having cast off the image of the eternal student politician". She noted that he was "very loyal to Kinnock" and "closely identified with the management of the leader".[10] Dick Clements proved not to be the kind of chief of staff that Kinnock required; though loyal to the leader, he was reluctant to engage in the type of party management that Kinnock considered essential. Clarke suffered from no such inhibitions. Gradually Clements was eased out and Clarke was promoted in his place.

Patricia Hewitt was another of Kinnock's early appointees who was ultimately squeezed out by Clarke. A former general secretary of the National Council for Civil Liberties and unsuccessful parliamentary candidate for Leicester East in 1983, she applied to work in any capacity for both Hattersley and Kinnock during their 1983 leadership campaigns. A former firebrand of the left, her ardour for radical socialism had cooled at the same time as Kinnock's, and so she was well qualified for a job in his office. Hewitt was keen on revamping the Party's publicity machine and placing a strengthened leadership at its centre. She was duly appointed Kinnock's press secretary.

From the beginning Hewitt saw herself as a kind of political general secretary, who would shape Party policy according to the leader's dictates. She was just as arrogant and ruthless as Charles Clarke, which guaranteed a clash of personalities. Clarke jealously guarded his status as Kinnock's closest personal adviser; he would not allow anyone else to establish the same degree of intimacy and trust. Hewitt, in turn, was determined to extend her power within the Party and indeed in the public domain. Both could not survive indefinitely within the limited space of the leader's private office.

Increasingly, Hewitt bore the brunt of criticism for the shortcomings of Kinnock's media performances. She was also scapegoated for what was considered to be a mishandling of the *Spycatcher* affair in early 1987 when her telephone call to the lawyer acting for Peter Wright in Australia enabled the Tories to attack Kinnock for an alleged lack of patriotism – always a sensitive spot for him. Following her return from maternity leave in spring 1989 she was moved from her post as press secretary and appointed "policy co-ordinator" with overall responsibility for the management of the Policy Review. She also became the leader's main direct liaison with the media professionals of the Shadow Communications Agency.

Once the Policy Review had been finalized at the 1989 conference, it was clear that Hewitt's new post would have little influence. Having lost the battle with Charles Clarke for the seat closest to the throne, Hewitt left Kinnock's employ altogether and took a post as a research fellow at the newly established centre–left think-tank, the Institute for Public Policy Research. Hewitt continued to enjoy considerable influence within the Kinnock circle, although this was now exercised from outside the private office. Right up to the 1992 general election, she was being entrusted with drafting and rewriting Labour's endless Policy Review relaunches. During the campaign itself Hewitt, working hand in glove with the Shadow Communications Agency, was the unelected official with the most day-to-day control over Labour tactics and activities. In the event of a Labour victory she had been widely tipped to head the Downing Street policy unit.

With Hewitt out of the office Clarke was in full possession of his domain. As the one person with unrestricted access to the Party leader, this unelected private staffer became a more powerful figure than any member of the shadow cabinet or the NEC. He regularly attended meetings of the shadow cabinet, intervened at will in the Policy Review process and was privy to the workings of every Party body. Disliked and feared, Clarke was serenely untroubled by his lack of personal popularity and positively revelled in his hatchetman image. It suited him to be feared by others, as long as he retained Kinnock's confidence. Theirs became almost an association of equals, based on mutual trust and understanding.

Clarke's own aide-de-camp was Neil Stewart, who was hired to deal with "Party relations" when Clarke's own responsibilities had become too large and onerous to supervise the everyday details of meeting-fixing and arm-twisting. Like Clarke, Stewart was a former president of the NUS. Unlike Clarke, he was elected on a National Organization of Labour Students (NOLS) ticket in opposition to the CP–Liberal Broad Left pact. His victory in 1982 made him the first in a line of less than inspiring, but electorally successful LCC-backed NOLS candidates for NUS president. Stewart was one of a number of career apparatchiks who beat a well-trodden path from student politics to Kinnock's door, and he was well suited to his duties: cajoling trade union officials, Labour MPs and Walworth Road full-time officials into line with the leadership.

According to one former employee of the Labour leader, "If Neil Stewart says 'we think that this ought to happen', there's absolutely no doubt that he means that Neil Kinnock wants it to happen."[11] Stewart, a heavy-handed operator who antagonized more often than he impressed, was not always successful and periodically caught the blame from either Kinnock or Clarke when plans went awry. In particular his attempt to act as Kinnock's man in the Walworth Road by-election teams – in which he tried to run the press briefings over the heads of the professionals – was considered inept by employees at Walworth Road.

Like many lifelong professional politicians, Kinnock was always ill at ease with economics. From the beginning he knew he would need a specialist adviser he could trust. Originally this was Henry Neuberger, who was appointed in 1983 when his Tribunite leanings and mildly interventionist economics seemed well suited to the Kinnock leadership.

Within a few years even this approach came to seem too radical to Kinnock, and Neuberger left Kinnock's staff and went to work for Bryan Gould. He was replaced by John Eatwell, a fellow of Trinity College, Cambridge, described by someone who worked with him on the Policy Review as having "the deep-seated political instincts of a Tory".

From 1987 onwards Eatwell's was the main voice coaxing Kinnock to endorse the irreplaceable supremacy of the free market. Like Kinnock himself, Eatwell was a late convert to economic orthodoxy. Indeed, as recently as 1985, in a *Tribune* article co-authored with Roy Green, he had advanced a sharp critique not only of Thatcherite *laissez-faire* but also of the "Keynesian compromise", which had been "fatally flawed by its dependence on traditional neo-classical assumptions concerning the market as a means for the efficient allocation of resources".[12] It was precisely this "dependence" which, on Eatwell's advice, was to constrict Labour's economic policy in 1992 to the dreary formula, "we will not spend what the country cannot afford".

Eatwell's advice was endorsed and fleshed out by others, notably economist Paul Ormerod, director of the Henley Centre for Economic Forecasting and a right-wing activist in the London Labour Party. Another adviser was Gavyn Davies, a leading economist with Wall Street investment banker Goldman Sachs, whose wife, Sue Nye, worked in Kinnock's office. It was rumoured that Davies refused an offer of employment within Kinnock's office on the grounds that he could command a much higher salary in the City. He was often touted as a possible economics supremo in a Kinnock administration in Downing Street, and the Labour leader often deferred to his advice on questions such as the European Exchange Rate Mechanism, interest rates and inflation.

Increasingly, Party policy was determined in the leader's office. The origins of the Policy Review itself lay in a private memorandum from Peter Mandelson to Charles Clarke in July 1987. Throughout its evolution the review was controlled, step by step, by the leader's office. Every Policy Review group and every report was closely monitored by members of Kinnock's private staff, working to precise briefs from Clarke and Hewitt. Besides Eatwell on the Productive and Competitive Economy group, Patricia Hewitt was a member of the People at Work and Economic Equality groups. According to Hughes and Wintour, their "aim was to stay close to the groups, report back to Kinnock how they were developing, and reflect Kinnock's views to the groups as necessary".[13] The crucial issue of defence policy, one of the most sensitive topics under discussion, was watched and nurtured with special care by Clarke himself.

This method of policy formation by a small inner circle of unelected advisers surrounding the leader, which became custom and practice during the Policy Review, grew quite blatant in the last years of the

Kinnock regime. Again and again the leader would let it be known through his private office what would and would not be Labour Party policy. The press grew accustomed to this and gave far more weight to these unattributable briefings than to the decisions of the annual Labour Party conference. The Walworth Road policy directorate became an irrelevance.

A case in point was Kinnock's attitude towards the Party's commitment to cuts in military expenditure and the transfer of resources to social needs. Few policies are as close to the heart of the movement as this one, expressing as it does a bedrock socialist conviction that capitalist society has its priorities wrong. Although in 1989 the leadership had succeeded in overturning the Party's non-nuclear defence policy, the commitment to defence cuts remained in place. With the collapse of the Stalinist regimes in Eastern Europe at the end of the year, the bloated military budget seemed more ripe for pruning than ever. After all, even the Tories had initiated a defence review.

But in the run-up to the 1990 conference, Kinnock made it clear that he would no longer countenance the Party's policy, even though it was backed by the GMB, NUPE, USDAW, TGWU and MSF (the successor of ASTMS), as well as the vast majority of constituency parties, and was therefore certain to be reaffirmed at Blackpool. Kinnock was doomed to defeat, but this did not trouble him. Indeed, he positively gloried in his isolation from the movement he was supposed to lead.

At the pre-conference NEC meeting, six "soft left" shadow cabinet members – Gould, Cook, Prescott, Beckett, Lestor and Richardson – plus front-benchers Clare Short and David Blunkett defied Kinnock by backing a composite motion committing the Party to defence cuts. Kinnock won the vote by fourteen votes to thirteen, the closest result on the NEC since the end of the miners' strike.[14] The leadership promptly unleashed its team of spin-doctors. In unattributable briefings to journalists, the shadow cabinet dissenters were accused of "blatant opportunism", "self-indulgence", "putting their personal positions before that of the Party" and of being "more interested in the outome of the NEC elections than the general elections". They were threatened with "punishment" in the shadow cabinet elections to be held the following month, a punishment duly meted out when under pressure from Kinnock's office a score of Labour MPs withheld their votes from Gould, Prescott and Cook. To justify his attack, Kinnock hinted at a hitherto unknown doctrine of "collective shadow cabinet responsibility in opposition".[15]

According to the *Guardian*, Kinnock had told the NEC that the arguments for defence cuts were "glib and simplistic" and that the role of NEC members was not "to impress the conference but to demonstrate to the country that we have considered and practical policies".[16] An indication that in Kinnock's eyes Labour conferences were held to "impress" not "the country" but the country's military establishment was to be found in the official conference guide, which boasted a full-page colour advert for the VSEL Challenger tank. Speaking in the conference debate, Martin O'Neill, Kinnock's defence spokesperson, denounced the defence cuts motion as empty rhetoric and urged conference to oppose it; he was greeted with hearty applause from the Party leader sitting on the platform. In the chair Jo Richardson refused to take a card vote on the composite, which might have given the motion the two-thirds majority needed to make it part of Labour's official election programme, and instead called twice for a show of hands before declaring the composite carried.

Kinnock hit back immediately. "Whilst I am Party leader and when I am Prime Minister," he declared, "the Labour government will always ensure that the defence policy we discharge will be a policy that best ensures the security and defence of Britain."[17] He went on to deliver a calculated attack on the conference: "We live in the world of realities, not resolutions. I can assure people now that what is the best defence policy for Britain will be ours, not some theoretical notion about some supposed average European defence budget."[18] It was a classic Kinnock outburst, mixing the rhetoric of statesmanship with heavy-handed mockery of his opponents within the Party.

The following year, 1991, resolutions calling for defence cuts poured in once again from constituencies and trade unions. This time, at the pre-conference NEC, Kinnock asked for the defence cuts composite to be remitted, rather than rejected outright. In practice remittal and rejection would amount to the same thing, but the proposal was enough to give the "soft left" NEC members the excuse they wanted to back the leader. This time Kinnock's majority was eighteen votes to five.[19]

On the morning of the conference defence debate the *Guardian* reported that "the leadership will shrug off the vote which does not commit it to anything in the current fluid climate".[20] Delegates could be forgiven for thinking that the leadership simply did not want them to show up at all for this debate. None the less, on a card vote, the composite was easily carried by 3,776,000 to 1,694,000. Although this two-thirds majority should have guaranteed defence cuts a place in Labour's election programme, the leadership was quick to assure the *Guardian* that "Labour is not going to make decisions about the country's defence policy based on a phrase in a resolution."

By the end of Kinnock's spell as leader, his office did not even bother with the formalities of party democracy. Clause Four was effectively disowned in the *Director* interview. Support for the US-led intervention in the Persian Gulf was declared by Kinnock while on holiday in Italy, without the slightest reference to the shadow cabinet or the NEC. The press was informally briefed that a future Labour government would not bring British Telecom back into public ownership and that Labour's commitment to ending male-only clubs would never be implemented. In January 1992 a dinner with journalists at an Italian restaurant was the occasion for an abortive announcement by the leader that Labour would phase in its promised increases in National Insurance contributions.

Instead of being answerable to the NEC or the Party conference, the Party's general secretary, Larry Whitty, organization director Joyce Gould and policy director Geoff Bish became mere functionaries of the Labour leadership. Some Walworth Road officials took instruction more willingly than others, but in the end all ceded the independence and authority of their offices to the leader's private bunker without a struggle. Whatever their foibles, Larry Whitty's predecessors as general secretary – Jim Mortimer, Ron Hayward and Morgan Phillips – were all substantial figures in the labour movement with priorities and loyalties of their own. All enjoyed autonomy from the parliamentary leader and some even challenged him directly. In contrast, Whitty became, in the words of one member of the NEC, no more than an "office boy in charge of the staples", receiving instructions not directly from the leader but second-hand from the leader's personal staff. Political favouritism ruled at Walworth Road. A division emerged between "insiders" known to be loyal to the leadership and "outsiders" whose loyalty was considered questionable. The former acted in effect as agents and observers for the leader's office, creating an atmosphere of mistrust and rivalry, which often hampered the functioning of the already creaky Party machine.

The Shadow Communications Agency provided the leadership with a publicity machine virtually independent of the Party's democratic structures (see pages 218–22). Formally, it was supposed to report to the campaign strategy committee. Informally, it reported directly to the leader's office and was accountable only to Kinnock's staff. Its boss, Philip Gould, seemed to perceive himself as a man of the elite generously placing his expertise at the services of the common people. He therefore seemed unwilling ever to consider the possibility that these common people might have traditions, values, needs or priorities more valid than his own. This made him an ideal vehicle for Kinnock's self-aggrandizement. Ignoring all polling evidence to the contrary, Gould insisted in both 1987 and 1992 that Neil Kinnock should be the central figure in all Labour's campaign imagery.

Like Gould, popular fiction writer Ken Follett and his image-consultant wife Barbara became fanatical Kinnock loyalists. In an interview in the *Guardian* in January 1992 Follett named Kinnock as his "political hero". He threw himself into fundraising efforts centred around the peculiar mystique of the leader for a section of affluent Labour supporters. Barbara, a former Labour parliamentary candidate in unwinnable Tory seats in 1983 and 1987, gained fame for refashioning the public appearances of leading front-bench lights such as Robin Cook and Harriet Harman. Cook was told to attire himself in autumnal colours and was instructed never again to wear his favourite National Union of Railwaymen tie. Harman, like other women Labour MPs and virtually all women parliamentary candidates, was told to power dress in bright, assertive reds and yellows. Like the advice offered by other experts and professionals close to the Labour leader, Barbara Follett's services, trivial as they might seem, were hardly politically neutral or ideologically value-free. Eatwell, Gould, Follett, and the others who clustered around Kinnock's private office brought to the Labour Party not only their technical skills but also, far more important, a freight of political assumptions about the need to conform to the status quo. Forming a mutual admiration society with the Labour leader, they confirmed each other's prejudices and elevated them to the status of science – and therefore beyond the remit of legitimate inner-Party debate. The result was to reinforce Kinnock's growing isolation and alienation from the movement he led and from the public he sought to woo.

Patricia Hewitt was replaced as press secretary by Julie Hall, who had previously worked as a political reporter for Independent Television News. Unlike Hewitt, Hall was a media professional whose function was to act as a barrier between Kinnock and the fourth estate. She followed the leader everywhere, protecting him from awkward questions and taking flak from frustrated journalists. Hall rapidly became one of the trusted insiders with close links to the campaigns and communications directorate. She married Mandelson's assistant, Colin Byrne, who served for some time as Walworth Road's chief press and broadcasting officer.

Kinnock's parliamentary private secretaries had the unenviable task of shielding the leader from the moods and pressures of the PLP. His first Parliamentary Private Secretary (PPS), Derek Foster, had always been solidly in the political centre of the Labour Party. As the Party's chief whip after 1985 he did not always meet with Kinnock's approval, but secured re-election several times despite Kinnock's lack of enthusiasm. In 1985 he was replaced as PPS by Kevin Barron, who was appointed within days of publicly resigning from the Campaign Group and denouncing the leadership of the NUM in the pages of *Tribune*. As an ex-left born-again Kinnockite, he was just the man for the leader's coterie.

After Barron moved on to join the front-bench energy team, Adam Ingram, yet another reformed leftist, became Kinnock's last PPS. Elected MP for East Kilbride in 1987, this former NALGO official and East Kilbride district councillor had a long record of association with left-wing causes. At one time he had been a supporter of Gerry Healy's notoriously sectarian Socialist Labour League, forerunner of the Workers' Revolutionary Party. As an unashamed member of the Labour right, Ingram's willingness to deploy the skills acquired in twenty years of faction-fighting made him exceedingly useful to Kinnock's office.

Central to Kinnock's command of the Labour Party was the control he painstakingly established over the National Executive Committee. Under Labour's constitution, the NEC is the Party's supreme authority outside the annual conference. It is charged with implementing the decisions of the conference and overseeing every aspect of the Party's work. In the 1970s the NEC was a powerful, independent body recognized as an authentic voice for the labour movement in the country at large. It defended the decisions of the Labour conference regardless of the wishes of the parliamentary leadership and challenged the policies and assumptions of Labour cabinets and shadow cabinets.

At the 1981 conference the Labour right gained effective control of the NEC. In alliance with the "soft left" (represented principally then by Neil Kinnock) their majority was tenuous at first but grew more reliable as the years passed. As leader, Kinnock was determined to exercise unchallenged control of the NEC. He did not want merely to win the votes; he wanted an enormous, guaranteed majority for whatever proposal he cared to present. He wanted to be seen by both the media and the public as the unchallengeable master of the Labour Party.

1985 and the "realignment of the left" was the watershed year for Kinnock's NEC. After that, the remaining left minority was gradually whittled away. Eric Heffer lost his seat in 1986 and Audrey Wise and Joan Maynard were deposed in 1987. In 1988 other left NEC members such as Jo Richardson and Margaret Beckett made their peace with Kinnock and began casting their votes with the leadership camp. In 1989, to the all-too-obvious public delight of the Labour leader, Ken Livingstone lost the seat he had won in 1987. The method for choosing the Young Socialists representative, which for years had been a virtual Militant sinecure, was changed to ensure the election of yet another leadership supporter. After the 1989 conference, Kinnock could expect to win most votes on the NEC by twenty-seven to two.

As leader, Kinnock spoke at NEC meetings at great length on nearly every issue. He would always respond to any criticism or disagreement and invariably had the last word. His office shaped NEC agendas and drafted virtually all the resolutions that were eventually carried by the body, however trivial the matter at hand. Kinnock himself or another member acting on his behalf moved or seconded every important proposal. There was no issue on which the Labour leader was not prepared to exercise his authority.

After 1989, Tony Benn and Dennis Skinner maintained a lonely opposition to the leadership on the NEC. They moved motion after motion but lost vote after vote. Although by virtue of seniority both men sat on the important NEC Home Policy and Organization sub-committees, they were hopelessly isolated. Many times they put forward arguments which others on the NEC knew were correct, but which they would not support because to back Benn or Skinner on anything was to court the leader's displeasure.

Under Kinnock's leadership, and with the help of key "soft left" NEC members such as David Blunkett, Robin Cook, John Prescott and Clare Short, Labour's once-mighty NEC became an ineffectual body, without the power or the will to form Labour strategy or policy or even to offer the leader and the shadow cabinet independent advice. At the end, its monthly meetings were almost entirely concerned with disciplinary matters or constitutional changes designed to strengthen the authority of the leadership and erode the rights of the members.

It has been said that the legacy of Thatcherism is a host of "little Thatchers" in every nook and cranny of public life. The same could be said about the "little Kinnocks" who have come to populate the Labour Party at all levels. Based as it was on a sharp distinction between insiders and outsiders, Kinnock's regime acted as a magnet for status-seekers, influence-peddlers and careerists of all sorts.

These "little Kinnocks" enabled their master to govern Labour with a rod of iron, but they could do nothing to enhance his standing with the electorate. In contrast to Jim Callaghan and Harold Wilson, Kinnock consistently polled well below his party. He had turned himself into the archetype of everything the public hates about professional politicians. He was seen as a man who would do anything or say anything, repudiate any conviction or embrace any prejudice for the sake of a handful of votes. In the end it was hard for many people, in the privacy of the polling booth, to vote for a man whose sole ambition was apparently to become Prime Minister.

Notes

1. "Aims and Values", NEC paper February 1988.
2. NEC minutes March 1988.
3. *The Times* 24 March 1988.
4. *Sunday Times* 26 June 1988.
5. *Director* September 1991.
6. NEC Report to Annual Conference 1991.
7. *Labour Party News* summer 1987.
8. *Independent on Sunday* 10 June 1991.
9. *Labour Weekly* 30 May 1975.
10. *Guardian* 4 October 1983.
11. *Guardian* 30 September 1991.
12 *Tribune* 22 February 1985.
13. Colin Hughes and Patrick Wintour, *Labour Rebuilt*, London 1990.
14. NEC minutes September 1990.
15. *The Times* 2 October 1990.
16. *Guardian* 2 October 1990.

17. *Guardian* 4 October 1990.
18. ibid.
19. NEC minutes September 1991.
20. *Guardian* 3 October 1991.

4

The Power of Patronage:
Labour's Parliamentary Elite

> The Thatcher administration is not so much a modern cabinet as a
> medieval court operating under a system of favourites.
> *Neil Kinnock, October 1989*

In the mid 1980s left opponents of the Labour leadership often accused
Neil Kinnock of trying to reverse the gains of 1979–83 by decanting power
away from the Party membership, the Party conference and the elected
NEC back into the hands of the Parliamentary Labour Party (PLP) and the
shadow cabinet. While it is certainly true that from his first days as leader
Kinnock set himself up as a bulwark protecting the traditionally right-
wing PLP from the marauding leftist hordes in the constituencies, in the
end it was within his own office that he concentrated power. By the 1992
general election the PLP and the shadow cabinet found themselves
stripped of any independent capacity to make policy or determine
strategy. Ironically, the first step on the road to this subordination of the
PLP and shadow cabinet was their liberation from the thrall of the Party's
elected bodies and dependence on the Walworth Road bureaucracy.
During the Kinnock years there evolved an ever more independent and
well-resourced PLP apparatus. With the help of "Short money" (state
funding given to opposition parties), grants and secondments from the
Party itself and disbursements from trade unions, the PLP assembled an
impressive battery of press officers, researchers and administrative
assistants, all collaborating to advance the political interests of the
parliamentary leadership. The post of PLP campaign co-ordinator was
first created in 1984. Unelected and unaccountable, it has been used to
assert parliamentary control over the full-time apparatus at Walworth
Road and to bypass the ever more indolent NEC. The proliferation of
shadow cabinet policy advisers, researchers and personal assistants
enabled the leadership to assert control over the policy-making process.

But securing the independence of the shadow cabinet from the rest of
the Labour Party served in the end only to bring about the subordination

of the shadow cabinet to the leader, his office and chosen personal advisers. Kinnock's regime thus became a mirror image of Margaret Thatcher's, a type of "Prime Ministerial government" exercised in opposition. Kinnock dispensed punishment and reward to Labour MPs not according to merit but in order to secure his own power in the Party and protect it from potential challenge. This tactic proved all too effective a means of dominating a PLP that had been denied real power to run the country for so many years. By the late 1980s, many Labour MPs had never served under a Labour government, even though some had been elected to the House of Commons three times. The height of political ambition became a place on the Opposition front bench. To be denied such a position was to be confronted with the premature end of a political career. Many Labour MPs could not stomach that prospect and agreed to pay whatever price the leadership demanded.

Thus was created an official parliamentary opposition united not by mutual respect or common political allegiance but by fear and ambition. In an alliance whose only glue was the patronage of a perpetually insecure leadership, there was no room for half-heartedness or compromise. To express even the mildest dissent was to risk all.

Kinnock's need to ostracize critics and bind a compliant majority with ties of personal loyalty led him to construct a massive payroll vote of front-bench MPs willing to accept whatever *diktat* was imposed on them. He ended up presiding over the largest front bench in Labour's history, whose size actually breached the standing orders of the PLP. In 1990 it encompassed over 90 out of 228 Labour MPs – more than 40 per cent of the total membership of the PLP – excluding chairs and members of Commons select and standing committees. There were more shadow ministers than government ministers.

Kinnock's ruthlessness in dealing with front-bench opposition was demonstrated by his summary dismissal of arts spokesperson Norman Buchan in January 1987. Buchan was an old-style left-winger and Tribune Group luminary, an ex-Communist and committed unilateralist who had been, along with Kinnock, one of the key abstainers in the 1981 deputy leadership contest. As a knowledgeable champion of the arts and an advocate of media reform, he had been a member of a joint NEC and shadow cabinet group which drew up the Party's arts policy for the 1987 election. Under his guidance the group submitted a paper to the NEC which proposed, in keeping with Party policy as passed at various conferences, to take supervision of broadcasting away from the Home Office and give it to a new ministry of arts.

The shadow home secretary, Gerald Kaufman, opposed the plan and lobbied Kinnock to secure its defeat. But it was not merely pressure from Kaufman that caused Kinnock to intervene to thwart the unwary Buchan. It was his own conviction that anything that could be seen as a challenge to the status quo in media control would provoke the wrath of the establishment. At the NEC home policy committee meeting in January 1987 the leader tabled amendments deleting Buchan's proposals and committing Labour to keep broadcasting within the Home Office remit. These were passed, to Buchan's dismay, by a one-vote majority.

The next day Buchan asked to see Kinnock privately and following a four-minute interview was stripped of his portfolio. Only moments after an astonished Buchan had left Kinnock's office, Patricia Hewitt notified the media that the arts spokesperson had been "dismissed". At this stage the full NEC had yet to view either Buchan's proposals or Kinnock's amendments.

Norman Buchan's mistake was not simply believing that Kinnock would support those who had supported him but failing to understand that Kinnock was determined to control all aspects of Labour policy. He protested in a speech to a meeting of the PLP that Kinnock was "not prepared to believe that he could be proved to be wrong". Kinnock answered, "I will sack people who do not accept the position of the front bench." In this case, that amounted to accepting the position of the front bench *as determined by the leader's office*. Kinnock claimed that it was "functionally necessary for a leadership to act that way".[1]

If Kinnock could treat an old associate and supporter so harshly over an apparently peripheral issue, then it can be readily imagined how he would treat old enemies with whom he disagreed over fundamental questions. That meant, above all, old enemies on the left, particularly Tony Benn and his associates. From the day Kinnock became leader he made it clear that membership of the left-wing Campaign Group of Labour MPs would be a bar to promotion within the PLP. He also made it clear that public repudiation of the group would be amply and swiftly rewarded. Jeremy Corbyn, Labour MP for Islington North and for many years Campaign Group secretary, remarked that the group was the biggest job creation scheme in the Palace of Westminster. Nearly every one of the twenty-odd ex-members of the Campaign Group sitting in the 1987–92 Parliament was appointed to the front bench shortly after leaving the group. Sometimes resignation and promotion were almost simultaneous. Mark Fisher, for example, was appointed to replace Buchan as arts spokesperson on the very day that he resigned from the Campaign Group.

Classic examples were the rapid promotions of Kevin Barron and Derek Fatchett after their break with the left following the miners' strike in 1985. Barron, MP for the mining constituency of Rother Valley since 1983, was an ex-miner whose arm had been broken by police when he was arrested in the course of a picket-line scuffle early in the dispute. Throughout the strike he had made no criticism, either public or private, of the NUM leadership. He was just turning forty; he held a safe Labour seat and faced no threat of deselection. Having attended a Campaign Group seminar in Chesterfield and sponsored the launch of *A Million Jobs a Year*, a Campaign Group pamphlet on economic policy, Barron quit the group the next day and denounced its leading members in an article in *Tribune*. Within days, he was appointed Kinnock's parliamentary private secretary. He then asked his research assistant to give him an undertaking that she would make no political statements with which he did not agree. Later, in 1990, as a junior member of Labour's front bench energy team, Barron was to play a leading role in fuelling the *Mirror*'s smear campaign against Arthur Scargill and Peter Heathfield.

Derek Fatchett, a former university lecturer on industrial relations, had replaced deselected right-winger Stan Cohen as candidate in Leeds Central prior to the 1983 general election. The local press had interpreted this as a triumph for the "revolutionary left" when it was nothing of the kind. Fatchett was a fair-weather leftist whose departure from the Campaign Group and subsequent denunciation of the left in *Tribune* remain the most highly publicized acts of his political career to date. He too was rewarded with a front-bench appointment, first as a junior whip and then as a member of Jack Straw's education team.

In the years to come, front-bench appointees Paul Boateng, Clare Short, Joan Ruddock, Margaret Beckett, Joan Walley and others were to find that resignation from the Campaign Group was the smartest career move they ever made. Kinnock wanted Labour MPs to draw lessons from these instant promotions. By making it obvious to all that a precondition for advancement in his PLP was not only a break with the left but a public repudiation of its leaders and policies, he intended to anathematize it and thus prevent it from exercising any influence within the PLP or the Labour Party at large.

The real effect of this anathematization was felt not by unwavering left-wing MPs such as Tony Benn, Dennis Skinner, Jeremy Corbyn, Bernie Grant, Bob Cryer or Mildred Gordon. They had never expected personal advancement under Kinnock's regime. The target of the exercise was the "soft left" in the Tribune Group, the very people who had provided Kinnock's original base in the PLP.

The Parliament elected in 1987 saw a massive intake into the Tribune Group, which expanded at one point to include more than half the PLP. Among its members were leading lights of the "soft left" such as Bryan Gould, David Blunkett, Michael Meacher and Robin Cook, Kinnock loyalists such as Gordon Brown, Jack Straw and Tony Blair, and out-and-out right-wingers like Peter Snape, the Labour MP for West Bromwich East. With Gould, Prescott and Meacher taking the first three places, the shadow cabinet elections of July 1987 demonstrated the strength of the Tribune Group in the new PLP. The Tribunite hegemony that had been heralded in the press seemed about to become a reality.

On closer scrutiny it became apparent that what had really happened was the forging of a political link between the right-wing Solidarity Group and the right wing of the Tribune Group. At a Tribune meeting held before the elections, Straw, Brown and Blair, clearly acting on behalf of the Labour leadership, had argued vehemently against any idea of a joint shadow cabinet slate with the Campaign Group. Thanks to the votes of Tribunite MPs who had been promised front-bench positions by the leadership, they won the day and a joint slate was rejected. The group then drew up a slate of ten names for the fifteen places and it was agreed that five slots would be left vacant. In the end most Tribune Group members used their five unallotted votes to ensure the continuing presence in the shadow cabinet of key Solidarity figures, notably John Smith, John Cunningham and Gerald Kaufman. Kinnock then handed the three major shadow portfolios to Solidarity stalwarts. Smith, rather than Bryan Gould, became shadow Chancellor; Kaufman became shadow foreign secretary; and Roy Hattersley took over home affairs. None the less, the economics team appointed by Kinnock was said to illustrate the newfound power of the "soft left". Gould was given responsibility for trade and industry while Michael Meacher was handed the politically sensitive employment brief.

The alliance of the "soft left" and the hard right illustrated by the 1987 shadow cabinet elections was a major breakthrough for Kinnock. From now on there was a solid bloc of 150–170 Labour MPs wedded to his leadership. So confident did this make the old right wing that in March 1988 the Solidarity Group voted to dissolve itself. An unnamed member told the *Sunday Times* that there were no more battles left to fight. "Kinnock is moving our way on defence, Europe and the economy and we've clobbered the nasties."[2]

With Solidarity dissolved and Tribune established as far and away the largest numerical grouping in the PLP, Tribune should have become, as its champions in the media predicted, the centre of gravity within the Labour Party. Instead, it declined steadily. In the words of one leading member, after 1987 the group was "colonized by the leadership". Kinnock supporters such as Brown, Straw, Blair, Barron, Snape and Adam Ingram displayed no interest in the group for months at a time, only to turn up *en masse* to ensure that crucial decisions – such as that on whether to support Roy Hattersley over John Prescott for deputy leader in 1988 – went the leadership's way.

The demise of the Tribune Group's influence was apparent as early as the 1988 shadow cabinet elections. Leadership acolytes had packed Tribune's slate-making meeting and once more blocked any alliance with the Campaign Group. They insisted that the Tribune Group run a slate of fifteen for the shadow cabinet places. *Tribune*, the weekly newspaper, which acted as a mouthpiece for what remained of the group's left wing, reported an "organized effort" to replace Tribune Group "soft lefts" – Michael Meacher, Jo Richardson and Bob Hughes – with Martin O'Neill, Tony Blair, Harriet Harman and Joan Lestor. The leadership's spin-doctors had briefed two Sunday newspapers to this effect the previous weekend. "Frustration is widespread on the left of the Group that it is becoming nothing more than a rubber stamp for the leadership," *Tribune* reported.[3]

Although the group ran a full slate, most of the leadership acolytes refused to back all fifteen candidates and switched their votes to established right-wingers. The result was that, while only eight Tribunites got elected, five erstwhile Solidarity supporters – Smith, Cunningham, Kaufman, Barry Jones and Donald Dewar – saw their votes increase substantially over the previous year. Prescott, Meacher and Gould saw their votes decline. But despite both leadership and Tribune Group support, Kevin McNamara, Clive Soley, Harman and O'Neill failed to win election. Kinnock's office let it be known that it regarded this as the fault of the left Tribunites, who had prioritized support for David Blunkett, Clare Short, Margaret Beckett and Jo Richardson.

Solidarity's confidence in the rightward trajectory of the leadership and, even more, in the inability and unwillingness of the Tribune Group to resist it, proved well founded. In 1988, when Tribune member Ann Clwyd, in defiance of a shadow cabinet instruction to abstain in the vote on the annual Defence Estimates, decided to follow conference policy by joining with with thirty-three other Labour MPs to oppose the government, she lost her front-bench education portfolio. No protests were forthcoming from the Tribune Group luminaries in the shadow cabinet, although a reduction in defence spending was supposed, at this time, to be one of their sacrosanct commitments. In an article in *Tribune* Clwyd took the moral high ground, justifying her disobedience by referring to the wickedness of high military spending. In less than a year, however, she made her peace with the Defence Estimates, won election to the shadow cabinet and was appointed spokesperson on overseas development.

Bryan Gould was one of those whose rise within the PLP was trumpeted by *Tribune*, the LCC and other voices of the "soft left" as a vindication of their strategy of "critical support" for Kinnock. First elected to the House of Commons from Southampton Test in 1974, Gould returned to Parliament in 1983, this time representing Dagenham, and in that year's leadership election was one of a handful of MPs to support Peter Shore, for whom he had worked in the last Labour government. Eager to make his mark and ambitious for advancement, he stood for the shadow cabinet in 1983 and though he received only twenty-five votes was given a front-bench job dealing with trade and industry. The following year Gould stood for the constituency section of the NEC and polled a mere 18,000 votes. Undeterred, he stood for the shadow cabinet again in 1984, and still received only twenty-five votes. In 1985, his vote increased to fifty-three but this still placed him well out of contention.

That year, John Smith took over the trade and industry team and Gould at last was given a chance to make a parliamentary name for himself. As the Labour spokesperson with responsibility for the City of London at the time of the deregulation of the London financial markets, Gould quickly established a high profile for himself. Standing out among so many lacklustre opposition spokespersons, Gould's confident, concise and well-informed performances at the Commons despatch box brought him to the attention of the media, won him increasing support within the PLP and a following in the Party, nurtured by the LCC, which saw in his addiction to "new ideas" a handy cover for its move to the right. In 1986 he secured eighty-two votes for the shadow cabinet and finally won a place, at the expense of Robin Cook.

Appointed by Kinnock to replace Cook as campaign co-ordinator, Gould turned this hitherto ill-defined brief into a high-profile position at the centre of Labour's campaign and media machine. By now he had become a trusted member of the Kinnock inner circle, which enhanced his authority within both the PLP and the Party apparatus. He took command of Labour's 1987 election campaign, and was credited with many of its successes whilst escaping blame for its signal failure. His stock in the Party rose accordingly and it was no surprise when at the October Party conference he was elected to the NEC constituency section on his second attempt with an impressive 344,000 votes. Gould topped that year's shadow cabinet ballot with 163 votes, 33 ahead of his nearest rival. He was appointed chief spokesperson on trade and industry.

Within two years, Bryan Gould was to find that he had fallen from grace, at least as far as the leadership was concerned. It was not that he had voted "the wrong way" at the NEC (where he was a consistent supporter of every Kinnock initiative between 1987 and 1992). It was certainly not that he had dared to dispute in public anything the leader said. But as the leadership moved ever further to the right, Gould, who had maintained his position in the political centre of the Labour Party, began to look every once in a while like a dangerous radical. Kinnock was particularly irked by his predilection for state intervention in industry, which was reflected in his work on the Policy Review which, in the words of one observer, "drove John Eatwell up the wall". Gould liked to develop his own ideas without prior reference to the leadership, a trait regarded as dangerous in the extreme by Kinnock's private office. Worse yet, like other leading "soft left" MPs, he enjoyed a personal power base in the constituencies independent of the leadership. From early 1989, stories to the effect that the leader was displeased with Gould began to appear in the press. The word went out in the PLP: he was no longer one of the trusted favourites.

In the shadow cabinet elections of 1989 Gould came ninth with 124 votes. In the big reshuffle that followed he was removed from the trade and industry team (to be replaced by Gordon Brown) and given the environment portfolio relinquished by Jack Cunningham, who became campaign co-ordinator. To Party members in the country the environment portfolio, with its responsibility for the perpetual headache of local government, is one of the most important. But within the Westminster hierarchy, it was definitely a demotion. At Kinnock's urging Gould let it be known that he had specifically requested the environment position. But it was no secret in Westminster that Kinnock had offered him no choice.

Gould was shocked at the sudden transformation in his standing, but he kept his discontent to himself. He found the petty vindictiveness of the last years of the Kinnock regime distasteful, but like so many others he could not bear to be an outsider looking in. Through assiduous application to his brief, polished parliamentary performances and a steadfast refusal to rock the Kinnock boat, Gould sought to rehabilitate himself. Against expectations he retained his NEC seat at successive conferences but saw his shadow cabinet vote slump alarmingly in 1990 when his 94 votes placed him seventeenth among the eighteen elected members. Other "soft left" shadow cabinet members also lost votes that year. John Prescott slumped from 116 to 85 votes and Joan Lestor lost her seat when she slipped from 129 to 78 votes.

As environment spokesperson, Gould was charged with formulating Labour's alternative to the Poll Tax, but his advocacy of a local income tax incurred the wrath of Kinnock's closest advisers and led to further sniping against him in the press. None the less, Gould redoubled his efforts to please the leadership. He kept aloof from the muffled front-bench protests over the Gulf War and played a leading role in the witch-hunt of left-wing Labour councillors in the London borough of Lambeth. He attacked Poll Tax non-payers. Gradually he clawed his way back on board the Kinnock bandwagon. With John Cunningham's performance as campaign co-ordinator coming under fire, Gould was recruited in late 1991 to serve as Cunningham's deputy in the run-up to the general election. During the campaign itself, he once again took command and with the Shadow Communications Agency was responsible for the day-to-day management of Labour's failed bid for government.

Gould's post-election candidacy for the Party leadership attracted less support than he (or the media) expected. He was fortunate to pass the 20 per cent nomination threshold introduced by the leadership (with

Gould's support) four years previously. In the electoral college, his following in the constituencies and the unions turned out to be even more derisory. He preached a "radicalism" bereft of radical policies, which failed to impress Party members who remembered the rhetoric of modernization he had offered them after the last general election defeat in 1987.

Another surprised victim of Neil Kinnock's disfavour was Michael Meacher, who as a member of the NEC had transferred his loyalty from the left to the leadership during the 1985 realignment. As employment spokesperson after 1987, he convened the People at Work Policy Review group, whose brief included the sensitive area of trade union law. After considerable consultation and debate, Meacher's review group proposed that union rulebooks should be compelled to include the right to pre-strike secret ballots and that individual union members should be able to take their unions to "independent tribunals" to get the rules enforced. But the document did concede that not "all supportive action" (so-called secondary industrial action) could be ruled out. There remained an assumption that the bulk of the Tory trade union laws would be repealed. This was still the official position of both the GMB and NUPE. The 1988 conference voted for both People at Work and a composite resolution, sponsored by the TGWU, which explicitly called for the repeal of all anti-union laws.

Meacher and his team went to work on the second phase of the Policy Review. With Kinnock's encouragement, Meacher set about examining new rights relating to mergers and takeovers and changes in company law to protect workers' rights. He believed he could forge a compromise acceptable to the trade unions, the members and the leadership. His idea was to retain parts of the Tory laws on union ballots while committing Labour to a "statutory enforceable right of union recognition, a broader definition of trade disputes so as to allow secondary action and the return of immunities to remove a union's liability in tort".[4] This seemed to him to answer the demands of the rank and file while providing the leadership with adequate election-time protection from the inevitable Tory jibes about Labour letting the unions hold the country to ransom.

When the review group's final report was submitted as part of "Meet the Challenge, Make the Change" to the NEC in May 1989, it included promises of a "charter of rights for employees" and a "right to a secret ballot" to be enforced by "an independent tribunal". For the first time the question of secondary action was given prominence. "We do not think that all forms of sympathetic action by other employees, following a majority vote, should be unlawful," the group argued (which was no more than echoing the norms stipulated by the International Labour Organization), but it added the crucial rider, "if workers have a genuine interest in the outcome of a dispute".

Meacher was satisifed with his work, but he had not understood that Kinnock was determined not only to appear to be independent of the unions but to hold actual power in government over them. He regarded Meacher's compromise formula as no more than a holding operation.

In March 1989, Meacher had argued in a BBC television interview that some secondary action was justified and that Labour would support it. Acting on Kinnock's behalf, both Charles Clarke and Peter Mandelson had warned Meacher not to give the interview, but the employment spokesperson saw it as an opportunity to put forward the policy that the review group was developing. Meacher was not aware that Kinnock and his office were already preparing to get rid of him and that anything he said implying anything other than complete hostility to solidarity action would be used against him. Following the interview, Mandelson's deputy, Colin Byrne, disowned Meacher's statements to the lobby correspondents.

Two weeks after the interview, the *Sunday Times* ran a front-page article under the headline "Row over union power" alleging that Kinnock was about to strip Meacher of the employment brief. It was the result of a briefing given by Mandelson, though nothing had as yet been said to Meacher himself. When the latter complained about the press story to Kinnock, the leader claimed he knew nothing about it. None the less, as the conference approached, the press repeated the story with growing confidence. Tony Blair, it was claimed, would replace Meacher, who would lose his shadow cabinet seat in the autumn poll. Charles Clarke made it clear to the media that the leader was not prepared to enter an election campaign with any policy that appeared to place the unions "above the law". In this period, in the opinion of lobby correspondents Wintour and Hughes, Clarke had effectively assumed the role of shadow employment spokesperson.[5]

At the Labour conference, Meacher's speech on trade union law was well received by most union delegates and was thought to be in tune with the thrust of the Policy Review, which the conference overwhelmingly approved, despite protests from the left. But throughout Meacher's speech, Kinnock sat on the platform talking to others; it was a remarkable public display of disaffection with a shadow cabinet colleague. Sensing the danger, Meacher canvassed hard for the shadow cabinet elections held in mid October and retained his seat with a slightly increased vote. Within days Kinnock moved him to social security spokesperson, without ever having directly expressed any criticism of his performance with the employment brief, which was duly handed over to Tony Blair.

While the mild-mannered Meacher was perhaps a predictable casualty of the Kinnock autocracy, the tough-talking John Prescott should have proved a harder nut to crack. Prescott prided himself on his public reputation as an outspoken working-class politician who could not be intimidated. But when it came to tackling Neil Kinnock's runaway authoritarianism, his bite proved less fearful than his bark. First returned to Parliament in 1970 for Hull East, Prescott was elected to the shadow cabinet in 1983. As employment spokesperson he was sidelined by the leadership in the run-up to the 1987 general election campaign, but in the shadow cabinet elections that followed he substantially increased his vote. He expected promotion and was furious when he was relegated to energy spokesperson. In response he let lobby journalists know that he intended to stand against Roy Hattersley for Labour's deputy leadership at the following year's conference.

In mooting his bid for the deputy leadership, Prescott took great care not even to hint at a challenge to Kinnock himself or to question any of the political changes wrought by the Policy Review. Instead, he focused on the Party's lack of campaigning activity and its weak membership base, without actually opposing the mass membership scheme then being pushed through by the leadership. This ruse, cooked up by Prescott's supporters in the LCC, did nothing to deflect Kinnock's rage when Prescott formally announced his challenge to Hattersley in December 1987. The leader denounced the move and mobilized all available resources to force the hapless would-be candidate into a humiliating withdrawal. Lobby correspondents were treated to a barrage of insulting but unattributable remarks and the patronage machine was wheeled out to cajole Prescott's parliamentary supporters into abandoning him. Leadership loyalists tried to force the Tribune Group to instruct Prescott to stand down, but had to be content with an expression of group opinion to the effect that it was heavily against his standing. The National Union of Seamen, Prescott's sponsor, was also lobbied by Kinnock's office, as were members of Prescott's Hull East CLP.

Prescott finally cracked under the pressure and formally ended his candidacy on 20 January 1988. A facesaving formula had been negotiated with Kinnock on Prescott's behalf by NUS leader Sam McCluskie and NUPE general secretary Rodney Bickerstaffe. It was claimed by the Prescott camp that in return for his withdrawal from the contest, the leadership had agreed that a "wide-ranging debate on the role of the deputy leadership" would be held at the 1988 Party conference. But Kinnock immediately issued a statement making it clear that he opposed such a debate. Prescott's camp claimed that their man had a copy of a draft resolution on the deputy leadership debate with manuscript amendments in Kinnock's own hand, but that did not deter the leader from mounting an all-out assault on him. The leader instructed Peter Mandelson, Hilary Coffman (one of his private staff), and David Hill, an adviser to Roy Hattersley, to tour the House of Commons denouncing Prescott to the parliamentary lobby. This public humiliation was unprecedented in Labour circles. Prescott had to be taught that preferment in the shadow cabinet was at the leader's discretion and that attempts to mobilize support from the constituencies or the trade unions would not be tolerated.

Prescott revived his deputy leadership bid in March 1988 after Tony Benn and Eric Heffer had announced their challenge to Kinnock and Hattersley. Insisting that he had no policy disagreements with the leader, Prescott claimed to make up one half of a "Kinnock–Prescott" ticket. For Kinnock this was the ultimate nightmare. Robin Cook, having previously pledged his support to Prescott, was placed under intense pressure from Kinnock's office and finally agreed to act as joint campaign manager with John Smith for the somewhat shopworn Kinnock–Hattersley "dream ticket".

In the end Prescott's ambiguous message – to support Neil Kinnock by despatching his deputy – held few attractions for either the unions or the constituencies (60 per cent of which supported Hattersley). Despite backing from the LCC, only two members of the shadow cabinet (Jo Richardson and Michael Meacher) and only half the Tribune Group supported Prescott in the ballot at the Party conference. In the days that followed, stories were planted in the broadsheet press to the effect that Prescott would be "demoted" from his post as energy spokesperson, where he had expected to lead Labour's opposition to electricity privatization, to the transport brief. After the 1988 shadow cabinet elections, in which Prescott's vote fell, he was duly replaced by Tony Blair. Kinnock could not have foreseen that the transport job was to prove an unexpected boon to Prescott. A series of horrific rail and air disasters gave him the opportunity to lambast the government both inside and outside Parliament and to destroy the career of the secretary of state, Paul Channon. In this role, Prescott became one of the most widely recognized and effective members of the shadow cabinet. As a result, at the 1989 conference he was elected to the constituency section of the NEC. His election was publicly welcomed by Neil Kinnock, delighted that "Johnny" (as he liked to call him) had replaced Ken Livingstone.

Kinnock was right to welcome Prescott on board the NEC. Over the next few years, the Hull MP backed the leader with regimental regularity. In the absence of recorded votes, he often found it convenient to hint to journalists that he had withheld his support from the leadership on certain issues – only to find himself publicly contradicted by the ever-watchful Dennis Skinner. Prescott's relations with Kinnock remained artificially jovial but deeply uncomfortable. Again and again Prescott would strain ever so slightly at the leash, only to come to heel at the first yank of the patronage chain. During the build-up to the Gulf War, Prescott seemed for the moment to be on the verge of breaking free, only to be slapped down forcibly and publicly. During the general election, he and his transport brief were kept out of the limelight by the Party strategists. Afterwards, during his second unsuccessful tilt at the deputy leadership, he made a number of public attacks on the outgoing leadership and the campaign style devised by the Shadow Communications Agency. But as a member of both the NEC and the shadow cabinet he had spurned many opportunities to voice his objections to Labour's strategy before the campaign, when they might have counted for something.

Whilst Prescott cultivated his tough-guy image, Robin Cook was always the real hard man of the "soft left". Cook had served as Kinnock's campaign manager in the 1983 leadership election and soon after won a seat on the shadow cabinet for the first time. Much to his dismay, Kinnock refused to give him the prominent portfolio he craved. Instead, he had to content himself with the backwater of the European and Community affairs brief. The following year, Cook almost lost his place altogether, coming last in the shadow cabinet elections, not least because he was seen as someone outside the leader's orbit. After the so-called realignment of the left in 1985, in which Cook and other "soft lefts" made clear their support for the Kinnock leadership, he rose to fifth place in the shadow cabinet ballot. There followed a meeting with Kinnock in which Cook, never one to underestimate his own abilities, asked to be appointed defence spokesperson in place of Denzil Davies. Kinnock rejected this request, not only because of his desire to downplay the defence issue at all costs, but also because he feared and mistrusted Cook's intelligence and abilities. The leader compelled him to accept the role of campaign co-ordinator, which at that time was an ill-defined and powerless post. Without an established parliamentary brief, Cook lost his place on the shadow cabinet the following year.

He learned the lessons of defeat and set about re-establishing himself as a major figure in the PLP and the Labour Party. Partly because of the strong support of the LCC, but also because he made it clear to Kinnock that he was not a rival or threat of any kind, Cook soon climbed back on board the Kinnock bandwagon. Having regained his shadow cabinet place thanks to the strong showing of the Tribune Group in the 1987 elections, Cook was made Labour's spokesperson on health. Here he flourished, attacking the Tories at their weakest point and making the right noises of support for the leadership at every critical juncture.

That year, in a statement circulated to constituencies in support of his candidacy for the NEC, he asked for the votes of all those who shared his "hunger for a Labour Party dedicated to defeating our enemies without, rather than denouncing enemies within". He claimed to oppose moves either to "rout the rump of the right wing" or to organize "pogroms against those who are pleased to regard themselves as to the left of us". Having finally secured a place on the NEC in 1988, Cook backed every one of the leadership's disciplinary initiatives and indeed all its other proposals on membership, finance, policy and organization.

Though Cook remained distant from the Kinnock clique, he knew that his sharp parliamentary performances made him virtually untouchable. He kept at arm's length the various abortive attempts to revive "soft left" influence and played a leading role in sabotaging Prescott's deputy leadership bid. After the 1992 election, he agreed to manage John Smith's leadership campaign, thus effectively jettisoning his links to what remained of the "soft left", including his long-time backers in the LCC. This sort of manoeuvre must have been what one shadow cabinet colleague had in mind when he privately described Cook as "an extremely fly operator".

By the spring of 1992 the Tribune Group had became a bulwark of the Labour establishment and an integral part of the Kinnock-led right-wing coalition. Forty-five Tribune members sat on the front bench in addition to the fourteen elected to the shadow cabinet. Despite the apparent success of individuals associated with it, the group as a whole had ceased to matter at all. Its once passionate and well-attended weekly meetings had dwindled to directionless once-a-month gatherings attended sometimes by as few as four or five MPs. The group had even ceased to run a slate for the shadow cabinet. Only a few years before it had been touted as the new powerhouse of the PLP but it was now an irrelevance, without ideology or purpose, eviscerated by the disease of leadership loyalty which overcame so many in the 1987–1992 PLP.

Many of those involved in the realignment of 1985, particularly those associated with the weekly *Tribune* magazine, were well aware of this dismal state of affairs and made repeated efforts to revive the "soft left" as an independent force in the PLP. In 1990 the informal meetings of what came to be known as the "supper club" were an attempt to build a kind of informal, semi-secret network that would not threaten Kinnock the way an openly organized parliamentary caucus would. The "supper club" had been meeting in one guise or another for some time before its existence became public during the build-up to the Gulf War. *Tribune* editor Phil Kelly, shortly before he left the journal to work for Michael Meacher, explained that members of "the supper club wanted a political space" between the "politically directionless" Tribune Group and the "automatically anti-leadership" Campaign Group, a "political space which would allow debate and which would not be dominated by the question 'Are you for or against Neil Kinnock?' " He quoted a bold, but predictably unnamed member as saying, "The political consequences of the flooding of the Tribune Group with self-styled supporters of Kinnock was to create a vacuum. That has now been filled." Kelly argued that the "semi-clandestine form of organisation" (invitation only, no agendas, no resolutions) was "a tribute to the responsibility of the club's members and an indictment of the prevailing atmosphere in the PLP".[6]

Far from challenging this "prevailing atmosphere", which indeed they themselves had helped to create, "supper club" members resorted to the off-the-record press briefings that they had despised when used against them by Peter Mandelson. They allowed themselves to be quoted, anonymously, complaining that "any deviation from the line is inter-preted as an attack on the leadership" and insisting "we are more loyal to Neil Kinnock than some of the so-called loyalists closer to him". Phil Kelly declared that the club would continue to meet, despite well-publicized threats against it emanating from Kinnock's office. The follow-ing week, when a *Daily Mail* reporter crashed a private "supper club" meeting, at least three of these brave souls dived under tables in an attempt to hide their identities from the public and, presumably, the leader's private office.

Kinnock knew he had nothing to fear from such people. In private many Labour MPs across the political spectrum expressed their con-tempt for Kinnock and his personal staff. But in public they were overcome by ultra-cautiousness, above all by a fear of being cast out or anathematized along with the "hard left". They were no match for the Kinnock machine. One demoralized leading "soft left" MP who had backed Kinnock in the crucial period of realignment admitted ruefully, "We created a Frankenstein."

In the end, those "soft lefts" who continued to regard themselves as independent from the leadership but were unable to do anything to prove it probably contributed as much to the suppression of honest debate within the Labour Party as even the most enthusiastic leadership acolytes. They hedged and trimmed their political convictions within the shadow cabinet or the NEC but always did so, they claimed, in the interests of Party unity. Terrified of being branded "oppositionists", they always found a reason to postpone or evade any confrontation with the leadership.

Despite many attempts, the parliamentary "soft left" were never able to work collectively to influence either the shadow cabinet or the NEC. At their gatherings they would exchange complaints about Charles Clarke and Peter Mandelson and would vow to work together to push "Neil" to the left. Then, when the moment of truth came at the shadow cabinet or the NEC, they would scatter for cover. Whoever was brave or foolish enough to stick his or her head above the parapet would wait for support from the others that never came. In this group, mutual solidarity was impossible. Over the years, they had watched each other abandon too many cherished principles.

The whole "soft left" parliamentary endeavour was a futile attempt to square a circle. They wanted an accommodation with the leadership that would give them power and position but still allow them to preserve some form of left credibility. But whenever there was a clash between these two objectives they chose the former. The reason was that when faced with an inner-Party battle Kinnock was never prepared to compromise, whereas they knew nothing but compromise. The result was that they actually helped to shift opinion in the constituencies from left to right, thus whittling away their own base of support. They wanted to be both independent and loyal – but in Kinnock's Labour Party they were not allowed to be both, so they failed to be either.

Kinnock's 1989 shadow cabinet reshuffle was his final declaration of independence from the "soft left". With the Policy Review complete and the non-nuclear defence policy abandoned, Kinnock no longer needed them. The reshuffle saw Meacher and Gould removed from their jobs as employment and trade and industry spokesperson respectively and replaced by those rising media and Kinnock favourites, Tony Blair and Gordon Brown. Leftist-turned-loyalist Margaret Beckett was made shadow chief secretary to the Treasury, completing a right-wing economics team under the supervision of shadow Chancellor John Smith. Frank Dobson was replaced as shadow Leader of the House by John Cunningham and shifted to the energy job. Robin Cook, a noted Commons performer, found his health and social security brief divided in two following the Tory division of the Department of Health and Social Security. One half was given to the discarded Meacher. Martin O'Neill, although not a member of the shadow cabinet, had already been established as defence spokesperson following Denzil Davies's resignation the year before. It came as something of a shock to the "soft left" to find that while they themselves had been pushed almost imperceptibly to the margins, picked off one by one, the old right, the Solidarity nexus, had installed itself at the centre of the shadow cabinet. Neil Kinnock now presided over a parliamentary constellation more right-wing than any Labour had seen for well over a generation. It should have been a shadow cabinet to the taste of Roy Hattersley, but Hattersley had been a semi-detached member of the Kinnock team for some years. Blamed for Labour's failure to present a convincing tax policy in the 1987 election campaign, he allowed himself to be removed as shadow Chancellor and returned to the home affairs brief he had already held between 1980 and 1983. Hattersley had said in public again and again that the Labour Party had been right to prefer Neil Kinnock to himself in 1983: Kinnock had been able to pull the Party to the right and marginalize the left in a way that Hattersley, with his right-wing background, could never have done. Yet he remained sceptical about the Shadow Communications Agency's approach and the Policy Review, which he feared had stripped Labour of unpopular commitments without replacing them with what he liked to call "vision". He disliked Kinnock's mode of operating, not least because it excluded him from all the important decision-making.

The home affairs brief should have been a natural for Hattersley, with his oft-proclaimed commitment to "freedom", but his refusal to challenge the establishment (not least the judicial establishment) always got the better of his libertarian instincts. His refusal to support the Birmingham Six (several of whom had been his constituents), the Guildford Four or the Tottenham Three before they were released from prison made it impossible for Labour to discomfit the government on the question of miscarriages of justice, which had become a major public concern since 1989. He wooed the Police Federation and downplayed Labour's commitments to greater police accountability. He climbed down on the Prevention of Terrorism Act and the Asylum Bill, and showed no interest in women's rights. Following any civil disorder he was quick to call for harsh punishments and "exemplary sentences". All of this was just what Kinnock wanted but it did not win Hattersley a place in the leader's inner circle. While he refrained from contradicting Kinnock in public, on the NEC or in the shadow cabinet, his unenthusiastic support for the leader was an ill-disguised secret. In the end, this old-fashioned right-wing social democrat, a man who had retained the same political worldview since he was first elected to Parliament in 1964, found Kinnock's Labour Party moving too far to the right even for him. In the run-up to the 1992 general election he shared a private joke with Tony Benn. When Benn mischievously asked whether Kinnock would find a place for him in his cabinet, Hattersley replied, "It would be nice to have someone to the left of me."

Gerald Kaufman, Kinnock's shadow foreign secretary, was never close to Kinnock but knew how to make himself indispensable at critical moments. For Kinnock, those critical moments were the reversal of the non-nuclear defence policy, and the Gulf War. Here Kaufman proved his value not only to Labour's old pro-Washington rearguard but also to its long-standing allies in the Foreign Office and US State Department.

Kaufman, the MP for Manchester Gorton, was first elected to the shadow cabinet in 1980. In 1981 he was a founder member of the right-wing Solidarity Group. From 1980 to 1983, as shadow environment minister, he did all he could to distance the Party from the new left in local government. As Kinnock's shadow home secretary from 1983 to 1987 Kaufman downplayed the Party's policies on racism and civil liberties and cultivated a studied neutrality whenever police were used against striking miners or printworkers. None of this endeared him to Party members in his own constituency, who tried to deselect him. In 1985, four of Gorton's six wards backed local councillor Ken Strath against Kaufman, who went on to win the reselection contest at the CLP general committee by sixty votes to forty – a surprisingly close result for a leading shadow cabinet member who had already held the seat for fifteen years.

Kaufman's base in Manchester was the Gorton Labour Club, a drinking club and bastion of the old-guard right wing. Through the Labour Club, Kaufman recruited members whose only loyalty was to him. He was able to place almost anyone he liked on the local Labour Party's general committee. In 1989, the Gorton constituency general committee had fifty delegates from branches and an extraordinary ninety-one from trade unions and affiliated societies, including batches from a local Fabian Society, the Gorton Co-operative Party, the GMB and the AEU, all of them Kaufman loyalists. There were two delegates from the EETPU white-collar section, EESA; both lived in Gorton but purported to represent the EESA General Office Branch based in EETPU head office in Bromley, Kent. In this "rotten borough" Kaufman himself was a delegate to the Gorton general committee from the Newcastle upon Tyne Staff Branch of the GMB.

In the reselection held that same year, 1989, John Nicholson, former deputy leader of Manchester City Council, was nominated by two Gorton wards, but Kaufman's supporters on the general committee voted to offer local Party members a shortlist of one: Gerald Kaufman. Walworth Road warned local activists that any attempts to canvass for a "no" vote in the affirmative ballot on the shortlist of one would result in disciplinary action. It was no surprise that Kaufman won his affirmative ballot, though the result was hardly a ringing vote of confidence. Only about two hundred of Gorton's thousand members bothered to participate.

In 1990–91 Kinnock allowed rumours to run unchecked through the Commons press lobby to the effect that Kaufman would not be appointed foreign secretary in a future Labour government. In the run-up to that year's shadow cabinet ballot, it was hinted that Kaufman might be replaced by his equally right-wing deputy, George Robertson, who had been a leading member of Labour's Foreign Affairs team since 1983. This story came to nothing when Robertson performed poorly in the shadow cabinet ballot. Indeed, what was most significant about the whole episode was that Labour sources were prepared to go to such lengths to undermine one of Kinnock's most trusted lieutenants, a right-wing mainstay within the shadow cabinet, not apparently for any political reason but simply to show who was boss. It seems that under advice from the Shadow Communications Agency, Kinnock's office had decided that Kaufman was a useful man in a national crisis but not a vote-winning face on the hustings. Sidelined during the 1992 election campaign, Kaufman announced his withdrawal from the NEC and shadow cabinet soon after Labour's defeat.

Another Solidarity stalwart who gained a leading place at Kinnock's side was John Cunningham. First elected to the shadow cabinet in 1983, he was given the environment portfolio by the new leader. This placed

him at the Party's local government helm during the ratecapping struggle. Despite repeated votes in all Party bodies affirming the strategy of
non-compliance with the government's Rates Act, Cunningham never
spoke out publicly for the strategy and did his best to stymie it behind the
scenes.

For many years, Cunningham acted as the parliamentary advocate-in-
chief for the nuclear industry. The Windscale/Sellafield nuclear processing plant is in his constituency and he enjoys close links with the British
Nuclear Fuels Ltd (BNFL) management. On his Commons office wall
hangs a large framed photograph of the plant. Cunningham fought a
successful rearguard action over several years against repeated attempts
at Labour's annual conference to commit the Party to opposition to
nuclear power. His most difficult hour came in 1986 when in the wake of
the Chernobyl disaster the anti-nuclear clamour was at its height. For a
while his shadow environment post seemed threatened but it soon
became apparent that Cunningham had made himself indispensable to
Kinnock, who went to extraordinary lengths to protect him from criticism. Cunningham survived, although he was forced to hand responsibility for environmental protection and Green issues over to another
right-wing member of the shadow cabinet, David Clark.

Cunningham retained his environment post after the 1987 election
defeat and was given command of Labour's campaign against the Poll
Tax. In this capacity he worked hand in glove with Labour's municipal
leaders to distance the Party from the insurgent movement against the
Poll Tax. Cunningham revealed a deeply reactionary cast of mind in his
response to the homophobic Section 28 of the Local Government Act of
1988. Speaking for Labour in a Commons standing committee, he initially
supported Tory MP Jill Knight's proposal to ban the "promotion" of
homosexuality in state schools. He was forced to recant only following
intense pressure at all levels of the labour movement.

Although Cunningham received only seventy-two votes in the shadow cabinet ballot in autumn 1989 (the lowest vote of any successful
candidate) Kinnock promoted him to shadow Leader of the House and
campaign co-ordinator. In this capacity Cunningham took charge of
Labour's election, organization and fundraising machinery. As the authority of Labour's general secretary, Larry Whitty, diminished by the
month, Cunningham increasingly behaved like a domineering trade
union boss, keeping a finger in every pie at Walworth Road.

Over the summer of 1991 there was a curious public hitch in what had
seemed to be Cunningham's cosy relationship with the Labour leader. In
August the *Sunday Times* quoted an unnamed "Labour source" criticizing
Cunningham for going fishing in Norway before the Commons had risen
for the summer, at a time when the shadow cabinet was supposed to be
on "full election alert". It was also put about that the leader's office

considered Cunningham no match for Chris Patten, who as the chair of the Conservative Party was effectively his opposite number. Six weeks later, at the 1991 Labour Party conference in Brighton, Cunningham, having made a passing humorous reference to the *Sunday Times* story, went out of his way to demonstrate his loyalty by describing Kinnock's conference address as "commanding and exhilarating" and "dramatic and moving". "Neil", he said, was the most "courageous, charismatic, inspirational and committed leader of any party in Britain".

Cunningham enjoyed a power base in the labour movement courtesy of the GMB, which made him supremely useful to Kinnock over the years. In contrast, Labour's defence spokesperson Martin O'Neill was of use precisely because he could claim no power base whatsoever, in the unions, the constituencies or within the PLP. Appointed to the front-bench defence team in 1984, O'Neill succeeded the frustrated Denzil Davies as defence spokesperson in June 1988 even though he was not an elected member of the shadow cabinet. Kinnock appointed O'Neill because he was determined that no person of any independent stature or political conviction should hold the sensitive defence portfolio. What was required, if the unilateralist policy was to be abandoned, was a lightweight, a spokesperson owing loyalty only to the leadership. In Martin O'Neill Kinnock found the ideal candidate.

His low standing was annually demonstrated by his abysmal showing in elections to the shadow cabinet. Despite receiving strong public backing from Kinnock and the full support of the arm-twisters in his private office, O'Neill never managed to get himself elected. His failure to win the confidence of his parliamentary colleagues did not stop Kinnock from reappointing O'Neill each year to his senior front-bench post while other competent parliamentary performers and elected members of the shadow cabinet were given lesser appointments.

Having tailored Labour's defence policy to the requirements of the establishment, Kinnock concentrated after 1989 on doing the same thing for its economic policy. The front-bench economic affairs team of John Smith, Gordon Brown, Tony Blair and Margaret Beckett first assembled in 1989 was for Kinnock the instrument through which he could demonstrate his commitment to the free market and gain respectability in the eyes of the City of London and the Confederation of British Industry. Its overriding commitment was to give no hostages to fortune in the form of specific spending pledges. In pursuit of this, the economic affairs team became the effective arbiter of Labour's policies on social security, pensions, childcare, education, health, transport, the environment and all other areas of public expenditure. The shadow cabinet members with responsibility for these areas could do nothing without the approval of the economics team, which from 1989 was stacked with Kinnock favourites. Although John Smith as shadow Chancellor was considered a dangerous rival, Gordon Brown, Tony Blair and Margaret Beckett, aided by junior spokespersons Chris Smith, Paul Boateng, John Marek and Nick Brown, were all in different ways loyalists depending for their standing on the leader's patronage.

John Smith was never close to Kinnock, who was always threatened by his political weight and experience. A former Secretary of State for Trade during 1978–79, Smith, with Roy Hattersley, was one of only two members of Kinnock's team with substantial government experience. Within Kinnock's office he was mistrusted as an independent figure with a sizable base of support within the PLP, which had elected him to the shadow cabinet in every year since 1979. Unlike so many others on the front bench, Smith had to be negotiated with rather than simply bought by the promise of preferment. Smith studiously avoided involvement in the inner-Party controversies of the early 1980s. Although firmly on Labour's right and a member of the Solidarity Group from start to finish, he rarely if ever made any direct attacks on the left. Unlike the "soft left", he did not have to. Nobody doubted where Smith, an old-style right-winger sponsored by the GMB, stood on the witch-hunt, unilateralism, the Gulf War or reselection. This put him beyond the reach of Kinnock, who had to rely heavily on him for any credibility in the economic sphere.

Smith was the model of a conservative shadow Chancellor between 1987 and 1992. He cultivated contacts in the City, criticized the Tories for imprudent fiscal management and, with the help of Gordon Brown and Margaret Beckett, curtailed the Party's spending promises. Contrary to the image presented by some newspapers, which used him as a stick with which to beat Kinnock, Smith was never a probing analyst or sophisticated economist. He was a pragmatist with the capacity to master the briefs prepared for him and to present them succinctly. This was precisely what Kinnock wanted him to do but it earned him an eminence that Kinnock resented.

Smith's adjutants, Gordon Brown and Tony Blair, were touted by the media as the rising stars of the new Labour establishment. They were sold as articulate, attractive, pragmatic politicians who enjoyed public confidence and were therefore the right people to lead Labour to victory at the ballot box.

When Brown had won the Dunfermline East seat in 1983 at the age of thirty-two he had already been, in effect, a full-time Scottish politician for a decade. A former student union activist turned television journalist, he had contested Edinburgh South in 1979 and was chair of the Scottish Labour Party in 1983–84. Within two years of entering the House of Commons he had made his way onto the front bench, attracting attention as a spokesperson on trade and industry before winning election to the shadow cabinet on the Tribune Group slate in 1987. As shadow chief secretary to the Treasury he stood in for John Smith while the latter was recovering from his heart attack in 1988, and seized the opportunity to make his name on the House of Commons stage. By this time he had abandoned the vaguely "soft left" credentials he had boasted prior to 1987 in favour of orthodox free market ideology spiced with invocations of the need for "partnership" between private industry and government.

Tony Blair was an establishment figure to his fingertips. Privately educated before moving on to Oxford and qualification as a barrister, he specialized in trade union law and worked in the chambers run by QC Alexander Irvine, who helped Walworth Road out of the legal mess created by the Militant expulsions in 1983 and 1986.

Blair was appointed to the front bench as a junior spokesperson on Treasury affairs within a year of being elected in the safe Labour seat of Sedgefield in 1983. After the 1987 election he was moved to trade and industry spokesperson and with support from Kinnock's office won a place on the shadow cabinet in 1988. After a year as energy spokesperson, during which his opposition to electricity privatization was couched in the most circumspect terms, he was considered the ideal person to replace Meacher as employment spokesperson. Back in 1982, when Blair had stood as the Labour candidate in a by-election in the safe Tory seat of Beaconsfield, he told *Labour Weekly* that he was entirely in sympathy with the need of trade unions to take illegal industrial action to defend their interests.[7] Eight years later, as Kinnock's employment spokesperson, he became the chief architect of the Party's commitment to retain nearly all the Tory laws against which the unions had chafed for more than a decade. Yet another Tribune Group member adept at swimming with the tide, Blair was a media creation who possessed no standing with the rank and file of the labour movement. Without the kind of aggressive eloquence that Brown could command, his meteoric rise within the PLP was attributable only to his televisual appeal and his willingness to say and do whatever the leadership wanted.

In contrast, Margaret Beckett's path to the top was more tortuous. As Labour MP for Lincoln between 1974 and 1979, she had already swung once from left to right when she had accepted a junior ministerial post in Callaghan's government. For a year in 1980–81 she sat on the NEC, where she voted solidly with the left. As a strong supporter of Benn in the deputy leadership campaign she made a much-publicized speech at the *Tribune* rally at Labour's 1981 conference denouncing Kinnock for having handed victory to Denis Healey. In 1983 she was returned to Parliament for Derby South and promptly joined both the Tribune and the Campaign groups. She cast her vote in that year's leadership election for Neil Kinnock and was subsequently appointed a spokesperson on social security, one of the very few members of the Campaign Group on Kinnock's first front bench.

With the support of the left, Beckett was re-elected to the NEC for one year in 1985–86 and again for a few months in 1987 when Betty Boothroyd resigned after becoming deputy speaker. Although she had been an inactive member of the Campaign Group she had paid her subscriptions and happily accepted the group's support for her repeated candidatures for the NEC and shadow cabinet. In 1988 she refused to back Benn and Heffer in their challenge for the leadership and made her ensuing break with the left as public as possible. Her reward was election to the NEC at the 1988 conference and to the shadow cabinet in 1989. Eager to use Beckett's assiduousness and her reputation as a former left-winger, Kinnock surprised nearly everyone by appointing her shadow chief secretary to the Treasury, effectively John Smith's deputy. As a leading member of Kinnock's right-wing economic affairs team, Beckett quickly became a model of fiscal rectitude. Her conversion to an almost Thatcher-ite *laissez-faire* policy may have been sudden, but it was followed through with astonishing rigour. Shortly before the 1992 election, *Tribune* columnist Hugh Macpherson wrote: "When Margaret Beckett was asked if Labour's plans contained an element of redistribution, she dissembled like a Victorian lady being asked if she harboured impure thoughts."[8]

Beckett's unshakable economic conservatism was complemented by her increasingly unquestioning support for the leadership line on the NEC. She was a godsend to the Walworth Road image-makers, who were desperately in need of a woman who was both politically reliable and capable of winning a place in the shadow cabinet. With strong support from Kinnock's office, she finished in the top three in both the 1990 and the 1991 shadow cabinet ballots.

As policy was increasingly formed by handpicked coteries, the shadow cabinet became more and more of an empty shell. One leading member privately revealed that he had only dealt with Kinnock on a one-to-one basis on three occasions over a two-year period. The weekly shadow cabinet meetings, which were supposed to formulate political strategy for the PLP, became less and less significant. Even behind their closed doors, open debate – the clear prerequisite for collective responsibility – was discouraged. Major policy decisions were prearranged beforehand in the leader's private office and then presented to the shadow cabinet for ratification. The only items the members were allowed to discuss freely were short-term considerations relating to Commons business for the following week. Even there, Kinnock insisted on personally intervening on nearly every agenda item, often betraying only that he did not fully understand the matter under discussion. His real interest was always parliamentary gossip: What is so-and-so saying about such-and-such? Can he or she be relied on? Is he or she "with us or against us"?

With the help of Charles Clarke and Peter Mandelson, Kinnock deliberately fostered rivalries between shadow cabinet members whose work he was supposed to be co-ordinating. As one member described it, the shadow cabinet is "not a team of colleagues but a disparate collection of competing individuals". Gordon Brown and Tony Blair, who enjoyed their own direct links to Kinnock's office, did not treat shadow cabinet meetings seriously and Brown in particular became an irregular attender who rarely bothered to stay to the end of a meeting.

Kinnock knew that it was fear of his power and not admiration for his abilities that motivated most members of his shadow cabinet. In order to protect his leadership he therefore had to prevent them coalescing into a coherent collective body. He adopted a similar approach to the PLP as a whole. The weekly PLP meetings in the 1987–92 Parliament were usually poorly attended, largely because it was seen as a powerless body which could not even co-ordinate the efforts and talents of its own members. Newly elected Labour MPs with local government experience were amazed to find that the PLP was less well organized and less democratic than the average Labour group on a local authority. Sometimes meetings would attract only thirty MPs, barely one tenth of the Parliamentary Labour Party; rarely did they draw more than seventy.

Front-bench loyalists would turn up to ensure the leadership came to no harm. Backbench dissenters were treated as cranks and mavericks with no contribution to make to the PLP as a whole. As a result, front-bench Labour MPs were reduced to the status of a leadership fan club and backbenchers were left to pursue their own individual concerns. In 1990 one in ten Labour MPs did not bother to cast his or her ballot in the shadow cabinet elections.

Despite their lack of formal power, PLP meetings were still taken very seriously by Kinnock. He attended nearly all of them and intervened continually on every issue, often subjecting MPs to lengthy, irritable lectures whenever it seemed that they had failed to grasp the absolute necessity of backing him at all times. With the help of the chair, Stan Orme, he was able to deflect occasional outbursts of backbench discontent, not least by the simple expedient of avoiding or even miscounting critical votes.

In March 1988 the PLP discussed the failure of many Labour MPs to attend debates in the Commons chamber. Kinnock subjected his fellow Labour MPs to ten minutes of angry abuse on this subject to which hardly anyone seemed to be listening. At the end of his diatribe there was no applause. A fortnight later, following Lawson's tax-cutting budget, which had provoked cries of "shame" from Labour MPs, Kinnock again attacked the assembled PLP members, this time for their lack of self-discipline in the chamber.

None of this would have been possible, however, if backbench Labour MPs and shadow cabinet members had been willing to stand up to the leader when they thought he was wrong. The culture of subservience and time-serving was the creation not solely of Neil Kinnock, but also of those MPs who colluded with it in order to gain or maintain parliamentary status.

What would a Kinnock cabinet have been like in government? Would it have ended up as a rerun of the worst of the Thatcher years? Although this fear remained unspoken in the years leading up to the 1992 election, it was in the minds of many Labour MPs. Although they all naturally wanted Labour to win, many could not help but wonder what Labour would become in government, with all that additional patronage to dispense, under a leadership so obsessed with the exercise of its own authority.

Notes

1. Benn diaries, 21 January 1987.
2. *Sunday Times* 21 February 1988.
3. *Tribune* 21 October 1988.
4. Colin Hughes and Patrick Wintour, *Labour Rebuilt*, London 1990.
5. ibid.
6. *Tribine* 15 February 1991.
7. *Labour Weekly* 16 August 1982.
8. *Tribune* 10 January 1992.

Paying the Piper:
Labour and the Unions

I know Neil is to the right of Margaret Thatcher on the unions.
Peter Mandelson to a shadow cabinet member, 1989

For Neil Kinnock, trade union links with the Labour Party were both an embarrassment and a necessity. He needed the block vote to push his policies through Party conference. He needed the approbation of the major union leaders if he was to be seen to carry the labour movement with him. And he needed union cash to finance his election campaigns. But the approval he sought from the British establishment required not only that he keep a safe distance between himself and the unions but that at critical moments he act as a public opponent of trade unionism. Following the advice of his private staff and the Shadow Communications Agency, he adopted a "tough posture" towards the TUC. He ensured that Labour adopted a harshly restrictive policy on trade union rights. Above all, he turned his back on workers engaged in industrial disputes.

After a long period of high-profile involvement in the Labour Party's affairs, the unions were told – so the story goes – to mind their own business and leave politics to the politicians. In striking this attitude, Neil Kinnock had the full backing of the establishment, which has always regarded Labour's links to the trade union movement as rendering it unfit and untrustworthy to govern. Increasingly, however, he was also backed by trade union leaders themselves. At the 1989 Labour conference, John Edmonds, general secretary of the powerful GMB, declaimed from the Brighton rostrum: "This conference must sound the death knell of the block vote. Let us say it clearly. The block vote must go. The trade unions should retain influence but must surrender control."

All the changes in the Party celebrated by the press (including the apparent reduction in union power) could only have come about with the willing co-operation of the unions themselves, or at least their top bureaucrats. The real story of Labour and the unions under Neil Kinnock was of a small number of union leaders wielding ever-increasing powers – through largely unscrutinized byways – at the expense of the Party conference, the NEC, individual Party members and, most crucially of all, their own union members.

Of course, there is nothing at all modern or radical about consigning the trade unions to the backrooms of Labour politics. The old division of responsibility – politics left to the Parliamentary Labour Party, industrial matters left to the trade union bureaucracies – always suited the PLP, union bosses and, above all, employers and the Tories. Following divisions in the 1970s between the trade union bureaucracy and the Labour leadership over Europe, pay policy and the Social Contract, this cosy arrangement came unstuck. Much of what happened in the 1980s was about re-establishing it in a new form.

The bedrock of trade union power in the Labour Party is, of course, money. Throughout its history, the Party has relied on the unions for finance. But the manner in which that finance is channelled to the Party has changed radically. For many decades, the bulk of it came in the form of affiliation fees, which are paid to the Party by each union according to the number of members it claims are paying its political levy. This number in turn determines the size of each union's block vote at Conference.

In the 1920s over one hundred trade unions were affiliated to the Labour Party and the block vote at its conference was dispersed accordingly. By 1980, the gradual swallowing up of old craft unions by larger general unions had reduced that number to fifty-four. A decade later there were fewer than forty, and a majority of the block votes were concentrated in the hands of four giant unions: the TGWU, the AEU, the GMB and NUPE, with further concentrations of votes in the hands of USDAW, MSF, UCW, UCATT, EETPU, and the NCU.

Total union affiliation rose in the 1970s, reaching an all-time high in 1979. It then declined sharply in the 1980s as unions lost members and ran into financial difficulties. In 1980 fees were paid for 6.5 million affiliated members; by 1990 the latter's numbers had been cut back by over 1.5 million, with severe consequences for Party finance.

In order to compensate for the decline, successive party treasurers and general secretaries asked for substantial increases in the union affiliation fee, but again and again the unions refused. Indeed, trade union affiliation fees between 1975 and 1988 increased much more slowly than individual membership fees, and well below the rate of inflation. This does not mean that the affiliated unions withheld money from the Party; on the contrary, the largest unions have steadily increased the total amounts they contribute. They have preferred, however, to make these contributions outside the constitutional channel of the affiliation fee, and thereby outside the scrutiny and control of the NEC or the Party conference.

The first steps in this direction were taken in 1979 with the formation of Trade Unionists for a Labour Victory (TULV). This was an independent body, formally separate from the Party machinery, whose stated aim was to mobilize financial and organizational support for Labour in the coming general election. From the outset, the GMWU, and in particular its then general secretary, David Basnett, was the dominant force in TULV. Following the 1979 election defeat, Basnett steered TULV on an ever more openly political course and it became in effect the arbiter between left and right in the Party's civil war.

All affiliated unions except the left-dominated NUM, the Fire Brigades' Union (FBU) and the footwear-workers' union NUFLAT were members of TULV, though the right-wing AEU-EETPU block kept its distance and eventually resigned. TULV's directors were Moss Evans of the TGWU, Clive Jenkins of ASTMS and Bill Keys of SOGAT. Its principal officer was Basnett's head of research at the GMWU, Larry Whitty (later Labour's general secretary), who kept close watch over all TULV expenditure.

On the ground, TULV was never more than a convenient shell; TULV regional organizers in six of the twelve Party regions were none other than the regional Party chiefs. In Bristol, TULV was used by local union right-wingers as a vehicle for organizing against Tony Benn in the selection of a candidate for the newly redrawn parliamentary seat of Bristol South. With John Golding, they played a crucial role in ensuring that Labour's chief whip, Michael Cocks, won the nomination for the safe seat, leaving Benn to face defeat in Bristol East.

Preoccupied with playing power politics in TULV, the trade union leaders made only a minimal contribution to Labour's 1983 general election campaign. Donations were substantial, though belated, but any other form of assistance was negligible. The workplace Labour Party branches set up with such enthusiasm in 1981 were starved of resources and given no role in the campaign.

During the 1980s, the Party's relations with the trade unions came under threat from Tory legislation. Under the 1984 Trade Union Act all unions had to hold secret individual membership ballots to determine whether they would maintain their political funds; if these ballots were lost, the unions would have to disaffiliate from the Labour Party. This was immediately recognized as a major threat to the Party and to trade union political power, not to mention the status of union leaders as political powerbrokers.

For once, action was swift and concerted. A Trade Union Co-ordinating Committee was set up to guide and service the political fund ballot campaigns in the unions; it was financed by TULV but otherwise independent of it. Graham Allen, the future MP for Nottingham North, was put in charge. The committee was based at TUC headquarters at Transport House and given £150,000 to run an eighteen-month campaign, preparing briefings for union activists, press events and advertisements, and giving legal advice over the wording and conduct of the ballots. In the end all the ballots were won comfortably. The mortal threat to the Labour Party's survival did not materialize.

This success indicated the potential for political action in the unions – when the leadership uses its resources and authority to put the arguments directly to members. But most of the unions involved steered away from mentioning the Labour Party in their ballot campaigns, in accordance with the strategy advocated by the Trade Union Co-ordinating Committee and developed in discussions at the TUC–Labour Party Liaison Committee. At a meeting of the latter held in August 1984, a representative from the left-wing union TASS took it upon himself to remind fellow bureaucrats that TULV was "absolutely banned from policy-making". In response UCW chief Alan Tuffin stated that he was not interested in a coy debate over the "non-political" role of TULV. Without hesitation he laid down the law: "the Party conference is crucial. It must be conducted in a civilized and disciplined way and the party image must be improved." Roy Grantham of APEX also rounded on the TASS representative, insisting that "TULV was set up to save the Labour Party". John Golding agreed. He told the liaison committee that most of his NCU members were "conservative" and "anti-Labour", an extraordinary admission for a man who had been his union's chief political officer for well over a decade and whose influence in the Labour Party was based on the affiliation fees paid by his members to it.[1]

Following the success of the ballots, union leaders decided they needed a new fundraising body with a broader base than TULV. Trades Unionists for Labour (TUFL) was established, with Bill Keys, now retired as SOGAT general secretary, its moving figure. Like TULV, it disclaimed any policy ambitions; but also like TULV, its very existence testified to the inadequacies of the traditional institutional links between the unions and the Labour Party, at least for the purposes of the trade union and Party hierarchies. TUFL was formally established and recognized by the NEC in 1986.

TUFL channelled a total of £4.1 million into Labour's 1987 general election campaign, including a flurry of emergency donations secured from the biggest unions in the last week of the campaign. Additional election-time donations and proceeds from fundraising outside TUFL amounted to a mere £140,000.[2] During the campaign, TUFL organized the seconding of a large number of full-time union officials to local parties in selected marginal constituencies. Their main charge was to maximize the trade union vote, but they often found themselves working to compensate for basic weaknesses in local party organization. Thus union full-time officials were substituting via TUFL for the Party's dormant mass base, just as TUFL centrally was substituting financially for the lack of any serious fundraising base outside the unions, such as a genuine mass membership.

In the election postmortem, the Labour leadership identified the Party's link with the unions as a vote-loser, even though a BBC exit poll showed that even among non-Labour voters only 27 per cent perceived this link as negative – well behind negative perceptions of the Party's economic competence, its tax policy or the trustworthiness of its leadership. None the less, it was decided that, in future, union influence would be wielded discreetly, not in full public view, where, after all, it might not only antagonize anti-union voters but union members themselves could observe and even try to influence it. No one had forgotten what had happened in 1979–81 when the block vote careered out of the parliamentary leadership's control.

After the 1987 general election, TUFL decided to place its fundraising on a more systematic base. At its annual meeting in October it agreed to establish a general election levy fund to which all affiliated unions would be expected to contribute. This ended TUFL's reliance on big one-off donations and enabled it to fend off some of the criticisms of elitism that had been levelled against TULV. Thus the unions finally met Labour's long-standing demands for an increase in the affiliation fee, but without ceding any control over expenditure of the additional amount to the Party's NEC or conference. To the union bureaucrats, Labour was a machine for winning general elections and nothing else; if it stagnated between elections, that was no concern of theirs.

Little effort was ever made to fulfil the non-financial parts of TUFL's remit: to encourage ordinary union members to become involved in Labour Party initiatives. At the outset of the Policy Review TUFL organized "Labour Listens to Unions" events in some areas and occasionally disseminated information about Party policy to union full-time officials. But these activities were sporadic at best and touched only a minute fraction of the affiliated membership. Neither individual union nor Party members can join TUFL. All its appointments and activities are determined from the top down. Where TULV had been run by Labour Party people, TUFL was purely a trade union affair. All its regional co-ordinators were officials of the GMB, TGWU or NUPE.

By 1990, TUFL was giving union money to all kinds of Labour initiatives. Very little of this was channelled through or even reported to the Party's NEC. TUFL cash went to fund the leader's office, front-bench researchers, by-election campaigns and new technology for the Walworth Road headquarters. The two TUFL full-time officials based in Transport House found their functions pared to the bone. Links between TUFL and the Labour Party operated solely at the highest level: through

Labour Party general secretary Larry Whitty, treasurer and NUS/RMT boss Sam McCluskie and the chair of the NEC's Finance and General Purposes Committee, John Evans.

TUFL itself was gradually marginalized as individual unions made grants to front-benchers and to specialist groups like Computing for Labour (an autonomous agency using the voluntary services of Labour-supporting computer experts but reliant on money from unions for purchase of hardware and development of software). Some prospective parliamentary candidates of suitable political colouring also received trade union disbursements. A Labour Party Business Plan was established in 1988 as a separate fund, intended to supply independent finance for major improvements in Labour's membership and fund-raising base. It was and is entirely underwritten by five major unions – the TGWU, the GMB, NGA, NUR/RMT, and UCW – and was financed, initially, by a £500,000 loan from the trade-union-backed Unity Trust Bank. Managed by representatives of the five unions, including NEC members Gordon Colling of the NGA and Tony Clarke of the UCW, it paid for much of the Party's press advertising in 1991–92 and financed the national membership system and the "high value donors" scheme, which resulted in the infamous £500-a-plate dinners.

In the thirty-page 1990 Labour Party NEC report a grand total of 150 words was dedicated to the topic "Trade Union Liaison/Trade Unionists for Labour". Noting that the post of trade union liaison officer at Walworth Road had remained unfilled for yet another year, the report admitted that "the level of communication between the Party and trade unions needs to be improved" but did not propose a single means of doing so.[3]

The following year the NEC again had to report that "the post of trade union liaison officer has yet to be filled, although the temporary appointment of Derek Gladwin has assisted with communications between the Party and the trade unions in the run-up to the general election".[4] Gladwin had just retired as a GMB official and was no longer chair of Labour's conference arrangements committee. His appointment (not only temporary but also unpaid) confirmed that "communications between the Party and the trade unions" were to be restricted to the top of the movement.

At the bottom, such communications have become more and more tenuous. TUFL organization seems to have evaporated in most of the country but here and there it survives as a power base for local political figures. For example, in Birmingham, TUFL is run entirely by its secretary, Keith Hanson, a former "soft left" who became both treasurer and trade union liaison officer of the Birmingham District Labour Party. In the run-up to the general election, he was made a temporary assistant regional organizer for the Party in the West Midlands and was given responsibility for the Birmingham marginals.

Hanson used his TUFL position to control trade union affiliations to local constituency parties. The use of TUFL offices for this purpose is well outside the organization's remit and contrary to Labour Party rules. The Party's director of organization, Joyce Gould, was forced to write to Hanson to complain about the practice but nevertheless a big effort was made to ensure maximum right-wing union influence in the selection of parliamentary candidates in Birmingham throughout 1990. Over £3,300 in affiliation fees was handled through Birmingham TUFL that year. £1,400 of this money came from a right-wing phalanx of twenty EETPU branches, ten GMWU/GMB branches, twelve APEX/GMB branches and five AEU branches. Compared to this, the £510 stumped up by the city's thirty TGWU branches was a political irrelevance.

One of the main targets for this influx was the Birmingham Small Heath CLP where the sitting Labour MP, Denis Howell, was retiring. The aim was to secure the Labour nomination for Roger Godsiff, the former APEX political fixer now ensconced in the GMB, with which APEX had merged. Howell himself was a former APEX president who apparently believed the parliamentary seat was in his union's gift.

Godsiff had been a union official since 1970, when he was twenty-four. He had been a councillor in Lewisham in south-east London for eighteen years; towards the end, he boasted the worst attendance record in the local Labour Group. He sent his children to private schools. His long record of service to the Labour right made him a natural for EETPU support. But in this case the EETPU had an additional incentive. In return for supporting Godsiff in Small Heath, it hoped to secure GMB support for EETPU political officer John Spellar (who had fought and lost Birmingham Northfield in 1983 and 1987), now hoping to be selected as candidate for the safe Labour seat of nearby Warley West.

What neither the GMB nor the EETPU counted on was the resentment that would be provoked by this attempt to steal a safe Labour seat for a trade union official who did not even live in the region, much less the constituency. There was a large black population in Small Heath and for some years black activists had been pressing for a greater say in the local Labour Party.

Godsiff knew in advance of Howell's plans to stand down at the next election. Accordingly, he began contacting sympathetic trade union branches. Three GMB branches affiliated to the CLP only two months before Howell's impending retirement was made public. Each one initially claimed five delegates to the general committee, which would have implied that they had at least 400 branch members living in the constituency. After complaints, the GMB national office ordered the branches to cut their representation to one delegate each.

But the real furore was caused by the EETPU delegates. It transpired that many of them had never been electricians and some were not even members of the union. Local activists took to sporting lapel stickers reading, "I am not, nor ever have been, an electrician." From mid 1990 a string of complaints about Godsiff's operation in Small Heath was submitted to Walworth Road. The NEC decided to proceed with the selection but delay the actual count until the allegations about the EETPU had been investigated. The selection meeting was held in November 1990; Joyce Gould then held a perfunctory investigation. She had already informed one CLP officer who had queried the GMB delegations that she had "no authority" to demand information from the union about the number of members claimed by the affiliated branches. On her advice, the NEC decided to proceed with the count (the ballots had been locked away for safe keeping, first with the police and then with a solicitor) and see if the disputed EETPU delegates actually made any difference to the result. The count was held in February 1991 and Godsiff narrowly lost the vote among individual members to his main rival, local councillor Mohammed Afzal, by 102 votes to 100. Godsiff walked away with the trade union vote, winning 17, plus the 4 disputed EETPU ballots, to Afzal's 4. This made him the winner, with or without the EETPU, and following a recommendation from Joyce Gould the NEC declared itself satisfied.

Then came a BBC *Newsnight* exposé and a flurry of stories in the press raising serious questions about the methods Godsiff had used to get the nomination. In a leaked letter from Godsiff to a GMB regional organizer, the would-be candidate had written the following:

> With regard to the delegates you are putting in Small Heath from the GMB, I trust the cheque I sent you was quite okay and the new GMB members have now been sent their membership cards, and I will ensure that they have them with them when they attend the January general management committee.[5]

It appeared that Godsiff had personally paid the GMB membership fees for a number of local supporters and then arranged for them to become delegates to the Party; some were not even aware that Godsiff was using them in this way and later complained that they had been led to believe that all they were doing was joining the Labour Party.[6] Godsiff had also written to Andy Dodds of the NUR pointing out that two NUR delegates to Small Heath voted with the "small left minority" and suggesting they might be removed in the future.

Following the media revelations, the NEC was forced to intervene again. Joyce Gould was asked to reinvestigate and a right-wing NEC panel was sent to interview Godsiff. It was reported to the NEC that Godsiff admitted he had behaved "unwisely" but the panel recommended that he should be endorsed anyway. Once more the NEC declared itself satisfied (with only Benn, Skinner and Clare Short dissenting) and Godsiff stood as the official Labour candidate in April 1992 in the Small Heath constituency where there was a swing against Labour of 2.5 per cent.

When a similar influx of EETPU delegates into the Birmingham Ladywood constituency seemed to threaten Clare Short, the NEC took a different line. It unilaterally removed a number of the spurious electricians, making the seat safe for Short and confirming the widely held view that some examples of trade union interference are more acceptable to the Labour leadership than others.

Whilst trade union membership and affiliation to the Labour Party has declined, the number of MPs sponsored by trade unions has grown. In the 1987–92 Parliament 56 per cent of Labour MPs were trade-union-sponsored – the highest proportion for decades. Of the 164 sponsored candidates in 1987, 129 were elected. Clearly, unions like to back winners. In a break from the past, two thirds of the 129 had no experience of manual work and an increasing number had mainly worked as full-timers for unions, including many who were sponsored by their former employers. This trend was even more pronounced in 1992, when an immoderate number of the 69 Labour MPs elected for the first time had worked as full-time trade union or Labour Party officials. In seventeen safe Labour seats the retiring MP had been replaced by a full-time union official or a Labour Party employee. These included the NUPE officials George Mudie in Leeds East and Jane Kennedy in Liverpool Broadgreen, Brian Donohoe of NALGO in Cunninghame South, as well as Godsiff and Spellar. In twenty-five key marginals Labour's candidate was a union official or a Labour Party employee; these include Andrew MacKinley of NALGO in Thurrock, Angela Eagle of COHSE in Wallasey, Keith Hill of the RMT in Streatham and Richard Burden of NALGO in Birmingham Northfield. It would seem that the trade union–Labour Party link is still very much alive, even if it is expressed more often in personal patronage than in policy formation.

The elevation of full-time union officials to Parliament has been accompanied by a steady decline in real trade union involvement at the base of the Labour Party. Workplace branches, in which so much hope was invested in the early 1980s, have withered. According to an NEC report, in 1985 there were 98 branches, including a 200-strong branch at Timex in Dundee. The one national "consultation" meeting ever held for workplace branches in Birmingham, in December 1985, was concerned entirely with rule revisions. Walworth Road would not make a list of workplace branches available to the branches themselves and it was therefore impossible to build any kind of national network. Neither the regions nor head office nor the unions supplied the branches with information or assistance of any kind. After the 1987 general election the

NEC reported receiving "no response from any workplace branch" during the campaign. A region-by-region survey later showed that only a handful of workplace branches were still functioning. By 1992, the Party had forgotten that workplace branches ever existed.

Although input from rank-and-file trade unionists to the Policy Review was negligible and the once-mighty TUC–Labour Party Liaison Committee was no longer even meeting by the end of the 1980s, Neil Kinnock was careful to ensure that the top union bosses were given places on all the review groups. This meant that by the time they were presented to the NEC the final Policy Review reports had all already been approved by these union leaders, without recourse to their own union conferences or any consultation with their members.

Of the twenty-nine members of the NEC elected each year at annual conference, eighteen are in effect elected by the trade unions (twelve trade union representatives, five Women's Section representatives and the treasurer). Kinnock relied heavily on union votes to give him the solid majority on the NEC he wielded so ruthlessly in the last years of his leadership. He knew he could rely on them to back him even when his proposals cut across the mass of union members' interests.

The twelve trade union representatives on the NEC are usually the number twos or threes in their own union hierarchies (Richard Rosser, general secretary of the TSSA, is a rare exception). Often they are obscure figures, long-serving full-time bureaucrats, whose actions within the Labour Party are virtually unknown to their own union members. They win their NEC places on the basis of a complex and ever-shifting pattern of inter-union alliances, not strictly based on politics. Indeed, the horse-trading among the unions to get their own people on the NEC has become legendary. For example, nearly all the unions, bar the EETPU and the AEU, back whomever the TGWU nominates because the TGWU, as the biggest union, can deliver vital block votes to candidates from smaller unions.

The twelve elected to the NEC in 1990 had an average twenty-five years' background as trade union officials, and thirty-one years' average Party membership. Their loyalty is to an organization – not a cause, not an ideology. They are creatures of the institutions of the labour movement and their primary drive is to maintain those institutions and the powers and privileges of the bureaucrats who run them. Most of them have a long-standing interest in Party affairs (many have been Labour councillors or stood as Labour candidates in general elections). Having secured the "Labour Party franchise" from their unions they pursue their own political interests within the Party with little regard to their unions' policies.

Since they are elected by a vote of all the trade union delegations at Labour's conference, rather than by their individual unions, it is hard to say just whom they represent or to whom they should be accountable. For several years Gordon Colling of the NGA print union (now GPMU) has acted as an informal whip for the trade union representatives on the NEC. He has worked at the NGA head office since 1961, was a former leader of the North Bedfordshire District Council and was Labour's candidate in Bedford in both general elections of 1974. Although Colling almost always backed Kinnock on the NEC, his first loyalty was to the corporate interests of the trade unions. Periodically he laid down the law to the parliamentary leadership, for example criticizing Tony Blair's instant policy-making on the closed shop (see page 162) and blocking the appointment of Colin Byrne as Mandelson's successor in 1990. A traditional right-winger, he backed Kinnock's expulsions, pushed for a leaner staff at Walworth Road and ever-tighter control from the top. He rarely spoke on policy issues.

In January 1988, with the nurses' one-day strike actions against cuts and for wage rises escalating and the National Health Service at the top of the political agenda for the first time in nearly six years, Colm O'Kane of COHSE and Tom Sawyer of NUPE brought a resolution on the dispute to the NEC. The resolution recognized that in their actions the nurses were "motivated by a concern for justice for patients", a statement tailored to the perspectives of the government and the press, who tried to pit patients against nurses. Tony Benn moved an amendment that "the NEC pledges full support for any strike action that may be decided upon by the nurses ... and calls upon the whole Labour and trade union movement and everyone who wishes to see the NHS survive to give all possible financial, industrial and moral backing to the nurses".[7]

Benn's amendment was greeted with fury by the trade union representatives. Sawyer in particular was embarrassed, knowing that his union, if left to its own devices, would back such a statement and demand that he do so as well. He raged at Benn, demanding that he withdraw the amendment. "We must not have a Labour split," he insisted. Andy Dodds of the NUR said the nurses had "no hope of other trade union support" while Tony Clarke of the UCW railed against "left splitters".[8] When put to the vote the amendment was defeated by twenty votes to four with only Benn, Dennis Skinner, Ken Livingstone and the Young Socialist representative in support.[9] When the nurses went on in July to win an increased pay award, the trade union representatives on the NEC voted to "congratulate the PLP for the way it has responded to this issue", but failed to congratulate or even mention the nurses themselves.

At the NEC in July 1989, Tony Benn moved a resolution supporting the industrial action recently taken by railworkers, dockers, local government workers and engineers. Again, the trade union representatives rounded on Benn. It was a moment that revealed a great deal about the priorities of Labour's governing elite and the paradox of the trade union link. McCluskie and Sawyer demanded that the resolution be withdrawn; it was, they told Benn, "none of your business". Ken Cure of the AEU condemned Benn's "interference" in trade union affairs. If this resolution had been put to a vote in almost any trade union meeting in the country, it would have passed with little dissent. But to the trade union representatives on the NEC, it was anathema.

Andy Dodds and Tom Sawyer came up with an alternative to Benn's motion, which recognized the "essential autonomy of the unions".[10] It was a candid restatement of the time-honoured division of responsibility between the two wings of the labour movement. The trade unions were saying to the politicians, "We'll leave the politics to you, you leave the industrial side to us." The result, as always, was a weakening of both the Labour Party and the unions.

It is perhaps not surprising that union people on the NEC have generally been hostile to recorded votes. In October 1989, Colling and Dodds moved the deletion from the standing orders of the chair's right to call a recorded vote. From now on a recorded vote would be allowed only with the agreement of a majority of NEC members, a majority which the union delegates, along with the women's delegates (effectively elected by the unions), can easily muster.

A 1990 survey of Labour Party members conducted for the Party by Patrick Seyd of Sheffield University revealed that two unaffiliated unions, NALGO and the NUT, account for the largest numbers of individual Party members, with 13 per cent and 10 per cent respectively. Another 10 per cent of members belong to the TGWU, 7 per cent to MSF and only 4 per cent to the GMB. In other words, only 2 per cent of the GMB's 650,000 levy-paying members are also Labour Party members in their own right. Yet the GMB was the key union player in Kinnock's Labour Party. Its rise and rise was one of the central stories of Labour in the 1980s.

In the 1970s general secretary David Basnett had moved what was then the GMWU from the right to the political centre of the labour movement without, however, loosening the grip of the bureaucracy. It became a mainstay of Labour's centre–left bloc in the early 1980s, and then of the centre–right bloc that has been dominant since. The union could only succeed in shifting the Party to the right because (in contrast to the AEU or the EETPU) it had shifted to the left earlier on. Basnett's role in TULV and the appointment of Larry Whitty, formerly the union's head of research, as Labour's general secretary in 1985 were key staging posts. Derek Gladwin, the union's Southern Region secretary, had already been the chair of the powerful conference arrangements committee for many years and only retired from this post in 1990.

After the debacle of the 1983 general election the GMB moved quickly to stake out a claim for leadership of the TUC and the Labour Party. Its 1984 resolution to the Labour conference set the agenda for Kinnock's reorganization, calling for efficiency at Walworth Road, improvements in publicity, more resources for the leader and deputy leader, the creation of a special by-election team and better regional organization. This set the agenda for much of the Party's internal reorganization in the years to come.

At the GMB conference following the 1987 general election, John Edmonds, who replaced Basnett in 1986, explained that "the GMB is the backbone of TUFL in the regions, and plays a major role in TUFL at national level". Noting that nine of twenty regional TUFL officers were GMB officials, Edmonds boasted that "during that campaign the GMB was the backbone of the Labour Party".[11]

Edmonds has spent his entire working life inside the bureaucracy of the GMWU and its successors. He inherited Basnett's seat on the TUC General Council, where his influence has grown steadily. He is a director of the Unity Trust Bank; a trustee of the Institute of Public Policy Research, a left-of-centre think-tank; and a governor of the London School of Economics. He has sat on a host of Labour Party bodies, including the Productive and Competitive Economy Policy Review Group and the key economic policy sub-committee, which vetted Labour's economic policy formulations in the approach to the 1992 general election. In effect, he became a one-man replacement for the TUC–Labour Party Liaison Committee that Tony Benn had set up in the early 1970s.

Since 1986, the GMB's representative on Labour's NEC has been Tom Burlison, boss of the powerful GMB organization in the north-east. A full-time union official from the age of twenty-eight, Burlison became chair of the Northern Regional TUC, a director of the Northern Development Company and the single most powerful individual in the regional Labour Party. Though he rarely contributes to NEC debates Burlison is a member of most of its principal committees, and major initiatives can succeed only with his support. In 1991 he was elected the GMB's first-ever deputy general secretary.

In a revealing incident in 1988 Edmonds demoted senior national GMB officer David Warburton, a traditional right-winger, long-serving supporter of Labour Solidarity, and editor of *Forward Labour*, a right-wing bulletin circulated among union full-timers. Warburton's crime was to write some carefully critical words about the performance of the Labour leadership. He even stated openly what everyone else believed at the time: that there was a "distance between the leadership and the rest of the movement". Such an expression of independence was one thing Edmonds would not tolerate, even from the right wing.

At the GMB's 1988 conference Edmonds made a cynical attack on Tony Benn and Eric Heffer, who were then standing against Kinnock and Hattersley for the Party leadership. "Just at the moment when we should be concentrating on this major review, this major modernization of the party's policy, two venerable gentlemen of pensionable age are stomping the country trying to persuade us to return to the manifesto of 1945."[12] Edmonds is no fool and he knew that Benn and Heffer were calling for policies far removed from 1945; the attack served as a warning to people in and out of the Parliamentary Labour Party that – at this juncture – the powerful GMB would tolerate no challenge to the leadership. Edmonds was never, however, a close personal supporter of Kinnock. "In private he let people know just how little he thought of the Labour leader," recalls one GMB insider. "And he let Kinnock himself know on several occasions that he had to improve his performance if he wanted continued GMB support."

At the 1989 GMB conference Edmonds advocated major changes in the constitutional structures of the Labour Party, including reforms in conference voting and in the election of the NEC. These became known as the "Edmonds proposals", although the detail came from other sources, including Kinnock's office. "We will give more power to this national executive because it will deserve more power and authority," Edmonds assured his members. "I would not give much power . . . to the present one." With the chutzpah that has become the Edmonds trademark, he argued that trade unionists "should not accept that I, as general secretary, should cast votes on their behalf without asking each of them individually what they thought on every issue".[13] In recent years, Edmonds has personally cast his trade union block vote at Labour conferences to prevent the direct election of the women's section of the NEC by women in the Party, to overturn his own union's policy on trade union law and to ensure the election to the NEC of trade union representatives who backed Kinnock uncritically, all without the slightest attempt to "ask" his members what they thought about the matters in hand.

At the GMB conference held in June 1990 a motion reaffirming the union's support for defence cuts was opposed by former APEX boss Roy Grantham, who claimed to be speaking with the authority of the union's executive (other executive members were not so sure). A show of hands was called and the chair – to universal disbelief and cries of outrage – declared the motion lost. When he then refused demands from the floor for a card vote, delegates staged an angry mass walkout. At last a card vote was permitted and the defence cuts motion was passed overwhelmingly. For once, Edmonds had to confess to Kinnock that he could not deliver his union's block vote; but he made no protest when Kinnock then set himself up against the Labour Party conference and announced he would pay no heed to its decision – which was also the decision of his own union.

The GMB dealt with the crisis of membership that afflicted nearly all the old blue-collar unions in the 1980s by seeking out mergers with like-minded organizations. The first was with the Boilermakers' union, which, like the GMWU, boasted a powerbase in the north-east and a leadership close to Labour Solidarity. Boilermakers' official Alan Hadden was already on the NEC and retained his seat there for some years, giving the newly formed GMBATU two out of the twelve trade union seats, a rare occurrence in the NEC's carefully balanced trade union section. Subsequently Hadden moved to the national constitutional committee, where he supervised expulsions.

The GMWU's old white-collar section MATSA incorporated a number of smaller white-collar unions, including the Greater London Staff Association, which in its previous incarnation as the GLC Staff Association had resisted many of the progressive policies of the Ken Livingstone regime. The union also swallowed up the tiny but politically important National Union of Labour Organizers, the long-established closed-shop union for Labour agents and organizers. At the end of the decade, the 100,000-strong APEX clerical union merged into the GMB, bringing with it a host of old-fashioned hard-right officials led by Roy Grantham, the general secretary. In 1991 the GMB swallowed up the National Union of Tailors and Garment Workers. More mergers are on the cards in the future as Edmonds pursues his vision of a "new unionism": a form of empire-building that owes little to mass recruitment and workplace organization and much to deals stitched up among union hierarchies.

During the 1980s the union put together an impressive list of spon-sored MPs, including Betty Boothroyd (former NEC member, now Speaker of the House of Commons), John Cunningham, Gerald Kauf-man, Kinnock's successor as Labour leader John Smith, Jack Straw, Don Dixon, Joan Lestor, Giles Radice, George Robertson, John Morris, Ann Taylor, Clive Soley, Paul Boateng, Alastair Darling and Nick Brown. By the end of the 1987 Parliament all but two of its twenty-five sponsored MPs were either current or former members of Labour's front-bench team. As Gerald Kaufman said, addressing the GMB conference in 1989, the GMB Parliamentary group "may not be the largest but it is certainly the most powerful".[14]

In contrast to the TGWU, politically isolated and riven by factional warfare, in the 1980s the monolithic GMB wielded increasing influence over other unions, notably the UCW and NUPE. Having placed itself at the centre of the trade union movement and acquired a reputation as a trend-setter, it helped to ensure that the bulk of the block vote at Labour Party conferences was always delivered to the leadership's requirements. This block vote accounts for over 90 per cent of the total votes at conference and is therefore of supreme importance to the Party leaders. Indeed, without the support of Edmonds and his like, Kinnock would have been defeated on unilateralism, the Gulf War and, ironically, trade union law.

Shortly after Tony Blair replaced Michael Meacher as employment spokesperson and convenor of the People at Work Policy Review Group, he declared in a television interview that Labour's support for the closed shop was at an end. The trade union representatives on the NEC were displeased, not so much by the contents of the announcement as by the manner of it. In a letter of protest to Larry Whitty, Gordon Colling complained that "a major policy statement was made by the spokesperson without reference to the NEC, to one of its committees or to the Policy Review process". He asked for assurances that such incidents would not be repeated. Although this was Kinnock's preferred method of policy formation, he was happy to give such assurances to the NEC and even apologized for Blair's action. The convention of deference to trade union status was thus preserved but – as every member of the NEC knew – the slow embrace of Tory anti-union law was nearly complete.

Blair's revision of the Party's policy was published in "Looking to the Future", the third stage of the Policy Review, which reached the NEC in May 1990. In accordance with a deal worked out in advance with John Edmonds and Tom Sawyer, the document emphasized "the rights of the individual" at work rather than the collective rights of trade unions. It also pledged not only to abolish the closed shop (in accordance with the European Community's Social Charter) but also to set up a "a new Industrial Court to deal with the whole area of industrial disputes". This court would comprise "expert industrial members" and be headed by a senior High Court judge. All industrial action would be unlawful without the "support of a properly conducted ballot" and supportive action would be legal only "where there is a direct interest between the two groups, of an occupational or professional nature".

This stiffening of previous Labour policy effectively ruled out secondary action by, say, teachers or miners in support of nurses or ambulance drivers. It left the unions even more hamstrung by the courts than before and the courts themselves as open as ever to employer manipulation. Worse yet, a new element was added: there would be a "right to picket peacefully, in limited numbers, in accordance with a statutory code of practice".

These new limitations on the right to picket caused concern among some trade union leaders. At the NEC, Sam McCluskie, whose NUS members at Dover had been involved in large-scale picketing, proposed removing the phrase "in limited numbers". This was agreed without much discussion at the first morning session of a special two-day meeting held in May 1990. During the lunch break, McCluskie left the

meeting for another engagement. Tony Blair, not a member of the NEC
but very much an interested party, lobbied Kinnock to have the limitation
on pickets reinstated. Charles Clarke swung into action and NEC
members were pressed to overturn their previous decision. When the
NEC reconvened after lunch, Gordon Colling announced that there had
been some mistake and that he was sure McCluskie had not quite meant
to remove all reference to limiting picket numbers. Kinnock agreed,
assuring the others that he knew that McCluskie would never support
such an omission. A new vote was then taken, a unique event at the NEC,
and, without debate, all the trade union representatives reversed their
votes of that morning and agreed to reinstate Blair's limits.

By the end of the Policy Review process Labour was committed to keep
the bulk of the restrictions on unions that had been imposed by the
Tories. Not surprisingly, the new policy package was heartily welcomed
by the press and by the British Institute of Management. There was some
discontent among left-leaning trade unionists, and a number of general
secretaries (including Rodney Bickerstaffe of NUPE) signed a statement
reasserting the rights to strike, to picket peacefully and to take supportive
action, an implicit rejection of the Kinnock–Blair line. But the trade union
dissenters were prepared to go no further. When the Scottish TUC
threatened to rock the boat, Ron Todd threw his weight around to ensure
that nothing was mooted which might be taken by the media as less than
unqualified support for the Blair package, whose progress through the
labour movement was being watched with keen interest by employers.

At the Labour Party conference most trade unions backed the Blair
proposals, to which Blair himself scarcely referred in an anodyne speech
from the platform. They did this even though hardly any of their own
union policies conformed to the proposals and privately many had grave
doubts about the whole thing. By now the watchword was loyalty to the
leadership. It had become clear that dissenters would be quickly isolated
and humiliated.

Blair's People at Work review group now focused on training and the
"labour market". "Opportunity Britain", the next year's instalment of the
Policy Review, reiterated the commitments made the year before on trade
union law but focused on the promotion of British workers' "skills".
When the Tories proposed to bring in yet another anti-trade-union bill,
Blair's only response was to demand why they refused to address his
agenda of improved training for the workforce.

Motions from the TGWU, UCATT and the NUM calling for a repeal of
all Tory anti-union laws were submitted to the 1991 TUC. As early as July,
Kinnock's office let it be known to all and sundry that it would not
countenance any regression on this question. Pressure was placed on all
union leaders to back Kinnock and throw out the left-wing motions.
When the TUC met, in Glasgow in September, Arthur Scargill moved the

pro-repeal resolution, pointing out that he was asking for no more than was supposed to be guaranteed under International Labour Organization conventions. Ron Todd, defying the mandate of his own union, attacked the resolution, arguing that nothing was more important than getting a Labour government elected. The AEU president, Bill Jordan, derided Scargill as a "blast from the past". He told journalists that Scargill's speech "may get the applause of lay members but it's the agreement between the trade union leadership that counts".[15] The Scargill motion was defeated by 5,809,000 votes to 2,270,000; the TGWU delegation voted with the right wing. Tony Blair was on hand to witness the victory and provide an instant soundbite. He welcomed the TUC vote as "laying to rest the arguments of the past".[16] That night Kinnock had dinner with the TUC General Council; he was ebullient.

In the aftermath of the 1992 general election defeat the Labour Party's link with the unions once again came under scrutiny. Although the unions had hardly featured at all in the campaign (despite Tory attempts to resuscitate the ghosts of the 1970s), pundits declared that Labour could win only if it broke its links with the unions. The controversy caught union leaders on the hop. They had dreaded another Tory term in government and had done nearly everything the Kinnock leadership had asked of them, including keeping silent during the election campaign. Now, with the prospect of a Labour government postponed yet again, many looked to Europe, to more mergers, to single-union deals, to anything in order to avoid the need to confront employers at the workplace. Some were tempted to write off the Labour Party as a waste of scarce resources, and others were furious to find their £5 million contribution to Labour's general election fund so airily dismissed. When Larry Whitty asked them to consider a massive increase in the union affiliation fee to save the Party from financial collapse, he was quickly rebuffed by the TGWU, the AEU and the GMB. "No say, no pay" was the bureaucrats' line, showing that it is one thing to talk about breaking or weakening the link with the unions and quite another to do it.

Trade union leaders, for their part, simply cannot afford to forfeit their political influence within the Labour Party; nor is it at all clear that their members, who need a Labour government, will let them. Union leaderships will go a long way with the PLP leadership, but in the end they will always intervene when their interests are at stake. They need the Labour Party and the Party needs them. Without the unions, Labour has no financial base, no link to the millions of people organized in the country's single largest political constituency and no counterweight to the Tories' big-business supporters.

Despite all the talk of weakening, abandoning or amending the link between the trade unions and the Labour Party, the Labour leadership's aim has always been to strengthen that link at the top of the movement while suffocating it at the base. The Kinnock regime leaned heavily on the trade union block vote, which acted again and again to ensure that its initiatives were carried inside the Party. The Labour leadership would no sooner discard such a political weapon than a bullfighter would cast away his picador.

The real choice facing the Labour Party therefore is not between breaking the union link and maintaining it, but between a further narrowing of the link to unaccountable deals cobbled up at the top and a major reform designed to widen and democratize it, to make it truly the property of the rank and file of both the Labour Party and the unions. The first step should be to bring the link with the unions out from behind closed doors, back into the open, onto the floor of Labour Party conferences, thus enabling both union and Party members to see it in operation.

Notes

1. Benn diaries, 1 August 1984.
2. NEC Report to Annual Conference 1987.
3. NEC Report to Annual Conference 1990.
4. NEC Report to Annual Conference 1991.
5. *Guardian* 30 September 1991.
6. ibid.
7. NEC minutes January 1988.
8. *Campaign Group News* February 1988.
9. NEC minutes January 1988.
10. NEC minutes July 1989.
11. GMB Annual Conference Report 1987.
12. GMB Annual Conference Report 1988.
13. GMB Annual Conference Report 1989.
14. ibid.
15. *Guardian* 6 September 1991.
16. *Guardian* 4 September 1991.

Kinnock's Footsoldiers: from Campus Caucus to New Establishment

> They threw their caps
> As they would hang them on the horns o' the moon,
> Shouting their emulation.
>
> *Shakespeare*, Coriolanus

The Labour Co-ordinating Committee (LCC) was formed in 1978 as a Labour left think-tank. Among its original sponsors were Chris Mullin, Michael Meacher, Frances Morrell, Stuart Holland, Audrey Wise and other rising stars of the Bennite political firmament. Though Benn himself never took an active part, in its early days the LCC was publicly regarded as his task force in the Labour Party. Such was the confidence then in the future of the Labour left that all manner of highly respectable campaigners, trade unionists and Labour MPs were happy to be associated with it. From the beginning, though, the LCC was a top–down organization reliant on media publicity for its credibility with the Party's grass roots.

The LCC was one of the main participants in the Rank and File Mobilizing Committee which backed Benn's deputy leadership bid in 1981, but the break within the Tribune Group over the Benn campaign and the emergence of Neil Kinnock as the leading abstainer heralded a turn away from the left. Several leading LCC figures, notably Peter Hain, argued that the left was in danger of overreaching itself and creating a backlash; they urged it to draw back from its offensive within the Party and to build a popular base outside. The LCC strategists denied that they were moving to the right; they insisted that their differences with Tony Benn and what emerged as the "hard left" were over strategy and tactics, not principle.

At this same time a group of political activists calling themselves Clause Four entered the LCC and became its footsoldiers. Hain and

others were well aware that the LCC's profile was out of all proportion to
its actual organizational capacity. Despite its reputation, the group at that
time had few direct links with constituency parties. The Clause Four
activists presented themselves as the answer to a prayer.

Clause Four had started life in the mid 1970s as a group of left Labour
students united by a visceral hatred of Militant and a determination to
remove it from leadership of the National Organization of Labour Students (NOLS), Labour's official student wing. It succeeded in doing this
in 1976 after a campaign entitled Operation Ice-pick – a choice of name
which suggests that even in those days the group was a good deal less
libertarian than its rhetoric implied.

Clause Four championed the Alternative Economic Strategy (which
called for reflation, import controls, extended public ownership and
planning agreements) and opposed the Callaghan government.
Immersed in a left-wing ambience, it did not hesitate to deploy the
traditional categories of Marxism against its enemies. Advocating what it
called a "third road" of mass, participatory politics, Clause Four rejected
both parliamentary reformism and "Leninist" insurrectionism. Some of
its members were veterans of Big Flame, a far-left libertarian-Marxist
group with a clutch of supporters in the north-west, one of whom was
Paul Thompson, later an LCC national chair. In 1980 Clause Four argued
that "however much we dislike the tactics of Militant it would be quite
wrong for Marxists and other democratic socialists to support the use of
organizational methods to drive Militant out of the Labour Party".[1] In
1986 it was to place itself at the forefront of a highly public campaign to do
precisely that.

Unlike the old Tribunites and other traditional Labour lefts, Clause
Four put a premium on organization. Its formation in the cauldron of
student politics seemed to have produced in it an obsession with secre-
tiveness and exclusivity. By the early 1980s, when it became the guiding
force in the LCC, it had become something of a freemasonry, a tightly
knit group of political activists driven by a fierce hatred of "Trotskyists" –
a label applied to anyone who opposed them from the left. Its technique
was to establish caucuses within caucuses, inner circles within inner
circles. In NOLS it operated mainly via the Democratic Left, the most
powerful factional grouping in student politics whose support, since
1982, has been the key to gaining positions within NOLS and the NUS,
including the plum prize, the NUS presidency. Within the Democratic
Left the LCC set the agenda and within the LCC, Clause Four pulled the
strings. Among the inner circle of Clause Four when it moved into the
LCC in the early 1980s were a number of master NOLS/NUS manipu-
lators, including John Mann, Neil Stewart, Phil Woolas, Phil Cole and
Sally Morgan. Many of them went on to occupy positions of influence

within the labour movement and all became arch-exponents of New Realism and fanatical opponents of the Labour left.

In the early 1980s, however, NOLS apparatchiks were very different creatures from the leadership loyalists they later became. Students had been drawn into the Labour Party by the rise of the Labour left. Both NOLS and Clause Four backed the Benn deputy leadership campaign and NOLS was affiliated to the Campaign for Nuclear Disarmament (CND), the LCC, the National Abortion Rights Campaign and the Labour Common Market Safeguards Committee. The attraction of the insurgent Labour left to students enabled NOLS to break from its long, suffocating alliance with the Communist Party-dominated Broad Left, which had included Liberals and "independents" of various hues. In 1982 NOLS finally succeeded in winning power within the NUS on its own, becoming the largest single bloc on the NUS executive and capturing the NUS presidency in the person of Neil Stewart. This was very much a triumph for John Mann, an archetypal backroom fixer who had been NOLS NUS Officer that year and was to become NOLS chair the next.

Succeeding generations of Democratic Left student politicians owe Mann more than they realize. He set up the machinery and established the strategy that has enabled them to dominate the NUS and control its sabbatical posts ever since. For Mann and other Clause Four activists, however, student politics was always a base for power in the Labour Party. Hence their move – en bloc – into the LCC.

They first became visible as a highly organized vanguard within the LCC in 1982 during the fight over the newly established register of unaffiliated Party groups, which was a snare to catch Militant. Many on the Bennite left regarded the register as an unacceptable interference in Party democracy, but this view was not shared by the constitutionalists of the left-wing Campaign for Labour Party Democracy (CLPD) nor by the LCC, which was keen to promote compromise within the Party on the basis of unity around the democratic gains of 1979–81. In collaboration with the CLPD leadership, the Clause Four activists turned up in force at the CLPD annual general meeting in order to outvote the "ultras" and ensure the pressure group complied with the register. However, within a year, the Clause Four activists had broken with CLPD. By 1987 they had branded the Campaign as "ultra-left" and decided to promote themselves as "*the* campaign for Labour Party democracy".

The general election defeat of 1983 opened up new horizons for Clause Four and the "soft left". The anguish felt by the rank and file was exploited by LCC leaders to justify their increasing reluctance to criticize the Party leadership. What was the point of winning the battle for control of the Labour Party, they asked, if Labour then lost the general election? The struggle for party democracy which had consumed so much of the left's energies during 1979–83, and which had secured for the "soft left" and the LCC their precious positions of influence, was now characterized as a distraction from the tasks of building a "mass orientated campaign-ing party", "popularizing socialist policies" and building "alliances with progressive social movements".[2] Arguing against such laudable aims was like arguing for sin. The problem was that they were always counterposed to any direct challenge to the power of the right in the Parliamentary Labour Party.

That year, the LCC backed Kinnock's campaign for Labour Party leader. He was portrayed as a politician of the left who could both consolidate recent gains and unite the fractured Party. The Kinnock campaign was managed by Robin Cook, who had close ties to the LCC and had been one of the original "soft left" abstainers in 1981. In addition, a number of prominent LCC members, including Peter Hain, were also involved. The "soft left" activists believed they had hit the jackpot with Kinnock's election; at last they would have the ear of the Labour leader. Kinnock recruited two leading LCC members, Patricia Hewitt and Charles Clarke, to work in his private office, but at the same time he denied leading positions within the shadow cabinet to LCC favourites such as Michael Meacher and Cook.

The LCC insisted that the left had to have a constructive approach to the new leadership; it argued that support for the Kinnock–Hattersley team was in no way incompatible with a commitment to unilateralism, mandatory reselection of Labour MPs and opposition to witch-hunts. Indeed, it portrayed its support for the leadership as a strategy for protecting and extending these positions.

The LCC was one of the key players in the 1985 realignment of the left, where it fell to the LCC to provide the parliamentary "soft left" with both a left rhetoric and the appearance of a grassroots base.

At its 1985 annual general meeting the LCC adopted a fourteen-point charter which reaffirmed its traditional commitments to "the need for campaigning based on effective parliamentary action working in tandem with strong workplace and community action". It declared that "a Left Alternative Economic Strategy" must emphasize "common ownership . . . planning the economy, planned trade, compulsory planning agree-ments". Labour's politics had to be predicated on "an understanding of the class nature of society" supplemented by "parallel hierarchies notably of race and gender". Support for "socialist internationalism" included "the closure of all foreign military bases in Britain and the simultaneous dissolution of NATO and the Warsaw Pact" and "the establishment of a non- nuclear defence policy for Britain". Membership of the EEC was opposed because it would "preclude implementation of the Alternative Economic Strategy". Within the Labour Party, "consoli-dation of the democratic constitutional advances made in the Party constitution since 1979 . . . and the maintenance and improvement of the mechanism of accountability for elected representatives" were considered essential.

Within three years, the LCC was to abandon all the commitments contained in its 1985 charter, which in retrospect reads like the kind of "fundamentalist" "ultra-left" document the latter-day LCC would have damned at first sight. Only the fourteenth and final point would still have been endorsed: in it the LCC rejected what it described as "the narrow sectarian perspectives and strategies of Trotskyism and the ultra left".

Despite praise in the media and encouragement from the leadership, realignment was an awkward manoeuvre for the LCC. Some of its discomfort can be glimpsed in an LCC executive paper written in early 1986. The executive denied that there had been "any major changes concerning policy or abandonment of principle involved in recent positions taken by the LCC". The controversy was about "different ways of realizing socialist objectives, not . . . discarding them".[3] The LCC knew that the base within the constituencies for realignment remained severely limited:

> The new NEC grouping, the *Tribune* and other initiatives and LCC's relations to them are often very much realignment at the top. With many constituencies still dominated by Briefing/Campaign Group or other politics, new initiatives have often lacked weight and have given a misleading impression of changes on the ground . . . our concern for radical realism in tactics and winnable demands can take on the appearance of a rightward outlook and association with the Kinnock leadership. This is particularly dangerous as there is little sign that a Kinnock-led government would break decisively with past models.[4]

And the executive paper did make some criticisms of Labour's Jobs and Industry Campaign, which it said contained "all the hallmarks of a Keynesian technicism reminiscent of Wilson in 1964 rather than a preparation for a radical assault on the power of capital".[5] Here the LCC demonstrated how wedded it remained to left rhetoric at the same time as its practice swung sharply to the right. In the field of economic policy, its claim to represent an alternative to both traditional Labourism and "ultra left oppositionalism" could be maintained only by criticism of Roy Hattersley's handling of the shadow Chancellor's brief, since it could find little to say in contradiction to the official policies of Labour's front bench. This set the pattern for the rest of the decade. Whenever the LCC felt obliged to distance itself from the Labour leadership, it made Hattersley, the embodiment of traditional right-wing Labourism, the target.

In the process of realignment women's rights, lesbian and gay rights and anti-racism were counterposed by the LCC to commitments to union rights, job security and public spending; "popular campaigning" based in diverse "communities" was counterposed to "revolutionary socialism" and "class reductionism". But when these commitments were put to the test in 1987 during the media's fierce "loony left" campaign, the LCC was quick to denounce as "posturing" every practical attempt to move beyond lip service. A new "maturity" ruled out any direct challenge to racism, sexism and homophobia as "gesture politics".

During this period, organized LCC caucuses existed in only a handful of localities and most of these were caucuses organized against the "hard left". The LCC depended for its influence on its media image, which was a product of its relationship to the leadership and the NEC/parliamentary "soft left". None the less, the LCC was optimistic about the progress of the "new left" of which it formed, in its own words, the "the most organized core". It hailed Kinnock's 1985 Bournemouth speech as "a watershed". "In attacking impossibilist gesture politics Kinnock gave voice to what many Labour activists and voters had been feeling, even if only admitting it to themselves." The purge in Liverpool was described as "a corrective action against a vanguard party that had hijacked Labour's administration in Liverpool for its own ends".[6]

But at this same time Peter Hain commented in an internal LCC memorandum on the "drift and even inertia" that seemed to have gripped the organization. The purpose of realignment, Hain had thought, was to rebuild and revive the left; he was disappointed that so little had come of it. What he failed to understand was that this "drift" and "inertia" perfectly suited the purposes of the Clause Four/NOLS clique that was now in control of the LCC apparatus. Their project was to destroy the left, not reconstruct it – for them the rest was window-dressing.

Their chance came in the wake of the 1987 general election defeat. With heavyweight support from Eurocommunist journalists, tired Fabians and SDP-leaning pundits, all of whom had been arguing for years that Labour's electoral base was withering away, the LCC argued that the 1987 defeat required a fundamental revision of the Party's policies, presentation and internal organization. Its previous arguments in favour of "popularizing" socialist policies now became simply a call for politics by public relations. Its old advocacy of mass campaigning politics was abandoned and replaced by fidelity to the policies and perspectives imposed by the leadership. As Labour's political centre of gravity shifted ever more to the right, older, established right-wingers like Peter Shore, Denis Healey, John Smith and Giles Radice watched in astonishment as the Party leadership rushed past them with the LCC in tow.

At the 1987 Labour conference, a group of prominent "soft" and "hard" left individuals – members of the LCC and Labour Left Liaison respectively – issued a call for "left unity". Ken Livingstone, Peter Hain,

George Galloway, Ann Pettifor and Vladimir Derer set out a list of fifteen political points on which they believed a new left unity could be founded. The idea was to try to heal the breach opened up by realignment two years previously and restore some of the influence that the left had clearly lost since then. Although the fifteen points were nearly identical to those contained in the LCC Charter published only two years before, the "left unity" call was denounced by the Clause Four apparatchiks now controlling the LCC executive. They would not permit copies of the statement to be circulated at the LCC fringe meeting held at Labour's annual conference and both Hain and Livingstone were attacked at the LCC executive meeting for having signed the statement. They were criticized for having gone public with the initiative without consulting the LCC executive committee, but sceptics believed their real crime was to offer a hand of friendship to the "hard left".

The bulletin distributed by the LCC at the 1987 conference spelled out the Clause Four position: "The last thing we need at the moment are fifteen-point shopping lists full of generalities everyone agrees with but which say nothing about the real problems before us." What was needed was "an alliance of the democratic left" that would exclude the "ultra-left bodies" which have "undermined the party's appeal with their gesture politics, sectarianism and opposition to new thinking".[7]

Within one year, Ken Livingstone had been removed from the LCC executive. George Galloway, one of the key builders of LCC Scotland, had become a target of abuse in the LCC bulletin *Labour Activist*. Hain, one of the most energetic and committed members of the LCC since 1979, saw his vote collapse at the LCC AGM. Increasingly disenchanted with the NOLS apparatchiks, who in turn became increasingly hostile towards him, he decided to retire from the organization's executive, voluntarily but quietly, before he was deposed in public.

The transformation of the LCC from advocate of "extra-Parliamentary campaigning" to vanguard of the Kinnock leadership was apparent in the daily bulletins it issued to delegates at the Labour Party's 1987 annual conference. These denounced "the willingness of delegates and visitors to applaud speakers mentioning Wallasey or Liverpool Broadgreen" (two left-dominated constituencies) and variously attacked the Campaign for Labour Party Democracy, *Labour Briefing*, Militant, Sharon Atkin, Tony Benn, Ken Livingstone and Eric Heffer. They also made great play of the "Sawyer proposals" to remodel Labour's youth organization.

The LCC had a special interest in the "Sawyer proposals". After Clause Four's victory in NOLS in the mid seventies it had turned its attention to the Labour Party Young Socialists (LPYS), long dominated by the Militant Tendency. Initially Clause Four aimed to instil some democracy into the LPYS, and even collaborated with other left groups to do so. But the LPYS proved a more difficult nut to crack than NOLS, not least because of its largely working-class make-up. When it became apparent that it would be impossible to do more in the LPYS than set up an opposition to Militant, Clause Four lost interest in it. Only John Mann persisted in believing that there must be a way around the problem.

Complaints about the sectarian manner in which Militant ran the LPYS were widespread, but Militant could at least claim that it ensured that the British Labour Party had a functioning youth wing. In 1983 there were 495 LPYS branches and the national LPYS was highly active. That same year Tom Sawyer had become chair of the Labour Party NEC's youth committee; alongside the mostly right-wing and elderly NEC members sat representatives from LPYS and from NOLS – the latter's was John Mann. This was the beginning of Mann's relationship with Sawyer, through which Clause Four/NOLS was to achieve its long-term aim, the destruction of Militant's base in the LPYS.

During the miners' strike, the number of LPYS branches rose to an all-time high of 581. A total 305 delegates and 1,350 visitors attended the LPYS conference in Blackpool and Tom Sawyer was the fraternal delegate from the Labour Party's NEC. Undaunted, Mann outlined his proposals for restructuring the LPYS in a private meeting with NUS activists in spring 1985. A year later, Mann and Phil Woolas, his old NOLS associate, co-authored a Fabian pamphlet entitled "Labour and Youth: the missing generation". Their call for reform of the LPYS – and an end to Militant domination of it – was picked up by the press, and excerpts appeared in *Tribune*. Mann and Woolas damned the "Militant stranglehold" over the LPYS, which they branded "moribund" and "insignificant". Their recommended remedy was "mass collective activity for young people and political education". Labour should aim its youth activities "almost exclusively at teenagers" and stage "large-scale cultural and social activities".

Stripped of their participatory rhetoric, the Mann–Woolas proposals soon became "the Sawyer proposals". These were submitted by Sawyer to the NEC in July 1986 and sent out for consultation to constituencies and affiliates. In the end, 85 per cent of all responses opposed the proposals. Objectors argued that the proposed national youth campaigns committee would not be elected by or accountable to young Party members. The "regional" campaign committees sounded suspiciously like a device to get rid of the regional LPYS conferences – which indeed is precisely what they did. The proposed lowering of the age limit for YS membership from twenty-six to twenty-one would strip the YS of half its membership and all its leadership at a stroke. The YS would be left with no independent policy or profile because it would have no independent national structure.

Apart from raising the new age limit from twenty-one to twenty-three, the NEC ignored the results of the "consultation exercise" and asked

Labour's 1987 conference to endorse what were in effect John Mann's proposals to gut the Party's youth wing. Most constituency delegates were mandated to vote against the package, but it passed easily thanks to union block votes.

The LCC, delighted with its long-awaited triumph over Militant, announced that it would now publish its own *Youth Activist* newsletter. One issue appeared. Ex-NOLS chair Ben Lucas, writing on behalf of the LCC executive, complained to Larry Whitty about "lack of initiative from the Party on youth work and the failure to implement and further develop the changes to Labour's youth work agreed at last year's Party conference".[8] This seemed to many to be nothing but the usual LCC attempt to escape responsibility for the consequences of its own political initiatives. Its real priority was the compiling of a political dossier on members of the Labour Party involved in youth and student work. A circular to LCC supporters requested details of local youth and student officers and asked respondents to classify them in the following categories: "LCC or other democratic left", "Militant", "other ultra left".

At the same time, Neil Usher, the outgoing chair of NOLS, was appointed the Labour Party's new Youth and Student Officer with wide powers over both the YS and NOLS. In the NUS, Usher had been nicknamed "the crusher" and presented with an ice-pick at a student revue because of his single-minded hatred of "Trotskyists". Under his aegis, the Labour Party's youth wing declined rapidly. The campaigning, educational and social activities promised by Sawyer, Mann and Woolas never happened. By 1990, there were only fifty-two YS branches left in the country – and in total they claimed only three hundred members. The Party's annual youth conference, which had replaced the national LPYS conference, was a miserable affair, poorly attended, dominated by Walworth Road officials and denied the right to take votes on policy issues. The effect of the LCC's scorched-earth policy towards the Militant-dominated YS was to leave Labour without any youth organization at all. Asked at the end of 1990 why Labour had no plans to revive the Red Wedge initiative for the coming general election campaign, Neil Usher explained, "Paul Weller and Billy Bragg are not the musicians we would use to attract new voters . . . there's not the same kind of buzz as there was in the eighties . . . we've got a healthy lead in the polls because of what we've got to offer rather than just what Billy Bragg says."[9] On 9 April 1992, for the first time in generations, the Tories drew more support from young males aged 18–25 than Labour.

Using the NOLS committee as their political base, Clause Four/LCC supporters continued to exercise a rigid control over the NUS apparatus. Their dominance coincided with a period of steep decline in the effectiveness and public reputation of student unionism. Simon Buckby acknowledged in an LCC mailing that "an apparent lack of openness and ideological expression by the soft left in the student movement . . . has permitted the development of both right and hard left".[10] Buckby's successor as LCC youth officer, Kerry Postlewhite, admitted that "the Democratic Left now operates solely as a vehicle for the selection of candidates and is quite likely to be winding itself up".[11]

NOLS itself stagnated. It submitted virtually identical annual reports of its activities to the Labour Party conferences in 1988, 1989 and 1990. Although it continued to be the most powerful electoral machine within the NUS, the quality of NOLS apparatchiks declined from the Mann/ Woolas days. Dependent on connections with the Labour front bench and practical support from Party full-time officials, the new generation of Democratic Left activists, having had their NUS positions handed to them on a plate, became a byword among students for incompetence and mediocrity.

One of the most salient features of Kinnock's regime was the heavy traffic on the career track from NOLS and the NUS to full-time employment in the upper echelons of the labour movement. In addition to John Mann and Phil Woolas, who went from NOLS to the AEU and GMB respectively, pioneers of the career track included Charles Clarke, Nigel Stanley, a member of the NOLS national committee in the 1970s and an LCC founder who became an adviser to Bryan Gould, and Neil Stewart, a former NUS president who also went to work for Kinnock. In recent years this trickle turned into a flood as upwardly mobile student politicians found their lack of qualifications or experience no barrier to securing paid positions in Kinnock's "new model party". (The table on page 183 illustrates the extent of NOLS/LCC infiltration of the labour movement as of early 1992.) These labour movement *arrivistes* brought with them a predilection for tight-knit caucus politics, for the deal struck behind closed doors, which they had acquired in student politics. As veteran opponents of Militant, Socialist Organiser and other forces to their left, they boasted well-honed skills in faction-fighting which were highly valued by the Kinnock leadership.

In the final years of the Kinnock regime a split emerged within the Labour apparatus between what might be called the old and new Labour Party establishments. The former NOLS apparatchiks formed a kind of "state within the state" at Walworth Road. Their loyalty was not to their immediate superiors, but solely to the leadership clique and to Kinnock's office in particular. They assessed the politics of their co-workers and made that assessment available to the leadership as and when needed. Those Walworth Road employees who were not included within this select circle regarded many of its members simply as agents of the leader's office. Certainly, LCC members provided a handy and informal link between Walworth Road and the parliamentary leadership, however little they provided for the Party members and trade unionists who had to foot the bill for their wages. Not surprisingly, friction arose between this Praetorian Guard and older, more established officials.

Late in 1987 the LCC set up its CLP Activists Network. This was presented as an attempt to identify one person in each CLP as an LCC contact; initially it covered one hundred CLPs, mostly in London. Its main work in its first full year of existence was, according to the LCC mailing, campaigning to elect Robin Cook and remove Ken Livingstone from the NEC. Soon, the Activists Network became the basis for the surreptitious introduction of a two-tier membership within the LCC. While a handful of politically trusted activists, mostly with NOLS connections, ran the organization via the Activists Network, the silent majority of LCC members merely paid subscriptions.

Although it continued to promote itself as "the largest pressure group on the left", the LCC in the years after 1987 became little more than a network of political acquaintances pledged to mutual assistance, a new freemasonry in the corridors of labour movement power. Having taken control of the LCC, Clause Four itself ceased all formal activities as an independent organization. It even ceased to register as an unaffiliated Party organization with Walworth Road. But the organization was still used to funnel money to the LCC, and a loan of £2,400 from Clause Four made up one sixth of the LCC's total annual income in 1988–89. In 1990 it was announced to those remaining on the Clause Four mailing list that there was no longer any need for a continued separate organization because "the enemy" had been defeated: the enemy in question being the "hard left".

Back in 1988, Peter Hain had described the LCC as being controlled by a "new majority whose politics is in practice defined by opposition to the hard left".[12] The contest for the Labour leadership held in that year was the last occasion on which the left face of the LCC was in evidence. There was general agreement within the LCC that the challenge of Tony Benn and Eric Heffer was, in the words of LCC veteran Trevor Fisher, "the gesture of a bankrupt politics, and hopefully the end of an era".[13] But the organization was divided by John Prescott's challenge to Roy Hattersley. Mike Craven, a leading member of the LCC executive, was an employee of Prescott and was organizing his campaign. The Kinnock camp, however, was backing Hattersley and had already condemned Prescott's candidacy.

The payroll vote of Walworth Road full-time officials, trade union employees, and parliamentary assistants and researchers was mobilized in an attempt to force the LCC to support Hattersley. In the end, however, Craven and his allies won the day and the LCC executive backed Kinnock for leader and Prescott for deputy. This displeased several of the LCC's parliamentary sponsors, including Kinnock's former parliamentary private secretary, Kevin Barron, who wrote in the LCC mailing for August 1988:

> I, like many other people who have left the Campaign Group, have taken on the ideological debate within the Party against the so-called hard left and see this campaign as a useful means of continuing [it]. We should not be misled by supporting a candidate who will only offer a smokescreen to the hard left (who have caused the election nobody seems to want) and not taking them on in the interest of the democratic left of the party.[14]

In an attempt to maintain at least a semblance of independence from the leadership, the Craven-led LCC executive majority then issued a strongly worded press release which declared that it was "not a Kinnock echo chamber and that we strongly oppose the increasing authoritarianism and centralization of Party decision-making in the leader's office".[15] But although the executive backed Prescott, many LCC members fell in line behind Hattersley. In a ballot of the LCC membership (the turnout was never published) Prescott received 59 per cent, Hattersley 33 per cent and Eric Heffer 5 per cent. The subsequent failure of the Prescott campaign convinced many in the LCC that there was no longer any mileage in even token public opposition to the Kinnock leadership.

The LCC liked to claim credit for stimulating the Policy Review and boasted often of its participation in it. Every year, the LCC submitted lengthy documents to Walworth Road combining pages of sociological jargon with empty paeans to "modernization". Every year, when its submissions were largely ignored, it would express disappointment with the review's lack of "vision", "strategy", "radicalism" or "priorities", then demand that Party members and conference delegates back it anyway.

The LCC finally crossed the Rubicon in the summer of 1989 when it decided to back the leadership's move against unilateralism. In an LCC mailing, Hilary Bernard referred to the non-nuclear defence policy as "simplistic", "nationalistic", "anti-European" and "romantic nonsense".[16] An LCC membership ballot on defence policy received widespread publicity and was referred to in the press as "the first significant test of grassroots Party opinion" on the leadership's change of heart. A total of 220 ballot papers was returned and unilateralism was rejected by 157 votes to 62.

The figures might have been taken to indicate just how small and unrepresentative a group the LCC had become. Instead, the media, prompted by the Labour leadership, treated the ballot as evidence of disenchantment with unilateralism at the base of the Party. More generally, the symbiosis that existed between the LCC, Kinnock's office and political correspondents of the broadsheet press enabled the LCC to raise its public profile far beyond any influence it wielded within the Party. Kinnock used the LCC to float initiatives that he wanted to push through the Party. The press, knowing that what the LCC said today Kinnock was likely to say tomorrow, kept an eye on its every pronouncement. Writing up the latest LCC press release (a practice in which Patrick Wintour seemed to specialize, at the *Guardian*) was an easy way to grab the inside track on an emerging story. The LCC itself, eager for publicity, encouraged journalists to believe that it had Kinnock's ear. First Lesley Smith, later to work in the Labour Party press office, and then Mike Craven, a public relations professional, served as LCC national press officers. Both made sure that the circle of mutual misinformation worked in the LCC's favour.

In 1989 the LCC published "Leaders and Members", its submission to the NEC's consultation on Labour's constitution. Wrapped in double talk about "member involvement" and "mass membership", the document called on the Party to substitute what it called "informal structures" suitable for "confidence building" for the traditional democratic mechanisms, which it dubbed "arenas for factional battles". Ward and constituency meetings, it seemed to think, were no place to discuss politics, which ought to be left to the professionals. Instead of holding debates and votes, Labour should emulate the Tories by organizing "luncheon clubs, garden parties, jumble sales, barbecues – there is no shortage of activities other than meetings".

"Leaders and Members" called for a break with the unions and a "move towards an individual member party". It warned, however, that "at the moment the unions act as a safety valve. It does not matter if the CLP delegates are sometimes to the left of the unions because they exercise so little power over decisions." It stated that the Party conference should consider "amendable" policy documents drawn up by the leadership instead of resolutions submitted by constituency parties and affiliated unions. It advocated the establishment of "policy commissions" composed of "MPs, union representatives and experts". It argued that the present NEC should be abolished and replaced by a smaller body in which the PLP would be separately represented. Taken as a whole, the effect of these reforms would be to entrench the power of the middle layers of the Labour bureaucracy and effectively to exclude rank-and-file Party members from any active role in decision-making. Suspicions that what "Leaders and Members" was really all about was creating a Labour Party in which LCC supporters could rise rapidly to the top were reinforced by the document's plea for the "development of a tier of lay activists who are able to be elected to the highest bodies of the party". For all its participatory rhetoric, this was a recipe for the perpetual domination of the Party by a politically reliable cadre of full-time apparatchiks, councillors, MPs and Party or union officials. While "Leaders and Members" stipulated that groups like the LCC should be permitted to operate freely within the Party, "Militant and some of the other Leninist organizations" should be proscribed. Revealingly, the document failed to call for members to be guaranteed any right to freedom of speech or opinion.

"Leaders and Members" also featured the usual LCC call for quotas for women in all Party bodies, a demand also backed by the left. The LCC's real agenda here was revealed by its argument that quotas would "remove the need for separate women's organizations to be resolutionary and electoral". In other words, there would be no need for direct representation by women of women within the Party; the promotion of individual women would take the place of the collective empowerment of women. For the LCC, the sole purpose of quotas was to improve women's representation in "Parliament and local councils, general committees and regional executive, on the shadow cabinet and the national executive".[17] Over the years, the LCC gave active support to the leadership as it first downgraded and ultimately all but abolished the established and autonomous Labour women's organization. It helped to organize the Labour Women's Network, a body with no democratic structures (yet officially blessed by the NEC) which offered advice to aspirant women politicians on how to get themselves selected for parliamentary seats.

Using the language of the women's movement to secure advancement within the Party for its own women acolytes was an LCC speciality, as was the claim that any criticism of an individual woman's politics was an attack on "feminism". The latter was a manoeuvre the Clause Four clique had perfected in student politics. People who opposed them from the left were branded as "anti-feminist", accused of indulging in "macho" political posturing or smeared as "aggressive" and "intimidatory". It seemed to some observers that the LCC had decided that political debate of any kind was a threat to "women" – by which they always meant women aligned to their own organization.

The 1989 Labour Party conference saw the LCC make a big effort to shift Tony Benn, Dennis Skinner and Ken Livingstone from the NEC. "It's time CLPs started to ask what these three individuals contribute to the work of the NEC. On most voting issues they have been in a hard left rump," the LCC fulminated.[18] This did not stop it from issuing a warning to Neil Kinnock on the morning of his speech to the conference:

> This is not a good time to concentrate on bashing an external or an internal enemy. . . . Kinnock needs to deliver today a statement of workable, practical radicalism, which could command an imaginative leap in popular thinking. If he does not, the opportunity to win the battle of ideas may have been lost for another generation.[19]

Though Kinnock failed to oblige his footsoldiers, they were not unduly perturbed:

> Behind all the jokes and Tory-bashing the message in Neil Kinnock's speech yesterday was that the way is now clear for a smooth run to victory at the next election. With the review complete we've got the policies sorted out and we're fit to govern again. . . . The Policy Review is making us more electable.[20]

This premature triumphalism was an indication that the LCC believed its war against the "hard left" had been won; like Clause Four before it, the LCC began to wind itself down. When Ken Hulme resigned his paid post as LCC organizer in 1989, the group decided not to replace him and abandoned its offices in Soho. Not everyone was pleased with this development. In 1989 Trevor Fisher, who was to depart the LCC executive the following year, wrote in the LCC members' mailing: "Although an organization of activists, it has not been an active organization." He criticized the organization for being London-dominated and for having "rarely sought to be a rank and file grouping".[21] He also criticized it for keeping big names on its executive who did no work; Labour MPs Chris Smith and Kate Hoey, two of the top three elected to the executive in 1988, never attended a single meeting.

Earlier in 1989, the LCC had launched an ambitious recruitment campaign to consolidate its base. The aim was to win five hundred new members within twelve months. Like Labour's mass membership drive, which the LCC had championed, its own campaign was a flop. Only fifty new recruits, mostly London-based, were attracted. In the early 1980s the annual meetings of the organization had regularly attracted two to three hundred individuals. The 1990 AGM held in London was attended by only seventy people, and a total of 103 ballots were cast in the executive elections. The annual report admitted that the level of official LCC activity had not been as high as in previous years. At Labour's annual conference, the LCC described its main activity as promoting the NEC candidature of Margaret Hodge. Despite its continuing reservations over the Policy Review's lack of "strategic direction", the LCC argued that "unity is essential because conference shows the Party at its most exposed. After four years of debate over policy changes, now is not the time to question fundamentals."[22]

In recent years, there has been a large turnover in the membership of the eighteen-strong LCC executive. Only eight members elected for 1988–89 remained on the executive elected for 1990–91. The previous year the executive had been so weak that it had been forced to co-opt Fiona MacTaggart, former leader of the Wandsworth Council Labour Group, and Lesley Smith, by now a full-time Party press officer. In 1990 there were twenty-four candidates for the eighteen executive places; most of these were NOLS insiders, straight out of student politics with little practical Labour Party experience.

Like other Party pressure groups, the LCC suffered from the severe crisis of activism that beset the last years of the Kinnock regime. In the absence of a sizable membership or any broad contact with the Party rank and file, the LCC came to rely solely on the press release, the mail shot and the off-the-record briefing to present its case. It still advertised itself as "Labour's Democratic Left", even though all those "soft left" activists genuinely committed to democracy had long since abandoned the organization, as had former key strategists like Nigel Stanley, John Denham, Peter Hain and even John Mann (who believed the LCC had made a mistake by linking its fortunes so closely to Kinnock's).

LCC recruitment literature was peppered with enigmatic injunctions: "ideals need ideas", "make connections", "articulate the alternatives" and "connect up". It asked: "Do you feel that our ideals can be put into effect if only we can think up the modern ways of giving them effect?"[23] Apparently if the answer to this puzzling query was yes, the LCC was the organization for you. Essentially the purpose of all the buzzwords was to indicate to the potential recruit that the LCC was *the* organization for anyone who wanted a place on the inside track in Kinnock's Labour Party.

The contents of the five "Activist" mailings issued in 1990 to the elite members of the LCC's "Activists Network" nicely illustrate the priorities of the group. They dealt with the "hard left", NEC elections, the far-left group Socialist Organiser, conference amendments and the future of Party conference. Each was intended solely to arm "activists" for internal Party manoeuvres. The bulletins on the "hard left" and on Socialist Organiser seemed to have more to do with state-security-style political surveillance than with political organization within the labour movement.

Between 1990 and 1992 the only *raison d'être* of the LCC seemed to be the destruction of old enemies on the left. In Haringey, Camden, Tower Hamlets, Lambeth, Brighton, Merseyside, Bristol and throughout Scotland LCC members used their standing with the media to spread damaging disinformation about the left; they used their connections with the Labour bureaucracy to initiate investigations and suspensions.

A paper by Sue Goss and Mike Craven "Labour After Thatcher", adopted at the 1990 annual general meeting argued that Labour now needed to "go on the offensive, highlighting specific policies capable of commanding the political agenda between now and the election".Too few firm commitments, it warned, "could be counter-productive".[24] But in the remaining eighteen months before the 1992 general election the LCC said not a word about the Gulf War or the tragedy of the Kurds, about growing unemployment, homelessness, hospital opt-outs or the crisis in state education. When Gerald Kaufman unilaterally altered policy on nuclear weapons in the pages of the *Guardian*, its only complaint was that he had failed to consult the shadow cabinet.

A woolly enthusiasm for all things "European" became the entirety of the LCC's foreign policy. It responded to the movement against the Poll Tax, a perfect example of the extra-parliamentary "mass politics" that the early LCC had championed, by attacking both its leaders and its grassroots activists. Support for Charter 88 and proportional representation became convenient substitutes for campaigns against racism, miscarriages of justice or a woman's right to choose on abortion. When the National Membership Scheme that it had welcomed ended up divesting the Party of a huge proportion of its paying membership, leading LCC members responded by arguing, privately at least, that mass membership political parties were a thing of the past and that Labour should rely on state funding in future.

This fascination with the prospect of state funding reflected the fact that the LCC had become nothing but a coterie of trainee professional politicians. Value-free, ambitious, convinced of their own inherent right to govern, their only interest in political ideas or political debates was to manipulate them to outflank rivals or promote favourites. Though all had passed through higher education, a number came from working-class backgrounds. For them the career track from student politics into the upper echelons of the Labour Party or the unions offered a unique chance for a rapid rise in living standards and social status. They formed a community of *nouveaux riches* in the Labour Party, proud of their youthful success and contemptuous of anyone who seemed to have other priorities in life. They saw themselves as winners, and despised their enemies on the left as losers, people who perversely insisted on bucking what the LCC took to be the inevitable march of "new times". Chanting the slogans of the hour, they spared no effort in making themselves useful to the powerbrokers of the Labour establishment, whose patronage they craved. They were the ideal footsoldiers for the Kinnock regime.

Thus, from under the stone of the 1985 "realignment of the left" had slowly crawled what was to become, by the 1992 general election, the new far right of Labour politics. The former prophets of the "third road" now argued for an abandonment of class politics, for a turn away from the poor and oppressed to the well-heeled and over-privileged. Some argued that privatization was the force of the future and that redistributive taxation was a thing of the past. Their contempt for the old right's "Labourism", in days gone by a token of their residual leftism, had become a function of their dedication to a new media-based politics run by and for a permanent professional elite.

But with Kinnock's failure, the LCC found itself suddenly bereft of high-placed friends. As the premier advocates of the Kinnock strategy at the base of the Party, the LCC activists feared they would be blamed for defeat. There were hasty efforts to resurrect their fortunes by renewing their old radical rhetoric, and they were the key backers of Bryan Gould's leadership candidacy, which they touted as a campaign for "new ideas". But by this point, apart from *Guardian* journalists, few people familiar with their track record were fooled. The overwhelming rejection of Gould by all sections of the Party was not only an expression of scepticism about the precise content of his "new ideas" but also a rejection of the careerism with which the LCC was associated.

Some activists with past or present NOLS/LCC connections and their positions in the labour movement as of April 1992

Charles Clarke – LCC member, NUS president, Chief of Staff to Neil Kinnock

Neil Stewart – NUS president – personal aide to Neil Kinnock

Lesley Smith – NUS vice-president – Parliamentary Labour Party press officer

Steve Morgan – NOLS member of the NUS executive – regional organizer, London Labour Party

Phil Cole – NOLS national committee member – regional organizer, London Labour Party

Phil Woolas – NOLS NUS organizer – GMB communications officer

Ben Lucas – chair of the NOLS national committee – UCATT researcher

Vicky Phillips – NUS president – Labour Party women's officer

Pauline McNeill – president of NUS Scotland – GMB full-time official

Jo Moore – vice-chair of the NOLS national committee - Labour Party press officer

Sally Morgan – NOLS national committee – Labour Party organization directorate

Simon Buckby – member of NOLS national committee – assistant to John Prescott

Rachel Brooks – NOLS member – GMB full-time official

Carol Judge – member of the NOLS national committee – personal assistant to Graham Stringer, Labour leader of Manchester City Council

Iain Watson – NOLS activist and LCC member – Labour Party policy directorate

Andy Pharaoh – NOLS national committee – temporary regional organizer, London Labour Party

Neal Lawson – LCC executive member – TGWU full-time official

Maggie Jones – LCC executive member – NUPE full-time official

Paul Simpson – LCC member – Labour Party political education officer

Rex Osborn – LCC member – Labour Party political intelligence officer

Cathy Ashley – LCC member – Labour Party policy directorate
Paul Convery – LCC secretary – Islington councillor, director of Unemployment Unit
Ian Wingfield – LCC executive – UCW researcher
Bill Gilby – LCC chair – NUPE political officer

Notes

1. *Paved With Good Intentions: the politics of Militant*, Clause Four pamphlet 1980.
2. "New Agenda for Party Democracy", *Labour Activist* September 1983.
3. "A Strategy for Labour's Democratic Left", LCC executive committee paper 1986.
4. ibid.
5. ibid.
6. *Labour Activist* May 1986.
7. *Labour Activist Conference Bulletin*, 29 September 1987.
8. LCC mailing March 1988.
9. *Tribune* 23 November 1990.
10. LCC mailing October 1988.
11. LCC mailing January 1989.
12. LCC mailing July 1988.
13. *Chartist* June–August 1988.
14. LCC mailing August 1988.
15. *Guardian* 17 June 1988.
16. LCC mailing spring 1989.
17. LCC "Campaign for Quotas statement", April 1989.
18. LCC summer mailing 1989.
19. *Labour Activist Conference Special* 3 October 1989.
20. *Labour Activist Conference Special* 4 October 1989.
21. LCC mailing autumn 1989.
22. *Labour Activist Conference Special* 1 October 1990.
23. LCC recruitment leaflet 1990.
24. "Labour After Thatcher", LCC paper 1990.

7

Neil Kinnock's War:
Labour and the Gulf

The hottest places in hell are reserved for those who, in times of a
great moral crisis, maintain their neutrality.

Dante

During the Gulf crisis and the war that issued from it, two well-established currents within the British labour movement contended for the Labour Party's heart and soul. A tradition of anti-imperialism and anti-militarism, deeply rooted in the rank and file, fought desperately against another tradition – equally deeply rooted among the trade union and parliamentary elite – of subservience to the dictates of the Foreign Office and the White House.

The Gulf crisis began on August 2nd 1990 when Saddam Hussein's army occupied Kuwait. The initial response from Western powers was confused and cautious; Iraq had been a long-standing ally of the United States and a key recipient of US military aid throughout the long Iran–Iraq War. But fearful of the future security of Middle Eastern oil supplies and eager to impose its authority in the region in the wake of the collapse of the Soviet Union power, the Bush administration soon adopted a belligerent policy towards its former friend. Operation Desert Shield was commissioned. Armed forces were sent to Saudi Arabia and war preparations began.

The foremost international supporter of the Bush strategy was, of course, the then Prime Minister, Margaret Thatcher. Initially, the government was worried that a war in the Gulf might be politically damaging if it was conducted without maximum "national unity". With the Conservative Party trailing in the opinion polls and in crisis over the Poll Tax, many Tory MPs feared the Gulf could become another Suez instead of another Falklands. But once Labour had made clear its support for the Tory policy, the government could breathe easy; "national unity", at least the kind of national unity that makes the headlines, was assured.

Labour's foreign affairs spokesperson, Gerald Kaufman, having consulted only Neil Kinnock and the chair of the NEC international subcommittee, Tony Clarke, was quick to give unreserved public backing to the war preparations. While still on holiday in Italy, and without consulting the shadow cabinet or the NEC, Kinnock went on radio to endorse Bush's response to the crisis. He even went so far as to claim that "by definition" Saddam Hussein was the type you did not negotiate with, which was well beyond the Tory government's official position.

It was not until a month after Allied troops were first sent to the Gulf that the Commons were allowed to debate the issue. Despite the urging of MPs including Tony Benn, Eric Heffer, Tam Dalyell and the Liberal Democrat leader, Paddy Ashdown, the Labour leadership had refused to press the government to reconvene Parliament. The Commons were recalled only when both Opposition and government front benches had privately agreed that a one and a half day debate conducted within definite limits would be held on September 6th and 7th; there was to be no motion placed before the House and no vote taken. It would be only a consultative exercise, a chance for both major parties to express their support for action against Iraq, not an occasion for democratic decision-making.

The Labour leadership rejected calls for an emergency meeting of the Parliamentary Labour Party and made no attempt to consult Labour MPs before the Commons debate. The NEC was not convened and the shadow cabinet was not consulted until after the Commons debate had finished.

Opening the debate for Labour, Kinnock gave unequivocal backing to the US-led intervention. Responding to what Thatcher called in her speech "our resolute approach", he advised the government to seek UN sanction for direct action against Iraq. This sanction, he made clear, should be regarded not as a restraint on the use of force but a method of legitimizing it. He failed to mention any need for the government to seek the sanction of Parliament before committing British forces to war. Instead, he tried to outgun Thatcher by stipulating "war aims" more far-reaching than the government's, including a permanent arms embargo on Iraq, the destruction of its chemical weaponry and the "continual" monitoring of its nuclear plant. He also demanded Iraqi "reparations, especially to the poor countries that have been further impoverished by its aggression". If this was a reference to oil-rich Kuwait, it left his audience quite baffled.

Kinnock was followed by a queue of veteran Labour MPs, among them Peter Shore, Peter Archer, Pat Duffy and Giles Radice, for whom the Commons debate seemed mainly an occasion for sententious discourse on foreign affairs. None of them offered any serious analysis of the costs and benefits of a possible war. A handful of mostly left-wing Labour MPs, horrified at the drift towards war, decided to force a vote on the procedural motion that the Commons adjourn. Thus, despite the best efforts of the Labour leadership, MPs were compelled to register their positions on the Gulf question. Throughout the Gulf crisis, it was to be the Labour left, in the face of deep resentment and obstruction from the front bench, including its "soft left" elements, that ensured that the Commons held debates and took votes on the greatest issue of the day.

In this first debate, Tony Benn rose from the backbenches to deny that war was the only possible solution to the Gulf crisis. He argued that neither the United States nor the British government was concerned with the freedom of Kuwait or the deterrence of territorial aggression. The real *casus belli*, he insisted, was the security of Western oil supplies. A terminally ill Eric Heffer, in his last speech to the Commons, delivered a memorable condemnation of Tory hypocrisy on human rights, democracy and international law, points that no one on the Labour front bench was prepared to raise.

Labour's defence spokesperson, Martin O'Neill, used his Commons speech to praise the preparations undertaken by the British armed forces. As David Lambie, the retiring MP for Cunninghame South and one of a number of mainstream Scottish Labour MPs to oppose the war, observed, O'Neill seemed not to be addressing the House at all but "the British military establishment and our so-called friends across the Atlantic". Norman Godman, another dissident Scot, intervened in O'Neill's speech to ask whether the medical facilities in the Gulf would be able to deal with gas attack victims. "The respect I feel for the British forces and those who lead them tells me that they would not put people in the field without the necessary support," O'Neill answered, revealing not only a political loyalty to the military establishment but a belief in its competence and concern for the lower ranks that astonished anyone familiar with military history.

Towards the end of the debate, the Foreign Office minister of state, William Waldegrave, referred to Benn's contribution. "I asked myself whether I would feel more secure in my arguments if he was agreeing with me," Waldegrave explained, "and came to the conclusion that I would not." To which, *Hansard* records, Kinnock rejoined from the front bench, "Join the club." Waldegrave immediately picked up the remark and repeated it to the whole House.

Only thirty-six Labour MPs voted against the government. Over half the Parliamentary Labour Party voted with the whip to support the Tories, including several shadow cabinet members who had made their names within the Party as peace activists. However, when the swollen front-bench "payroll" vote was discounted, it appeared that only 41 per cent of backbench Labour MPs had been prepared to join the Party leadership in backing Thatcher's drive to war.

The first effect of Labour's endorsement was to assure the government and the US that if war started the leaders of the Opposition would back them. This relieved ministers of a potentially huge burden – the burden of having to convince the public that war was necessary and justified. Within days, the government despatched the first British ground troops to the Gulf.

Just how deeply committed to war the Labour leadership had become was revealed when it rejected out of hand Ted Heath's proposals for a diplomatic solution. In September, in the run-up to the 1990 Party conference, the first batch of opinion polls on the crisis was published. They showed that 19 per cent of the British public and 26 per cent of Labour voters opposed US–British military intervention. Public opinion was still fluid.

Within the Labour Party, there was revulsion at the base of the movement over the idea of a war for oil, over the hypocrisy of the Bush administration and the Tory government and over the supine position of the Labour front bench. Within the local and national groupings that quickly emerged to oppose the war, Party members were often central. One of the first local parties to react was Roy Hattersley's Sparkbrook Constituency Labour Party; clearly, opposition to the leadership stance spread well beyond the usual confines of the left. More than forty emergency resolutions against a war in the Gulf were submitted to the 1990 Labour conference.

At the pre-conference NEC Dennis Skinner and Tony Benn were alone in opposing the drive to war. All other NEC members voted against the emergency resolution submitted by the Fire Brigades Union (FBU) which did no more than demand that United Nations authorization be secured before any military action was commenced. The NEC approved a statement drafted by Gerald Kaufman which praised the Bush administration, endorsed military action to remove Saddam Hussein from Kuwait and suggested some form of indefinite control over Iraq.

At 9.15 a.m. on Wednesday October 3rd, Peter Mandelson assured journalists that the conference debate on the Gulf crisis would be short. He had already scheduled it to conflict with BBC children's programmes so that it would not be seen on television, a form of censorship usually reserved for resolutions on Ireland, and on lesbian and gay rights.

In his conference speech, Gerald Kaufman argued that by backing the UN on the Gulf Labour could ensure action by the international community on Palestine and Central America, questions he knew were dear to the hearts of the rank and file. He opposed the FBU resolution, he said, not because he was against securing UN approval for military action but because it would not be helpful to specify what type of sanction military action would require: "it could be with forces under national command but with UN authorization. . . . We should not opt for some specific form of action which would tie the hands of the international community in circumstances we cannot foresee."[1] Kaufman, like other Labour leaders, was well aware of the cynical and selective use of UN resolutions being made by the Western powers; he knew perfectly well that a UN-sponsored war in the Gulf would not lead to justice for the Palestinians or to an end to US interference in Central America.

During the debate, Jo Richardson, in the conference chair, refused to call Tony Benn, who stood directly in front of her with his hand raised throughout the session. It was a dramatic illustration of just how far the Party had travelled in a few short years. Richardson, a vice-president of CND, was clearly under instructions not to allow Benn to speak. She did, however, call Denis Healey and John Edmonds, who, visibly carried away by the rhetoric of war, opposed the FBU resolution because, he said, it would inhibit commanders in the field from taking "pre-emptive strike action".

The carve-up of the debate infuriated many delegates. After all, Tony Benn was the leading anti-war spokesperson in the country. One leading television correspondent was flabbergasted, privately describing it as "a disgraceful stitch-up, even by their standards". Kinnock's spin-doctors counterattacked, deriding Benn as a "vain old man" and claiming he had no right to speak from the floor because he was a member of the NEC. In fact, Benn himself was careful never to claim he had any automatic right to speak in the debate and confined his public response to objecting to John Edmonds' insensitive remarks.

Although the FBU resolution was defeated by 4,862,000 votes to 623,000, it won the support of over 80 per cent of constituency parties. Although a number of the larger unions present already had executive policies similar to the FBU resolution, none of them was prepared to vote for it. At the last minute, NUPE's Tom Sawyer had arranged for Clare Short to replace the anti-war MP Alice Mahon on the NUPE delegation. The delegation then voted by a majority of one not to back the FBU resolution, which certainly would have been passed at any NUPE conference.

In a Commons debate held on November 8th Gerald Kaufman praised the "wise words" of foreign secretary Douglas Hurd on the need to ensure "maximum support" for the international coalition against Saddam Hussein. "During the past three months," he told the Commons, "we have proceeded parallel to the government and we hope that will continue." In his speech Martin O'Neill went further. He took the view that "military action will come and that when it does we will have to use the force of arms with care but with some regret because we sought a peaceful solution". There was no alternative because "all the signs are that there is little likelihood of the Iraqi authorities expressing any interest in a negotiated settlement". O'Neill then suggested that it was necessary to humiliate Iraq. "It is fair to say that if we realize our objectives by peaceful means but do not at the same time secure either the dismantling by treaty or the destruction by force of arms of Iraq's nuclear and chemical capabilities, any solution that we achieve will be a pyrrhic one."

On November 11th a further brief debate in the House saw another vote on an adjournment motion, thanks once again to the determined cadre of anti-war Labour MPs. This time, thirty-nine Labour MPs voted against the government. The opposition front bench and the Labour whips continued to voted with them. Among Labour dissenters were a number of MPs never previously associated with the Campaign Group, including the newly elected MPs for Paisley North and South, Irene Adams and Gordon McMaster, as well as David Lambie, Harry Ewing, Norman Godman and John McAllion. In a further vote in December, Labour's anti-war ranks swelled to a total of forty-two MPs.

The UN Security Council imposed a January 15th deadline for Iraqi withdrawal from Kuwait; after that, it warned, military action could start at any time. As the deadline neared, the Labour leadership grew uneasy about its ability to maintain Party unity if war commenced. It began putting new emphasis on the importance of sanctions – which up till then had hardly featured in front-bench speeches. O'Neill announced that Labour would "take into account" the findings of the Security Council's sanctions committee before "reaching its own decision about whether war is necessary". It soon transpired, however, that the sanctions committee had no plans to produce any report.[2] Just how out of touch O'Neill had grown was revealed when his own Clackmannon CLP voted to invite Tam Dalyell, a prominent opponent of war, to address a public meeting in the constituency.

Stories began appearing in the press claiming a revolt over the Gulf was brewing in the shadow cabinet. John Prescott fuelled speculation by telling reporters, "Labour supports the UN but there is a healthy suspicion within the shadow cabinet that this is not the view of the US or British governments. . . . I fully support the use of force if it is shown to be necessary, but the momentum seems to be in favour of war, not peace."[3] A few days later Robin Cook chose to tell the BBC's On the Record that all possible options had to be explored "to avoid any precipitate military action". It was necessary, he said, to consider "whether sanctions have yet had time to do the job".[4]

Cook and Prescott were sending a signal via the media to the Labour Party leadership. The day after Cook's remarks were reported, an article by Kaufman appeared in the Guardian saying that sanctions should be given a chance beyond the January 15th deadline. Kinnock seemed to confirm the new posture when he emerged from a 35-minute talk with US Secretary of State James Baker to tell the world that he was in favour of "the prolonged and patient pursuit of sanctions . . . if force becomes necessary it will have to be because sanctions are proved to be not capable of achieving the objectives".[5]

Meanwhile, the spin-doctors let the press know that Kinnock had assured Baker that Labour still backed the Tory government on the Gulf and that Labour would "support British soldiers if a war started, regardless of its reservations about the timing of the use of force".[6] The leadership's sudden interest in sanctions was intended only for internal Labour Party consumption. The dissenting shadow cabinet members quickly told the press – unattributably, of course – that the statements made by Kaufman and Kinnock would "unite the Party" and were like "opening a safety valve that was about to blow".[7]

All of this was part of a ghastly game played by the leadership, the "soft left" and the media over Labour's Gulf policy. For "soft left" members of the front bench, dropping hints to the media was a punishment-free way of making their dissent over the coming war known to the Party rank and file while at the same time maintaining their loyalty to the leadership. For the leadership, such muted, often coded opposition was easy to control and, in any case, gave it another chance to show the establishment that it was tough enough to tame internal dissent in times of "national crisis". Press reports of front-bench dissent were inevitably followed by denunciations and threats of discipline issuing from the leader's office.

The media made much of the existence of the "supper club" of leading "soft lefts" who were allegedly unhappy with Kinnock's hawkish stance on the Gulf. Among the front-bench members named in the press as attending its meetings were John Prescott, Michael Meacher, Robin Cook, Margaret Beckett, Clare Short, Joan Lestor, Joan Ruddock, Jo Richardson, Chris Smith, Joan Walley and Mark Fisher. In fact this so-called club had been meeting on and off for some years and its most distinctive feature was the complete inability of any of its members to stick together on any issue. The media did not discover the "supper club", nor did they expose any plot against Neil Kinnock. There was no such plot. The "minutes left on a photocopier" that supposedly brought the existence of the club to light were a deliberate leak. No one was sure at this stage how the war would develop and how public opinion would respond to it, and they were keeping their options open.

If front-bench "supper club" members had collectively decided to oppose war they would have enjoyed the support of a large segment, possibly a majority, of both the Parliamentary Labour Party and the Party membership. Certainly any attempt by Kinnock to purge the entire front bench of anti-war sentiment would have led to a backlash. By their silence, their refusal to take joint action to change Labour's position, these MPs helped Kinnock to keep the Party in line behind the war. And this, in turn, was vital to George Bush's international alliance, without which he could not have proceeded with the war. The equivocation of the "soft left" was therefore a contributory factor – only one among many, but a real one nevertheless – in the avoidable and inexcusable Gulf War.

Some Labour MPs seemed to regard peace in the Party as more important than peace in the Middle East. On a free vote, a majority of Labour MPs would probably have refused to back the government's policy uncritically. Because the Labour front bench could not get enough Labour MPs to speak for war it connived with the Tories to truncate the debates for fear that anti-war MPs would dominate them. Tony Benn pressed the Speaker, the Labour leader and even the new Prime Minister, John Major, for a debate on a substantive motion on the crisis throughout December 1990 and early January 1991 but was always rebuffed. From the beginning of the crisis until the war ended in February 1991, the only debate about the war or war-related issues in opposition time was that held by the Scottish National Party.

On January 14th, the day before the UN deadline, the NEC international committee met. Benn brought a motion calling on the Labour leader to take a personal initiative for a peaceful solution. Another motion from the National Graphical Association (NGA) national council called for sanctions to be given more time to work and urged the leadership to call for diplomacy to resolve the crisis. Kinnock dismissed Benn's motion as "cynical populism", insisting that "we cannot signal weakness to Saddam Hussein". Warning of the "devastating consequences of Saddam Hussein retaining status as a superpower", Kinnock informed the NEC that, in his view, "you cannot postpone a war against Iraq".

It was easy to dismiss Benn but not the NGA. Tony Clarke and SOGAT official Ted O'Brien put together an emergency motion which incorporated much of the sentiment of the NGA statement but insisted that the "freeing of Kuwait" was necessary. The motion did, however, clearly stipulate that "UN authorized forces should not undertake military action before sanctions have been in operation long enough to have the maximum effect".[8] This motion was passed unanimously by the committee with support from both Kinnock and Benn. It represented a shift in the Party's line away from outright warmongering and reflected the pressure the unions and the rank and file could still exert on the leadership.

Later that same day, however, Jack Cunningham told the Commons that the major debate on the war scheduled for January 14th and 15th "will enable us to place on record our emphatic support for the United Nations and for all efforts to find a peaceful solution. If, regrettably, armed conflict occurs – we have never ruled that out – the British forces will have our total support." At this time opinion polls showed up to half the population was still doubtful about the use of force.

In the shadow cabinet Kinnock had come down hard against Labour putting any motion or amendment in the debate, and he refused to bring forward the regular Wednesday morning meeting of the Parliamentary Labour Party so that it could precede the Commons vote. Bradford West MP Max Madden organized an informal meeting for Labour MPs to discuss the issues before the public debate; it was attended by twenty-two MPs, who agreed to send a delegation to Kinnock to urge him to change his line on the Gulf. Kinnock rejected their proposals out of hand, including their plea that he give public backing to a last-minute peace proposal from the French president, François Mitterrand.

The leadership connived with the Tories to ensure that once again no substantive motion on the Gulf would be put to the House on January 15th. In the debate, backbench Tory MP Edwina Currie, oblivious to the irony, urged the Commons to emulate the unanimity of the Iraqi parliament in backing government war policy. For his part Neil Kinnock seemed to agree. In his speech he disparaged negotiations, peace conferences, linkage between the Palestine question and the Gulf crisis, and described Saddam Hussein as a menace who had to be dealt with. It was left to Edward Heath to point out that the logic of this position was the military conquest of Iraq itself.

Once more dividing the House on a procedural motion, fifty-seven MPs voted against the government, making January 15th the high point of parliamentary opposition to the war. The Labour dissenters ranged far beyond the usual confines of the Campaign Group left and included such figures as Alex Eadie, Terry Davis, Jim Cousins, Andrew Faulds, Doug Hoyle, Mike Watson and Bob Litherland. Another thirty-one Labour MPs abstained. Maria Fyfe and John McFall voted against the government and then resigned their front-bench portfolios. Fyfe complained about the pressure from Kinnock's office to turn every issue and every vote into a loyalty test. "When people are putting lives on the line, to attempt to turn it into a leadership issue is contemptible."[9] Clare Short, who up till now had toed the leadership line, abstained. She told Tribune that the vote went "very badly" for the Labour Party; the failure to table a resolution meant that there seemed to be no clear distinction between Labour and the Tories.[10]

When the Parliamentary Labour Party finally met on January 16th, the day after the Commons debate and two days before war broke out, the MPs for Edinburgh East and Bristol South, Gavin Strang and Dawn Primarolo, joint convenors of an ad hoc group of anti-war MPs, put forward a motion stating that force should not be used before sanctions had had more time to work. This motion was identical in content to the motion passed at the NEC international committee and therefore was ostensibly the Party's official line, which made it impossible for the leadership to oppose it openly. Kinnock, near hysteria, told assembled Labour MPs that "we must save the Party" and that although he would back the Strang–Primarolo motion "we don't control the timetable . . . if we don't back the war we will be destroyed . . . we must make clear we are not pacifists . . . " Later, the official minutes of the meetings carried a toned-down version of Kinnock's speech in which he was said to have argued that "we had voted in the same lobby as the government but we had been voting to extend the authority of the UN". Kaufman was more controlled and more aware of the stakes. Avoiding the question of military action altogether, he said there could and should be Party unity around the need for more time for sanctions.

The Strang–Primarolo motion was passed unanimously. This was clearly a setback for the leadership, which had been cornered into making a modest break from the bipartisan consensus on the Gulf. But soon Kinnock's media management team got to work. The vote was presented as a victory for the leadership; once again Kinnock had united the Party around his position and isolated the openly anti-war faction. *Tribune* also bought the story; it reported with a straight face the comment of an anonymous but supposedly authoritative source that the new position meant "sanctions should be given at least a year". But it was compelled to note that "little seems to have resulted from the moderate and conscience-racked rebellion in the Shadow Cabinet . . . there is no logic in a position which states that, although war now would be wrong, if one starts, we will support 'our troops' ".[11]

On January 15th Larry Whitty sent all CLPs and affiliates a letter outlining Labour Party policy on the Gulf; it was Walworth Road's first and last communication on the subject. Confused and contradictory, it emphasized the role of the UN and the need for continuing use of sanctions so that the desired outcome be achieved without further use of force. The PLP Campaign Briefing sent to Labour MPs at the end of January by Jack Cunningham was less equivocal; it offered "clear and total" support for British troops fighting in the Gulf and criticized calls for any ceasefire that might "give substance to Saddam Hussein's propaganda". Cunningham added:

> After this war we cannot allow the situation of insecurity and suffering in the Middle East to continue . . . the war in the Gulf has removed any possibility that there can be a return to pre-war conditions when the fighting ends . . .

In reality, he and the rest of the Labour leadership had no intention of pressing the Tory government or the United States to redress the long-standing injustices that made the Middle East a powder keg. But they offered just this post-bellum prospect as an inducement to wavering Labour MPs to climb aboard the pro-war bandwagon. When the war ended, the rapid return to pre-war conditions in the region was not greeted by any protest from the Labour front bench.

The problem Cunningham was wrestling with was highlighted by the strong resistance to the war among Labour Members of the European Parliament (MEPs). On January 15th, thirty of Labour's forty-five MEPs, including several normally associated with the leadership, signed a statement against the use of military force. A week later, a motion calling for a ceasefire was put to the European Parliament and won the support of twenty-four Labour MEPs; only sixteen voted against it and two more abstained. Heavy pressure from Kinnock's office, outraged at this sudden outbreak of disloyalty, had little effect. The MEPs were far from Westminster, not dependent on Kinnock's personal favour for advancement within the European Parliament, and less sheltered than most MPs from the realities of international politics.

War finally commenced in the early hours of January 18th, three days after the expiry of the US–UN deadline, when the bombing of Iraqi targets began. Kinnock rose in the Commons to tell the nation, "our forces naturally have our complete support". He commended the "dual aims of maximizing the disabling of Iraqi military strength and minimizing any harm to civilians". This was actually a broader set of aims than those laid down by John Major, who stuck to the simple objective of getting "Iraq out of Kuwait". Liberal Democrat leader Paddy Ashdown picked up the discrepancy and said it was "reassuring . . . that the Prime Minister laid out so clearly the limited aims of the operation".

Only anti-war backbenchers raised the question of civilian casualties and challenged the carpet bombing of Iraqi cities. Tony Benn told a silent Commons that in spite of all the pro-UN rhetoric, shooting had started without any authorization from the UN Secretary General. This point should have been at the heart of contributions from the Labour front bench if the statements agreed by the conference, the NEC international committee and the Parliamentary Labour Party had been anything other than fig leaves to cover the nakedness of Labour's support for a US-led war.

The following day *The Times* reported that "ministers have joined forces with their Labour counterparts to minimise backbench opposition to government policy in the Gulf".[12] The government motion for the major debate on the war scheduled for January 21st had been agreed in advance with the Labour leadership. The Labour amendment to it had likewise been agreed in secret beforehand.

At a special meeting of the Parliamentary Labour Party, convened before the debate, Gerald Kaufman told MPs that Labour had to support British troops. Declaring that a ceasefire would serve no purpose, Kaufman again referred to the need for a solution to the Palestinian problem, and to the need to end the arms trade. There was, he said, "a huge agenda which could only be tackled by the authority of the UN", which, he predicted, would be enhanced by a successful resolution of the Gulf crisis. Kinnock emphasized that Labour must do nothing to allow itself to be accused of being "anti-war or anti-troops". He urged Labour MPs to support the Allied action "not because it is popular" but because Labour "must support the UN".

In the Commons debate on the 21st of January, for the first time in the Gulf crisis, a substantive motion was put by the government and a complementary opposition amendment was tabled. In the debate the government announced that it had accepted Labour's anodyne amendment. The machinations of both front benches thus denied MPs the opportunity to vote on an amendment that actually opposed the war and offered an alternative to the government's course. In the vote that followed the debate, thirty-six Labour MPs voted against the motion proposed by the government and amended by their own front bench. All were described by the *Daily Star* the following day as "treacherous swine". Another forty-nine Labour MPs did not vote at all; a total of eighty-five Labour MPs thus defied the whip. Among those voting against the government were Tony Banks and Leeds North West MP John Battle, both of whom promptly resigned from the front bench.

At the January meeting of the NEC, the leadership tabled a two-page statement which "regretted" that sanctions had not been given longer to work but went on to call for "the substantial disarming of Iraq" including the "complete removal of chemical, biological and nuclear weapons and the means of making them".[13] Not content with the official objective of securing the expulsion of Iraq from Kuwait, Labour was calling in effect for a permanent occupation of Iraq – a major extension of the war aims. The Labour leadership had trapped itself in this posture because it knew it could not sell the real war aims to the Party. In a desire to appear more serious than the Tories about the long-term issues raised by the crisis, it stumbled onto an agenda that could only have succeeded in hopelessly widening and prolonging the war had the government adopted it.

Benn and Skinner put forward an amendment calling for the reconvening of the UN Security Council, an immediate ceasefire and a peace conference to examine all Middle Eastern issues. In the ensuing debate, Robin Cook argued that although sanctions would have worked and war should not have started, there could not possibly be a ceasefire now and therefore the NEC had no alternative but to support Kinnock's position. Reading from a prepared statement, John Prescott went out of his way to make clear that he had never had any differences with the leader. He disclaimed reports of his doubts about the war and concluded that neither a ceasefire nor a UN meeting would help. He therefore "backed Neil", as did Clare Short, who thought that Kinnock's resolution was good but did not go far enough because in her opinion Syria (a member of the anti-Iraq coalition) should also be disarmed. David Blunkett also declared himself against a unilateral ceasefire. Neil Kinnock chose to sum up the debate, stating that Labour now faced a shooting war with British troops involved and a new Tory leader enjoying a honeymoon with the public. Again and again he argued that Labour had no choice but to support the war if the Party was to win the coming election. Benn's amendment was defeated with only Benn, Skinner and the MSF representative Barbara Switzer voting for it. Blunkett, Cook, Gould, Prescott, Jo Richardson and Short all voted against and supported Kinnock's resolution widening the war aims.

Speaking at the Royal United Services Institute on January 24th, Kinnock criticized the lack of "instinctive European Community cooperation over the Gulf" and called on Germany and Japan to contribute more funds to the war effort. He said Labour would once more review its defence policy in the light of the Gulf crisis and went so far as to claim that the UK had a "right of influence" in the Middle East.[14] The leadership had shifted from trying to out-Europe the Tories to trying to out-Kipling them: left-wing critics accused Kinnock of adopting the ideology of the "white man's burden".

Despite his volte-face at the NEC, John Prescott found himself attacked by Kinnock's office in the newspapers. The *Observer* claimed:

> According to a senior Kinnock aide, "Neil thinks it is incredible that someone who aspires to ministerial office in a matter of months should behave in this treacherous way." When he is Prime Minister he will not have to stick to those elected to the Shadow Cabinet. He can include or exclude who he likes.

To rub salt in the wound, the anonymous source also raised Prescott's recent conviction on a driving offence.[15] *The Sunday Times* went further, citing an unnamed Kinnock source to the effect that Prescott would not become secretary of state for transport in a Kinnock cabinet.[16] Later the press reported that Prescott and Kinnock had met and resolved their differences, which apparently had only ever existed in the minds of the media. Kinnock vigorously denied having anything to do with placing the stories in newspapers; Prescott, meanwhile, continued to tell reporters that the "supper club" was working to influence Kinnock from the inside.

Labour MPs Harry Barnes and John McAllion put a resolution to a Party meeting on February 6th that disclaimed any extension of the war aims beyond the removal of Iraq from Kuwait. Terry Davis and Norman Godman wanted to amend the NEC statement to include among the Party's war aims the establishment of a democratically elected government in Kuwait. Whilst Bradford South MP Bob Cryer proposed an amendment attacking the hypocrisy of the Tories on arms sales and the hijacking of the UN by the US, Clare Short proposed that the meeting should welcome and reaffirm the NEC statement which, her amendment claimed, did not extend the war aims.

Kinnock and Kaufman opposed all the resolutions and amendments and insisted that the meeting endorse the NEC statement as a whole without qualification. Only seventy-four Labour MPs, 32 per cent of the Parliamentary Labour Party, bothered to attend the meeting. Kaufman declared a ceasefire "unthinkable", whilst Durham North MP Giles Radice told the meeting, "if we behave responsibly we will win the election". His definition of responsibility was, evidently, uncritical collusion with the government's war policy.

Once again, Kinnock, on the verge of hysterics, addressed the MPs. Labour, he said, "must win the election" and the NEC statement would work to Labour's "political advantage". "We can't limit the war aims," he declared frantically, dismissing the efforts of the French and Soviet governments to initiate peace talks and adding for good measure that sanctions would have to continue after the war. Finally, he demanded that Labour MPs "stop these weekly services in the religion of distrust". When put to the vote all the amendments were defeated and the Barnes/McAllion resolution was withdrawn. About one third of the Labour MPs present voted against the leadership.

The killing of several hundred civilians by the bombing of a Baghdad bunker on February 11th galvanized latent disquiet about the war both inside and outside the Labour Party. In the House, only anti-war MPs Tam Dalyell, Dennis Skinner, Tony Banks and Tony Benn tried to press the government over the event. There was no reappraisal from Kinnock, despite his earlier insistence on minimizing harm to civilians. He told the Parliamentary Labour Party, "the tragedies of the Iraqi people would be used by Saddam Hussein to obscure the atrocities he had committed".

But as news of the level of civilian casualties came through, the unity of Labour MPs came under strain. Robin Cook expressed concern about civilian casualties. In the course of being interviewed on radio about health issues, he went out of his way to explain that he thought it was unnecessary "to blow up every power station, water supply, every bridge in Iraq". The next day the *Daily Mirror* asked "whose side" he was on, but Cook was quick to assure inquiring journalists that his remarks had been cleared by Kinnock's office, which then reminded Cook, again via the newspapers, that Labour's war policy was "outside his portfolio".

Joan Ruddock, a junior transport spokesperson, was also disquieted by the bombing, which, she said, was beginning to go beyond what the UN intended. Ruddock had gained national prominence as the spokesperson for CND and on this basis she had been selected as a Labour candidate in 1987 by the Deptford constituency in south London. After abstaining on the crucial January 21st vote, she explained her position to the angry members of her general committee. She felt she could not jeopardize her work as a front-bench spokesperson and told the meeting that Kinnock's position on the war would have been even worse without the efforts of the "supper club". At one point she claimed she had not abandoned any of her principles, but conceded that she wrestled with her conscience and considered resignation. After her public remarks on the Baghdad bombing, Ruddock was summoned by Kinnock, who told her that she had to stick to her front-bench transport brief or face the sack. She chose the former.

At the same time Clare Short became the fifth Labour MP to leave the front bench over the war. She had abstained in the January 15th vote before war actually commenced and then joined the pro-war lobby in the crucial January 21st vote. She had voted for Kinnock's NEC resolution extending the war aims and made clear her support for the destruction of Saddam Hussein and his "war machine". But after the Baghdad bombing, Short changed her position and criticized the US military strategy. According to some accounts she was then sacked from the front bench following a private meeting with Kinnock; according to others she resigned. Short herself seemed confused about which scenario would play better. In any case, she was quick to assure the media that she had not criticized the leadership and had left the front bench not because she disagreed with the war policy but because she wanted to be free to speak her mind.

Neither Short nor any of the other "soft left" MPs played any role in organizing opposition to the war inside or outside Parliament. Without their help, a small core of openly anti-war MPs worked tirelessly to raise the arguments against war in the Commons, through the media and at hundreds of local public meetings. In so doing they became for a time the real leaders of the opposition in Britain. Though isolated within Parliament, they enjoyed substantial support elsewhere in the labour movement. A number of trade unions affiliated to the Labour Party voted to support the Committee to Stop War in the Gulf. Among them were BETA, FBU, MSF, NUM, TGWU Region 1, NGA London Region, MSF West Midlands Region, MSF Eastern Region. Members of the TGWU, NUPE, UCATT and AEU executives backed various anti-war initiatives, as did scores of TGWU, NCU, UCW and UCATT branches. A demonstration against war in Glasgow on January 12th was joined by ten Labour MPs and three Labour MEPs, as well as the assistant general secretary of the Scottish TUC. At the last minute a message of support was sent to the rally by the Scottish Labour Party executive.

Throughout this period there was a solid base of public disquiet over the war that an anti-war Labour Party could have mobilized and educated. A study by Hull University showed that 32 per cent of the public were "worried by the violence of the war"; only 12 per cent "felt good because of British and allied successes"; even 40 per cent of *Sun* readers thought the paper "glorified the war too much"; and 37 per cent thought the most acceptable war aim was "a Middle East peace settlement, including the Palestine question".[17]

When the Iraqi leadership put out the first peace feelers at the beginning of the third week of February, Gerald Kaufman told the Commons that the land attack should go ahead, because nothing less than "unconditional surrender" should be acceptable. At that week's meeting of Labour MPs Bill Michie and Terry Davis proposed that Labour call for a ceasefire and a new round of diplomatic initiatives. Joan Ruddock suggested that Michie's motion ought not to be discussed at all because of the Soviet initiatives then in progress. Kaufman, however, was not interested in compromise; he wanted the motion defeated. Kinnock once more lectured MPs about their responsibility to win the next election: "We are professional politicians and if we do not take account of short-term electoral considerations why the hell are we drawing our salaries?" Although the leadership won the vote with the support of some 90 Labour MPs, lobby correspondents were told that 210 MPs had attended the meeting and voted six to one to support Kinnock. The only surprising thing about this preposterous lie was that the media swallowed it whole.

Some days later the land war was finally launched. As Allied forces swept through Kuwait and southern Iraq it soon became apparent that Saddam's "war machine" was not as fearsome as the public had been led to believe. On February 26th, in the House of Commons, Kaufman and foreign secretary Douglas Hurd congratulated each other on the success of Operation Desert Storm. No Labour front-bench member asked why the war was continuing when Saddam Hussein's troops were in the process of withdrawing from Kuwait or why Allied planes continued to bomb and strafe retreating Iraqi soldiers.

The next day at the regular NEC meeting Benn and Skinner again proposed a ceasefire. Even now, with George Bush and John Major themselves contemplating such a move, with the Iraqis ousted from Kuwait and in full flight up the road to Basra, Kinnock would not relent. He claimed that thanks to his efforts Labour would now be able to rebut Tory smears that it was soft on defence. The statement he submitted to the NEC was nearly two pages long but contained little of substance. It insisted on proceeding with the war until Saddam Hussein's "full compliance" with UN resolutions was clear, and noted that this would be difficult to determine given "Saddam's continual inconsistency and dishonesty". It also had the cheek to welcome "the government's statements limiting the war aims to those previously specified by the Labour Party and its spokespeople".[18]

David Blunkett proposed an amendment to Kinnock's statement to the effect that the UN should not be dominated by the United States. John

Prescott objected to the slaughter of retreating Iraqi troops and argued that the war should stop now. He also proposed an amendment to Kinnock's statement. Clare Short wanted Kinnock's proposals to dismantle Iraqi nuclear and chemical capability amended so that they would apply to all the powers in the region.

Kinnock was livid at the spectacle of the "soft left" shying at the last hurdle. "We know the UN is ineffectual but we can't say it now," he said, "it would be used against us." He then launched a bitter attack on anti-war campaigners by charging that "some people are waiting for the body bags to come home to justify their positions" and insisted that because no one could trust Saddam Hussein the ground war must continue. He added, in a reference to the coming general election, "We have a war to fight." Labour, he said, was "powerless" to affect the course of the war. "Sanctions would not have worked." Personally, he declared, he hated the "creepy crawly" business with the Tories across the despatch box over the war, but he did it "to help the Party".

After this outburst, Prescott withdrew his amendment. Blunkett toned his down so that it merely said that the UN should not be dominated by "a single power", omitting specific mention of the US. Kinnock still rejected it. The vote against Benn's proposal was eighteen votes to five. Blunkett's was defeated by fourteen votes to seven. Clare Short's was defeated by thirteen votes to ten. The main resolution from Kinnock was then agreed by the margin of eighteen votes to three.[19] Twelve hours after Labour's NEC had rejected a ceasefire in the Gulf, Bush and his allies declared one and ended the shooting war.

Throughout the Gulf crisis, Labour's leaders had helped cloak the US-led military adventure with the respectability of "international support". Bipartisanship in the House of Commons hamstrung the anti-war movement, depriving it of legitimacy and resources, and helped block the emergence of a genuine, nationwide debate on the war. ITN editor Stuart Purvis explained the almost total absence of anti-war comment on television: "The role of the opposition party in Parliament is important to our news coverage. Labour is synchronised to government policy so that the level of debate on television matches the level of debate in Parliament."[20]

During the general election campaign just a year after the Gulf War ended, the Tories were too embarrassed to raise the war as they had raised the Falklands in 1983. There was too much unfinished business, too many question marks over the real aims and effects of the military action. 110,000 Allied sorties had been flown and the equivalent of 88,000 tonnes of TNT, equal to seven Hiroshimas, had been dropped on Iraq. The Allied bombardment had destroyed the economic infrastructure of Iraq. The Pentagon estimated that some 250,000 Iraqis had been killed.

Kuwait was still a corrupt despotism. The Palestinians were still stateless. The Kurds were still under attack. Saddam Hussein was still in power.

Had Labour opposed the war, it could at least have challenged the government's record on all these questions; it could have asked what kind of government sacrifices human life for economic interest. Labour's performance throughout the Gulf crisis won it few friends. The Party leader was bellicose and bullying. Rather than address the serious moral and political issues raised by war, the shadow cabinet played word games with the media and with each other. Fear of losing a minor job on the front bench seemed the main motivating factor for scores of MPs. It was a profoundly alienating spectacle for anyone, young or old, who believed that politics was about something more than personal advancement.

Notes

1. *The Times* 4 October 1990.
2. *Guardian* 4 January 1991.
3. ibid.
4. *Independent* 7 January 1991.
5. *Guardian* 8 January 1991.
6. ibid.
7. *Tribune* 10 January 1991.
8. NEC International Committee minutes January 1990.
9. *Tribune* 22 February 1991.
10. ibid.
11. *Tribune* 18 January 1991.
12. *The Times* 19 January 1991.
13. NEC minutes January 1991.
14. *Guardian* 25 January 1991.
15. *Observer* 10 February 1991.
16. *Sunday Times* 10 February 1991.
17. *New Statesman and Society* 8 March 1991.
18. NEC minutes February 1991.
19. ibid.
20. *Free Press*, "Campaign for Press and Broadcasting Freedom", March 1991.

One Member, No Vote

8

Everything Must Go!
Selling Labour to the Media

> A political party does not truly exist unless it is
> divided against itself.
>
> *Hegel*

Campaigning and Communicating

Throughout the 1970s, Harold Wilson and Jim Callaghan pursued their own personal media strategies from a beleaguered 10 Downing Street. Both were obsessed with cabinet leaks and both saw the principal enemy as the left, notably Tony Benn. The media's appetite for splits between the Labour Party and the Labour government was insatiable. Wilson and Callaghan responded by posing as national leaders above Party control. This only succeeded in confirming the view that Labour was dangerously extreme and therefore not to be trusted with power; it also enabled the media to portray the leader as unable to control his own Party and therefore unable to govern the country. Kinnock and his advisers were to draw important lessons from this experience.

It would be hard to have a worse press than Labour had in the early 1980s. Week in, week out, the Party was portrayed as divided, chaotic, extremist, incompetent and dissembling. Fleet Street was given ready assistance by shadow cabinet members and Walworth Road employees, who supplied a flow of hostile quotes and unflattering stories. As for Labour Party activists, their voices were heard only during the direct television broadcasting of Labour's annual conference. Apart from that they had to put up with being routinely traduced by their Party leaders as well as by the media. The story is not simply one of media unfairness to the Labour left but of collusion between the media and the Labour leadership in attacking the left, to the detriment of the Labour Party as a whole.

By now it ought to be axiomatic that the media will give the Labour leadership favourable coverage when it is battering its own left wing or its trade union supporters but that when it moves against the Tories or any part of the British establishment it will be given a hard time. The hostility of the media has long been a popular theme of Labour politics, but seldom is anything done about its root causes. As Roy Hattersley admitted at a Campaign for Press and Broadcasting Freedom conference a few years back, "There is no media policy other than pragmatic policy." The Labour front bench, in and out of government, even at the height of Wilson's paranoia, has always backed the broadcasting hierarchies and the undemocratic, secretive system that maintains them. Again and again, Labour conferences have demanded media reform, some minimal tilting of the balance away from the Conservative Party and the employers, but again and again Labour in Parliament has declined to pursue these demands, even when they were begging to be raised, as during the debates on the Broadcasting Bill in 1990. Complaints about the role of the Tory tabloids after the 1992 general election carried little weight because the Party's front bench had been so unwilling for so many years to raise the underlying problem of media ownership.

Since the Labour leadership under Kinnock had no intention of challenging the bias of the media (not to mention the concentration of media ownership), it faced a major problem: how to deal with the reality of flagrant media hostility to the Labour Party, its personnel and its policies? Its way out of this problem was to try to recast the Party in the image preferred by the media, to do its bidding on issue after issue, to perform all the ritual exorcisms demanded by the pundits.

Following Labour's 1983 general election defeat there was a clamour at all levels of the Party for major improvements in Labour's "image" and hence in its media and campaigning strategy. Kinnock, the GMB leadership, the "soft left" and others exploited this sentiment; they argued that the Labour Party needed to adapt to the new realities of the televisual age. It needed to present its message in a more co-ordinated, professional fashion. In so doing they were always careful to assure Party members that this would require no changes in policy. In effect they offered a technical solution to what everyone – left and right – knew was a political problem.

The first fruit of the new approach to public relations was Labour's Jobs and Industry campaign, described by the *Guardian* as the "biggest and most expensive campaign ever undertaken" by the Labour Party.[1] Launched in April 1985, its purpose, according to Kinnock, was to "increase Labour's credibility as a party that can manage the economy competently and fairly".[2]

The initial launch document declared that the purpose of the campaign was to "present Labour as a party of production", not "a well-meaning party which prints money for social objectives".[3] This rhetoric was periodically reinvoked over the coming years and was dusted off in the 1992 general election, when it became clear that the one thing the Party's campaign machine had utterly failed to do was to establish Labour as a credible manager of the economy.

Jobs and Industry was originally scheduled to run to the 1985 Labour conference and then to be relaunched in a "second phase" for another year after that. In effect it drifted right up to and through the 1987 general election. In its first year the campaign consisted of nine booklets or "charters" touching various employment-related subjects, six leaflets (most of which sat undistributed in head or regional offices) plus sweat-shirts, stickers, beermats, paper hats, videos and a poster. Dissemination of all of these was confined almost entirely to circles of Party loyalists. Waste was enormous.

The buzzwords that made up the bulk of the Jobs and Industry campaign, like those in Freedom and Fairness (1986), Meet the Challenge, Make the Change (1989), Looking to the Future (1990), Opportunity Britain (1991) and Made in Britain (1992), were the subject of lengthy debate among public relations consultants, Walworth Road full-time workers, staff in the leader's office and a handful of selected shadow cabinet members, but none of them ever struck a chord with the public. The real message of the whole package, as interpreted by the media, was twofold. First, Labour had at last discovered the modern science of public relations, which the media considered good news because it was an acknowledgement of their own power and importance. Second, Labour was playing down its radical policies and trying to appear sensible, which also pleased the media, not least because they enjoyed the spectacle of Labour struggling to conform to their own prejudices.

Inevitably, the need to transmogrify Labour's image was used to justify changes in policy. Here the so-called lessons of the 1983 manifesto, the "longest suicide note in history", were cited in support of a strategy of curtailing the volume and detail of Labour's commitments, as if the problem was one of sheer quantity and not one of content and internal consistency. In 1985 Geoff Bish, newly appointed as Labour's first Director of Policy after a decade of running the research department, proposed to cut back sharply the number of political pledges made by the Party. This was in his view a step by which Labour would not only "avoid giving the impression of making promises which will not be believed; but we will also avoid making unnecessary enemies".[4] Thus, as early as mid 1985 the interdependence of Labour's media and policy strategies was being openly articulated; Bish had spelled out the principle that was to guide Labour into and out of the 1987 defeat and was to disarm the Party disastrously in 1992.

Enter Mandelson

In September 1985 the NEC appointed Peter Mandelson as the Labour Party's first ever Director of Campaigns and Communications. The idea of having a single post responsible for all publicity and campaigning at Walworth Road, first mooted in the Labour Co-ordinating Committee document written by Patricia Hewitt in 1983, was taken up by the review committee established to overhaul Labour's full-time apparatus in 1985. The review recommended the establishment of a campaigns and communications directorate (CCD) responsible for Party campaigns, press and publicity, broadcasting, political and psephological intelligence, printing and design and sales and marketing. The new director would be among the Labour Party's most senior full-time officials, working directly under the general secretary and accountable to the NEC.

Mandelson has claimed that he was headhunted for the job by Charles Clarke, Kinnock's senior personal adviser. In fact Mandelson himself sought out Clarke as soon as he heard about the new post; the head would appear to have done all the hunting on this safari. Mandelson's politics were on the far right edge of Labour's hard right. Party members who remembered his interventions on the Streatham CLP's general management committee and as a Lambeth councillor from 1979 to 1982 were surprised when he failed to defect, along with most of his colleagues, to the SDP.

By 1985 Charles Clarke and Peter Mandelson had known each other for well over a decade, going back to the days when Clarke was NUS president and Mandelson was chasing round Oxford colleges garnering votes for local student union elections. When Clarke was head of the International Youth Council, Mandelson was working for its British wing. Later, when Clarke became a Hackney councillor, Mandelson was employed as a community liaison worker with the council. After a stint as a researcher for MP Albert Booth, then Labour's transport spokesperson, Mandelson decided to leave politics; associates recall that he had given up on the Labour Party as hopelessly left-wing. For a while, he worked as a producer on LWT's *Weekend World*.

His principal opponent for the job was Nita Clarke, who had been Ken Livingstone's press officer at the GLC and had played a key role in managing the council's highly effective campaign against its own abolition by the Thatcher government. In those days advocates of "professionalization" and believers in the potential effectiveness of a bold, new campaigning strategy liked to point to GLC campaigns as the way forward; their populism, high public profile, humour and skilful exploitation of the media were held up as models for the rest of the Labour Party.

But many on the NEC in 1985 did not regard Nita Clarke's GLC connections as a recommendation. Mandelson, on the other hand, made a big impression; in the words of one observer, he was "tough, confident and thoroughly nasty". He told his interviewers that Labour should offer voters a choice of a "Swedish Britain rather than an American Britain". Its campaigning approach needed to be based on polling, competent leadership and, above all, discipline. He promised to "get rid of the dead wood". When asked his view of the Party conference, Mandelson said it would be nice to abolish it but that it was not worth the trouble. The NUM, Black Sections and the Liverpool councillors were all "negative influences" which had to be offset with "positive ones". At conference speakers should be organized to show that the floor and the platform were both competent and in harmony. When asked about women, he replied that Labour should appeal to them as parents and as part of a family team.[5]

Though Mandelson was clearly Kinnock's choice, the NEC was divided. On its first ballot 11 votes were cast for Mandelson, 10 for Clarke, and three for two other candidates. On the second Mandelson won with 14 votes to Clarke's 10.[6] Tom Sawyer privately explained that he had voted for Mandelson because Kinnock had promised in return to issue a strong statement in defence of local government. Such a statement was never made.

Mandelson believed that Labour's basic problem was that it appeared too left-wing and "extreme". The images of disorder and division in which the media had revelled in the early 1980s had to be replaced by images of harmony, competence and discipline. In other words, the public had to be convinced that Labour was a "safe bet". The best way to do this was to win over the mainstream media, to speak in their language and offer them the kind of stories they would present as "positive". Mandelson faced a number of obstacles in pursuing this strategy. One was the Party's membership, which he regarded as hopelessly infected with the virus of extremism and therefore a major liability. Another was the Party's policies, notably unilateralism and support for trade union rights, which he knew the media would never accept as legitimate. In this context Mandelson's preferred option was to promote the leader himself. He chose this course partly because he worked for Kinnock and it was what Kinnock wanted for himself and partly because it was the most effective means of undermining the membership and policies that he believed were damaging the Labour Party.

In contrast to Michael Foot or even, in a different way, Jim Callaghan, Kinnock had to be seen as someone with authority over his own Party. To demonstrate strength by virtue of a vigorous attack on Britain's political and economic establishment was ruled out from the start – after all, the whole point was to court the media, not antagonize it. An enemy within was required. Again and again in the following years Kinnock's only memorable public interventions were in intra-party controversies – attacking Militant, the miners, Liverpool, left-wing councillors, Black Sections, unilateralism, Poll Tax protesters, opponents of the Gulf War, the Campaign Group of Labour MPs, the leadership challenge of Benn and Heffer.

Mandelson quickly established himself as an independent power at Labour's Walworth Road headquarters. He cultivated his direct links to Kinnock's office and exploited them without inhibition. Whenever Mandelson took an initiative outside the knowledge of Larry Whitty or the NEC – to whom he was supposed to be accountable – he was always able to say that he had already cleared it with Kinnock. Mandelson, after all, could offer Kinnock a great deal that Whitty could not – direct access to the media, independent advice predicated on the well-being of Kinnock's career rather than that of the Party as a whole – without the baggage that Whitty brought with him, such as trade union connections, responsibility for an unwieldy apparatus and greater accountability to the NEC. Although nominally Mandelson's superior, Whitty was sidelined, effectively left to run the shop while Mandelson got on with the politics.

Immediately after his appointment, Mandelson had turned to public relations consultant Philip Gould. In December 1985 Gould presented a 64-page report which was circulated amongst a small number of people approved by Kinnock's office and Mandelson himself. Its recommendations included: centralized concentration on the mass media, rather than localized campaigning by CLPs; the simplification, repetition and orchestration of the Party's message via the mass media; total control exercised by the director of campaigns and communications; and the setting-up of a pool of volunteer media professionals with a full-time co-ordinator.

Over the next few months, Mandelson assembled his Shadow Communications Agency (SCA), an ever-changing team of volunteer advertising agents, TV producers, designers, copywriters and marketing experts completely independent of the paid staff at Walworth Road and of the NEC. Its nucleus came from the advertising agency Boase, Massimi, Pollitt, which had handled the highly successful GLC campaign (within a year its reputation on the left was to be severely blemished by its tasteless campaign for the ill-fated *News on Sunday*). Only Philip Gould and his professional partner Deborah Mattinson were to be paid by the Labour Party for their services. In March 1986 the existence and functions of the SCA were ratified at the NEC, which thereafter assumed the role of passive spectator as the SCA redesigned Labour's campaigning strategy and its political priorities. SCA volunteers were mostly high-powered professionals in their late twenties and early thirties. Many were genuinely keen to help Labour win the next election; very few were aware of the role their outfit was playing in changing not only the image but also the substance of the Labour Party. Most, indeed, were vaguely left-wing, confirmed unilateralists and members of CND. They had despaired over Labour's disastrous performances of 1979 and 1983 and were keen to offer their services. Almost none of them, however, had any practical political experience.

At the March 1986 NEC the SCA made an hour-long presentation entitled "Society and Self" based on a "qualitative survey" in which thirty groups of eight people had been interviewed for 90 minutes each. In effect, the Labour Party had paid several hundred thousand pounds to ascertain the views of 240 people. Some of these might have been Labour voters, though previous voting preferences were not ascertained. The object was ostensibly to develop a clear understanding of the "target voters" and to devise an appropriate campaigning approach. At the NEC members of the SCA flashed up a sequence of quotations from the interviewees expressing a range of social prejudices and platitudes. "It's nice to have a social conscience but it's your family that counts" was one example. The SCA concluded: "self-interest is the best guide to what people think . . . the government has legitimized self-interest . . . people were concerned with their health, their wealth and their safety . . . the breakdown of the family and the rise in crime".[7]

These revelations were followed by a presentation on the Labour Party's image and how it was perceived. The public, the SCA argued, was more interested in people than ideas; therefore the leadership image was crucial. People like Ken Livingstone, it was asserted, did great damage. Labour was said to be too associated with the poor, the unemployed, the sick, the disabled, pacifists, trade unions and minorities, all of which placed it at a great disadvantage to the Tories, who were increasingly seen to be "for everyone". Labour was seen as "yesterday's party" and did not appeal to those who saw themselves as "above average". Specific issues were transient in the voters' minds and faith in the Labour Party's competence in government was all. Internal disunity, lack of government experience and left-wing "infiltration" all damaged this faith. The SCA quoted one interviewee as saying: "If I had a brick I would throw it in Arthur Scargill's face." Another was quoted as saying: "Why should we give money to the gays?"[8]

To improve the leadership's image the SCA recommended "decisiveness, toughness and direction". Mandelson had always believed that "strong leadership" should be the core of the Labour Party's appeal and now had empirical "evidence" to back him up. In August 1986 Bob Worcester of MORI sent a memo to Kinnock and his team which warned that although the leader was liked he was not perceived as "strong". Other Labour MPs, especially front-benchers, needed to do more to "publicize Neil Kinnock's assets".

In tandem with Kinnock's office, Mandelson concentrated on cultivating a handful of influential contacts in the broadsheet press which, he knew, set the political agenda for the much more powerful broadcast media. He believed that no direct appeal to the electorate made by Labour could possibly have the same effect as positive media coverage. He therefore set out to win over a few lobby correspondents and a handful of editors by feeding them the kind of copy they wanted, by tailoring Labour's political priorities to their preferences and prejudices. This would set the framework for television and radio coverage, which was the real prize.

But this offensive served another function, equally vital to the leadership. It knew that the vast majority of labour movement activists rely for their information about the Party on the national press. No leaflet, circular, newsletter or public meeting can hope to gain anything like the attention that a single line in the *Guardian* receives. Again and again over the years, Kinnock's office was to use leaks, off-the-record briefings, press releases, "speeches" (that is, press releases) by shadow cabinet members to their constituency parties and so forth to set the agenda for debate within the Labour Party. The principal conduits for this material were a handful of Fleet Street journalists pounding the Westminster beat. Over the years they included Patrick Wintour, Andrew Grice, Donald MacIntyre, Nicholas Wapshott and others.

The effect of these media blitzkriegs was to pre-empt debate within the Party by giving the impression that the leadership had set its course on a particular matter and could not be swayed. In this way each and every issue was turned into a test of loyalty. For rank-and-file Party members, whether they agreed with Kinnock or not, attending meetings came to seem pointless since the decisions had clearly already been taken at the top.

As important to Mandelson as what he got into the media was what he kept out of it. One of his first moves was to try to keep Tony Benn off the air. In February 1986, Benn was scheduled to appear on the BBC's *Question Time* the day after the NEC considered the expulsion of the Liverpool Militants. Benn was apprised by sources within the BBC that Mandelson was trying to keep him off. He wrote a letter of protest to Larry Whitty, who passed it straight on to Mandelson, who then despatched a handwritten letter to Benn assuring him that his only concern was "about the legal implications of any NEC member" appearing on television and saying anything about the Liverpool expulsions, which were being contested in the courts. Of course, Mandelson's department had nothing to do with the expulsions or their legal consequences; the fact that he never made any effort to keep other, more right-wing NEC members off television over similar issues speaks for itself. The BBC producers concerned wrote a sharp letter of protest to the Labour Party about Mandelson's attempts to dictate whom they could and could not put on the air.

Control of the annual conference agenda was another vital tool in shaping the public view of Labour's internal life. Both Kinnock and Mandelson insisted on vetting all proposed conference agendas before they were seen by the conference arrangements committee, a nominally autonomous body elected each year to oversee the compositing of motions and the timetabling of discussions. After 1987 the Policy Reviews and documents, "Looking to the Future" and "Opportunity Britain" were used to structure and restrict the entire week's debate at Party conference, forcing policy initiatives from outside the Walworth Road/ shadow cabinet axis off the conference agenda. Mandelson was assisted in this work by Sally Morgan, a veteran of Democratic Left student politics who became secretary to the conference arrangements committee in the mid 1980s. With the help of Derek Gladwin, the long-serving GMB Southern Region secretary who was chair of the committee for over fifteen years, they ensured that the leadership's preferred policy options were given prominence regardless of the feelings of constituency delegates. The numbers of potentially embarrassing motions were kept to a minimum and their discussion was scheduled for times at which they would get least media exposure.

The weekly meetings of the Parliamentary Labour Party proved another useful vehicle for media manipulation. In his efforts to build up Kinnock as a "strong" leader, Mandelson released excerpts from Kinnock's remarks, sometimes before Kinnock had opened his mouth. Succinct examples of Kinnock's "common sense" were repeated in the press as if these were verbatim reports from meetings at which their journalist writers had been present. Labour MPs often observed that there was no correlation at all between Kinnock's rambling lectures to the PLP and the remarks attributed to him the next day in newspapers. Even voting figures from these meetings were misrepresented, with dissent usually minimized and backing for the leadership usually exaggerated. Not surprisingly, attendance at PLP meetings dwindled.

Mandelson also briefed the media about leadership initiatives and likely debates at the NEC before the NEC had actually met. Hence the stories which frequently appeared in the run-up to meetings telling readers what Kinnock would be demanding at the coming NEC. The loyalty factor was thus called into play, so that for the NEC to do anything other than rubberstamp the leader's initiative provoked a major furore. As soon as NEC meetings concluded, Mandelson would be in position as NEC members filed out of the building, telling camera teams whom to film and attempting to steer journalists to the NEC members whom he knew would loyally repeat the leadership line.

The staff whom Mandelson inherited upon his appointment in 1985 were pleased to have him after the directionlessness of the preceding period. His appointment was a signal that the new professionalism seen in the Jobs and Industry campaign would be encouraged and rewarded. New press officers were hired and the Party appointed its first ever "political intelligence officer" to analyse opinion-poll data and liaise with MORI. The suspicions of the NEC and trade unions about the use of modern public relations methods were being swept aside. The authority Mandelson derived from links with the leader gave his staff added confidence and zest.

"Peter Mandelson's skill was in taking the risks necessary to open up the Party to new techniques," said one former associate at the campaigns and communications directorate. In those days, Mandelson's office door was always open and advice, new ideas and fresh input were welcomed. By all accounts the CCD was a happy team, happy because the Party seemed to value its work. The size of the directorate mushroomed, accounting for more than half the twenty-five new posts created by the Party in the two years following the 1985 reorganization. Its budget soared from £35,000 in 1983 to over £300,000 in 1986.

There was as yet no clear hierarchy within the CCD, and every employee seemed to have equal access to Mandelson, whose enthusiasm for the job was in noted contrast to the attitudes displayed by most other senior Walworth Road staff. He was never a hands-on manager and made few contributions to the actual design or production of new material. He conducted staff relations with an informality that was at first attractive but later became loathed because of its openness to manipulation and favouritism.

Out of the Shadow Communications Agency's first experiment in "qualitative research" was born the Freedom and Fairness campaign, launched in April 1986. Its main slogan was "putting people first", a slogan which had been coined several years before by NALGO for use in its campaign against public sector cuts. In contrast to the Jobs and Industry campaign, the emphasis in Freedom and Fairness was "shifted from charters and statements to shorter, more accessible party brochures and leaflets".[9] The ostensible political content of Freedom and Fairness was hardly touched on in the press; all the coverage was about the Party's new image and its decision to appeal to the individual and the consumer.

At a meeting of the campaign strategy committee held in May 1986, just after the launch of the Freedom and Fairness campaign, a letter from David Blunkett to Peter Mandelson was circulated describing his "value-free approach to campaigning and presentation" as a "grave mistake". Mandelson's response was to boast that the coverage of the Freedom and Fairness campaign press launch was worth £1 million in free publicity for the Party's "new look". He thus demonstrated that he knew the price of everything but the value of nothing.

Mandelson Triumphant

The 1987 general election campaign resulted in a huge boost to Mandelson's prestige, both inside and outside the Labour Party. With the initiation of the Policy Review at the 1987 conference, his direct influence over the politics of the Labour Party increased dramatically. Innocently, Bryan Gould had articulated the logic that was to give Mandelson a degree of political power never before held by an employee of the Party. "The popular appeal of policies must be a prime consideration, not an afterthought," Gould had told a Labour Co-ordinating Committee conference shortly after the 1987 defeat.[10] This principle was to become the lodestone for the Kinnock leadership throughout the 1987 Parliament.

Redundancies at Walworth Road caused by the Party's post-elections financial crisis left the campaigns and communications directorate largely unaffected. Morale was low virtually everywhere except in the directorate, whose personnel, proud of their performance in the general election campaign, saw themselves as the Party's "pacesetters". Some of the workers taken on temporarily during the campaign were given permanent posts.

Much of 1988 was given over to the Labour Listens campaign, which Mandelson described as "a substantial programme of listening to public opinion".[11] It was a calculated fraud perpetrated against both Party members and the general public, a device designed not to enfranchise the public but to disenfranchise the membership and transform the political direction of the Party. "For the first time," the Labour leadership boasted, "a political party is saying to the people: 'Tell us what you think. How best should Labour play its role in the Britain of tomorrow?' Now you have that opportunity; we are listening."

The original idea was that the Labour Listens campaign would generate thousands of responses from groups and individuals, which would be "fed into" the Policy Review groups "on a regular and systematic basis", as Geoff Bish put it to the NEC and shadow cabinet in November 1987.[12] Enthusiastic Labour strategists declared that "as a campaigning device the Labour Listens approach should be continued as part of a regular constituency organization up to the next election."[13]

The idea of Labour Party members spending their time "listening" to the general public rather than arguing among themselves appealed to many. But for activists on the ground, some of whom tried to take the leadership at its word, the Labour Listens campaign ended up a frustrating exercise. They could not help but wonder just whom they were supposed to be listening to. The implicit assumption of the campaign was that the general public was homogeneous and that if you listened to enough people you would end up with a "common sense" consensus. But, of course, in any given community there would be conflicts, minority views and contradictions. How were Labour's listeners supposed to sort these out?

And what mechanisms were to be used to enable Labour to "listen"? Public meetings, street-corner surveys, door-to-door or telephone canvassing? None of these would produce scientific, reliable or precise results. And how did you go about codifying these results so they could be "fed in" to the Policy Review process? Where would the information solicited via these mechanisms wind up? What weight would be attached to it? Wouldn't it become clear to the public that Labour Listens was a publicity stunt and that the Party wasn't actually listening to them at all? Such cynicism was well placed. In the various papers on the Policy Review submitted to the NEC by Geoff Bish, Larry Whitty and the chair of the NEC home policy committee Tom Sawyer, who was to take credit for the entire exercise, there was never any proposal for a structure to channel the findings of the Labour Listens initiative into the Policy Review.

Party members also wondered how they should respond to what they heard when they "listened". Should they not defend and argue for those policies that had been democratically approved by the Party conference? Wasn't that what they had joined the Party for in the first place? If the public demanded the return of capital punishment, an end to abortion rights, or the mass repatriation of "foreigners", should Labour listen politely and redesign its policies accordingly?

Worse yet, activists found that for specific constituencies with specific demands on Labour – the peace movement, black people, lesbians and gays or trade unionists – there was no way into Labour Listens. Infuriatingly, the process seemed to give priority to the views of those who were hostile to the labour movement and little weight to those who were part of it.

A full-time Labour Listens unit was set up at Walworth Road to oversee a series of regional publicity stunts, "targeted" events and the production of a huge amount of superfluous promotional material. Amidst a public relations fanfare, the first Labour Listens event was staged in Brighton. An invited audience of about 150 people was given two hours to put views to the panel of listeners, which included Roy Hattersley and Bryan Gould. This audience included members of the local chamber of commerce, various local employers and charity groups, but no members of the local Labour Party. Participants were told that a videotape of the event would be "fed into" the Policy Review. This meeting was followed by similar events in Plymouth, Manchester, Nottingham and Birmingham. All have been described by eyewitnesses as poorly attended, dull, disorganized and sometimes embarrassing. The purpose of these "flagship events", as they were dubbed by the campaigns and communications directorate, was not to collect data on public opinion but, in Mandelson's words, to "raise public awareness" of the Labour Listens exercise. Clearly what was important was not actually listening to anyone but being seen to listen to everyone.

In March 1988 Mandelson solemnly reported to the campaign strategy committee that all these events "were successful although at one or two the attendance has not been as good as we would have liked".[14] In fact, the events had been humiliating for the front-benchers involved. They attracted large numbers of cranks eager to ride their hobbyhorses in public, and the press lost all interest after the first shindig in Brighton. Mandelson refused to note any of these realities in his thirteen-page report to the committee. Instead, he asserted that Labour Listens formed the "basis of a three-to-four years' strategy to build up the campaigning capacities of CLPs" and that it was all "about reaching out to the public . . . enlisting and mobilizing the public".[15]

When questioned about the exclusion of Party activists from the Labour Listens events Mandelson told the press, "You don't have to be someone who attends meetings seven days a week to deserve a say on policy."[16] In fact, it seemed increasingly clear that the one guarantee of not having a say in Labour policy was attending Labour Party meetings.

The Labour Listens campaign stumbled on into the autumn of 1988 with "targeted" events on social security, pensioners, housing and co-operatives, but to all intents and purposes the exercise was dead. It had served its purpose the moment it had been launched. It had cleared the decks for the Policy Review by suggesting not only that the Party was in the procees of reconsidering all its policies but also that Labour would from now on conform to what passed in the media as "common sense". Labour Listens, which was supposed to form the basis of local campaigning in the new model Labour Party, was quietly dropped after eighteen months.

At the 1988 conference Labour's latest logo: "Labour values . . . your values" was unveiled. The "our" in "Labour" was highlighted, a bold assertion of the Party's new-found empathy with the general public. Larry Whitty announced that the new slogan emphasized "the enduring values which we believe Labour shares with the great mass of the British people", which he said included "a conviction that people need the strength of the community to express a common will".[17] Nobody seemed aware of the unpleasant authoritarian associations of some of the phrases employed in Mandelson's attempts to imply a direct and almost intuitive link, unimpeded by Party activists, between the Labour leader and the "people".

Since Mandelson's real power derived from his direct relationship with Kinnock's office, he could dispense with the niceties of Walworth Road's formal hierarchy. He rarely attended the regular meetings of the four directors that were held under Larry Whitty's supervision, which were supposed to be the forum for Walworth Road's senior management. His approach to industrial relations with Walworth Road employees was crude and one-sided; he dealt not in negotiation but in threats and ultimata. In private he made it clear that as far as he was concerned the unions were a nuisance and the sooner they were expelled from Labour headquarters the better.

There was a spreading feeling within Walworth Road that some of the Party's employees were more equal than others. The criterion for success in Mandelson's bailiwick was no longer talent and eagerness, but "political reliability". This meant unquestioning loyalty to the Party leader; any broader loyalty – to the shadow cabinet or the NEC – was mistrusted. Members of the NOLS/LCC network, unremittingly hostile to the left and loyal to the leadership, found their way into the campaigns and communications directorate as to elsewhere in Walworth Road. As the Policy Review unfolded these new apparatchiks became more and more confident, unwilling to entertain any notion that anything they undertook in the Party's name was less than a complete success. Walworth Road employees with honest doubts of any kind – including some genuine Kinnock supporters who had worked flat out in the 1987 election – were designated untrustworthy and unpromotable.

Colin Byrne, Lesley Smith and Jo Moore, veterans of NOLS/LCC faction fighting, were all hired by Mandelson in this period. They interposed themselves as crucial conduits between the media and the Labour Party. Smith was quickly moved to the PLP press office, where she tended to the career anxieties of various front-bench spokespersons, while remaining technically in the full employ of the Party itself. Moore, a former vice-chair of NOLS, had worked briefly as a press officer for the London Labour councils of Haringey and Islington. She proudly described herself to colleagues at the CCD as "the hammer of the Trots in Haringey" where she was an active Party member; she was not ashamed to admit her real credentials for the job. On the fiftieth anniversary of the murder of Leon Trotsky in August 1990 she announced to startled co-workers that she was annoyed with herself for having forgotten to mark the date by wearing her ice-pick brooch.

Increasingly, Peter Mandelson abandoned any pretensions at mass campaigning for off-the-record briefings of favoured journalists. He was highly skilful at giving chosen journalists the pleasant sensation of believing they were in the know when their colleagues were not. Mandelson could do this only because journalists felt that talking to Mandelson was as good as talking to Kinnock himself. Indeed, it was better, because

Mandelson could say things that Kinnock had to keep to himself, not least his opinions of shadow cabinet colleagues. Of course, most of the professional journalists involved in this game were perfectly well aware of what Mandelson was doing. They ran the stories he gave them because no one could afford not to be in Mandelson's confidence and write with any authority on the Labour Party. Their editors would not have tolerated it.

The closest parallel to the Mandelson regime was its counterpart run from 10 Downing Street by Bernard Ingham. Joe Haines called Ingham "a ventriloquist's dummy with ideas of his own", an apposite characterization of Peter Mandelson. Indeed, all the dubious practices for which Ingham was pilloried by more critical members of the fourth estate were carried out by Mandelson. The *Guardian* and *Independent* made a principled protest against Ingham's methods by withdrawing from his system of unattributable press briefings. They did so with considerable fanfare and not a little self-congratulation. But at the same time they remained key players in the shadow system of unattributable briefings run by Mandelson on behalf of Kinnock's office.

From his early days Mandelson cultivated *Guardian* journalists and in particular Patrick Wintour. Wintour's political odyssey was a familiar one. He moved from the far left at Oxford, where he was a member of the old International Socialists (forerunner of the Socialist Workers Party), to the *New Statesman* and the Labour left. He became a member of the executive of the Campaign for Labour Party Democracy until he abandoned it to become a supporter of the "soft left" Labour Co-ordinating Committee and ultimately a Kinnock camp-follower. Mandelson, who had known Wintour at Oxford, entrusted the *Guardian* journalist with the work of disseminating the leadership's latest initiatives to the Party membership and the general public. Around the House of Commons, Wintour became known as "Mandelson's amanuensis".

The game had many other players. Also at the *Guardian* there was Alan Travis, another disenchanted veteran of far-left politics. Andrew Grice, who had worked on Maxwell's short-lived *London Daily News*, was known as a Labour right-winger before he moved to the *Sunday Times*, where for several years he regularly reproduced comments made by Mandelson and members of Kinnock's office. Politicians in the House of Commons came to regard his columns as a reliable gauge of what the Labour leadership was thinking, of who was in or out of favour.

In the final years of his regime, Mandelson perfected the art of the "black briefing", in which negative but unattributable comments about individuals are disseminated via off-the-record press briefings. Mobilizing the media against internal opposition – real or imagined – increasingly came to dominate the work of the CCD, causing considerable tension within the directorate. The professional journalists there – as opposed to the political apparatchiks – refused to take part in the negative briefings and felt their own status was undermined by them. The method had become all too predictable: Mandelson would summon one of his loyalists to his office, the door would close, and the next day a personal attack on a left-winger, a shadow cabinet or NEC member, even on a few occasions the deputy leader of the Party, would appear in the press.

During Mandelson's carefully orchestrated campaign for the Hartlepool parliamentary selection in 1990, some of his CCD staff, on his instructions, used the Labour Party's facilities to issue Mandelson's personal statements to the press. This was in flagrant violation of Party rules on campaigning in selection contests and broke the code of neutrality that might be thought to govern the conduct of the Party's servants. The NUJ father of the chapel at Walworth Road was asked by irate staff to intervene and Mandelson was instructed to desist.

Mandelson grew increasingly addicted to grandiose strategic pronouncements. The period running up to the 1989 elections to the European Parliament, including the county council elections in May and the crucial weeks in which the Policy Review papers would be made more or less public, was proclaimed a "ten-week campaign offensive". In a paper to a campaign strategy committee meeting in the shadow cabinet room in Westminster in January 1989, Mandelson said the campaign would involve "a series of co-ordinated events and publicity-seeking initiatives" and that Labour would need "a central driving message which applies to both sets of elections". That "driving message" was to be "a new deal for Europe and a square deal for Britain". He informed the committee: "Our publicity materials will be based on creative concepts which reflect the central message of the overall campaign."[18] The sloppy, fatuous language was typical of Mandelson's presentations, but no shadow cabinet or NEC member challenged it, such was the timidity – and the fear of the stab in the back – that gripped the highest echelons of the Labour Party during his reign.

During Mandelson's 1989 offensive, green issues came unexpectedly to the fore. Labour's response was a full-page advert, placed in the *New Statesman and Society* and elsewhere, designed to appeal to potential green voters. Its rambling prose surrounded a photograph of a young, white, attractive, middle-class mother and child. It was a litany of actual and potential environmental catastrophes but offered not a single word about Labour's proposed remedies. Not surprisingly, given Labour's recent abandonment of unilateralism and of any opposition to nuclear power, the approach typified by this advertisement left the green vote to the Green Party, which secured a remarkable 15 per cent of the poll. Afterwards, Mandelson's only answer to the threat posed by the Greens was to conclude that that the voters had been duped. Apparently they had failed to realize "the extremity and full nature of the Greens' policies".[19] Labour's counter-strategy would be to highlight this "extremity", in other words, to run a kind of updated red scare against the Greens.

For the leadership, the whole Policy Review process had been from the beginning a publicity exercise, for which the "ten-week campaign" was primarily a showcase. Overriding importance was attached to the construction put on the Policy Review group reports (and their reception at the NEC) by the media. On the morning of May 8th 1989, when details of the newly completed review had not yet been made available to Party members or to affiliated unions, the national papers ran almost identical stories in which Kinnock was portrayed as being on the verge of a great political breakthrough. The ultimate test of his leadership was to be his success in forcing Labour to abandon unilateralism, and other residual left policies. "Labour sheds ideological baggage", the *Financial Times* healined. "Kinnock set to scrap unilateralism", the *Independent* announced, adding "Labour leader poised to defeat left". On the front page of the *Guardian* Patrick Wintour outlined the main changes in the Policy Review in a detailed and accurate report. Some NEC and shadow cabinet members wondered why Wintour seemed to know more about the contents of the Review than they did. Joe Haines, in a *Daily Mirror* editorial that morning, advised Labour to "adopt the new policies which can win elections and abandon the old shibboleths which have lost us the last three".

After the NEC meeting that approved the bulk of the Policy Review, Mandelson gave the press what purported to be a blow-by-blow account. *Today* headlined: "Fighting Kinnock routs shopping-list socialists". "Kinnock hits at shopping-list socialism," the *Times* declared, reporting that, as Tony Benn spoke:

> Mr Kinnock interrupted him and told the Executive, "This is an attempt to devise policies to inoculate ourselves from the capitalist system. It is the system we live in and we have got to make it work more efficiently, more fairly and more successfully in the world market place."

Kinnock, in fact, did not interrupt Benn. Mandelson had taken an agreed quote and inserted it creatively for dramatic effect.

The presentation of the Labour leader's long-awaited confrontation on the nuclear bomb on May 10th, following the second day of the meeting, was perhaps Mandelson's master work. The *Independent* headlined: "Kinnock crosses defence rubicon" and the *Guardian* followed suit: "Tough Kinnock speech dominates debate on defence in the NEC". The *Mirror* rejoiced: "Kinnock sweeps to nuke arms victory . . . defeats left in policy battle", which might have given some readers the impression that Kinnock had vaporized Tony Benn in a thermonuclear strike. The

Independent ran the whole of what purported to be Kinnock's speech to the NEC. *Today*'s headline combined all the elements, the leadership's loyalty test plus the implication of violence in the suppression of left-wing heresies: "Back me or sack me: Kinnock challenge as he crushes left over nuclear arms".

This proved to be the best press coverage Neil Kinnock ever received in the nine years that he was the leader of the Party. Not one of the journalists who wrote up the epic two-day NEC meeting was actually present. The sole source for their stories was Peter Mandelson. The violent language, the deliberate use of military metaphors to describe Kinnock's "victory" against the unilateralists, the focus on the leader's determination to force the Party into line, were all components of the long-nurtured strategy of building Kinnock up at the expense of the Labour Party and its traditions.

The Decline and Fall of Mandelson

The Kinnock leadership was unable to turn its temporary triumph of 1989–90 into anything durable. The favourable press that accompanied the Policy Review and the thrashing of the left vanished as the general election clash with the Tories approached and the stakes became higher.

In 1989, following the NEC's decision to disallow amendments to the Policy Review, Mandelson told reporters that the "soft left", which had hesitated on the issue, had been put in its place by the usual "tough talk" from the leader. The "soft left", in the persons of David Blunkett and Clare Short, was none too pleased. Blunkett complained: "The briefing given afterwards distorted the decision of the NEC and sought to place the leadership in confrontation with party activists. The message that the briefings seem to give is that the party is winning when the activists are defeated." Short agreed: "For years, the briefings have been about how Neil smashes the left and Peter Mandelson obviously thinks that enhances the leader's reputation. But to misrepresent things so that the leadership seems more aggressive than it actually is, is just daft."[20] For once the "soft left" had been on the receiving end of the Mandelson treatment and did not like it.

Mandelson regarded the "soft left" as politically unreliable and personally weak. His strategy for dealing with them was a mixture of flattery, bribery and threat. Anyone who stepped out of line – as did, on rare occasions, John Prescott, Michael Meacher, David Blunkett and Clare Short – would receive the full Mandelson treatment. Those who toed the line would be rewarded with favourable publicity and advancement in the Party hierarchy.

It was clear at the 1989 conference that Blunkett had patched up his quarrel with the Walworth Road press office, which made strenuous efforts that year to raise his public profile. Before the conference had even started, a two-page press release was issued detailing Blunkett's activities in and around Blackpool that week, claiming the Sheffield Brightside MP was "set for a whirlwind week at Labour Party conference in Blackpool – including major conference speeches and a range of fringe meetings". At the time this was issued the NEC had not yet decided who would be speaking on its behalf in the conference debates. The press release claimed that Blunkett had "his finger well and truly on the political pulse", advertised his forthcoming column in *Tribune* and offered flattering biographical details, from which all reference to his tenure as leader of Sheffield Council was omitted.

But the real rising star among Labour MPs that year was Tony Blair, who was about to become the Party's employment spokesperson. Like other favoured members of the shadow cabinet, he was given a high profile by the campaigns and communications directorate at press conferences, and the opportunity to appear in party political broadcasts; he became the subject of a stream of flattering newspaper profiles.

The press, which had boosted Kinnock from the Vale of Glamorgan by-election through the Policy Review process, became more critical of him after mid 1990. The launch of "Looking to the Future", the next phase of the Policy Review, was greeted with much more scepticism by the media. The glossy colour cover for the statement – the briefest of all Labour's "programmes" – depicted a young, blonde, professional-looking but casually dressed woman with a squeaky-clean child. Mutterings about the "Aryanization" of the Party's image were heard not only amongst the rank and file but also in the shadow cabinet and even amongst journalists, who knew a cynical appeal to prejudice when they saw it.

Now that the dragon of the left had been publicly slain, Mandelson was forced to look further afield for the "enemies within" needed as sparring partners for the leadership. He became obsessed with manipulating the platforms at press launches, ensuring high-profile placements for favourites such as Brown and Blair and obscurity or calumny for others. Much time was spent devising a formula to exclude selected individuals (notably Michael Meacher) from the platform of the "Looking to the Future" press launch.

According to Mandelson, Labour's campaign strategy in the first half of 1990 was supposed to be devoted to "attacking the Tories for not delivering on the economy". "Looking to the Future" was launched at the end of May. It allegedly "shifted the emphasis of the Party's campaign strategy" and "presented an attractive and practical vision of Britain under a Labour government in the 1990s". This, Mandelson promised, "will provide Labour with campaigning momentum beyond the Party conference and forward to the election". He warned that the whole strategy "depends on heavy promotion of the personal benefits of Labour's programme", but he failed to notice that the determination to promise as little as possible, to minimize specific commitments, was a major obstacle to such promotion.[21]

By now Peter Mandelson had come to believe his own propaganda. He was the whizzkid with the magic wand. Profile after profile of the great man appeared in the press and in specialist magazines. But he over-reached himself. The leadership was ambivalent about his selection as the parliamentary candidate for Hartlepool, which had been arranged not through the leader's office but by Mandelson's own contacts with the powerful GMB. Having decided that he would need time away from Walworth Road to pursue his own political career, Mandelson needed someone personally loyal and politically reliable to run the office in his absence. Colin Byrne, who as a former NUS and ILEA press officer was very much a member of the NOLS/LCC clique, had already been appointed senior press officer. In the summer of 1989 Byrne's position was further enhanced when he became chief press and broadcasting officer, in effect Mandelson's deputy, a post that had not existed pre-viously. He was placed in authority over Tony Beeton, the experienced broadcasting officer who had been his main competitor for the job. Journalists and politicians trusted Beeton, a media professional whose career owed nothing to Mandelson, which was presumably why the latter considered him an unsuitable deputy.

Mandelson originally intended to remain as director of campaigns and communications for as long as possible in the run-up to the general election. But key members of both the shadow cabinet and the NEC did not like the idea. His off-the-record briefings and his growing arrogance had irritated many who agreed with his politics and thought he had done a useful job for the Party at a critical time. They were alarmed at the idea of Mandelson operating as a parliamentary candidate as well as a Walworth Road employee, which was in any case in violation of traditional restrictions on Party full-timers. Gordon Colling of the NGA, the chair of the NEC communications committee, to which Mandelson was nominally responsible, mobilized a number of other NEC trade union representatives to force Mandelson to relinquish his Walworth Road empire.

Mandelson had no alternative but to accept this reversal, assuming that he would be able to secure the appointment of Colin Byrne as his successor and thereby maintain his influence within the campaigns and communications directorate. But he radically misjudged the situation. Many people in the Labour hierarchy, and particularly within the NEC, recognized that Byrne was nothing but a cypher for Mandelson. Although Neil Stewart lobbied NEC members from Kinnock's office on Byrne's behalf, neither Kinnock nor Charles Clarke felt able to campaign openly for him. At the NEC meeting that appointed Mandelson's successor Kinnock voted for Byrne but did openly canvass support for a candidate who would be defeated.

At this meeting the NEC rejected not only Byrne, but also David Hill (Roy Hattersley's researcher) and former NUS president Phil Woolas (another NOLS veteran with useful links to Kinnock's office). For once, the trade union representatives and "soft left" NEC members made their weight felt. They did not want another politician, loyal only to the leader's office, in this sensitive post. Accordingly they gave the job to television producer John Underwood, who was little known inside Labour Party circles. Underwood was the most experienced and best qualified candidate, which is perhaps why so many commentators described him as a "surprise appointment". He was a media professional and had offered himself as a servant of the Party and the NEC, without any ulterior political connections or ambitions.

Reeling from this rebuff, Mandelson was soon to find himself stymied at another hurdle. He cautiously let his press contacts know that he would be joining Kinnock's office as a personal adviser to the leader. But his long-time ally, Charles Clarke, hoisting the spin-doctor by his own petard, used the press to make it clear that Mandelson would not be joining Kinnock's office in any capacity. He was concerned here not only to protect his own supremacy in the leader's office but also to maintain the unassailability of the leader himself. Mandelson had come to enjoy too high a public profile, and his personal ambitions meant that his loyalty to Kinnock might not always be relied upon. He was too much of a loose cannon to be allowed on the captain's deck. The spurned Mandelson was forced to take a part-time job with an industrial consultancy run by some old comrades from the Lambeth Labour right, a post he combined with a lightweight weekly column in the Maxwell-owned *Sunday People*.

When his retirement was ritually announced from the platform at the 1990 Blackpool conference there were scattered boos from delegates but not a single clap. In his final report to the Labour Party as director of campaigns and communications, issued two months before Margaret Thatcher's demise, Mandelson had proclaimed that "the aim of the Party's campaign strategy throughout the year has been to consolidate and deepen our support so as to withstand any serious swing back to the government".[22] On this test his regime in its last year was a spectacular failure.

What, in fact, had the CCD been up to in that year? It had come up with a slogan: "Labour: the people who can, not the people who con", which was used with mixed results during the 1990 local elections but was shelved with the onset of the Gulf crisis and the fall of Thatcher. Besides producing its usual reams of paper for distribution at annual conference, the entire product of the campaigns and communications directorate comprised: the production of ten "mini-manifestos" whose contents were supplied by the policy directorate; a briefing on the Tory government's record; one issue (the last) of *RED*, the Party's youth magazine, intended as a replacement for the defunct *Young Socialist*; a Christmas and summer sales catalogue; lottery tickets; a local election briefing pack; sixteen brief leaflets on various unrelated topics; the "Looking to the Future" booklet (also written elsewhere); a "Winning the 1990s for Women" pack; and a booklet for Trade Unionists for Labour. It also provided platform staging and exhibitions for the GMB conference, the Party's press conferences and a handful of other public events. "0898 – Labour Line", a fundraising telephone hook-up on which Party supporters could listen to recorded messages from Kinnock, Hattersley, John Cunningham, *et al.* (at a cost of 48p per minute, peak rate) proved unprofitable and was closed within a year. The directorate also published the 1991 Labour Party diary, which devoted a full page to a list of some of the country's most expensive hotels and restaurants.

In his written report to the 1990 conference, Mandelson explained to puzzled delegates that Labour had undertaken a host of "campaigns" during the previous year. Only a handful of delegates had heard of these and virtually none had participated in them. Among them was something Mandelson called Industry 2000, which, it was alleged, "boosted Labour's image of economic competence". Then there was the Best Health Care campaign, which had apparently taken place over the summer of 1990 and had been "a major national and local campaign on opt-out hospitals". He also insisted that there had been a Labour campaign on education entitled Invest in Tomorrow featuring otherwise unspecified "press and campaign initiatives", and a transport campaign called Moving Britain into the 1990s.[23] All of these "campaigns" were simply rubrics dreamt up by Mandelson for his year-end report. None of them featured in his regular reports to the campaign strategy committee or the NEC.

When the Gulf crisis first broke in August 1990, Mandelson, who, with the leader and his coterie out of the country, had been anticipating a quiet summer, was unsure how to respond. After a few days' delay, his team came up with the idea of having energy spokesperson Frank Dobson appear on television to publicize Labour's effort to monitor petrol price rises. Labour's image-makers seemed to have decided that the British motorist was the main casualty of the Gulf crisis. Dobson had himself filmed at Walworth Road with Labour staff members shown ringing up petrol stations to get price information, which was then apparently entered onto computers. The whole scene was a fraud. Nothing was entered on computers and there never was any effort to monitor petrol prices at Walworth Road.

The technical quality of the campaigns and communications directorate's product ebbed as the initial impetus of 1985–86 was spent and the talents drawn in to help revitalize Labour became disillusioned and left. The red rose had rapidly become as unprepossessing and nearly as invisible as the old flag. The "new look", the logos, the typefaces, the layouts and all the other visual totems of Mandelson's directorate began to fray at the edges. The old "ransom note" style returned as staff were asked to produce literature with no particular aim or audience in mind. They seemed unable even to settle on a single style of punctuation. The copywriting became turgid and at times ungrammatical. Kinnock's message to the Party faithful in the autumn 1990 issue of *Labour Party News* makes interesting reading, not least as a specimen of the disjointed stream of New Realist consciousness that had become Labour's literary house style:

> We are Looking to the Future in all areas. Even more, we are seeking power in order to help people to prepare for the future . . . the idea of a new world order for global security is moving from being just a hope of idealists to an expressed purpose of international leaders. . . . Our positive policies and the Tories' negative record, our determination to make the future work for the people, the Tories' readiness to leave the future to chance, are all factors which give us strength and support.[24]

Mandelson Rises from the Dead

On succeeding Mandelson in the £28,000-a-year job, John Underwood let it be known that he intended to work for the whole of the NEC, the whole of the Labour Party, and not for one faction only. He tried to eradicate the "them and us" mentality that divided his staff and to put an end to the favouritism that had demoralized many workers. He informed Party audiences at special training days that Labour faced an extremely difficult task in the coming general election, pointing out just how much of an electoral mountain it still had to climb and how ambiguous the messages from the opinion polls really were. All this won him the instant enmity of Kinnock loyalists, who had come to rely on mindless triumphalism to maintain their sway over the Party.

Kinnock and members of his private staff made no secret of their dismay at Underwood's actions. Soon the leader's office and sources at Walworth Road began to place stories in the press citing critical remarks about Underwood from unnamed Labour MPs. Unattributable sources claimed that Underwood was not doing enough to project the Party's policies, that he was putting up a wall between Party spokespersons and the press, that he did not know how to handle the parliamentary lobby and that in general he was spending insufficient time cultivating the media. Quickly, Underwood found himself marginalized at Walworth Road. Without Kinnock's ear the director of campaigns and communications became just another apparatchik. It was widely reported that in the light of Underwood's alleged stonewalling of the press, dealings with the parliamentary lobby would switch to Colin Byrne, who was at that very moment finalizing plans for his marriage to Julie Hall, Kinnock's personal press officer.

Underwood was hampered by the acute financial crisis that had dogged Walworth Road since 1987. Staff vacancies were left unfilled and advertising was cut back. In his previous jobs Underwood had impressed colleagues as an extrovert and an enthusiast, but in Walworth Road he became cautious and taciturn. In the Kinnockite hothouse there seemed to be no room for an honest public relations worker.

Of course, he had been immediately confronted on taking the job with the almost impossible task of presenting Labour in an appealing light following the fall of Thatcher and the Tory retreat on the Poll Tax. In his paper to the campaign strategy committee at the end of March 1991, Underwood was cautiously optimistic but could come up with few arresting campaign initiatives. Negative attacks on the Tories, particularly on "John Major's personal responsibility for the recession", were to be backed up by promotion of Labour's alternative on the economy, which he summarized as follows: "Our determination to combat recession and, with the right policies, simultaneously to build foundations for durable economic success."

Underwood argued that following the collapse of Thatcherism and the onset of recession, the "individualism" of the 1980s upon which the entire edifice of the Policy Review had been constructed was now on the wane. He wanted to see what he called "a shift in emphasis to the positive promotion and projection of Labour's programme" and an assertion of the importance of collective values. But he faced the daunting Kinnockite caveat that was always heard in the run-up to general elections: "we will only promise what we know we can afford, particularly in terms of our commitments in areas such as transport and regional policy".[25] For three years, the Party had been announcing an imminent shift in emphasis to the positive benefits offered by a Labour government. The problem was that the Policy Review process and the concentration of power in the leader's office had left the Party with no positive programme to promote.

Members of the shadow cabinet and the NEC had been privately complaining for some time about the CCD's exclusive focus on the leader. With Mandelson out of the way they began demanding a fairer share of the media spotlight. At a campaign strategy meeting in January 1991 Underwood found he was pushing at an open door when he argued that "the profile of shadow cabinet members should be enhanced . . . to make them more recognizable to the electorate". He announced a "change of emphasis" which would see a higher profile for shadow cabinet members and "in particular, the economics team".[26] In April, director Hugh Hudson produced his second party political broadcast for Labour. This featured John Smith, Gordon Brown, Margaret Beckett and Tony Blair and emphasized their educational qualifications, technical expertise and political conservatism.

With Mandelson gone and an outsider in his place, Kinnock's office began to discharge many of the functions previously allotted to Mandelson. Within the CCD Colin Byrne, taking over Mandelson's favoured press conduits, acted as Kinnock's eyes and ears, promoting favourites and disparaging critics. Journalists rapidly realized that the stories they wanted would not be forthcoming from Underwood, so they went straight to Byrne or to Charles Clarke in the leader's office for the kind of copy they used to receive from Mandelson. Members of the shadow cabinet had also by now acquired the art of the off-the-record briefing and discovered just how useful it could be to settle political scores or promote a personal initiative within the Party or the PLP. Week after week, Brown, Blair, David Blunkett, Cook, Prescott, and of course Kinnock himself sent frantic signs to each other, to the Party, and to the public via the political columns of the quality press.

For the increasingly isolated and undermined Underwood, the final straw came in the spring of 1991 with Kinnock's personal appointment of Peter Mandelson as the Labour press officer in the crucial Monmouth by-election. The clear implication was that the leadership did not regard Underwood as being up to the job. During the campaign, Mandelson took every opportunity to seize the limelight. A feature appearing in the *Independent on Sunday* in mid-campaign glorified his role as the Party's "image maker" but failed to mention once the name of the Labour candidate. Labour won the by-election, overturning a 9,350 Tory majority on a swing of 12 per cent, thanks mainly to popular anxiety over the government's plans to force local hospitals to opt out of the NHS. But readers of Sunday newspapers following polling day would have been forgiven for thinking that Labour's victory had been the work of Peter Mandelson. Mandelson's self-aggrandizement angered Underwood and upset many Labour MPs and Party activists who believed that they too had played a part in Labour's success.

In the aftermath of the by-election the press, well briefed by Mandelson himself, speculated that he would be named as the public relations supremo for the general election. A furious Underwood decided that he had to act. He declared that Mandelson would play no role, official or otherwise, in the Labour campaign and also moved, at last, against Colin Byrne, who, with his fiancée Julie Hall, was now sharing a London address with Mandelson. One Underwood supporter within the CCD told *PR Week* that Underwood felt that neither Kinnock nor his office was supporting his position. "This was compounded by sniping that John was not up to the job and had a poor relationship with lobby journalists. He felt he was not getting the full support of Colin and wanted to move him from the deputy slot."[27]

Underwood demanded Byrne's removal as chief press and broadcasting officer and soon secured the agreement of Larry Whitty that Byrne should be redeployed to another post within Walworth Road. But Byrne refused to go and Kinnock supported him. He had tolerated Underwood's appointment but would never back him against one of his own loyalists. Underwood had no choice but to resign his post in June 1991, after only eight months in the job. The "soft left" on the NEC, who saw Underwood as a friend and Byrne as an enemy, were livid. It was obvious that Underwood had paid the price for his even-handed approach to the job. When the NEC, following Underwood's resignation, met to consider his replacement Dennis Skinner proposed that the new director be instructed to work for the NEC and the Labour Party as a whole. This attempt to reassert political control over senior Labour officials was defeated by five votes to sixteen and, with the exception of Joan Lestor and Jo Richardson, failed to attract the support of the "soft left".[28]

But in the wake of Underwood's departure it was clear that the NEC would never appoint Byrne to fill his vacancy. Walworth Road staff were told that applications for the post from internal candidates would not be welcomed. The deadline for external applications came and went with hardly a single serious candidate emerging. A headhunting agency was hired to seek out suitable personnel but failed. After the public humiliation of Underwood – and with its principal author, Colin Byrne, still in post as the number two at CCD – it was no wonder that people with the skills and status to do the job steered clear.

The NEC had no choice but to return to David Hill, whom they had rejected the previous year. He had a long background in Labour politics, primarily as Roy Hattersley's aide-de-camp, but little direct experience in the media. Hill was a compromise candidate who alone could secure majority support from the NEC.

At the 1991 Labour Party conference Byrne remained the chief spin-doctor and was seen lurking in the press rooms with Mandelson at his side. But he soon left the Party's employ to work for the Prince's Trust, promoting the Business in the Community project and the Prince of Wales's Business Leaders' Forum.

After the election defeat the following spring, an embittered Byrne wrote a long letter to the *Guardian* on behalf of the Kinnock circle in which he claimed, among other things, that he had resigned in protest at an alleged "plot" to undermine Neil Kinnock on behalf of John Smith. This claim was about as credible as his assertion in the same letter that Roy

Hattersley was a "pacifist" who had opposed the Gulf War.[29] Byrne had left Walworth Road because his career there had come to a halt.

The first noticeable effect of David Hill's tenure as director, which began in July 1991, was the sudden promotion of Roy Hattersley as a spokesperson for the Party. By the autumn of 1991 the entire workload of the CCD had been compressed into what the NEC report called "the relentless activity of the intensely pro-active team of press officers" who organized, it was claimed, some twenty press conferences a month.[30] In 1990–91 the directorate produced for general public consumption a grand total of three leaflets: on health, pensions and the Tory budget. Like Underwood and Mandelson before him, Hill declared it was time to prioritize the Party's "positive messages". He told Labour candidates in September 1991 that "spelling out the choices and the benefits that will come from a Labour government will dominate everything that we do".

Although Hill refrained from attacking members of the Party through off-the-record press briefings he, like Mandelson, saw campaigning and communicating as entirely a matter of mass media news management. He adopted an aggressive approach to journalists and broadcasters who gave the Party less than favourable coverage, and urged his staff to do likewise. He engaged in a highly public battle with the *Sunday Times* in early 1992 over the newspaper's "Kremlin files" story, which purported to expose relationships between Labour leaders and the now-defunct Stalinist regime of the USSR. Hill claimed the *Sunday Times* story was part of a co-ordinated smear campaign against Labour and even telephoned daily newspapers to denounce it on the Saturday before it was published. Hill's real target was not the absurd Kremlin story: he knew that the newspapers set the agenda for broadcasting; he hoped by attacking them that he would force the broadcasters to treat that agenda critically.

Many in the Party hierarchy found what one newspaper called "the new-found combativeness" of Labour's media team refreshing, especially after Mandelson's sycophantic courtship of the parliamentary lobby. But in the absence of an alternative means of communicating to millions of voters it could have little effect. During the election campaign, with the leader's office and the Shadow Communications Agency managing Kinnock's ceaseless rounds of photo-opportunities, Hill and his press officers spent much of their time harassing the press. One Fleet Street veteran commented: "I'm a Tory supporter and my paper is a Tory paper. But if Labour gives us a story with some substance we'll run it. There's no point at all in missing our deadline then calling us up the next day and being personally abusive about what we've printed." He added that he was "sick and tired of being shouted at by incompetent, arrogant and unpleasant" Labour Party press officers.

Since 1985 Labour had launched one "campaign initiative" after another, each one going off with a contrived bang and fizzling out with an inaudible whimper. They had little impact on the electorate and were of no assistance in persuading people to join the Party. The only thing which the campaigns and communications directorate ever effectively promoted was itself. If it is judged by its professed aims, above all the promotion of the leader and the projection of the Party as competent to run the economy, then it stands damned even by its own favourite yardstick, the opinion polls, which revealed in 1992 that the most members of the public mistrusted Kinnock and regarded the Labour Party as less able to deal with the economy than the Tories, even in the midst of a recession. On April 9th, the verdict of voters at the ballot box confirmed these findings.

Notes

1. *Guardian* 2 April 1985.
2. *Guardian* 3 April 1985.
3. ibid.
4. NEC paper September 1985.
5. Benn diaries, 24 September 1985.
6. NEC minutes September 1985.
7. Benn diaries, 24 March 1986.
8. ibid.
9. NEC Report to Annual Conference 1986.
10. *Tribune* 10 July 1987.
11. NEC Report to Annual Conference 1988.
12. NEC paper November 1987.
13. NEC Report to Annual Conference 1988.
14. Campaign Strategy Committee minutes March 1988.
15. ibid.
16. *Tribune* 15 January 1988.
17. *Labour Party Annual Conference Report* 1988.
18. Campaign Strategy Committee minutes January 1989.
19. NEC paper July 1989.
20. *Tribune* 3 February 1989.
21. NEC Report to Annual Conference 1990.
22. ibid.
23. ibid.
24. *Labour Party News* autumn 1990.
25. Campaign Strategy Committee minutes March 1991.
26. Campaign Strategy Committee minutes January 1991.
27. *PR Week* May 1991.
28. NEC minutes June 1991.
29. *Guardian* 13 April 1992.
30. NEC Report to Annual Conference 1991.

Ploughshares into Swords

Wherever the Stars and Stripes goes to secure and protect freedom
you will find the Union Jack by your side.
Clement Attlee to a US audience, 1950

Unilateralism and its Discontents

Though unilateral nuclear disarmament has long enjoyed a solid base of
support among the rank and file of the Labour Party, it is most certainly
not among what the apologists for the Policy Review like to call Labour's
"traditional" commitments. For the Party's parliamentary leadership, the
real traditional commitments – retained to this day – have been to nuclear
weapons, the alliance with the United States and large-scale military
budgets. Only twice since the end of World War Two has Labour moved
to break with that tradition. And on both occasions the parliamentary
leadership deployed all its political resources to force the Party to turn
back the clock to the policies of the Cold War consensus.

In response to the growth of the Campaign for Nuclear Disarmament
(CND) in the late 1950s, Labour's 1960 Scarborough conference committed Labour to a policy of unilateral nuclear disarmament. Party leader
Hugh Gaitskell denounced the decision from the conference platform
and publicly vowed to defy it. Within a year he was able to mobilize
enough trade union block votes to get the policy overturned.

Twenty years later in Blackpool a Labour conference once again voted
for a non-nuclear defence policy. As with the 1960 decision, this was an
expression within the Party of a mass movement outside it. In the late
1970s and early 1980s, in response to the breakdown of detente, the
emergence of what became known as the Second Cold War and moves by
both NATO and the Warsaw Pact to "modernize" (that is, enlarge) their
nuclear arsenals, the peace movement in Europe grew rapidly. Millions
were mobilized in a series of major demonstrations in capital cities across
the world.

In Britain, the focus of public opposition was NATO's decision to site
cruise missiles on British soil and the commissioning of Trident nuclear-

armed submarines to replace Polaris. After two decades in the doldrums CND found its membership increasing twenty-fold in two years. Its campaign against cruise missiles and for a nuclear-free Europe drew enormous support within the Labour Party. Tens of thousands of Party members rallied to the CND banner. Nearly one third of constituency Labour parties affiliated, as did several major trade unions.

The strength of feeling within the Party was demonstrated by the submission of 143 resolutions on defence policy, nearly all of them favouring unilateralism, to the 1980 conference. But this upsurge of anti-nuclear passion, coupled with increasingly outspoken criticism of the Atlantic Alliance, found little echo in the Parliamentary Labour Party, which remained firmly enmeshed within the traditional Cold War bipartisan consensus. Such was the strength of feeling on this issue, however, that in July 1980 the national executive committee, defying the advice of leader Jim Callaghan, voted to support the major CND demonstration in London in October.

Shortly before that demonstration, the Party conference met in Blackpool and passed a unilateralist resolution on a show of hands. Labour's defence spokesperson Bill Rodgers was isolated. Official Party policy was now to oppose "any British participation in any defence policy based on the use or the threatened use of nuclear weapons" and, when next in government, to "close down all British and American nuclear bases located on British territory".[1]

This decision represented not only a repudiation of the course pursued by the previous Labour government, but also a radical break from Labour's traditional subservience to establishment opinion on foreign and defence policy. Representatives of the establishment, in Parliament and in the media, recognized this with dismay and campaigned to repair that break throughout the following decade.

But success was long in coming and required more tortuous tactics than the establishment had anticipated. In November 1980, Labour MPs elected Michael Foot to succeed Callaghan as leader. Foot was well known as a unilateralist and veteran supporter of the peace movment. His election indicated the extent to which even pro-nuclear Labour MPs recognized the mood of the Party and the need to give rank-and-file activists a leader with whom they could identify.

The Party's pro-Washington right wing was driven onto the defensive as never before. Suddenly, it found its base of support narrowed down to a small circle of Labour MPs and the hard-right leaders of a handful of unions that were marginalized within both the Party and the TUC. It was powerless to resist as the mainstream of the Party embraced unilateralism as a non-negotiable principle. In 1981 even Denis Healey, ardently in favour of the Atlantic Alliance, found it expedient to declare in his manifesto for the deputy leadership that he was committed to "genuine disarmament", a reduction in defence spending and the cancellation of Trident.[2] In 1982, conference backing for unilateralism reached the two-thirds majority necessary to force the leadership to include it in the Party's election programme. The next six annual conferences were to reaffirm that commitment.

By the mid 1980s the only voices heard publicly disagreeing with the Labour Party's anti-nuclear policies were those of the AEU and EETPU leaders. Of course, the absence of open argument at Party conferences was no proof of a new consensus in the Party. Opposition to the non-nuclear policy remained deeply ingrained in the parliamentary leadership.

Foot was personally committed to the unilateralist policy, and enjoyed the backing of conference and a majority on the NEC, but because of his fear that the parliamentary right would bolt from the Party or otherwise damage the Party's electoral prospects he refused to stop its ceaseless campaign of sabotage against the policy. The trump card held by the pro-nuclear faction was simply this: that though they were heavily outnum-bered in the Party's policy-making bodies they controlled the handful of parliamentary posts that determined its presentation to the public. Throughout the nine years in which Labour's official policy was unilater-alist, the shadow cabinet spurned every opportunity to use the House of Commons as a platform to argue for that policy. No motion in support of it was ever tabled in the House by Labour's official spokespersons; if the subject came up at all it was only because the Tories raised it, usually with the help of their supporters in Fleet Street. No sustained public cam-paign, no series of rallies or leader's speeches were dedicated to it. Attempts to link the Party to the powerful grassroots movement against the Bomb – which could boast a cadre of hard-working activists in every town and city in the country – were confined to local constituencies and backbench MPs. Indeed, throughout this period the Labour Party's least well guarded secret was that most of its leaders had nothing but con-tempt for its single most important foreign policy commitment.

From the beginning, the Tories were keen to exploit this contradiction. They knew that they could not lose by making defence a major issue because the Labour leadership would be unwilling and unable to coun-terattack. They emphasized the alleged threat to British security from the Soviet Union and claimed a Labour government would leave the country defenceless. Since most of the shadow cabinet accepted the existence of a Soviet threat and similar assumptions underlying the Cold War, their responses in Parliament to the Tory jibes were either obscurely technical or half-heartedly moralistic. Where the Tories appeared clear and confi-dent, Labour seemed confused and shamefaced. This allowed the Tories to score heavily with the millions of voters who were undecided on the issue.

Successive Labour defence spokespersons Bill Rodgers, Brynmor John and John Silkin time and again repudiated the Party's policy in private conversation with journalists. None ever saw his primary remit as arguing for non-nuclear defence, either inside or outside the Commons. Even Denzil Davies, later to resign in a famous dispute with Kinnock over the issue, rarely mentioned the policy unless pressed to do so.

Unilateralism Sabotaged

Labour went into the 1983 general election campaign clearly committed to a non-nuclear defence policy, cancellation of the Trident nuclear-armed submarines programme, removal of cruise missiles and closure of all nuclear bases on British territory within the lifetime of a Labour government. The Party was also committed to substantial reductions in defence spending and the long-term dissolution of all military blocs, East and West. It was the most radical and coherent defence policy the Party had ever offered the electorate.

On the specific question of the fate of Polaris, however, there was already confusion. The manifesto stated, in contravention of clear instructions from the Party conference, that Polaris would be included in multilateral and bilateral negotiations with the Soviet Union; it also implied that in the end Polaris would be removed unconditionally, regardless of the outcome of any such negotiations. This ambiguity, the direct result of pressure from Denis Healey and the parliamentary right – and Foot's willingness to accede to such pressure – proved a hostage to fortune. The Party's opponents could use it to present Labour as hopelessly incoherent when it came to the country's defence. Those inside the Party who disagreed with the non-nuclear policy – including Callaghan and Healey – could use it to present their own views to the public rather than those of the Party.

When Neil Kinnock stood for the leadership of the Labour Party in 1983 one of his strongest suits was that he was considered to be a staunch unilateralist and was therefore in tune with the rank and file on the single most emotive issue facing the Party. His first major public engagement as Labour leader was an address to a huge CND rally held in Hyde Park in late October 1983. This event was billed as the new Labour leader "coming home" to speak directly to the constituency closest to his heart: the peace movement. At the rally he reiterated Labour's commitment to non-nuclear defence to an audience of over a quarter of a million. Reactions to his speech were mixed – some criticized it as hesitant, nervous, lacking in clarity – but no one predicted that it was to be the last occasion on which Kinnock would speak at a peace movement event.

Kinnock spent his first few years as leader working out a new accommodation with the Labour Party's Atlanticist right wing. A crucial part of that accommodation was an attempt to refashion not the unilateralist commitment itself (still endorsed by the overwhelming majority of the rank and file) but the context in which it was presented. Out went the moral case against possession or use of nuclear weapons. Out went the political critique of the division of Europe between East and West or indeed any scepticism at all about the institutions of the Cold War. Out went any repudiation of Washington's sway over British foreign policy. Instead, Kinnock emphasized Labour's willingness to work within NATO to protect the security of Western Europe. Labour in government would pursue its non-nuclear policy in conjunction with its partners in NATO for the purpose of "collective security" through a strategy of "defensive defence".

Although at this stage the leadership avoided referring to a direct military threat from the Soviet Union, it went out of its way to insist on Labour's preparedness to defend Britain from any external attack. Kinnock wanted everyone to know that his concern for "national security" was as strong as Margaret Thatcher's. Labour's argument with the Tories shifted from moral and political to pragmatic grounds: nuclear weapons, it was said, were an inadequate means by which to defend the country.

The first step in this direction was taken at the 1984 Party conference, at which the NEC statement "Defence and Security for Britain" was agreed by 5,300,000 votes to 1,300,000. The statement reiterated Labour's commitment to a non-nuclear defence policy, cancellation of Trident, removal of cruise and all other nuclear weapons based on British territory. But it also pledged that under a Labour government Britain would remain a loyal member of NATO. Moreover, any financial savings achieved through scrapping nuclear forces would be reallocated within the overall defence budget to meet the costs of "strengthened" conventional defences.

The statement had originally been drafted by full-time researchers at Walworth Road and was presented to the June 1984 NEC international committee by the new leadership of Kinnock and Hattersley on a take-it-or-leave-it basis, a practice that was to become common in the future. Attempts by the left to amend it were voted down by seven votes to six.[3] When two weeks later the paper came to the full NEC, Tony Benn again proposed a series of amendments setting out the Party's oppositon to warmongering and rejection of the myths of the Cold War. Kinnock acknowledged the logic of Benn's arguments but insisted that it would look as if Labour was "soft on the Russians" and was undermining the

United States. Besides, he told the executive, the existence of Soviet missiles was evidence of a Soviet intention to attack.[4] Benn's amendments were defeated.

Reservations within the Labour Party were swamped by assurances that this was the only way unilateralism could be sold to the public. The Party's defence spokesperson, Denzil Davies, told conference that the NEC statement was "morally right and militarily sound" and promised that it would show the country that "this Party wants to defend our country".[5]

Left-wing speakers in the conference debate treated the NEC statement as secondary to the TGWU composite, which reiterated the defence policies passed in the previous four years. Their fear was that the small minority that did not believe in the policy would seek to sabotage it, as they had done in the past. "It is about time that everybody in the Party supported nuclear disarmament, instead of just 95 per cent," cried the delegate from Orpington CLP. "I make a plea to people who have been appointed as Labour spokesmen for defence," added Eric Clarke of the NUM, "if you don't like the policy, don't take up the portfolio."[6]

With the exception of the diehards in the AEU and EETPU, the right backed the 1984 NEC statement and others like it because the arguments all remained firmly within its own pro-Washington perspective. Jim Callaghan made this clear when he told the conference that the NEC statement was "a great improvement" on what the Party had said before and described it as part of an "emerging policy" with which he could agree – as long as dangerously "destabilizing" unilateral moves were avoided. Denis Healey also announced that he was able to support the NEC statement, while still telling delegates that the only hope of avoiding a nuclear catastrophe was to exercise "British influence inside NATO".[7]

Key centre-left trade unions such as NUPE and influential "soft left" MPs like Robin Cook, were also prepared to back the statement because they saw it as a means of protecting the non-nuclear policy from direct assault. However, the centre did agree with the left that the Party needed to mount a vigorous campaign to win public support for that policy. Accordingly, a 1984 composite proposed by the TGWU, opposed only by the AEU and the EETPU, called for "a more determined campaign, inside and outside Parliament, to win support for Labour's peace policies". The composite included wide-ranging proposals for campaigning on such issues as arms conversion, civil defence and nuclear-free zones.[8] Similar calls for a public campaign had been issued at the 1983 conference and were to be repeated in 1985 and 1986. Not one speaker at any of these conferences ever took issue with such demands. Yet neither the national Labour Party apparatus at Walworth Road nor the Parliamentary Labour

Party ever mounted the campaigns that successive Party conferences demanded.

For the Labour leadership's new media strategists, the less said about defence the better. Whenever they were forced to address the defence issue – usually by virtue of an attack by the Tories in the House of Commons – Labour spokespersons concentrated on Labour's determination to defend the nation by conventional means. Voters were assured at every opportunity that Labour's policy was entirely in keeping with the pro-Washington tradition of post-1945 British foreign policy.

At the 1986 conference, Kinnock used his leader's speech to respond to criticism of Labour's defence policy from the Reagan administration. He promised that a Labour government under his leadership would pursue its non-nuclear strategy as a loyal member of NATO. "I would die for my country," Kinnock declared, "but I would never allow my country to die for me."[9] A new NEC statement was approved, warning yet again that a Labour government might have to use savings on nuclear weapons to meet increased conventional defence needs; again there was little debate. For the seventh consecutive year, conference reaffirmed its support for unilateralism, this time by a margin of five to one.

In late 1986, as a general election loomed, the leadership at last took steps to launch the defence campaign the Party had been demanding for so long. It was to be embodied in a document entitled *A Modern Britain in the Modern World: the power to defend our country*.

At a meeting of the campaign strategy committee in November a paper from Peter Mandelson stated that the NEC initiative would generate huge and positive publicity and would "reassure" people employed in the defence industries and the public in general about the willingness of a Labour government to shoulder its responsibility for the defence of the nation. Kinnock advised the NEC that the mass media would be on the lookout for anything too explicit; he believed the thrust of the campaign should be to "build up the confidence in the Party among the opinion formers". Robin Cook, ostensibly a committed unilateralist, was concerned only about increasing funds for polling research and personnel at Walworth Road. Kinnock was delighted to agree.[10]

On November 25th, Kinnock declared publicly that a Labour government implementing the Party's non-nuclear defence policy would still welcome US ships carrying nuclear weapons into British ports. On November 26th, the NEC agreed by twenty-six votes to six to launch *Modern Britain in the Modern World*, even though the NEC itself had not been allowed to amend the proposed statement and had been given no opportunity to approve the initiative in the first place. Tony Benn moved that long-standing conference policy calling for the mutual dissolution of NATO and the Warsaw Pact be incorporated into the document. Kinnock knew that if it was put to a direct vote on the NEC, Benn's motion would win; he moved that it not be taken at all – and was backed by a majority of those present.[11]

The long-awaited "campaign" was unveiled on December 10th 1986. It consisted entirely of a glossy brochure – its cover swathed in a Union Jack – with an accompanying party political broadcast on radio and television. The media were fascinated. They had been extensively briefed about the leadership's battle to sanitize the document. Their response was to seek out and find all the traces of political fudge, all the verbal contortions and cautious qualifications and display them for the whole country to see. The document's lack of clarity and consistency was made all the more obvious by the intensity of the hype surrounding it. *Modern Britain in the Modern World* emphasized the Labour Party's commitment to strengthen Britain's conventional forces. The Tories, it declared, should cease investing in "nuclear pretence in favour of strong defence"; they were even accused of running down the country's defences. The document described NATO as "a partnership of democracies", ignoring the fact that Turkey, Greece, Spain and Portugal had all been members while under military rule. It argued that the Alliance must continue as long as there was a potential threat to Western Europe from the Soviet Union. Later the same people were to argue that it must continue even though the Soviet Union was no longer a threat to Western Europe. While confirming the Party's commitment to non-nuclear defence the document also made clear the willingness of a future Labour government to shelter under the US nuclear umbrella.

The inconsistency and dishonesty of these formulations could not be disguised from either the Party's friends or its enemies. Within the Party, there was disappointment and confusion. Kinnock told members that Labour's priorities were "an absolute commitment to a sound national defence policy and to membership of NATO" – not nuclear disarmament.[12] This was not what the Party had been waiting for. Even strong supporters of the leadership in the constituencies refused to have anything to do with *Modern Britain in the Modern World*. However, the "soft left" *Chartist*, linked to the Labour Co-ordinating Committee, declared that for all its inadequacies the document should be endorsed: "we will have to bite our tongues".[13]

Most of the first issue of *Labour Party News*, published in early 1987, was taken up with excerpts from *Modern Britain in the Modern World*. Cartoon graphics courtesy of the *Sunday Mirror* depicted tanks, submarines, missiles and soldiers scattered across a map of Europe. Later, Mandelson complained about the poor Party response to the initiative:

> Despite heavy promotion and the considerable immediate impact of the campaign in the media some resistance was encountered among CLPs and trade unions to engaging in the campaign. This may have been related to

public reaction, which indicated higher identification of the party commitment to conventional defence and to NATO but no growth in support for the
Party's non-nuclear defence strategy. Responding to public interest many
CLPs preferred to make economic and social policy a higher campaign
priority.[14]

In fact, Party activists had found the content and form of the defence
document deeply alienating. As for Fleet Street, it soon concluded that
the policy was neither one thing nor the other; Labour in government still
could not be relied upon to protect the military establishment. The Tories
were delighted at what they saw as proof positive of Labour's internal
inconsistency on defence. How could Britain remain a non-nuclear
member of a nuclear alliance? How could a Labour government give up
nuclear weapons when the country it now openly named as the chief
potential aggressor, the Soviet Union, possessed so many of them? Why
did it say it was in favour of talks on multilateral disarmament when it
would give up its own weapons regardless of what happened in those
talks? The leadership was unwilling and unable to answer these questions because to do so would require a searching critique of all the
premisses of the Cold War and the Atlantic Alliance.

For Kinnock the campaign was an attempt to square a circle. The
balance of political forces inside the Party made it impossible to jettison
the non-nuclear defence policy; yet the Party leadership was convinced it
was an electoral liability. Even more important, that leadership, including Kinnock himself, was convinced that the unilateral abandonment of
nuclear weapons would never be tolerated by the British establishment.
It was fear of confronting that establishment – not the supposed impossi-
bility of winning majority support for nuclear disarmament – that prevented Labour from ever launching the real campaign on defence for
which conference kept asking. At each stage the "soft left" justified the
leadership's tortured formulations (and its own willingness to compromise with the pro-nuclear right) as pragmatic means of protecting
unilateralism. But the main effect of those formulations and compro-
mises was to discredit unilateralism and lay the basis for its
abandonment.

Kinnock's response to the Zircon scandal which broke five months
before the 1987 general election revealed just how deeply embroiled he
had become with the military establishment. When the government
forced the BBC to ban journalist Duncan Campbell's television film about
the Zircon spy satellite system, Kinnock backed it in the House of
Commons, criticizing only its "incompetence" in protecting official
secrets. He had previously been given a confidential briefing on aspects
of the film that were said to endanger "national security". Attorney
General Michael Havers was thus able to assure the High Court that the

Opposition would back the government on this issue in Parliament. Following the leader's craven performance, Kevin Barron, his parliamentary private secretary, was besieged by dismayed Labour MPs in the Commons tearoom.

When Special Branch officers knocked down Duncan Campbell's door in their search for incriminating material, Kinnock still refused to condemn the government, confining his intervention to a demand for more government consultation with the BBC. Later, police officers interrogating Campbell said to him, "The Leader of the Opposition thinks that revealing the existence of the Zircon satellite was a threat to national security. Why do you presume to disagree with him?"[15] When the police conducted a trawl for evidence through the offices of BBC Scotland, the *Guardian* placed the blame on Kinnock's shoulders. During the emergency Commons debate on the trawl, Kinnock and Hattersley were absent. Deputizing for them, home affairs spokesperson Gerald Kaufman argued that the government should have acted earlier to contain the secrets. Kinnock stuck to the same theme, attacking the Tories for "eight months of complacency followed by two weeks of intensive bullying or attempted bullying".[16]

As the general election of 1987 approached, Labour's defence policy was in as much disarray as in 1983. Bryan Gould, the campaign manager, kept promising but never delivered a counterattack to the mounting Tory jibes. In his Fabian Society tract, *Labour's First Hundred Days*, Gould failed even to mention nuclear disarmament. At the end of January, a Labour Party delegation visited Lord Carrington at NATO headquarters to assure him of Labour's loyalty to the alliance. Among the party was Nigel Williamson, at that time still editor of *Tribune*; within a week of his return Kinnock had designated him the first editor of the new *Labour Party News*. While Thatcher visited Moscow and sealed her friendship with Gorbachev in front of television cameras, Kinnock planned a visit to Washington in the spring. In the second week of February, a Marplan survey revealed that Gorbachev was far more trusted by the British public than Reagan, but Kinnock had his sights set on Washington. Just before going, he announced that a Labour government would accept cruise missiles if progress was made at the disarmament talks in Geneva. This was a direct contravention of agreed Party policy, but the "soft left" kept its counsel; the Labour Co-ordinating Committee urged Kinnock to moderate his announcement by setting a twelve-month limit on the provisional acceptance of cruise missiles, but the leader rejected the idea immediately.

The nature of the Labour Co-ordinating Committee's commitment to unilateralism became clear when a member of its executive, Lesley Smith (soon to be a Labour Party press officer), urged Joan Ruddock, ex-chair of CND, to stand for the NEC not in order to bolster support for the non-nuclear defence policy, but as the "best chance of reducing the votes of Tony Benn and Dennis Skinner".[17]

In his *Guardian* column in February, Ian Aitken wondered: "What on earth has happened to that great campaign on defence policy which we were led to believe the Labour Party was going to conduct in advance of the election?"[18] Polling evidence indicates that had such a campaign been conducted, it would have met with a positive response. In the months before the election, a Marplan poll found that 27 per cent were in favour of cutting military expenditure and only 17 per cent favoured increasing it. While 34 per cent were for dismantling nuclear weapons, 56 per cent disapproved of US nuclear weapons being based on British soil. And 86 per cent saw no great military danger from the USSR.

Instead of appealing to and consolidating the potential support for a non-nuclear policy, Labour was engulfed in parliamentary chicanery. On March 10th, during a defence debate initiated by the SDP–Liberal Alliance, Jim Callaghan launched a well-publicized attack on Labour's defence policy. "It is my experience that any concession that you make to the Russians they will pocket it, say 'Thank you', and give you nothing in return," he told the Commons. Trident, he added, should be completed. The former Prime Minister's swan song was soon being reported to the entire country. It demonstrated, just as he had intended, that the Party hierarchy remained as unreconciled as ever to the non-nuclear policy. The following day – the morning on which Labour was launching its programme for jobs, supposedly the centrepiece of its general election strategy – there was chaos in the PLP. John Prescott upbraided Callaghan in the Commons tearoom in full view of Tory MPs.

Labour MP John Gilbert, a former defence minister and a long-time NATO champion well connected to the US establishment, appeared on Channel Four to tell the voters that Labour's defence policy was "an albatross and a burden . . . opposed by many of the shadow cabinet and the PLP".[19] On March 12th an article attacking unilateralism appeared in *The Times*; its author was Richard Heller, research assistant to shadow cabinet member Gerald Kaufman and a former political adviser to Denis Healey. Kaufman explained to the press that he did not agree with Heller's view and was sacking him. In the Commons, Margaret Thatcher congratulated Callaghan on his speech. Kinnock's only response was to urge Labour MPs to follow his example of "self-discipline".

Kinnock's pilgrimage to Washington, which was meant to bolster his credentials as a world statesman on an equal footing with Thatcher, proved a debacle. The White House made its preference for Thatcher plain and its contempt for Kinnock and hostility to his Party's unilateralist policy unequivocal. It added insult to injury by giving Kinnock an audience lasting only some fifteen to twenty minutes. The effect of this insult was compounded by Charles Clarke's ill-advised decision to enter into a public wrangle with the White House staff over the exact length of time Ronald Reagan had allotted Kinnock.

During the 1987 election Labour politicians usually known for their astuteness in dealing with the media kept managing to slip up when it came to defence. John Smith was mauled on a phone-in programme by a straight question from an ex-soldier. Kinnock told David Frost in a Sunday morning interview on May 24th that Britain had no need to rely on nuclear weapons because "you have to make any occupation totally untenable".[20] His muddled syntax and dubious logic attracted adverse headlines and made Labour's defence policy look just what the Tories had been saying it was: an invitation for Soviet troops to invade. This impression was only confirmed a few days later when Kinnock, in an attempt to justify his remarks on the Frost programme, cited the Mujaha-deen's success in resisting the Soviet Union's forces in Afghanistan. At the daily untelevised press conferences campaign co-ordinator Bryan Gould simply refused to answer questions about what the tabloids had dubbed Kinnock's "Dad's Army" proposals. The Party also refused to nominate a spokesperson for a Radio Four discussion on the issue. Kinnock, still touring Britain in search of photo-opportunities, was accused by the press of avoiding cross-examination. Meanwhile the Tories ran a series of adverts in the papers showing a soldier with his hands raised in surrender with the slogan "Labour's policy on arms" emblazoned underneath.

Ronald Reagan got in on the act, letting it be known that if Labour won the election, the US would have to persuade it of the grievous error of nuclear disarmament. Healey and Kinnock answered by repeating their earlier promises to keep cruise missiles while negotiations amongst the superpowers were going on; in effect they acknowledged that nuclear weapons did defend the country and thereby further undermined the Party's case against them. Lack of confidence at the top was felt at the bottom. Fewer than half of Labour's local election addresses mentioned defence; nearly three-quarters of these, however, stressed Labour's commitment to increased conventional defence.

Opinion polls showed that during the course of the campaign defence rose to the top of the political agenda – but certainly not because the Labour leadership wanted it that way. According to the study of the 1987 general election by David Butler and Dennis Kavanagh, only 20 per cent of those interviewed on May 18th named defence as a major campaign issue; ten days later – with less than two weeks left till polling day – 60 per cent named it as such. On May 18th, 57 per cent said Labour would handle the country's defence badly; ten days later it was 66 per cent. This was the only issue on which any discernible movement of opinion occurred as a result of the campaign but, as in 1983, the movement was against Labour. The Party had only itself to blame.

Unilateralism Dumped

Immediately after the 1987 election defeat, pressure began to build for the leader to disavow unilateralism. Key members of Kinnock's office and staff in both the policy directorate and the campaigns and communications directorate made their feelings known. Some were surprised to find they were knocking on an open door.

Kinnock and his closest advisers recognized that the strong emotive and political support for unilateralism within the Party at every level meant that the leadership would have to proceed with great caution. While some members of the shadow cabinet counselled Kinnock to reject the policy in a grand public gesture, others knew that this would precipitate a confrontation which, at this juncture, the leadership could not be sure it would win. The ground had to be prepared. A key role was to be played by erstwhile champions of unilateralism on the "soft left", including Joan Ruddock, who had made her name and won her safe Labour seat entirely on the basis of her role in the peace movement. She wrote in *Tribune* in July 1987 that in the light of Gorbachev's initiatives, "the political gap between multilateralists and unilateralists in the Labour Party has narrowed dramatically, in fact to the point where the traditional distinction has become obsolete".[21]

When the launch of the Policy Review was endorsed by a compliant Party conference in October 1987, the leadership was careful to stress that there was no hidden agenda involving the abandonment of unilateralism. All policies should be reconsidered from time to time, it was argued, in a spirit of open intellectual inquiry; it was natural that defence should be among these. But for those closest to the Kinnock leadership, from the outset one of the primary purposes of the Policy Review was to engineer a change from "unilateralism" to "multilateralism" – that is, from a determination to end British participation in the nuclear arms race to a willingness to retain and even threaten to use the country's nuclear capacity.

At the conference, for the eighth year running the non-nuclear defence policy was reaffirmed by a large majority. However, the AEU and EETPU now changed tack: instead of outright opposition, they called for the next Labour government to hold a national referendum on the question; this was rebuffed by a large majority but it was a foretaste of things to come. In off-the-record briefings the leadership opined that the distinction between "multilateralists" and "unilateralists" was much overstated. Tony Clarke, the chair of the NEC international committee, attacked Ken Livingstone from the conference plaform; Livingstone's sin was to have questioned the leadership's commitment to the cause of nuclear disarmament.

The domination of the Policy Review process by Kinnock's office and selected members of the shadow cabinet was clearly illustrated by the manipulation of the defence brief. Gerald Kaufman, the new shadow spokesperson on foreign affairs, and Tony Clarke were appointed co-convenors of the Foreign and Defence Policy Review Group; they were joined by Denzil Davies, the Party's defence spokesperson, George Robertson and Stuart Holland from the Parliamentary Labour Party, Gwyneth Dunwoody and Joan Lestor from the NEC, and Ron Todd, the TGWU general secretary. Kaufman, Clarke, Robertson and Dunwoody were all pro-nuclear and pro-Washington; Lestor, Davies and Holland were less certain but pliable. Only Todd was a committed unilateralist. Charles Clarke kept a watching brief as a co-opted member representing the leader's office. Throughout the two-year process that led to the rejection of unilateralism Clarke, acting for Kinnock, was to remain in close contact with Kaufman, guiding and pre-empting the review group's every move.

The group's first key decision was to postpone any fundamental review of defence policy (as opposed to foreign policy as a whole) until the second year of the process, 1989. The ostensible reason for this was the rapidly changing international situation. The real reason was uncertainty among the leadership as to whether it could at this stage face down the Party on this crucial issue. This explains the strange, repeated but hesitant exercises in anti-unilateralist kite-flying in which Kinnock engaged in 1988. In February he went out of his way to send congratulations to CND on its thirtieth anniversary and stressed the need "to make and win the arguments for non-nuclear defence".[22] Then came the Benn–Heffer leadership challenge; Kinnock was in no doubt that he would trounce Benn, but the contest still made him uneasy. As so often when he was uneasy he resorted to arrogant self-assertion. And as so often his arrogance led to blunders.

On May 10th 1988, the *Independent* published a front-page story headlined "Kinnock set to modify nuclear weapons policy". The paper's political editor, Anthony Bevins, reported remarks made by Kinnock to the effect that he was now prepared to retain Trident nuclear submarines, that nuclear weapons could be used as a means of negotiating with the Soviet Union, and that Britain's continuing membership of NATO did indeed imply acceptance of the US nuclear umbrella.

Kinnock and his advisers claimed the *Independent* story was a breach of confidence; the remarks had been made in an off-the-record private conversation. In retrospect, however, it is hard to avoid the conclusion that the briefing was yet another attempt "to lead from the front" by floating proposals in the press before consulting the Party itself. Kinnock was perfectly aware in speaking in this manner before a journalist of Bevins's standing that such remarks would reach a wider audience. He was, however, unprepared for the backlash they caused within the Party: the *Independent* article seemed to confirm the now widespread belief that the leadership was determined to jettison the non-nuclear policy. This impression was buttressed by other statements made by Kinnock at this time, including a speech to the Socialist International in Madrid in which he alluded obscurely to the Soviet Union's military capacity "not being purely defensive in all conditions and eventualities".

On June 5th 1988, in the course of an interview on BBC Television's *This Week, Next Week*, Kinnock stated that, in the light of "changed international circumstances", "there is no need now for a something-for-nothing" unilateralism because "the fact is now that it can be something-for-something".[23]

Kinnock came under fire for his apparently spontaneous alteration of the Party's policy, especially as the Policy Review group had made such a point of freezing the whole discussion. As a result, his leadership was questioned by many who none the less backed him strongly against the challenge from Benn. In a direct response to his media outbursts, the hyper-cautious general executive council of the TGWU defied general secretary Ron Todd and refused to nominate either Kinnnock or Hattersley for the Labour leadership. On June 13th, in a late-night telephone call to a friendly journalist, Denzil Davies dramatically resigned as the Party's defence spokesperson. He made it clear that he had been hopelessly undermined by Kinnock's style of leadership. Davies did not seem to object to the moves to get rid of unilateralism, just to the manner in which they were being made. He was a cautious politician who had backed Healey against both Benn and Silkin in 1981. A barrister with a firm command of whatever brief he was given (unlike either his predecessor or successor as Labour's defence spokesperson), he had a grasp of the detail of defence policy and a mind of his own. There was, therefore, no place for him in the Kinnock team.

The "soft left" was dismayed by the Davies episode and by Kinnock's use of the media. Robin Cook, David Blunkett and Joan Ruddock made protests directly to the leader. Blunkett called his attention to the "confusion and genuine concern" felt throughout the Party at Kinnock's apparent change of position and urged him to retract.[24] "Soft left" support was vital if Roy Hattersley was to see off the deputy leadership challenge from John Prescott. For once, Kinnock felt obliged to disregard his advisers; he withdrew his earlier remarks. To the relief of the "soft left", he made a public statement in the *Independent* on June 20th reaffirming his personal support for the existing non-nuclear policy.

Following Davies's resignation Kinnock appointed Davies's deputy, Martin O'Neill, as his successor. O'Neill, whose annual failure to win a place on the shadow cabinet in the vote of the Parliamentary Labour Party was to become a running embarrassment to the leadership, saw his function simply and solely as representing the views of the Party leader. One of his first acts was to pen an article in *Labour Party News* deriding the "outdated" divisions between "unilateral" and "multilateral".[25]

O'Neill's role on the Policy Review group was entirely subordinate to Gerald Kaufman, the foreign affairs spokesperson whose allotted task was to sort out the details of the Party's new defence policy. Kinnock's office, and Charles Clarke in particular, took on the job of mobilizing support within the Party for the change. Although defence was not supposed to be discussed as part of the Policy Review at the 1988 conference, the leadership knew that unilateralists would once again seek to have the existing policy reaffirmed. According to the account given in *Labour Rebuilt* by Colin Hughes and Patrick Wintour (whose sources included members of Kinnock's own staff) Kinnock and his office were to go to extraordinary lengths to ensure that a resolution reflecting the intentions of the leadership would be placed before the 1988 conference. Even if it failed to win outright, they reasoned that it would garner a substantial block vote and pave the way for the work of the review group.

In the spring of 1988 Mike Gapes, then the International Officer at Walworth Road and now Labour MP for Ilford South, was asked by Charles Clarke to draft a resolution that proposed reductions in Britain's nuclear capacity by "multilateral, unilateral and bilateral means". It may have seemed innocuous to many, but the insertion of "mutilateral" and "bilateral" in this context had only one meaning: that a Labour government would retain nuclear weapons for an indefinite period. This resolution was given by Kinnock's office to Tony Clarke, deputy general secretary of the UCW. As chair of the NEC's international committee, Clarke was ostensibly the elected officer to whom Gapes was accountable; in this case the chain of accountability seemed to have been reversed. The strategy was for Clarke and his general secretary, Alan Tuffin, to get the UCW to submit the Clarke–Gapes resolution to the Party conference. But the majority of the UCW executive committee kept faith with its own conference policy by amending the text of the resolution to remove reference to "bilateral and multilateral", thus making the resolution exactly what Kinnock's office did not want: explicitly unilateralist. Kinnock's office then turned to John Edmonds. He arranged for the GMB to submit an amendment to the UCW resolution reinserting the words "bilateral and multilateral".

In the end, forty-six resolutions from constituency parties and trade unions were submitted to the 1988 Party conference calling for the reaffirmation of Labour's non-nuclear defence policy. At a private meeting in Blackpool the UCW leadership, defying the mandate it had received from its own conference, accepted the amendment tabled by the

GMB. The conference arrangements committee immediately agreed to prioritize the resulting composite for debate, although it could claim only the support of the two unions, in contrast to the broad-based support that existed for the unilateralist composite. The conference was thus invited to debate two positions on defence policy: Composite 56, which contained an unequivocal commitment to unilateral nuclear disarmament, and Composite 55, the UCW/GMB alternative, supported by the Labour leadership. Had it passed, Composite 55 would have provided an escape route for the leadership, allowing it to ignore all the other resolutions calling for unilateral action. After pressure from Kinnock, the NEC voted to ask for remittance of the unilateralist Composite 56, knowing that the movers of the resolution would refuse to remit and that the NEC would then have to ask the conference to oppose it. It was the first time since 1980 that the NEC had opposed a straightforward unilateralist motion.

In his speech to the conference Kinnock once again laid great stress on his personal commitment to the cause of nuclear disarmament, but he also made clear that he believed that "changing international circumstances" meant that "bilateral" and "multilateral" negotiations had now to be considered. In the defence debate the balance of speakers was crudely fixed by Gwyneth Dunwoody, who had been placed in the chair by the NEC. Of the many delegates seeking to speak in support of Composite 56 only one, Ron Todd, was called by Dunwoody, while five people, including John Edmonds, Denis Healey and Martin O'Neill, were given time to oppose unilateralism from the rostrum. Just how far the leadership was prepared to go in rigging the debate was revealed by Dunwoody's decision to call one Ann Kean to speak. A personal friend of the Kinnocks, Kean was attending conference as a visitor, not a delegate, and thus had no right to speak in debate. But when the accredited delegate from her constituency, Brentford and Isleworth, failed to turn up, Kean was appointed delegate by persons acting on behalf of the NEC. It was an unprecedented manoeuvre. In her speech to the conference she talked of her previous commitment to the unilateralist cause and her subsequent recognition – in the light of "changed international circumstances" – that such an approach was out of date and other options had now to be explored. Her speech bore the unmistakable imprint of Kinnock's office.

Despite these machinations, Composite 56 was passed on a card vote by 3,715,000 votes to 2,471,000. The alternative promoted by the leadership, Composite 55, was defeated by 2,942,000 votes to 3,277,000 – a narrow margin of 335,000 votes. Clearly, several unions had voted for both composites, naively believing that they could doff their caps to the leadership while still supporting the non-nuclear policy. The leadership now set about targeting those unions, knowing that it needed only a handful of block votes to kill off the policy the following year once and for all.

The Policy Review group led by Gerald Kaufman set about drawing up proposals to be submitted to the 1989 conference. Martin O'Neill was charged with the task of preparing public and Party opinion for the impending change. Kinnock's personal staff undertook the job of persuading key trade unions to support the new policy; they targeted the UCW, NCU, NUPE and USDAW. Kinnock made known his repugnance for those trade unions that in his view gave the impression of "perpetually frustrating the direction of the Party".[26] It was obvious he was referring to the TGWU, whose biannual delegate conference was to be held in the summer of 1989.

Following review group "fact-finding missions" to Moscow and Washington, which were little more than public relations stunts, Kaufman drafted the final version of its report, which was submitted to Kinnock for approval before it was shown to any other members of the review group. Ron Todd did not attend the final sessions of the group, allegedly because he was preoccupied with a dock strike; it seems likely that he had read the writing on the wall some months before. Although there were minor objections from a minority of group members (notably Stuart Holland, who had just resigned his parliamentary seat) the report was agreed and submitted to the NEC. Up till then it had been classified "top secret" by the Party leadership. Even Roy Hattersley was forced to read it in Kaufman's office and was refused a copy to take away. None the less, few NEC members were surprised to find that the report "Britain in the World" abandoned the Party's commitment to a non-nuclear defence. In its place were pledges to cancel the fourth Trident submarine but to keep the other three, to maintain the "independent nuclear deterrent", to allow US nuclear bases to remain on British territory and continue to shelter under the American nuclear umbrella.

The NEC met in special session on the 8th and 9th of May 1989 to ratify review group reports. Kinnock was assured of the support of the traditonal right wing, but it was the "soft left" which was crucial to his success. A few weeks before, with the Labour leadership's imminent abandonment of unilateralism being trumpeted in every newspaper in the country, a number of prominent "soft lefts", including NEC members David Blunkett, Clare Short, Jo Richardson and Margaret Beckett, signed a *Tribune* statement reaffirming their support for the non-nuclear defence policy. On the evening of May 8th, Blunkett called a meeting of fellow "soft lefts" Cook, Beckett, Richardson and Short to try to save the one commitment which they had all always claimed was non-negotiable. Robin Cook, it transpired, had already met Kinnock and struck a deal to the effect that Labour would reserve the right to enter bilateral negotiations with the Soviet Union if multilateral talks were delayed. Blunkett himself had also already met with Kinnock; he wanted the leader to agree to a time limit for the removal of Trident submarines, but by this time Kinnock was confident of winning the vote and saw no need to make any concessions. Clare Short was confused. She was pushing a series of peripheral amendments on such matters as nuclear proliferation and the use of the deterrent outside NATO; none of the others expressed any interest in these. In the account of this period that Short later gave to Wintour and Hughes, she claimed that she had undergone a painful self-education in defence matters and had come to feel that "much of the unilateralist argument had been made out of ignorance".[27] Observers are still waiting for evidence of her new-found nuclear expertise to emerge in the Commons or elsewhere.

On May 9th, Gerald Kaufman presented the "Britain and the World" section of the Policy Review to the NEC. Tony Benn moved to delete the whole defence section of the review and substitute for it his own paper reasserting unilateralism and Labour's internationalist commitments to peace and disarmament. He pointed out that Kaufman's proposals amounted to a new policy of unilateral nuclear *rearmament*. The completion of the three Trident submarines would constitute a nine-fold increase in Britain's nuclear capacity at a time when both the United States and the USSR were reducing theirs. Ron Todd had written a letter urging the NEC to stay unilateralist and arguing that the basic logic of the Policy Review – that we had to keep nuclear weapons to get rid of them – was indefensible.

Kinnock announced he was not interested "in history" and that he would never again argue for what he now dismissed as "one-sided" disarmament. "I have been to the Kremlin, to the White House, to the Elysée Palace arguing for unilateral disarmament. They couldn't comprehend the idea of giving up weapons with nothing in return. They couldn't understand something for nothing." Clearly, that resonant phrase had never been discarded after its premature outing the year before. Kinnock went on to cite "patriotism and common sense" as his reasons for abandoning his earlier position. "I have ambitions for a non-nuclear world . . . but we want partners in negotiations. We must get into power."[28]

The hard right clapped the speech. Much play was made of this by the leader's office and an account appeared in somewhat exaggerated form in the press the next day. Sam McCluskie said he would vote for the document; he made it clear this was a vote of confidence in the leadership and that therefore the trade union representatives should ignore any union policies to the contrary and vote for the document. Bryan Gould also supported the new stance. He argued that Labour would inherit these weapons from the Tories and that they should be used to help start negotiations. He dismissed supporters of unilateralism as "seekers of theological purity".

Martin O'Neill was also present at the meeting and argued that the cancellation costs on Trident would be so high that it made financial sense to keep the system to use as a "negotiating card". Kinnock backed him up, saying that a Labour government could not decommission Trident because Gorbachev wanted it as a partner in negotiations.[29] As so often in the debate about nuclear weapons, "negotiations" were presented as an end in themselves rather than a means to an end – disarmament – which might be achieved a good deal more quickly, and more assuredly, by direct action. This reprise of Aneurin Bevan's famous "naked into the conference chamber" argument was all the more unconvincing in that since Bevan had made that case Britain had not been allowed to participate in the SALT 1, SALT 2 or START negotiations, despite its possession of nuclear weapons.

Blunkett proposed an amendment stipulating that if at the end of five years a Labour government had still not achieved a non-nuclear Europe through negotiations, it would take "independent steps to remove nuclear weapons and bases from our soil". Opposed by Kinnock, it was defeated by sixteen votes to nine – the usual left-wing foursome of Benn, Skinner, Livingstone and the Young Socialists representative was augmented this time by Blunkett himself, Richardson, Short, Beckett and Eddie Haigh (following TGWU policy) but not Robin Cook, Bryan Gould or Joan Lestor.[30]

Kaufman accommodated most of Clare Short's proposed amendments (which he privately regarded as trivial) but he was unhappy with Kinnock's deal with Cook. He was horrified at the thought of Britain going it alone in "bilateral" negotiations with Moscow. In the end he accepted a meaningless fudge which incorporated a weak reference to "bilateral" talks in order to save Cook's face. Cook's proposal was speedily dropped once his support for Kaufman's document had been secured.

Ken Livingstone's proposal that the NEC reaffirm the existing conference commitment to remove all nuclear weapons in the lifetime of a single Parliament was defeated by eighteen votes to eight. Among the eight were Blunkett, Beckett and Richardson. Clare Short abstained.[31] Tom Sawyer made a point of being absent at this moment: he was still bound by NUPE's unilateralist commitment. On a recorded vote, the document as a whole was then endorsed – with the same eight who had voted for Livingstone's amendment opposing it. Three others abstained on it: Short, Ted O'Brien from the print union SOGAT (which had a long-standing unilateralist policy), plus Sawyer, back in the room for the final vote.[32]

Kinnock's majority on the NEC was larger than his advisers had predicted. Even they had not counted on the eagerness of the "soft left" and the trade union representatives to please the Party leader. Kinnock staffers moved rapidly to exploit this success by briefing the press to the effect that the Party leader had delivered a stunning oration and faced down the demons of the hard left.

During the debate Livingstone had asked whether or not Labour would now actually be willing to press "the nuclear button". Bryan Gould, well aware that this would become an issue, told the *Daily Telegraph*: "The purpose of retaining a deterrent is not to use it or even to threaten to use it"[33] – which rather made a nonsense of the entire debate. Over the next few weeks Livingstone raised the question repeatedly in public. Kinnock, determined to show the world that he was too tough on defence to be fazed by Livingstone's goading, told the Welsh Labour Party conference on May 12th that he would hold to a policy that "never says 'yes' or 'no' to the question 'will you press the button?' ". A Labour government would keep nuclear weapons and "as long as the weapons exist the assumption by others will inevitably be that there may be circumstances in which those weapons might be used".[34]

Already, Kinnock had discarded the arguments he had used at the NEC, which had been told that nuclear weapons were to be kept in order to get Britain a seat at the negotiating table, not as a "deterrent". He was, however, still keen to make sure Party members knew he was keeping his membership of CND, and stories to that effect were fed to the press. He also agreed that "down the road" there might be a time when Britain would give up its nuclear weapons even though the superpowers still kept theirs – a concession to the unilateralists which he was to retract two years later.

At a reconvened NEC meeting held on May 17th, Livingstone moved an amendment to the final report to the effect that nuclear weapons should not be used by a Labour government. Kinnock personally moved a further amendment which ran to sixty words compared to Livingstone's twenty. Its evasiveness did not obscure its basic point, which was that the NEC recognized that "circumstances could arise in which [nuclear weapons] might be used". The right derided Livingstone's proposal as "mischievous", which meant that they could not think of a good reason to vote against it. Kinnock simply attacked Livingstone for "doing the Tories' work for them". Reversing his previous position, Gould argued that Labour had to accept the possibility of the use of nuclear weapons because it was "our negotiating strength".[35] In the end only four members of the NEC were prepared to disavow the use of nuclear weapons by backing Livingstone's amendment. Haigh, Richardson and Sawyer abstained while Cook, Gould, Blunkett, Short and Lestor all voted with Kinnock.[36]

Livingstone then moved another amendment rejecting the idea of a US nuclear umbrella for Britain. Kinnock again amended it at length: "This

NEC understands and has long understood that as a matter of reality as long as the US possesses nuclear weapons the Soviet Union will too – and vice versa." Kinnock's proposal was carried by the same vote as before: the NEC thus concluded that Britain had to accept the US nuclear umbrella. On the final vote on the "Britain and the World" report as a whole, Cook, Gould, Lestor and Short all joined with Kinnock and the right; Blunkett, Richardson, Haigh and Beckett backed Livingstone, Benn and Skinner.[37] Although Tom Sawyer abstained, he advised others to back Kinnock, explaining that his own hands were tied because of NUPE's unilateralist policy.

Months before, over the isolated opposition of Benn, Livingstone and Skinner, the NEC had declared that the report of each Policy Review group would be presented to Labour's conference on a take-it-or-leave-it basis; no amendments would be allowed. The NEC had also decreed that should any motion be passed by the conference which conflicted with the Policy Review, then the review would take precedence. This turned the whole matter into a test of loyalty to the leadership; it would not be possible to reaffirm nuclear disarmament without throwing out the whole Policy Review package, which only the firmest elements of the left were prepared to do.

The USDAW leadership skirted a direct confrontation over the policy change by putting to its conference an amendment to "broaden" existing USDAW support for unilateralism to include, in addition, support for multilateral initiatives. This enabled them to claim a mandate for casting the union's block vote in support of the Policy Review. But it was the 600,000-strong vote of NUPE that was the real prize for Kinnock. Tom Sawyer as NUPE deputy general secretary played a decisive role in delivering it. First, he persuaded the NUPE executive to reject the advice of its general secretary, Rodney Bickerstaffe, and to back Kinnock's Policy Review. Then, at the union's annual conference in Scarborough in June, he high-pressured delegates into agreeing to welcome the Policy Review by a majority of three to one.

Sawyer and his allies argued that the union's first priority was not ideology but the return of a Labour government, which, he implied, was blocked by the unilateralist policy. In this speech he also played his trump card, misleading some delegates into believing that the rejection of unilateralism would mean a greater commitment to cuts in military spending and the corresponding transfer of resources to areas like the NHS, education and local government where NUPE members worked. Even as he spoke Sawyer knew that the review made no mention of reductions in defence expenditure and that the Labour leadership was strongly opposed to the idea.

With USDAW, NUPE and a few other unions swinging behind him, Kinnock was assured of winning the vote at conference and no longer had to worry about the TGWU, for thirty years the bastion of unilateralism within the labour movement. At its biannual delegate conference in Bournemouth that summer Kinnock, invited to deliver a fraternal address to the delegates, abused the occasion by making an aggressive attack on his hosts for having dared to reaffirm their long-standing non-nuclear policy. Kinnock's real audience, of course, was not in the conference hall; he wanted to show voters at home watching the televised soundbites – and even more the pundits who would interpret them – that he was not beholden to "trade union barons" and that as Prime Minister he could be entrusted with the security of the realm.

After a year of arm-twisting and highly publicized leadership interventions, the outcome of the defence debate at the 1989 conference was something of a formality. Gerald Kaufman assured delegates that the Party's non-nuclear ideals (which he had never shared) were intact. The Policy Review changes, he said, were merely to ensure that "Britain could play its full part in bringing about a non-nuclear world".[38] AEU president Bill Jordan and others from the old pro-Washington hard right were more frank: unilateralism was a vote-loser and should have been dropped years before. But as in 1988 the key speech came from a self-designated former "lifelong supporter of unilateralism". This time it was one Sylvia Heal, called to deliver a pro-nuclear speech by prearrangement with the chair. Heal, another personal friend of the Kinnocks, was attending the conference as a delegate from the Surrey North West constituency, which had mandated her to support unilateralism. Disregarding the mandate, Heal claimed to have been persuaded by "changing international circumstances" to recant her previous unilateralist views. But she also made clear that the real motives for dropping the non-nuclear policy were electoralist: "I am not prepared to put the election of a Labour government at risk by clinging to a unilateralist policy."[39] Later she was to be rewarded with the Labour nomination in the Mid-Staffordshire by-election – won by Labour at the height of the agitation against the Poll Tax but lost two years later.

The "Britain in the World" Policy Review document was carried at the 1989 conference with a majority of 1,182,000. A resolution which reaffirmed support for unilateralist policy was defeated by 1,204,000. These votes did not reflect any shift of opinion within the labour movement on the question of nuclear weapons. The overwhelming majority of constituency delegates continued to back unilateralism; even those unions that had switched their block votes and provided Kinnock with his majority were induced to do so not by a new-found commitment to the Atlantic Alliance or the theory of "deterrence" but by the received wisdom that the leadership must be backed if Labour was to win the next election.

In the run-up to conference, there had been little effort to mobilize Party opinion against the policy change. The rank-and-file left was disunited and demoralized. The parliamentary and trade union leaders who might have been expected to take up the cudgels for nuclear disarmament contented themselves with token gestures such as statements in *Tribune* and letters to the *Guardian*. After the conference, scores of MPs and other leading Party figures who had championed unilateralism in public for many years abandoned it without a murmur. Robin Cook, Bryan Gould, Harriet Harman, Richard Caborn, David Blunkett, Nick Brown, Tony Blair, Kevin Barron, Margaret Beckett, Roland Boyes, Robin Corbett, Chris Smith, Clive Soley, Frank Dobson, John Prescott, Allan Rogers, Joan Ruddock, Clare Short, Jo Richardson, Stan Orme, Mo Mowlam, Alf Morris, Kevin McNamara, John Maxton, Derek Fatchett, Bob Wareing, Jack Straw, Joan Lestor and at least twenty other Labour front-bench MPs had all been happy enough to be associated publicly with CND during the early and mid 1980s. Now they went to ground. This was not just a question of presenting a united front to the public. These people even gave up arguing for the cause within the Party itself – because to do so would have meant destabilizing the leadership, and that was the unforgivable sin in Kinnock's Labour Party.

Within three months of Labour's embrace of nuclear weapons, the Berlin Wall came down and Stalinist regimes throughout Eastern Europe began to collapse, without the Soviet Union lifting a finger to defend them. The Cold War was declared at an end. At the very moment when a non-nuclear and anti-militarist policy would have been most apposite, Labour found itself saddled with an anachronistic commitment to weapons of mass destruction and to high military spending. As a result, Kinnock could find nothing to say in response to the momentous events in Eastern Europe that the Tories could not say better.

Learning to Love the Bomb

Despite the about-turns on unilateralism the commitment to commission only three Trident submarines and to cancel the fourth had remained in place. From 1989 on the Labour leadership promised defence industries that a Labour government would protect them from the wave of cuts in defence manufacturing that all experts agreed were on the way. With Kinnock's encouragement, Martin O'Neill visited the VSEL yard in the marginal seat of Barrow-in-Furness where the Tridents were under construction. He told the unions there that Labour was not set on cancellation of the fourth Trident. John Hutton, Labour's parliamentary candidate in Barrow, welcomed the announcement and declared that it was now "inconceivable" that Labour would cancel.

In July 1991 Gerald Kaufman published an article in the *Guardian* stating that under a Labour government Britain would continue to retain nuclear weapons as long as other countries possessed them.[40] Labour spokespersons rushed to confirm that this was in line with Party policy, which was news to the membership. The usual Walworth Road sources then let it be known that both Neil and Glenys Kinnock had allowed their long-standing memberships of CND to lapse. It was now clear that under Kinnock, the life-long disarmer, Labour would not undertake any disarmament initiatives, unilateral, bilateral or even multilateral.

Shortly before the 1991 conference opened, President Bush announced major unilateral cuts in the US strategic arsenal. The logical response would have been to cancel Trident, since it represented an upgrading of Britain's strategic nuclear weaponry. But at its Sunday pre-conference meeting the NEC, locked into the remorseless logic of Kinnock's desire to be as "tough" on defence as the Tories, voted by twenty-one votes to four to reject motions calling for such a step.[41] According to his office, Kinnock had assured the NEC that "Britain's status as a nuclear power can be used constructively".[42] The conference backed the leadership on this by the surprisingly narrow majority of 3,230,000 votes to 2,232,000. Obviously, unilateralist sentiment in the Party was still very much alive.

The conference also agreed, without debate, a paper drafted by Gerald Kaufman outlining what purported to be Labour's response to the Bush initiative. The small portion of it that did not consist of anodyne clichés without practical meaning was simply a reaffirmation of loyalty to NATO. The Bush initiative gave Labour the chance to embarrass the Tories on defence; the leadership's approach ensured that the government would face no criticism for their slowness to disarm. It also offered Labour a chance to point out how far in advance of the world's leaders the Party had been for some time; but by now Labour was incapable of making a positive, distinctive contribution.

In January 1992 the government staged a Commons debate on defence in an attempt to embarrass Labour in the run-up to the general election. The Tories tabled a motion reiterating their faith in the nuclear deterrent and their determination to retain nuclear weapons come what may. The Labour leadership responded with a pledge to "maintain an effective defence for the UK based on the necessary level of forces provided with the appropriate equipment and weaponry", which it supplemented by a call for arms talks among the eight current nuclear powers. Left Labour MPs put forward an amendment, which was not taken in debate, calling for the decommissioning of the Polaris submarines, the cancellation of the Tridents and the renunciation of all nuclear weapons.

In the debate the Tories concentrated on attacking Labour's prior history on disarmament. When defence secretary Tom King boasted that the Tories 'pro-nuclear policy had brought down Communism, whereas Labour's policy would have let communism win, there was no answer from the Labour front bench. How could there be? Its members had accepted all King's premises. Instead, Labour spokespersons attacked

Tory mismanagement of the defence review and tried to outflank the government by praising the Bush administration and NATO.

Labour's amendment, silent on the question of the fourth Trident, to the government motion was put to the House and defeated by the Tory majority. Following instructions from the Labour whip, 164 Labour MPs abstained on the final vote on the government's pro-nuclear declaration. The motion was opposed by the Liberal Democrats and Welsh and Scottish nationalists, who were joined in the lobby by 28 Labour MPs still committed to unilateralism.

The Tory government's commitment to the fourth Trident submarine was finally made unequivocal at the beginning of February 1992; it was another attempt to embarrass the Labour leadership. At a stroke, this decision increased British nuclear firepower by 20 per cent – from the equivalent of 3,000 to 4,000 Hiroshimas. The Labour leadership made no public objection. During the 1992 general election campaign Gerald Kaufman, in a rare public appearance, issued the only major statement the Party was to make on defence policy. He not only reiterated Labour's commitment to NATO but pledged that a Labour government would make Britain "self-reliant in our defence policy, able to respond to any threat to British security from beyond the NATO area". He also re-emphasized that "the Labour government will retain British nuclear weapons as long as other countries possess such weapons".[43]

There was, of course, absolutely nothing new in the pro-nuclear policy to which Labour returned under Kinnock. The shortness of memory that seems to be an occupational requirement for many political correspondents enabled them to celebrate as a "modernization" what was in fact a regression. For all but ten of the forty-seven years that have passed since the invention of nuclear technology Labour has supported its acquisition, possession and potential use. It was under a Labour government that Britain first acquired a nuclear capacity, in the late 1940s. During the 1950s the Labour leadership supported the construction of the hydrogen bomb. The first Wilson government accepted the deployment of Polaris submarines in 1964–66, thereby promoting the myth of the "independent British nuclear deterrent". The Callaghan government secretly commissioned the modernization of Polaris through the Cheveline Project in the late 1970s and gave British government blessing to the introduction of cruise and Pershing II missiles into Western Europe.

The adoption of unilateralism in 1980 was the result of an enormous groundswell of popular support for a non-nuclear defence policy; it was achieved by means of countless model resolutions, fringe meetings, debates in Labour ward meetings and general committees, all backed by a rising tide of mass demonstrations and direct action by the peace movement. In contrast, the readoption of the pro-nuclear policy in 1989 was entirely the result of manoeuvres emanating from the very top of the

Labour Party. There was virtually no pressure for such a change from below; in 1989 not a single resolution from a constituency party demanded the abandonment of unilateralism.

In the end, Labour simply closed ranks with the Tory government. It even tried to ape the Tories' national chauvinism. Since 1989, journalists had been told that Neil Kinnock's greatest personal attribute was his "patriotism". Labour's policies, the Party campaign managers now boasted, were "made in Britain". The Union Jack was given new prominence on Labour's public platforms and in its campaign literature.

Kinnock's great victory was to ensure that in 1992, unlike in 1983 and 1987, defence was not a political issue, in spite of a feeble Tory attempt to scare the public with tall tales of Labour leaving Britain defenceless. But what kind of victory was this? Whom did it really serve? The National Health Service would not have been an issue in the election campaign had Labour chosen to endorse opt-outs, privatization and cuts in the health budget. For the Labour leadership, defence and foreign affairs could only be vote-losers for the Party. Behind that conviction lay an assumption that to deviate by one iota from the establishment line on these matters was to court electoral disaster – because the election was assumed to be in the gift of the establishment, because the electorate was presumed to be impervious to informed debate and rational argument.

The tragic irony was that despite all Labour's attempts to appease the establishment, it still refused to back the Party against the Tories when the general election came. It still did not consider Labour a safe bet. It was aware that underneath the imposed changes there existed a deeper stratum of rank-and-file hostility to militarism, to the continuing imperial pretensions of the Foreign Office and to Britain's alliance with the United States. It knew that the subversive (in the best sense) defence policy adopted in 1960, overturned in 1961, adopted once more in 1980 and overturned again in 1989, could one day re-emerge as Labour policy.

Notes

1. *Labour Party Annual Conference Report* 1980.
2. Denis Healey's statement of candidature for the deputy leadership, May 1981.
3. NEC International Committee minutes June 1984.
4. Benn diaries, 27 June 1987.
5. *Labour Party Annual Conference Report* 1984.
6. ibid.
7. ibid.
8. ibid.
9. *Labour Party Annual Conference Report* 1986.
10. Benn diaries, 24 November 1986.
11. NEC minutes November 1986.
12. *Labour Party News* January–February 1987.
13. *Chartist* winter 1987.
14. NEC Report to Annual Conference 1987.

15. *Tribune* 27 February 1987.
16. *Guardian* 4 February 1987.
17. *Tribune* 15 May 1987.
18. *Guardian* 9 February 1987.
19. *The Times* 12 March 1987.
20. *Guardian* 25 May 1987.
21. *Tribune* 17 July 1987.
22. *Sanity* February 1988.
23. *Guardian* 6 June 1988.
24. *Observer* 26 June 1988.
25. *Labour Party News* July–August 1988.
26. *Tribune* 14 October 1988.
27. Colin Hughes and Patrick Wintour, *Labour Rebuilt*, London 1990.
28. *Guardian* 10 May 1989.
29. Benn diaries, 9 May 1989.
30. Special NEC minutes 9 May 1989.
31. ibid.
32. ibid.
33. *Daily Telegraph* 10 May 1989.
34. *The Times* 13 May 1989.
35. Benn diaries, 17 May 1989.
36. NEC minutes 11 May 1989.
37. ibid.
38. *Guardian* 3 October 1989.
39. ibid.
40. *Guardian* 15 July 1991.
41. NEC minutes September 1991.
42. *Guardian* 1 October 1991.
43. *Guardian* 15 March 1992.

10

The Purge

The nature of political parties makes the definition of disrepute
a difficult and subjective task; this could lead to a dangerous
escalation of the use of disciplinary action for factional or
malicious purposes . . . no action should be taken relating to the
expression of opinion and ideas.

NEC document, 1986

From Bournemouth to the National Constitutional Committee

By the end of Neil Kinnock's tenure as leader of the Labour Party,
investigations of local parties and disciplinary action of one kind or
another had directly affected party members in over eighty constituencies in all regions of the country. Local parties in London, Leeds,
Birmingham, Coventry, Liverpool (and indeed the whole of Merseyside),
Bradford, Bristol, Brighton, Glasgow, Edinburgh, Hull, Nottingham and
Sheffield had all been disturbed by suspensions, expulsions or the
imposition of candidates – as had such hotbeds of subversion as Steven-
age, Luton, Exeter, Leigh, Eastbourne and Hemsworth. Eddisbury in
Cheshire, a constituency with a 12,000 Tory majority, expelled eight
Labour Party members for Militant Tendency connections in 1992.

The witch-hunt had its origins in the backlash against Bennism of the
early 1980s. The Labour right singled out Militant for attack but its real
target was always wider, as was indicated by its sabotage of the Bermondsey candidacy of Peter Tatchell between 1981 and 1983. The establishment of an official register of unaffiliated Labour Party groups at the
1982 Labour conference was denounced by the left as an attempt to turn
the clock back to the bad old days of proscriptions and mass expulsions.
But defenders of the register insisted that no political purge was contemplated. All that was at issue here, they said, was the alleged abuse of the
Party constitution by the Militant Tendency. The following year six
members of the *Militant* editorial board were expelled, again amid
assurances that no wider witch-hunt would follow.

While at this time the "soft left" argued that the way to beat the

Militant and the rest of the "ultra-left" was through political debate, the Labour right was always convinced that bureaucratic measures would be necessary to remove the cancer of Bennism from the Labour Party. During his campaign for the Party leadership Neil Kinnock refused to pledge an end to the witch-hunt, but in his first two years he was cautious and urged restraint on the more gung-ho elements of the right. But with the defeats of the miners and of ratecapping struggles and the subsequent realignment of 1985, the door was open for a renewed attack on the rank-and-file left.

Kinnock's speech to the 1985 conference in Bournemouth excoriating Liverpool Council was the signal for an investigation into that Militant stronghold. An NEC team, led by Charles Turnock of the NUR, visited Liverpool, where they received "evidence" of Militant misbehaviour in a designated "safe house", terminology by which they intimated that ordinary Party members walked in fear of Militant "intimidation".

In May 1986, the NEC held an exhausting meeting, lasting from 9 a.m. to the early hours of the following morning, to consider the case against eleven Liverpool Labour Party members named in Turnock's report. For this purpose the accused were placed in a "dock" surrounded on three sides by NEC members and Party officials. General secretary Larry Whitty was to act as the prosecutor and NEC members as the jury. In the event all eleven accused were disciplined and all but one, Harry Smith, who had ridiculed the proceedings with a witty and effective defence, were expelled from the Party.

The expelled Liverpool members took legal action against the NEC, which had acted as prosecutor, judge and jury, for breaches of natural justice. As a result, the leadership determined to take steps to make expulsions easier and to prevent future cases from receiving the publicity the Liverpool people had enjoyed. It proposed the establishment of a special body, the national constitutional committee (NCC), elected by the Party conference and independent of the NEC, to adjudicate on disciplinary cases referred to it by the NEC or local constituency parties.

At the 1986 conference, Larry Whitty assured delegates the new disciplinary mechanism would "protect individual members from victimization". He also claimed that the NCC would relieve the NEC of its tedious disciplinary responsibilities, leaving it more time "to decide vital policy issues . . . and to direct our campaigning activities".[1] In fact, the NEC in the years to come was to become more preoccupied than ever with disciplinary business. Proposals for or reports of investigations or suspensions came before nearly every single one of its meetings in 1990 and 1991.

"Powers of discipline should be used sparingly, with tolerance," Whitty advised. The NEC document outlined the strict parameters within which the new committee would be expected to act: "If discipline is required then it should be proportionate to the offence"; "nobody should be at a disadvantage while the procedures are still being exhausted"; "efforts at mediation should be tried and exhausted"; "warnings should normally be given before any disciplinary action is taken"; the charges were to be "adequately specified".[2] All of these safeguards, on the basis of which the conference approved the NCC, were to be violated as a matter of routine by the NCC, the NEC and Party officials in coming years.

Charges of "bringing the Party into disrepute" should be used with care, the NEC document had warned, and it included a proviso "that no action should be taken relating to the expression of opinion and ideas".[3] This proviso, of course, proved to be honoured far more in the breach than not, even though, in response to claims made by conference delegate Eric Segal from Folkestone and Hythe that the NCC proposals were simply an attempt to "ease the path of expulsions", Larry Whitty had stressed again, "because one or two people have not heard me", that "nobody will be subject to discipline under the new rules for mere expression or publication of views or for individual acts of conduct".[4]

The only commitment given by the NEC in 1986 which has honoured to date is that "when disciplinary forces are actually used, they should be enforceable and not subject to interference from outside". This was the main concern of a leadership determined to be able to discipline members at will, without having to worry about either legal interference or the whims of Party conference.

The only case ever heard by the full NCC was that of Sharon Atkin. She had been removed as the candidate for Nottingham East before the 1987 general election, and charged by the NEC with various violations of the constitution because of remarks said to have been made at a Black Sections public meeting. Larry Whitty presented the NEC's case against Atkin, who was defended by the formidable Lord Gifford QC. Gifford argued that the charges against Atkin defied common sense. He expressed "utter astonishment that they are being seriously put forward. Each one is fundamentally misconceived." Gifford pointed out the legal, logical and factual errors in the NEC's case against Atkin and tore Larry Whitty's presentation to shreds. The NCC was forced to recognize that no grounds could be found for expulsion and had to settle for delivering a "reprimand". Simply dismissing the charges, as Gifford demanded, would have caused too much embarrassment to the leader, who was seen lurking outside the room in which the NCC meeting was being held, anxiously awaiting the verdict.

Aside from the Atkin case, all other cases have been heard by panels of three NCC members, agreed by the NCC as a whole. Since the political balance on the NCC has always been two to one in favour of the right, it has been easy to ensure that nearly all the panels comprised two right-wingers and one left-winger. Results were more often than not predetermined along political lines, and no right of appeal to the larger NCC, the NEC or the conference was allowed.

Mandy Moore, a member of the NCC since its inception, once observed, "The chances of proving your innocence are minimal. Many cases are the result of personal grudges or political differences which should be dealt with at constituency level." NCC panels solemnly received in evidence almost any piece of uncorroborated or even anonymous hearsay. Photographs of individuals selling the *Militant* newspaper or their appearance in published lists of donors to Militant-associated causes or their attendance at caucuses with others alleged to be Militant supporters would be sufficient to prove membership and ensure expulsion. Part of the evidence submitted by a Labour MP against one Scottish member was that he had been seen "clapping" a speech at a local meeting against the Poll Tax.

Between 1986 and 1990, the NCC dealt with 251 disciplinary cases, 150 of which ended in expulsion. Of the 119 members charged with Militant membership, 112 were expelled. Other charges preferred either by local CLPs or by the NEC have ranged from the ubiquitous "sustained course of conduct prejudicial to the Party" to "insulting the Party leader". Even-handedness was rarely on display at NCC hearings and left-wingers would find their carefully documented arguments brushed aside in moments. In contrast, when a Party member in Bristol who had openly campaigned against the official Labour candidate, left-winger Dawn Primarolo, in the 1987 election came before the NCC (defended by former MP Michael Cocks, who had been deselected by Primarolo) he received only a reprimand. Similarly, David Prendergast, a leader of the breakaway Union of Democratic Mineworkers who had publicly opposed the official Labour candidate in Mansfield in 1987 and who did not even bother to attend his NCC hearing, was suspended from Party membership for two years. In 1991, forty left-wingers were expelled forthwith, while a Party member accused of racist behaviour was suspended for two years.

In 1991 Hassan Ahmed, a potential parliamentary candidate in Nottingham East (where Sharon Atkin had already had trouble with the Labour leadership), was suspended by the NCC for three years. The investigation into him had lasted eighteen months. In his defence he had submitted 110 pages of evidence. It took eight hours for the prosecution to present its case and Ahmed took eight hours to respond. When the NCC panel then adjourned to discuss their verdict it took only ten minutes to find Ahmed guilty and pronounce sentence. The panel refused to tell Ahmed which of the ten charges against him had been proved and he was expelled from the Labour Party.

The trade union places on the NCC have never been openly contested; by a mysterious process each year there are only as many nominations as there are vacancies. In 1991 Shelley Burke, at that time employed as a personal assistant to Islington Council leader Margaret Hodge, became the first right-winger to be elected to the national constitutional committee's constituency section. Nearly one third of constituency parties chose not to participate in the ballot. In 1983, when Burke was active in student politics at Sussex University, she had joined a right-wing breakaway from the official Labour Club that ran candidates, including Burke herself, against official Labour candidates. With such a background it was ironic that she would now have the right to sit in judgement on the Party loyalty of others.

That same year, in a further irony, Eric Segal, the Folkestone and Hythe delegate who had warned against the excessive powers of the NCC at the 1986 conference, was referred to the NCC at the request of his CLP and subsequently expelled.

Vauxhall

In the midst of Labour's "ten-week offensive" in the spring of 1989, Stuart Holland announced his resignation as Labour MP for the south London seat of Vauxhall, which lies in the London borough of Lambeth and includes part of Brixton. As soon as Holland's resignation was announced demands arose that the vacancy be filled by a black Labour MP. A wide variety of black politicians expressed an interest in the seat and it was obvious the selection would be hotly contested.

The timetable and procedures for the selection were agreed by local Party officers with the director of organization at Walworth Road, Joyce Gould. Technically, Stuart Holland had been imposed by the NEC on the constituency party shortly before the 1987 election because the local black section, unrecognized under national Party rules, had participated in the selection contest that had chosen him. This time the black section, determined to give the Party leadership no excuse to block a black candidate, made a tactical decision not to take part, relying instead on its political influence within the Vauxhall Labour Party as a whole.

Would-be candidates attended special ward, trade union and women's section meetings. By Labour Party standards, participation by members was substantial. At the end of this process, sixteen individuals had received at least one nomination and five had received three or more. Emerging as the clear front-runner was Martha Osamor, who had received eight nominations: from three of the constituency's eight wards, from the women's section and the Lambeth Women's Council, and from TGWU/ACTSS, MSF and NUR branches.

Osamor was far more than just another Labour left-winger. She had spent many years outside the Labour Party as a community activist in Tottenham in north London. Born in Nigeria, she had earned her spurs as a genuine grassroots leader during more than fifteen years' activity. She had been prominent in local campaigns against police abuses and was closely linked with community organizations on the Broadwater Farm estate, where police and local youths clashed violently in October 1985.

After working with local Labour left-wingers in the ratecapping campaign of 1984–85, Osamor had joined the Labour Party and was soon selected to stand as a Labour candidate for Haringey Council. Elected in 1986, she immediately became a leading member of the Labour Group, defending its controversial lesbian and gay rights policy. When leader Bernie Grant stepped down to be replaced by Steve King in 1987, she became the group's deputy leader. However, within months the entire left leadership was ousted when the local Party and the Labour Group split apart over the borough's financial crisis. Osamor opposed the cuts strategy advocated by the right wing, which was guided by a nucleus of Labour Co-ordinating Committee members who had moved into the area over the previous few years.

In the course of the Vauxhall nomination meetings, Osamor presented herself as someone who wanted to get into Parliament in order to support struggles taking place outside it. The response from local Party members was enthusiastic. This was the kind of MP the people of Vauxhall, among the most impoverished and oppressed in the country, required.

But Osamor's selection was the last thing the Kinnock leadership wanted. The heavily publicized two-day NEC meeting that approved the Policy Review and overturned unilateralism had taken place in the middle of the nomination process. It had been clear from the start of the process in Vauxhall that the NEC would use the new powers given it by the 1988 Party conference to screen by-election candidates. What few expected, however, was just how far the leadership would go in ensuring that the candidate of its choice would be the Labour nominee.

Along with Osamor, others nominated included Kate Bennett, a local left-winger, Greater London Labour Party chair Glenys Thornton, former Lewisham East parliamentary candidate Russell Profitt, former Fulham MP Nick Raynsford, former Lambeth Council leader Linda Bellos and black sections activist Marc Wadsworth. A local LCC caucus which decided to back Thornton was attended by regional organizer Phil Cole, who was subsequently rebuked for this impropriety by GLLP general secretary Terry Ashton. At Walworth Road, situated just outside the constituency boundaries, officials were aware of the potential problems posed by the combination of a left-wing constituency and a large local black population. Just before the close of nominations, a Lambeth Council UCATT branch submitted the nomination of Wesley Kerr, a black television journalist hitherto unknown as a Labour Party member.

Kerr, a friend of Peter Mandelson, had been been cajoled into standing in order to ensure that at least one black candidate acceptable to the leadership would be on offer. The UCATT branch was the fiefdom of UCATT's then national local government officer, Alan Black, who was well connected to both the Labour right and the local Labour Co-ordinating Committee; he was happy to use his dormant branch to do the Labour hierarchy's bidding.

Unlike Kerr, Kate Hoey had actually made a big effort to win nominations from the Vauxhall wards and affiliated unions. After a brief stint in Trotskyist politics in the 1970s she had joined the Labour Party and become a Labour councillor in Hackney, where she served alongside Kinnock's chief of staff, Charles Clarke. In 1983 and 1987 she had been Labour's parliamentary candidate in marginal Dulwich and had been elected a Southwark borough councillor as recently as 1988. She enjoyed a modest public profile as a campaigner on sports and recreational facilities. It seemed that at the next general election the Dulwich seat would be hers for the asking; apparently, she just could not wait. Despite her record and local connections, Hoey failed to receive a single nomination from any local branch. A grand total of five Party members voted for her in all the wards she addressed. In the end she entered the reckoning only by virtue of a nomination from the South East Political Committee of the Co-operative Wholesale Society, which was affiliated to the Vauxhall Labour Party. The committee had nominated her at a meeting at which no member of the Vauxhall CLP was present. In attendance, however, was John Cartwright, then SDP MP for Woolwich, who had left the Labour Party eight years before but had retained his involvement in the CWS. Although he did not vote, he was to have more say in selecting the Labour by-election candidate than any members of the Vauxhall Constituency Labour Party.

The NEC set up a panel to interview the nominated candidates. Its members were Eddie Haigh of the TGWU, John Evans, Joan Lestor and Tom Sawyer of NUPE; it was chaired by Roy Hattersley assisted by Peter Mandelson and Joyce Gould. On the morning of the scheduled interviews, an article by Patrick Wintour entitled "Labour risks row over candidate" appeared on the front page of the *Guardian*, illustrated by a photograph of Osamor. "The Labour leadership is expected today to risk a confrontation by refusing to short-list a unilateralist for the Vauxhall by-election in south London," it said. It noted that though Osamor had won the largest number of nominations, the "NEC is expected to rule her out tomorrow since she is under investigation by the District Auditor. . . . Party sources made it clear last night that the leadership would not tolerate Ms Osamor and would if necessary impose a candidate. They insisted that the Party could not put at risk the programme of recent months by suffering another disastrous by-election like Greenwich in 1987."[5]

In fact, the only people investigating Osamor at this time were her Labour opponents in the Haringey Council leadership, which alleged that community organizations in which she was involved were guilty of financial improprieties. At this stage Osamor herself had not been informed of the details of the allegations and the *Guardian* article enlightened no one. The leadership was delighted at the wording and prominent placement of the article; it needed the smear story to disguise its real reasons for keeping Osamor off the shortlist.

At the interview later that day, Osamor was told that her views on Ireland, the witch-hunt and the Policy Review were not in accord with those of the NEC. She was asked why she had made criticisms of the leadership. When she was told not to speak to the press about the interview she asked how it was that the *Guardian* that very morning had been able to quote "Party sources" to the effect that the decision about her candidacy had already been made. She was assured by panel members that they knew nothing about the story and that no decisions had yet been made.

Hattersley's panel recommended a shortlist of Hoey, Thornton, Raynsford, Pat Moberley (a local right-winger) and Wesley Kerr, the sole black person included. Gone were not only Osamor but all the other black candidates, who together had received twenty of the thirty-four nominations. The NEC shortlisted candidates could claim only ten nominations between them. Not one was a unilateralist.

At the NEC meeting the following morning, Tony Benn and Ken Livingstone moved that Osamor be reinstated to the shortlist. What Livingstone described as a "poisonous" debate ensued in which Hattersley explained that Osamor was clearly unsuitable as a parliamentary candidate. "If there was ever anyone who has been used by extreme elements, it's Martha Osamor. She's a simple woman, of that sort. She could never have got elected to Parliament."

Livingstone described the panel's recommendations as "racist". Kinnock replied by calling him "a prat" and accusing him of "ignorance and prejudice". Jack Rogers of UCATT said he had lived in an area with black people for years and had never had any problems. Haigh insisted that "race played no part" in the panel's deliberation and then warned Livingstone, "If you say any of this outside, I'll sue." When Livingstone asked why Russell Profitt, who had stood for Parliament before and was regarded as an experienced and able mainstream black politician, was deemed "unsuitable", he was told that it was because Profitt worked for Brent Council. Only the four left-wingers voted to reinstate Osamor to the shortlist; Jo Richardson, Clare Short, David Blunkett and Robin Cook all backed Hattersley.

The leadership's argument that the purpose of the new by-election procedure was to ensure the Party had candidates who could stand up to the heat of a campaign conducted in the glare of national media attention was hardly consistent with its inclusion of Wesley Kerr, who had no previous political experience whatsoever. Kerr was never a serious candidate, as the panel well knew. He was there to allow the NEC to claim it had shortlisted a black person. Under pressure from black activists, Kerr decided not to allow himself to be used as a token black and withdrew from the shortlist, making it an all-white affair.

Meeting that night in Lambeth Town Hall, the Vauxhall Labour Party general committee voted by thirty-three votes to ten, an unexpectedly decisive majority, to ask the NEC to reconsider and expand the shortlist in line with the CLP's own long-standing policy to include at least one black person on all shortlists.

The four remaining shortlisted candidates had been locked away during the meeting in the council leader's office. Following the local Party's refusal to interview them, they were whisked away to the House of Commons across the Thames, avoiding angry black protestors by exiting via the back door of the Town Hall. At the Commons Hattersley's panel was already assembled, fully expecting the Vauxhall Labour Party to reject its list and more than prepared to make the final choice on its behalf. Without further consultation with the NEC, the panel chose Kate Hoey, whose sole qualification over the others was that she had no support whatsoever in the constituency; all the rest had been nominated by one local Party branch each and could boast some support independent of the NEC itself. Perhaps that was why they were all rejected.

In the House of Commons Margaret Thatcher used the furore to score a cheap point about democracy: "We are glad to note that the Soviet Union is well ahead of the Labour Party in relation to what is happening in Vauxhall." The *Daily Mail* commented, "As a future Prime Minister Mr Kinnock may continue to lack credibility, but as an old style Chicago party boss nobody can hold a violin case to him."[6] In response to the less opportunistic criticism pouring out from the black community, Labour offered feeble tokenism. At the grand Policy Review press launch held that month a spot was found on the platform for the black Labour MP for Brent South, Paul Boateng, who had just been appointed to the Labour front bench.

Asked about her lack of support in the local Party, Kate Hoey explained, "I am the democratically elected candidate of the Labour Party nationally."[7] Local activists largely boycotted the ensuing campaign, which was heavily dependent on Party employees, one of whom was assigned to each of the Party's eight wards. In the midst of the nationwide European elections, this was an extraordinary concentration of resources in a safe Labour seat. On polling day Hoey won with a reduced majority on a low turnout.

At the NEC meeting following the by-election, it was proposed that Labour MPs elected at mid-term by-elections should not have to stand for reselection before the next general election. This was a transparent attempt by the leadership to protect imposed by-election candidates from deselection by local Party members. At the NEC, the "soft left" backed the leadership to force the rule change through, despite the fact that for once the left were joined by five trade union representatives who bridled at such blatant manipulation.

But this was not the end of Martha Osamor's mistreatment at the hands of the Labour leadership. Vauxhall had made her a national name; her base in Haringey was strong. She refused to slink off into a corner to lick her wounds. The Labour Co-ordinating Committee in Haringey redoubled its attack on her. Despite its repeated efforts to get the police and the district auditor to act against her, these agencies made it clear that there was not sufficient evidence to justify an investigation and declined to be drawn into what was obviously an internal Labour Party feud.

The source of the allegations against Osamor was Dolly Kiffin, the self-styled "community leader" of Broadwater Farm. Osamor had crossed Kiffin by refusing to support her arbitrary sacking of several childcare workers from a local voluntary group. The local Labour Co-ordinating Committee and the council leadership convened a kangaroo Labour Party court to "investigate" Osamor, but persistently refused to detail any specific charges against her or to produce any evidence of wrong-doing. Instead, for several months they maintained a steady flow of half-truths and insinuations to the local media and local Party members. Osamor was enraged to find her reputation and her years of work in the Tottenham community besmirched by a cabal of Labour politicians. She denied and continues to deny all the allegations.

In the end Osamor was expelled from Haringey Labour Group for her refusal to co-operate with the kangaroo court. But that was not enough for her opponents. For good measure they expelled her again a month later (though she had not been readmitted in the meantime) for voting against the council's 1990 budget setting the Poll Tax. Osamor, who had been reselected for her council seat with strong support from local Party members, was therefore barred by the NEC from standing in the May elections. That the allegations against her, which Labour right-wingers had described as being so grave as to require police action, were trumped up for use in a politically motivated smear campaign was proved by the speed with which they were dropped once Osamor had been removed from the Labour Group. Undaunted, Osamor remains active in a host of local and international struggles and is still a member of the Labour Party.

Birkenhead

Frank Field, who was first elected Labour MP for Birkenhead in 1979, was always a fervent champion of his own right to say or do anything he liked. In April 1987 Field appeared on BBC television to advise voters to back the SDP–Liberal Alliance in seats where Labour came third. At the following NEC Tony Benn suggested that Field be asked to issue a statement calling on all electors to vote Labour. Kinnock replied that this was unwise because Field might refuse. This was the same meeting that had removed Sharon Atkin as Labour candidate in Nottingham East. In the general election that followed, Field's call for tactical voting was used by the Liberals against the Labour candidate in Southend West. The latter asked Field for a statement which he could use to rebut the Liberals but Field declined, saying, "I stand by what I said on tactical voting and I don't issue statements of support for anyone."[8]

At around the same time Field was denouncing the Labour candidate in the neighbouring Wallasey constituency, left-winger Lol Duffy, in the local press. Although he had never met Duffy, Field wrote in a private letter that was widely circulated in the area, "I can tell you in the most definite terms that I will not be supporting Duffy. I have refused to appear on any platform with him and I hope that Cammell Laird workers similarly refuse to give him a hearing when he tries to gatecrash on our factory gate meetings during the election campaign." This letter, written on May 5th, was published on the front page of the *Wirral Globe*, a local newspaper, on May 21st under the heading "Marxist Lol slammed by Frank Field".

The Wallasey CLP ran a vigorous local campaign and Duffy succeeded in cutting Tory MP Lynda Chalker's majority from 7,000 to 279 votes. Without Field's intervention, Duffy would probably have won the seat. The MP's treachery angered local Labour Party members, many of whom were already alienated by his aloof and dismissive attitude towards his Birkenhead Party members. Field's views on such issues as training and taxation were not in keeping with the views of most Party members or indeed with Kinnock's own Policy Review. He had strongly opposed the workers' occupation of the Cammell Laird shipyard and was hostile to trade union activity. In the Commons he was a right-wing maverick, earning plaudits from Tories and the media but annoying many Labour MPs.

In the selection contest held in Birkenhead in late 1989, Field was beaten in the electoral college by Paul Davies, chair of the Wirral District Labour Party and a local TGWU official, who secured 50.5 per cent of votes to Field's 45 per cent. In the individual members' section of the college, Field had won by 165 votes to Davies's 113. In the unions' section

Davies took 35 votes to Field's 16. The postal votes went to Field by a wide margin.

Field stormed out of the meeting, making it plain that he would not accept the local Party's decision. Although earlier he had raised no complaints about the conduct of the selection, now he cried foul to the press. He intimated that he would resign and fight a by-election if the Party leadership failed to defend him. He then embarked upon a high-profile media campaign to save himself, indifferent to any damage he would cause to the Labour Party or even its leadership.

Davies was not a member of the Militant Tendency, despite Field's attempts to hint to the press that he was, but a mainstream left-wing TGWU activist. This meant that his opponents found it difficult to redbait him and had to resort to accusing him of thuggish behaviour. According to Field, Davies had physically threatened a fellow trade unionist and had intimidated children attending a Sunday School. Davies was able to produce evidence to disprove both these allegations.

In response to a question from Tony Benn at the December NEC Neil Kinnock admitted that he had had a private meeting with Frank Field. The leader said he had told Field that any evidence of malpractice in the selection procedure should be submitted to the NEC. Accordingly Field drew up and submitted an extraordinary 150-page dossier.

The Field dossier, compiled by a group of the MP's Birkenhead supporters, was a farrago of bizarre and largely untruthful allegations about a number of personalities in the Wirral Labour Party. It also raised the by now familiar spectre of "intimidation" and claimed that both Birkenhead and the neighbouring Wallasey constituency parties had been infiltrated by "Trotskyists" and "Militants". According to the dossier, twenty-two Militants and eleven Socialist Organiser supporters lived in the two constituencies. This rather contradicted Field's earlier claim – made to explain away his defeat in the selection contest – that his local Party membership was 40 per cent Militant with an additional 20 per cent Militant "fellow travellers".

Invitations to members of the public who wished to submit evidence to the dossier were placed in the local press by Field's supporters. The finished product was ineptly written and singularly unconvincing. It asserted that "the political antics of some Labour members of Wirral Council have brought the name of the Party into disrepute". The "evidence" for this claim was provided by three "independent Labour councillors" who had been expelled from the Labour Group for persistently voting with the Tories. Included in the dossier as "evidence" of the unacceptability of Paul Davies as a Labour candidate was a letter from the deputy leader of the Wirral Council Conservative Group.

One entry in the dossier read: "Tom Scilly, ward secretary (clerk with the TGWU, Liverpool office) works closely with the left in the party. He has a relationship with Tina Moran of Liscard ward who has been the constituency assistant secretary." What were these people being accused of? Working for the left? Working for the TGWU? Having been constituency officers? Having a relationship? Another entry referred to "the vice chair Jane Fairburn, common-law wife of Mark Cushman" and alleged, falsely, that she "organized the printing of T-shirts for the anti-Poll Tax cause". One contributor to the dossier explained informatively that a certain Party member "lives with a lady of the same opinions, whose name I can't remember". Another saw fit to bring to the readers' attention the fact that a particular Party member was "a Welshman". Militant supporters, described as "hard men, hit men", were said to be at the forefront of a campaign of "intimidation" in the Wirral, though the dossier derided one of them for being only "5 feet tall with duck feet". As evidence of the serious charge of "intimidation" Field cited incidents in which members of the Birkenhead general committee had laughed at him.

Field's dossier argued that the parliamentary selection was invalid because membership checks were not undertaken. He claimed that more members had voted at the reselection conference than were eligible to do so. He also attacked TGWU affiliations to the Birkenhead CLP and called for nine of the thirteen affiliated branches to be investigated by the national TGWU. This theme nicely complemented the ongoing "soft left" campaign, supported by the media, to exclude trade unions from the selection process. The Labour Co-ordinating Committee jumped on Field's bandwagon and issued a press release protesting against the role of the unions in deselecting Field. Although Field denounced the TGWU for affiliating to the CLP on the basis of inappropriate membership (unemployed workers who had retained their union cards) he was himself, though no dockworker, a member of the TGWU Dockworkers Branch TG 6/506.

The Field dossier was sent to the press at the same time as it was submitted to the NEC. Field's strategy was to use the media to apply pressure on the NEC to act in his defence. He presented himself as an innocent man of principle hounded by raving, bullying, cheating extremists. For the media he was Marlon Brando in *On the Waterfront* or Gary Cooper in *High Noon*, a brave individualist standing alone against a mob of evil-doers. Paul Davies was affronted by the charges made against him. In the good humour which, in marked contrast to Frank Field, characterized his approach throughout the dispute, Davies claimed that on the basis of the portrait contained in the Field dossier "even my mother would not vote for me". But few people in the media and none at all in the Labour leadership appeared to be remotely interested in hearing Davies's case.

In January 1990 the NEC solemnly agreed by twenty votes to three (Benn and Skinner were joined on this occasion by Eddie Haigh of the TGWU) to institute a wide-ranging inquiry into the Labour Party on the Wirral. Many NEC members agreed with Roy Hattersley that much of Field's "evidence" was irrelevant, yet they all voted to back Field by launching what was, in effect, a crackdown on the left in the Wirral. It was not that any of them had much time for Frank Field. Most NEC members considered him a liability to the Party. Many declared, in private, that Field should not be allowed to hold the Labour Party to ransom. But time and again they came to his rescue at the NEC. They were as determined as Field himself that he should continue to be the Labour MP for Birkenhead – for the simple reason that the NEC dared not allow itself to be seen by the media as defending the Labour left against Frank Field.

The February 1990 NEC considered an interim report from Joyce Gould, which acknowledged that not one of Field's allegations relating to the selection procedure could be substantiated. The NEC majority responded with a call for a further investigation not only into Field's allegations but also into the activities of the Socialist Organiser group in the area. Forced to concede that no Party rules had been broken, the NEC fell back on the old standby of "far left infiltration".

Among those who had confirmed that the original selection was perfectly valid was Peter Kilfoyle, the Party's right-wing regional organizer who had overseen the entire procedure. He resented what he saw as a slur on his professionalism and went on record refuting Field's allegations. Joyce Gould had also been forced to concede that the allegations made against Paul Davies were bogus and that there were no grounds on which he could be disbarred from standing as a candidate should the NEC decide to rerun the selection. As Davies said, "The only thing wrong with me is that I am not Frank Field."

Field, meanwhile, kept up his one-man campaign against the forces of darkness in the Labour Party and reiterated his threat to resign and fight a by-election. The June 1990 NEC received a further report from Joyce Gould. The meeting had no alternative but to conclude that there had been no irregularities in the conduct of the original Birkenhead selection contest and to confirm that all the trade union affiliations were bona fide. None the less, by seventeen votes to eight, the NEC ordered the selection to be rerun. The NEC also accepted Gould's charge that six members of Birkenhead CLP, including Geoff Barker, the deputy leader of Wirral Council, were supporters of Militant. They were referred to the national constitutional committee and subsequently expelled from the Labour Party. At the same meeting the NEC agreed to undertake a separate investigation into the activities of Socialist Organiser.

The rationale for a new selection contest thus turned out to be not any objections to the conduct of the previous one but simply to the participation in it of half a dozen people alleged to be members of the Militant Tendency. The NEC made no recommendation about when the Birkenhead selection should be rerun, but did authorize a continued investigation into the activities of Wirral Labour Party members. The effect was to provide Field with a free hand to continue his campaign of blackmail against the Party and to give Joyce Gould the discretion to delay the reselection indefinitely.

Shortly after the NEC meeting, an informal approach was made to Davies to see if he would give up his claims in Birkenhead in return for the Party's nomination for the Bootle by-election. This proved once again that there was no objection to Davies himself, simply a determination not to upset Frank Field. Davies, a local activist who had spent years building a local base, was not interested.

In the late autumn it was widely rumoured in the press that Labour would rerun the Birkenhead selection in March 1991. Regional organizer Peter Kilfoyle made it clear that the Birkenhead Labour Party was ready to proceed. But Field declared that he would not stand in any new selection until the left in Birkenhead and Wallasey had been routed. He issued yet more statements demanding the Labour leadership root out "left-wing infiltration". As before, his outbursts in the media forced the leadership to take action on his behalf. The December 1990 NEC decided by seventeen votes to six to defer the Birkenhead reselection. Outside the NEC David Blunkett, who had voted with the NEC majority, declared his impatience with "Frank Field going on the TV and abusing the Party when it is doing what has been asked to be done".[9]

The Birkenhead selection was finally rerun in June 1991, eighteen months after the original ballot. This time, Field won the individual members' ballot by 159 votes to Davies's 99. In the unions' section Davies won 25 branches to Field's 18. That made Frank Field the overall winner in the electoral college by 53 per cent to 45.5 per cent.

One of the reasons that Field had finally agreed to let the ballot go ahead was the presence of new blood in the regional office. Peter Kilfoyle was on his way to Parliament courtesy of the Walton by-election and had been replaced by Eileen Murfin. Kilfoyle was passionately anti-Militant and clearly on the Party's hard right, but he was prepared to tolerate traditional trade union left-wingers like Davies and had little time for a self-publicist like Field. Murfin, on the other hand, knew exactly what was expected of her by the leadership and proceeded to do it.

Two trade union branches, GMB No. 275 and No. 11, and two affiliated societies, the Christian Socialist Movement and the Co-operative Party, all of which voted for Field, were allowed by Murfin to participate in the ballot despite the fact that their delegates had failed to fulfil the voting precondition of attending at least one general committee meeting of the Birkenhead CLP in the past twelve months. In addition, the Christian Socialist Movement branch had not paid its affiliation fee for 1990. Up to sixteen Field supporters who had not paid any subscription to the Party during 1990, despite written reminders, were allowed to vote in the second contest even though they had been ruled ineligible by Kilfoyle in the first.

Paul Davies and his supporters claimed that if it had not been for these breaches of the rules he would have won the selection ballot by 50.3 per cent to 48 per cent. Davies had drawn the attention of the national Party to these irregularities before the selection meeting had been convened but had received no response. Birkenhead CLP chair Sue Williams publicly charged the Labour hierarchy with manipulating the procedure to get the desired result. "I am absolutely appalled that the Labour Party has stooped so low to get the result that they wanted," she said. "It's an absolute disgrace. I have never seen such a shambles of a meeting. They have altered the voting and the membership."[10]

Davies documented his complaints to the NEC but, in contrast to the treatment given the discredited Field dossier, his submission received short shrift. NEC members were presented with it only when they arrived at the July 1991 organization sub-committee meeting, which was expected to endorse Field. Tony Benn asked for more time to read the document but "soft left" members insisted there was no time available. Kinnock moved to endorse Field immediately. When Benn raised the question of Field's disavowal of an official Labour candidate in Wallasey there was no response. John Evans defended Eileen Murfin and Clare Short described criticism of the regional office as "outrageous". Only Benn, Skinner, Eddie Haigh and Barbara Switzer of MSF voted against endorsing Field.

The NEC then moved to silence grassroots protests about the conduct of the rerun selection by suspending the Birkenhead Labour Party. The excuse was once more a complaint that local Party officers had sought to "intimidate" members at the conclusion of the selection meeting. In response to Field's claim on television that he had been physically sick before attending local Party meetings, local Party secretary Paddy Reynolds had quipped, after the ballot result was declared, "Frank Field has another four years of feeling sick to look forward to." This casual comment was intended by Reynolds as a joke and taken that way by everyone else present. But for the Party leadership and the media it was evidence of the "intimidation" Field and his supporters had endured from the local left.

If anyone was guilty of running a campaign of intimidation it was Frank Field, who used the media to slander local Party members whose only crime was that they preferred to have someone else as their Labour

MP. These were not public officials or national figures. These were not members of organized left-wing groups. They were grassroots activists with strong political commitments who had made every effort to abide by the rules of the Labour Party only to find that they were denied even the semblance of fair treatment. For the Party leadership, appeasing Frank Field and his backers in the media was far more important than protecting the rights of Party members to select a parliamentary candidate of their own choosing.

Proscribing Socialist Organiser

In the course of his campaign against the left in Birkenhead Frank Field had attacked members of the neighbouring Wallasey CLP. Despite Field's 1987 denunciation, the Labour candidate, Lol Duffy, and his colleagues had built Wallasey into a dynamic local Party with a high profile in the community. In recent years it had taken a number of seats from the Tories in council elections. Ten years of hard work, aided by continuing economic recession, had turned this former Tory stronghold into one of the tightest marginals in the country.

Field pointed the finger at Socialist Organiser, the left-wing group with which Duffy had been associated and which boasted a number of supporters on the Wirral. In response, the NEC agreed to investigate the group. It was Socialist Organiser's misfortune not only to have crossed Frank Field but to have tangled in the bear garden of student politics with the Labour Co-ordinating Committee. For some years Socialist Organiser had opposed the Democratic Left/LCC student faction in both NOLS and the NUS. For Socialist Organiser's old enemies, now ensconced in the Labour hierarchy, the Field attack was the perfect excuse to exact revenge.

Joyce Gould presented the results of her investigation to the June 1990 NEC. There was little about Socialist Organiser's role in the Wirral; instead there was an indictment of the group as a whole and especially of the editor of its newspaper, Sean Matgamna. Gould's document was in some ways even more preposterous than the Field dossier because where the latter consisted mainly of petty gossip the former took off into realms of pure fantasy.

For nearly five months Gould had been ostensibly investigating Socialist Organiser, but in late August, two months after she had completed her paper and one month after the NEC had banned the group, the librarian at Walworth Road wrote to the *Socialist Organiser* newspaper to complain that the Party library had not received its subscription copy since autumn 1989. Wherever Gould had been looking for information about Socialist Organiser it was not in the Labour Party library, which might have been supposed to be her first stop. Nor did she make any attempt to contact Socialist Organiser or to reply to its many letters and phone messages offering to supply her with any information she required.

Instead, she relied on Socialist Organiser's old enemies in the student movement. Her paper was largely a rehashed version of an old Democratic Left dossier on Socialist Organiser. This was supplemented by revelations supplied by one Rachel Pitkeathley, who had been a student supporter of Socialist Organiser for a little over a year, during which time she had secured a place on the NOLS national committee. Following a dispute within Socialist Organiser which resulted in the exodus of a number of its leading student activists, an embittered Pitkeathley found herself without a political base. She was quickly lured into the Labour Co-ordinating Committee camp and soon found a job as a researcher for a Labour MP. At the urging of her new-found confederates Pitkeathley provided information and documentation about Socialist Organiser, heaping calumny on her former associates.

Joyce Gould's submission to the NEC was a remarkably sloppy piece of work, littered with major and minor inaccuracies and downright impossibilities. Much of it dwelt on the career of Sean Matgamna. Apart from misspelling the English form of his name (under which he edited *Socialist Organiser*), it got his year of birth wrong and alleged falsely that he had once been a member of the IRA. Gould reported that Matgamna had "fled" to England after "rumours that Matgamna was on the IRA hit-list as an informer". In fact, Matgamna had come to England with his parents at the age of twelve and was a known opponent of the IRA.

The document catalogued in bizarre detail Matgamna's alleged career in and out of a variety of left-wing groups. The focus on Matgamna seemed to imply that his prehistory was shared by all other Socialist Organiser supporters, which was untrue. The smear seemed to be a substitute for efforts to prove that either Matgamna or Socialist Organiser had actually done anything to disrupt or damage the Labour Party. Indeed, no evidence or arguments to that effect were ever put to the NEC.

Gould's document claimed that Socialist Organiser's bureaucracy was run "by about ten people, most of whom live at 54a Peckham Rye". In fact, no one associated with the group lived at that address at the time the dossier was submitted. This detail, like much else in the report, was inserted in order to paint Socialist Organiser supporters as abnormal people inhabiting unnatural environments while engaging in conspiratorial activity. It was a picture worthy of the *News of the World*.

The leadership's willingness to take action on the basis of a dossier filled with the sort of information usually of interest only to the intelligence services disturbed many who had no sympathy with Socialist Organiser's politics. Matgamna sent his answer to the document, which had been leaked to him by journalists, to NEC members, thus forcing Joyce Gould to issue a revised version to the July meeting of the NEC. This time she supplemented her report with "evidence" in the form of half a dozen Socialist Organiser internal discussion bulletins provided by Pitkeathley.

On behalf of Socialist Organiser, Martin Thomas wrote to all members of the NEC, pointing out that Socialist Organiser had first learned about Joyce Gould's report from a *Sunday Times* article published on June 17th alleging that Labour planned to "outlaw" the group. He asked to be informed of all allegations and of all evidence in support of these allegations and requested a hearing at the NEC. He received no reply.

The NEC approved Gould's document in July 1990 and voted in effect to ban Socialist Organiser. The first communication on the matter that Socialist Organiser or any of the individuals named in the Gould report received from Walworth Road was a letter from Joyce Gould sent on August 1st informing them of the NEC decision. She explained that the NEC had declared Socialist Organiser "ineligible for affiliation" because it was, in effect, a party within the Labour Party, with its own "programme, principles and policy" and "branches within the Party".

This was the same verdict that had been pronounced on Militant some years previously and was the one thing that Joyce Gould's report did appear to prove. Gould quoted internal discussion bulletins in which there were clear references to recruitment and to the various national and local structures of the organization. But it was never clear whether it was the mere fact of having organizational structures and membership (something common to dozens of internal Labour Party pressure groups) or the type of organization which made the group "ineligible for affiliation" (for which they had not applied in any case). If the issue was the unacceptability of "democratic centralist" forms of organization, this was never spelt out, though it was frequently hinted at, especially by the Labour Co-ordinating Committee. Nor were the "principles and policy" that allegedly separated the group from the rest of the Party identified. The effect, however, was that Party members could be deemed in breach of the constitution and liable for expulsion simply for being Socialist Organiser supporters.

Socialist Organiser responded to the ban by publicly winding itself up. It offered to make any amendments to its organization or practices needed to bring it within Party rules, if only someone at Walworth Road would tell its supporters what these were. Of course, this was a calculated move designed to expose the illogicality of the NEC's decision. By emphasizing the NEC's violations of natural justice and its threat to free speech in the Party, Socialist Organiser mounted a formidable campaign against the ban, which drew surprisingly wide support. In a speech to a public meeting called to protest at the NEC actions, *Tribune* editor Phil

Kelly commented, "By this decision and the manner in which it was taken the NEC has raised unnecessary doubts about Labour's commitment to a pluralist society, freedom of speech and open government."

At the 1990 Labour Party conference, thirty-five emergency resolutions protesting against the ban were submitted, including one from the Co-operative Retail Society (CRS) Political Committee. Constant lobbying by Socialist Organiser and others ensured that a debate on the resolutions was finally taken on the last morning of the conference week. John Wilton, the parliamentary candidate for Birmingham Edgbaston, came to the rostrum holding up a copy of the *Socialist Organiser* newspaper in one hand and a copy of *The Times* in the other. "Comrades, I am not a supporter of either of these newspapers," he began. "This one supports the Tory Party and says Vote Tory at a general election. This one supports the Labour Party and says Vote Labour at a general election. What is being proposed by the NEC . . . is that if you write for this one and support it," he held up *The Times*, "there is no problem about you being a Labour Party member. If you write for this one," he held up *Socialist Organiser*, "and support it, you cannot be a member of the Labour Party. . . . How can we persuade people we are serious about civil liberties and justice if we don't practise it in our own Party?"[11]

An extremely irritated Tony Clarke replied for the NEC. "The history of tolerance is something that we will defend," he said, "but there comes a time when you have to say that tolerance when abused has to be spoken out against."[12] Despite his speech, the NEC won the vote by the heavy margin of 5,200,000 million votes to 488,000. Although Socialist Organiser's right to free speech and free association within the Party was backed by only a handful of small unions it had won the support of well over half the constituency parties.

After the 1990 conference debate, some at Walworth Road were worried that a general purge of Socialist Organiser was not worth the embarrassment it might cause. For the Labour Co-ordinating Committee this was frustrating. Rachel Pitkeathley was asked once again to attach her name to an article on Socialist Organiser in a committee newsletter. She gave a lurid account of her life as a supporter of the group, which was picked up by the press. "The changes are simply cosmetic," she told Patrick Wintour, "the inner vanguard party remains intact."[13] The *Guardian* declined to grant Socialist Organiser's request for a right to reply.

One result of the move against Socialist Organiser was to delay the parliamentary selection in Wallasey. Lol Duffy, the local favourite, had publicly severed all his links with the banned group. The Wallasey Labour Party officers pressed for a prompt start to the selection procedure. After all, this was now a highly winnable seat and it made sense to have a candidate in place as early as possible. The national Labour Party and the regional office prevaricated; it seemed that the leadership was waiting for a general election to be called so that a candidate other than Duffy could be imposed.

In December 1991 the regional office was forced at last to agree a selection timetable with the constituency officers. Duffy received over 70 per cent of the nominations including the support of five of the six local party branches, the women's section and numerous trade unions. His twenty-four nominations far exceeded the tally of five achieved by his nearest rival, Angela Eagle, a COHSE full-time official, former chair of the Oxford University Fabian Society and a supporter of the LCC.

In January 1992 the NEC decided that the imminence of a general election demanded the intervention of an emergency 'by-election panel' to interview potential candidates and shortlist contenders in those constituencies without a Labour candidate already in place. Quite why an NEC panel could operate any faster than local Party officers was not explained. During the panel's interviewing of Wallasey candidates, Roy Hattersley asked Lol Duffy how he would reconcile his personal beliefs – notably his support for unilateralism and repeal of all anti-union laws – with the Party's present policy. From a man who had regularly denounced Party policy in the past, this was pure cheek. Duffy made it clear that he would have no problem with this. Many other candidates found themselves in the same position, but to no great surprise, Hattersley's NEC panel excluded Duffy from the Wallasey shortlist. John Evans explained to reporters the panel's reasoning: "On almost every area Mr Duffy said that although he would campaign on agreed policies he didn't personally agree with them."[14] In other words, Duffy was being punished not because he was personally unsuitable but because he did not share the politics of the Labour leadership.

Under the rules of the Labour Party, if more than 50 per cent of those who vote in a parliamentary selection return blank ballot papers the selection must start from scratch with new nominations. Contrary to Party rules, no independent scrutineer was allowed into the Wallasey count held at the regional office in Warrington. When pressed, Eileen Murfin admitted that the officials had not bothered to count the blank votes, again in contravention of the rules. But sources leaked the total to the media, which reported that 163 blank papers had been returned by local members in protest at the exclusion of Lol Duffy. Only fifty-seven votes had been cast for the "winning" candidate, Angela Eagle. Under the Party constitution the selection was null and void; but Party officials glossed over this detail. To add insult to injury, the NEC not only dismissed the complaints of Party members but threatened to mount yet another "investigation" of the constituency after the general election.

Lol Duffy worked diligently for Angela Eagle during the general election. "I'm not going to go off and sulk just because the NEC has broken every rule in the book to prevent me being a candidate," he said.

Thanks to the years of hard work put in by himself and others in the constituency the seat was taken from the Tories and Eagle became the first Labour MP for Wallasey.

Lambeth

Lambeth Council's stand against ratecapping in 1985 resulted in the surcharging and disqualification of council leader Ted Knight and thirty-six other Labour councillors. In the elections which followed in 1986, a new batch of Labour councillors took control. There followed a period of instability, in which contending right, centre and left factions swapped places in the Labour Group leadership. For a while, an LCC-dominated administration, led by Dick Sorabji, held sway, but in less than a year in office it antagonized the local Labour Party and the bulk of the Labour Group. It was replaced in mid 1989 with a new left administration led by Joan Twelves.

That year, the Lambeth local government committee was suspended by Walworth Road, in an attempt to protect some of the Sorabji group from deselection. The manifesto for the May 1990 council elections was drawn up by the regional office. Already, Poll Tax enforcement was becoming a sensitive matter. "Only as a last resort", ran one crucial passage of the regional office manifesto for Lambeth, "will we carry out the obligation imposed on local authorities of taking legal action to collect this iniquitous tax."

Unlike the Labour Party elsewhere in London, the Lambeth Party achieved good results in the May 1990 elections. That year David Blunkett praised the council for busting the government's Poll Tax cap, which restricted local authority expenditure. Throughout this period left policies were supported by two of the borough's three CLPs. Though the Labour Co-ordinating Committee had a base in Streatham its councillors were perpetually frustrated by the ability of the Twelves administration to survive one crisis after another and still keep the support of a majority of the Labour Group and the local Party. At the beginning of 1991 the committee decided that enough was enough.

The spark was two special council meetings held in February. The first was on the Gulf War. Before the war commenced on January 18th the Labour Group officers had prepared reports with the help of staff on the possible impact of a war in the Gulf on Lambeth residents. There was nothing exceptional about this; both Tory and Labour authorities up and down the country were routinely doing the same. Among the recommendations put to a Labour Group meeting held on January 21st was the calling of a special council meeting on the war at which a motion would be put by the Labour Group.

Joan Twelves tabled a draft of this motion which, along with the recommendations in the officers' reports, was thoroughly discussed in what observers recall as an even-tempered Labour Group meeting. Josh Arnold-Foster, a Lambeth councillor who worked for Martin O'Neill, Labour's defence spokesperson, tried to amend the officers' recommendations but was defeated. In the end the group voted with only two against and five abstaining to hold the special council meeting and to put to it a strong anti-war resolution. This was supported in the days that followed by both Norwood and Vauxhall constituencies.

Alerted by the Lambeth Labour Co-ordinating Committee, Joyce Gould wrote to all members of Lambeth Labour Group on January 30th. She advised them that "this matter is not germane to the functioning of the council in Lambeth" (despite the fact that the Association of Metropolitan Authorities (AMA), the Association of London Authorities (ALA), the London Fire and Civil Defence Authority (LFCDA) and other bodies had issued advice on the Gulf crisis to local authorities) and that therefore in this case Labour councillors would not be bound by the Labour whip. Gould's letter was sent out without any effort to contact the Lambeth Group officers or the chief whip, Julian Lewis.

The special council meeting attracted wide publicity. The public gallery was packed and the debate was heated. At one point the sound system failed; this was due not to a left-wing conspiracy but to the effects of an industrial dispute. The Tories' pro-war amendment was defeated by the Labour majority, although eight Labour councillors abstained on the vote. Twelves moved the Labour Group's official anti-war resolution, which was passed by a narrow twenty-six votes to twenty-four. Seven Labour councillors joined the Tories to vote against Labour Group policy and three more abstained.

A week after the Gulf War meeting the council held another, even more contentious special meeting. This time the subject was the use of bailiffs to collect the Poll Tax. For two years the Labour Group and the Labour Party had been embroiled in a debate about Poll Tax non-payment and non-enforcement. The Twelves leadership antagonized some of its left supporters when it abandoned its initial line of total resistance and began, grudgingly, to set the wheels in motion to collect the tax. Twelves's strategy was to keep within the law but push it to its limit. She could cite not only the Labour Party's local manifesto (written by the regional office) but also advice from the Association of Metropolitan Authorities, council officers, the National Consumer Council and the Law Commission on the disadvantages of "distress", that is, the use of bailiffs, as a remedy for Poll Tax non-payment, which was inevitably high in this borough of poverty and unemployment. There were numerous shades of opinion on this matter within the Labour Group and the local Party but the bottom line for most had always seemed to be refusal to use bailiffs, which was seen as a form of physical harassment of the poorest people in the borough. This position had been supported unanimously by the Vauxhall general committee as late as November 1990 and by the Labour Group in December by an overwhelming twenty-one votes to five and again in January by twenty-two votes to two. On this issue, the LCC had found itself completely isolated.

The Labour Group's agreed policy on bailiffs contradicted the formal advice from paid officers who were acting, in effect, under legal instructions. It was agreed that both the officers' recommendations and the Labour Group's amendment to them would be put to a special council meeting on February 7th. Again, the gallery was packed, this time with supporters of Lambeth Against the Poll Tax, one of the most vigorous groups opposing the Poll Tax in Britain. The whip had been imposed by democratic agreement and this time there was no letter from Joyce Gould to contravene it. None the less, the officers' recommendations to use bailiffs were passed with the support of five Labour councillors as well as of the Tories and Liberals. Official Labour Group policy was never put to the vote.

The council's decision to use bailiffs was greeted with uproar from an enraged public gallery. Lambeth councillor Cathy Ashley, a full-time employee at Walworth Road and a supporter of the Labour Co-ordinating Committee, went straight to the press to claim she had been subject to "intimidation" and "harassment". She implied that after the meeting her car tyres had been slashed by her left-wing political opponents. It was said that "scab" had been daubed on the door of another right-wing Labour councillor. The usual Labour Party "sources" then hinted broadly that Lambeth would have to be "dealt with". A two-page spread in London's *Evening Standard* quoted extensively from unnamed Party officials and Labour MPs to the effect that the Lambeth Labour Group was a menace which had to be eliminated.

All this was manna from heaven for the Tory press, aware that the Tory Party's fortunes in the capital were sagging. Lambeth left councillors were depicted as urban gangsters engaged in thuggery and criminal acts. Joan Twelves became the latest addition to right-wing demonology. Ironically, at this very moment she was retreating from some of her earlier left-wing positions, paying off her Poll Tax and making substantial cuts in Lambeth jobs and services.

The Labour Co-ordinating Committee skilfully exploited the media brouhaha. The February members' mailing was mostly given over to a vitriolic attack on Lambeth Council and the roles allegedly played by various left-wing groups and individuals in the borough. Written by Ben Lucas, a former NOLS officer now living in Lambeth and working for UCATT, the article rehashed Ashley's allegations of "intimidation" and contained extravagant accounts of the two council meetings. It was sent straight to the press. This gave birth to another spate of bad publicity for the Labour Group and a new set of legends about "loony" Lambeth, which were to form the basis of the original NEC investigation into the Labour Group.

On February 2nd, the *South London Press*, reporting the special Gulf War council meeting, had claimed on its front page that during the meeting "Steve French and some colleagues chipped in with cries of 'Victory to Iraq' ". This was illustrated with a ten-inch-square photo of French, a left-wing councillor who was opposed to the cuts Twelves was making. French wrote to the newspaper pointing out that he had said no such thing at the meeting (or anywhere else) and demanding a retraction. The *South London Press* refused to print his letter. Significantly, at this point not a single other newspaper had attributed any such remarks to French. Not even the *Sun* had picked up the inflammatory allegation.

But in his article for the Labour Co-ordinating Committee mailing Ben Lucas claimed that "Steve French was heard repeatedly shouting 'Victory to Iraq' and 'Bomb Israel' during the debate." Lucas had not been present at either this meeting or the subsequent council meeting on bailiffs, but failed to mention this either to his readers or to the journalists to whom he spoke. He also failed to cite any other source for his claim about Steve French, a claim that he knew would be terribly damaging both personally and politically for French. In fact, French had not even spoken in the council debate. Out of over one hundred people in attendance at the meeting the only people who ever claimed to have heard this remark were a tiny group of LCC supporters.

Lucas's article formed the basis for a Patrick Wintour article in the *Guardian* on February 28th 1991. Wintour failed to inform his readers that his source was a Labour Co-ordinating Committee members' mailing and implied that Ben Lucas was an independent witness. The "Victory to Iraq" and "Bomb Israel" allegations were printed as fact. French complained to the *Guardian* but the paper refused to concede there was anything wrong with its story or to print French's letter correcting the misinformation.

At the urging of the Lambeth Labour Co-ordinating Committee, Joyce Gould recommended to the NEC organization sub-committee which met at the end of February that the Party should launch "an urgent investigation into the activities of the Lambeth Labour Group". She reported that she had written to the Labour Group telling them not to obey the whip in the Gulf meeting because the resolution being put was "in opposition to the policy of the Party". In the case of the bailiffs meeting, she informed the NEC incorrectly that "there was some doubt as to the Group view on this issue" and implied that it was an offence for the whip to be used to compel Labour councillors to vote against council officers' recommendations. But the most important point she made was that both meetings had been "conducted against a background of personal abuse, disruption and threats of intimidation to individual councillors". Her only source of information for this assertion was the press and the Lambeth Labour Co-ordinating Committee. The organization sub-committee and later the full NEC approved Gould's recommendations with only Tony Benn and Dennis Skinner dissenting.

Vauxhall MP Kate Hoey and Streatham parliamentary candidate Keith Hill, a full-time NUR official, were consulted by Gould throughout the course of the Lambeth investigation. Thanks to an inside tip-off, Hoey and Hill were able to issue a press release welcoming the decision to launch the Lambeth inquiry on the very day it was made. They denounced what they called "the antics of an unrepresentative minority". At the Greater London Labour Party conference held on March 1st, the new London press officer, Jo Scard, spent much of her time briefing the press on the Lambeth allegations. An emergency resolution against the latest witch-hunt was heavily defeated by union votes. During the debate, Ted Knight asked rhetorically, "We don't want purges, do we?" Labour Co-ordinating Committee members around the hall clamoured back, "Oh yes we do!" Among those seen applauding the attacks on Lambeth made from the rostrum was Phil Cole, the London regional officer in charge of the Lambeth inquiry. Cole, a former student politician, was also a member of the Labour Party in Lambeth and a supporter of the Labour Co-ordinating Committee.

Joyce Gould met the Lambeth Labour Group officers, including Joan Twelves, on March 15th. The officers wanted to know if the NEC investigation was based solely on reports in the press and if so which ones they should try to respond to. Gould was evasive, and claimed that members of the NEC had asked for an investigation "very quickly indeed" because they had been concerned about what they read in the press and what certain people had told them.

The officers asked about the Ben Lucas article. "I don't know anything about Ben Lucas," she said. "I've never communicated in any way with Ben Lucas. Why should I?" She then acknowledged that she did know about Lucas's paper but assured the Lambeth councillors, "It's not gone to the NEC. That is a completely separate paper." The councillors pointed out that they had not yet received any formal notification of the investigation and were aware of it only from reports in the press. They wanted sight of everything the NEC had seen regarding their cases since that was the only way they could answer accusations. Gould explained, "Reports that go to the NEC are private and confidential to the NEC. It is for them to decide what it is you see and what you don't see."

There was strong local support for the Lambeth councillors now under investigation. The Labour Group itself voted to condemn the investigation, as did two of the three constituency Labour parties and most town hall unions. A 1,000-strong NALGO meeting, convened to discuss opposition to the Twelves cuts package, resolved with only three voting against to condemn the witch-hunt against her.

At the March NEC thirteen councillors, including the entire Labour Group leadership and all its left-wing critics, were suspended, along with two local Party members involved in the campaign against the Poll Tax. They were barred from holding any Party office or attending any Party meetings besides their own ward meetings. Even before the NEC had met, the *Guardian* had printed the names of the fifteen, supplied by the usual "sources".

In her report to the NEC Gould cited a number of concerns about Lambeth Council. One purported to be discontent among the manual trade unions with the Twelves leadership. This assertion was based entirely on a letter from a right-wing Lambeth UCATT official, complaining that the council leadership was "veering wildly from one position to another". An official letter from the joint committee of the council and unions disclaimed the UCATT statement and opposed the investigation. Gould seemed to be shocked that the local Labour Party wielded influence on the Labour Group: "Such was the importance of local Party support in influencing Group members' actions that Group leadership elections were preceded by hustings around the ward meetings to obtain nominations."[15]

The central allegation against Twelves read "that over the last two years there has been a lack of decisive leadership . . . the leader . . . has on many occasions been in breach of the decisions and policies of the Group". This was a strange assertion since over the previous two years the Labour Group had endorsed nearly every one of Twelves's proposals. Twelves was also accused of "having a history . . . of advocating a strategy of confrontation with the government", which could also be said about most other Labour council leaders in the country. Finally, Gould claimed and the NEC agreed, without a scrap of supporting evidence, that there had been "intimidation" of councillors. "Although there may be no connection it cannot be proven – one woman councillor had her door daubed and another her tyre slashed"[16] (sic). If no connection could be proven then why was this grave allegation of criminal behaviour included in the report at all?

After the NEC decision, Joyce Gould finally wrote to all the suspended councillors asking them to respond to the "charges". Those who decided to avail themselves of this facility found Gould in person defensive and confused. In July, she presented her final report to the NEC. David Blunkett tried to get the charges against three of the suspended councillors – the experienced and highly respectable trio of Lesley Hammond, George Huish and Bill Houghting – dropped, but he could not muster a majority. All fifteen councillors were accused of "a sustained course of conduct prejudicial to the Party" (the two local Party members were further accused of association with Militant) and referred to the national constitutional committee. Gone were the references to lack of "decisive leadership" and complaints from manual unions. The original false allegations of intimidation and thuggery had also vanished, although they were the reason the NEC had launched the investigation in the first place.

The "charges" against the individual councillors consisted of a bald list of dates followed by a note of a vote at a council or Labour Group meeting or some public statement or internal Party document or even just an assertion that the individual in question had supported "an illegal budget". In some instances the fact that an individual had been referred to in an article written by one of the others was listed as a separate "charge". There was no indication of just how these unrelated events amounted to a "sustained course" of anything.

The litany of offences in one case read: "April 1988 – opposed cuts; September 1989 – article in Briefing opposing views of Group; Summer 1989 – statement in NALGO journal opposing all aspects of Poll Tax; July 1990 – moved to invite Sinn Fein councillors." The specifications varied with each councillor, but all included two particular items that obviously constituted the real offence: "February 1991 – voted for resolution on Gulf; February 1991 – voted against use of bailiffs." On both of these issues all thirteen had voted in accordance with Labour Group and local Party policy; they had obeyed the whip; it was the Labour Co-ordinating Committee councillors, now priming the witch-hunt, who in this instance had broken the whip and voted with the Tories.

Gould's report managed to get the date of the council meeting on bailiffs wrong throughout. Far more disturbing was the documentation submitted to the NEC in support of the "charges": copies of Labour Group minutes, a 1989 bulletin by "Councillors Against the Cuts", clippings from Labour Briefing, the South London Press, the local NALGO journal, letters in the press, strategy papers circulated by the leader or others within the Labour Group and the local Party, a pre-election Party newsletter, an unsigned account of a Labour Group discussion on Sinn Fein.[17] Where did all this material come from? Who had been compiling it over the years and why? No one at the NEC, with the exception of Tony Benn and Dennis Skinner, seemed the least perturbed by these questions.

Despite the baffling style of presentation, it was now obvious to the thirteen that their real offences were political. The councillors involved had opposed cuts, challenged the use of bailiffs to collect the Poll Tax, opposed the Gulf War and invited Sinn Fein representatives to speak in the borough. On all these issues they had acted with the support of their local parties; in most instances they were also following the Labour whip;

in many they had been joined in voting this way by other Labour councillors who for mysterious reasons had escaped the attention of the NEC.

The breaches of whip over the cuts had already been dealt with under the rules of the Party through joint meetings of the local Labour Group and representatives of the local constituency parties. These bodies had debated the various breaches and decided democratically not to discipline the councillors involved. The thirteen claimed that for them to be prosecuted for this offence a second time amounted to "double jeopardy". In any case, if breach of the whip was the real issue, why were none of the right-wing councillors who had broken the whip over the bailiffs being charged?

The Sinn Fein allegation was welcomed by the press, who could use it to reiterate the long-standing claim that Labour was soft on the IRA. In 1986 Lambeth Council, along with many others, had invited a group of elected Sinn Fein councillors to address them. In 1989 councillors and tenants' representatives had gone on a fact-finding visit to Northern Ireland where they once again met Sinn Fein councillors. There had been no objection from either Walworth Road or the LCC to either of these initiatives. Then in mid 1990, Rachel Webb, a left-wing councillor, had submitted a report to the Labour Group which suggested that Lambeth tenants might defend themselves from crime in the same way that IRA "punishment shootings" defended tenants in nationalist areas in Northern Ireland.

This absurdity was roundly rejected by the Labour Group, which went on to pass a resolution moved by Steve French calling on the council to organize a visit from Sinn Fein "to exchange information especially vis-à-vis safety on council estates". This was passed by eighteen votes to fifteen. At the following Labour Group meeting Greg Tucker proposed that the Group officers should start work immediately "to invite Sinn Fein councillors to visit the borough this calendar year". This was passed by fourteen votes to ten – and it was this vote to which Joyce Gould objected. No formal Labour Party policy banned intercourse with Sinn Fein. Other councillors across London had done no less than the Lambeth thirteen and had not been disciplined. Obviously the Party was opposed to Sinn Fein, but it was also opposed to the media ban on Sinn Fein and in favour of a united Ireland. This "charge" was included only because it was a handy means of smearing the Lambeth group by linking it to the IRA and terrorism.

Nine of the thirteen suspended Lambeth councillors had their cases heard in July 1992, fifteen months after they were initially suspended and three months after the general election. The final revised sets of "charges" and evidence to support them had only been given to the accused a matter of weeks before the national constitutional committee hearings. The existing charges were augmented by alleged offences committed since the councillors had been suspended. There were seven letters from Lambeth Party members plus a letter from Hoey and Hill (recently elected Labour MP for Streatham with help from some of those suspended) making highly generalized (and political) judgements on the thirteen as a group and alleging that their reinstatement would be a disaster for the local Labour Party and Lambeth Council. All these submissions had been written within a two-day period in mid June 1992, and all were from people known to be connected with the Lambeth Labour Co-ordinating Committee. They were backed up by a 29-page submission from Kim Dewdney, a former LCC executive member and Lambeth councillor who had acted as chief whip under the discredited Sorabji regime in 1988–89. Over sixty errors of fact were discovered in Dewdney's document, which was nothing but an attempt to vindicate the LCC's brief term at the top in Lambeth and blame its various failures on the intransigence of its left critics in the Labour Party and the Labour Group.

Larry Whitty and Joyce Gould, with regional officer Phil Cole at their side, took turns presenting the NEC's case against each of the individual councillors. No one seemed to think it extraordinary that the general secretary of the Labour Party would spend a whole day "prosecuting" two local councillors whose crimes amounted to half a dozen breaches of the Labour whip. Nor did any member of the national constitutional committee panel comment on the failure of either Gould or Whitty to prove the charge of "sustained conduct prejudicial to the Party". When representatives of the accused reminded Whitty of his own assurance to Party conference in 1986 that the committee would not concern itself with the "holding or expression of opinion", he repeated that the councillors had broken the whip and that that alone was tantamount to "conduct prejudicial", but produced no evidence to corroborate this assertion.

Counterposed to the flimsy evidence offered by the NEC were scores of detailed statements in support of the thirteen, both as a group and as individuals, from the majority of their fellow Labour councillors, from their local ward and constituency parties, from a wide range of trade unions and community groups, from council officers, members of the public and Norwood MP John Fraser. The evidence of the substantial contributions made to the local Labour Party and community by the thirteen was incontestable. All of this should have been weighed by the national constitutional committee panel in favour of the suspended councillors, but all the councillors who appeared before the committee in July 1992 were found guilty as charged. The committee, as is its custom, refused to explain exactly which of the councillors' acts had justified this verdict. Nor was any explanation given for the inconsistent sentences: some of the councillors were expelled and some suspended (from either the Party or the Labour Group) for periods of six months to two years. The national constitutional committee had vindicated accusations that it was nothing but the Labour leadership's kangaroo court.

Terry Fields and Dave Nellist

The attacks on Militant and the rest of the left in Liverpool did not come to an end with the expulsions of 1986. Initially regional officer Peter Kilfoyle, appointed by the NEC to clean out Merseyside, had promised to build a grassroots opposition to the Militant through intensive political education and union mobilization. But the problem Kilfoyle faced was that the left's strength in Liverpool arose not out of manipulation of Labour Party rules but out of the city's appalling poverty and its tradit-ions of working-class solidarity. Kilfoyle was "forced to abandon nice-ties", as the *Guardian* put it, in his battle against the Militant.[18]

Kilfoyle and the regional office intervened at will in every Labour Party body in the city. The district Labour Party was repeatedly closed down. Dissenting wards and constituencies were threatened that reports about them would be sent to Walworth Road. In March 1989 the Liverpool Broadgreen CLP had only just been reopened following an investigation when it was suspended again and placed under the control of the regional office. At the NEC meeting which approved this move, Tony Benn warned that the decision was the first step in getting rid of Terry Fields. Joyce Gould denied the allegation.

In the late 1980s Liverpool City Council had come under a new, non-Militant but left-leaning leadership headed by Keva Coombes. For the first time in years, the ever-fraught Liverpool Labour Group achieved some stability. However, the first meeting to set a Poll Tax, in March 1990, saw numerous councillors voting against the tax, in accordance with local Labour Party policy. Sixteen were immediately suspended by the NEC, which thus handed control of the Labour Group to the right-wing rump led by Harry Rimmer. Coombes was removed as leader and the Rimmer faction immediately began dismantling everything the left had achieved in its years of power. Cuts, redundancies and rent rises were pushed through with the aid of the Liberal Democrats against the opposition of left councillors. As a result more councillors were sus-pended, bringing the total excluded from the Labour Group to twenty-nine. The Rimmer leadership worked hand in glove with Peter Kilfoyle and boasted frequently that it had the full backing of Neil Kinnock. Its decision to privatize rubbish collection precipitated a bitter dispute with the workforce. The battle lines were drawn. Walworth Road had deliber-ately engineered a major split in the city's labour movement.

Rimmer-supporting candidates were imposed in a number of left-wing wards before the May 1991 council elections. In response, the local Broad

Left, in which Militant was heavily involved but which was certainly not an exclusively Militant operation, decided to stand its own candidates. To Walworth Road's dismay, five out of six of the Broad Left candidates won, with majorities varying from ninety to nine hundred. Clearly, the Liverpool left enjoyed a substantial base of public support in the city.

The previous year, Peter Kilfoyle had won the selection to succeed the retiring Eric Heffer in Liverpool Walton. It was a closely fought contest, with Militant supporter Lesley Mahmood losing to Kilfoyle only by a margin of less than 4 per cent. Mahmood lodged a number of complaints about irregularities in the ballot but they were all ignored by Walworth Road. Her chief grievance was that Kilfoyle had been allowed to stand as a candidate at the same time as he continued functioning as a regional organizer responsible for overseeing parliamentary selections, including his own. Among other things, he had been able to canvass among members whose names and addresses he alone was privy to.

With the death of Eric Heffer in May 1991, a by-election was held in Walton. Flushed with their success in the council elections, Militant and the Broad Left decided to run Mahmood as a "Real Labour" candidate against Kilfoyle. For the Labour leadership it was a godsend. Militant had come out into the open, it was said, doing at last what the right wing had always dared it to do, running under its own colours.

The by-election campaign was conducted in the glare of national publicity which painted Kilfoyle as the champion of the forces of reason against the irrational extremism of Mahmood, an impression reinforced by the simultaneous broadcasting of Alan Bleasdale's television drama *GBH*, on Channel Four. At the outset of the campaign the chair of the local Party wrote to all Labour Party members urging them to "observe other members" campaigning for Mahmood and take note of "name, time, date and circumstances". Socialist Organiser supporters, keen to prove their loyalty to the Party, actually canvassed for Kilfoyle but found "the stench of witch-hunting was unbearable".

> When we returned from our first leafleting runs, "Militant Tendency Incident Forms" were handed out for people to write down details of Mahmood supporters seen. When we refused to give the names of a Leeds University *Militant* seller, supposedly spotted, one Kinnockite suggested a form should be filled out about us too.[19]

A huge effort, supervised behind the scenes by NEC member John Evans, went into collecting data about Mahmood supporters. A van was parked near the Mahmood campaign headquarters and photographs were taken of anyone who went near it. A ladder was braced against the back of the room and more photographs were taken through the windows. A note was made of every address displaying a Mahmood poster and these were then checked off against a list of Labour Party members.

The Mahmood candidacy put both Terry Fields and Dave Nellist, Labour MPs who had long been associated with the Militant Tendency, in an embarrassing position. They were harassed throughout the by-election by the press, who demanded to know whether they had been canvassing in Walton. None of the MPs said a word that could be construed as a refusal to support the official candidate, nor did they offer any public support to Mahmood. True, they did not appear in Walton to canvass for Kilfoyle, but neither did over one hundred other Labour MPs.

On June 26th, in the middle of the campaign, the Conservative Party chairman, Chris Patten, press-released a letter to Kinnock urging him to take action against both Fields and Nellist. The Labour leader refused to denounce Patten's letter for what it was: an obvious attempt to make media capital out of Labour's internal divisions.

On polling day official Labour humiliated Real Labour in Liverpool Walton. The Broad Left tried to put a brave face on it, pointing out the low turnout and the decrease in the percentage of the Labour vote, which dropped 11.4. per cent on Eric Heffer's 1987 result. There was also an 11 per cent swing against Labour to the Liberal Democrats, further proof, if proof were needed, of who really benefits from Labour's fratricidal civil wars. But Mahmood herself had secured a mere 2,600 votes, some 6.6 per cent of the total.

Certainly this was no personal victory for Peter Kilfoyle but confirmation that the loyalty of the Labour-voting electorate was to the Labour Party and not to any faction within it. Militant supporters were learning the painful lesson taught years before to the breakaway SDP, which despite media support had failed to supplant Labour in working-class areas. The Tories were humiliated with a mere 1,155 votes, some 2.9 per cent of the total, showing that on Merseyside at least even Militant was more popular than the government. But the Tory campaign strategists knew the whole episode was good news for them. "Senior ministers believe", it was reported, that "the atmosphere of crisis surrounding the Labour-led council, which proposed widespread redundancies . . . played a part in re-establishing national support for the government," which was slowly gaining on Labour in the opinion polls.[20]

None of this stopped the Labour leadership from a highly public display of jubilation at the Walton result. At last, the "enemy within" had been beaten in open combat. David Blunkett, who had been in close contact with Rimmer and, in his capacity as Labour's local government spokesperson, had advised him to proceed with redundancies and privatization, announced that the ghost of the Militant Tendency had been laid forever. On the night of the by-election, Jack Cunningham confirmed to the press that Labour would draw up a list of Mahmood supporters for expulsion and that the report going to the NEC on the Walton affair would cover the behaviour of Terry Fields.

The following Sunday, the *Observer* reported that "senior Labour members are convinced the time is right to move against the remaining Militant elements in the Party, even if it means expelling an MP". According to the usual "senior Labour source" up to two hundred "Trotskyists" would be expelled. "It would be a mistake to let this drag on through the summer," the "source" opined, "when political reporters have little else to write about."[21]

In the second week of July Terry Fields was jailed for sixty days for non-payment of Poll Tax. As the first public figure to be imprisoned, he attracted extensive publicity. His was clearly a stand based on principle, as even those who disagreed with it acknowledged. An anonymous Labour Party spokesman offered no sympathy: "Neil Kinnock has made it clear that the Labour Party does not and never will support breaking the law." Mr Fields, he concluded, was "on his own".[22]

Days after Fields's imprisonment, the NEC organization sub-committee met to consider, among other items, a report on the Walton by-election drawn up by John Evans and presented by Joyce Gould. In the middle of the discussion, Kinnock introduced a motion on Fields that had not previously been circulated. The motion referred to the MP's imprisonment and his involvement with the All-Britain Anti-Poll Tax Federation, which had been declared a "Militant front" by the NEC in spring 1990. The motion called on the director of organization to investigate the circumstances of the imprisonment and report to the full NEC the following week.

Roy Hattersley was uneasy about the reference to prison, as were Larry Whitty and Joan Lestor. The deputy leader suggested that the motion refer only to the Anti-Poll Tax Federation. "I can't vote to kick him out for that," Anne Davis said, "a lot of members in my area are part of the Anti-Poll Tax Federation and they've got nothing to do with Militant." Blunkett opined that Fields's Militant links were a sufficient basis for action. Robin Cook, who was not a member of the sub-committee but was present anyway, referred to a speech Fields had given in the Commons in which he had referred to "our programme" for "taking over the commanding heights of the economy". This was taken by Cook to be a reference to the Militant programme, though in fact the phrase was Aneurin Bevan's. Clare Short came to the rescue by amending Kinnock's motion so that it simply required the director of organization to "enquire into the activities of Terry Fields". This was passed by seventeen votes to two, with only Benn and Skinner voting against and Anne Davis abstaining.

At the same meeting the sub-committee voted to initiate disciplinary proceedings against sixty-two Party members who had allegedly been involved in the Mahmood campaign in Liverpool Walton. Joyce Gould explained that she would be examining more of Evans's photographs and would issue an expanded list of up to two hundred names to the full NEC.

Charles Clarke briefed the press on behalf of Neil Kinnock. In his version of the meeting, the Labour leader had told the NEC that he had nothing but "contempt for the irresponsibility of those who do not pay the Poll Tax when they can afford to pay". He also informed them that Joyce Gould would be investigating Fields's links with the Anti-Poll Tax Federation, despite Clare Short's amendment. All this happened while Terry Fields was in prison and unable to respond.

Dave Nellist was not named during the debate but was clearly in the firing line. Senior right-wing Labour MPs argued that the same charges could and should be made against Nellist as against Fields. Ray Powell, a Labour whip, went on record to say that the next Labour government could not afford to be "looking over its shoulder" to see what Nellist was up to.

Once again Chris Patten wrote to Kinnock:

> I was delighted to read in the newspapers this morning that you are attempting to rid your party of the extremist elements that have done so much to threaten the fabric of society, encourage law-breaking and wreak havoc in local government. It will be for the good of the country, if this time you do the job properly, rather than treat the whole exercise as a PR stunt to show you are not completely in hock to the left-wingers in your Party.

Patten went on to argue, not without reason, that since everyone had always known Fields was a Militant supporter why had Kinnock endorsed him as a candidate not once but twice? He then argued that if Fields was being disciplined for involvement in the Anti-Poll Tax Federation, consistency would demand that Kinnock move against the twenty-three other Labour MPs who had supported it at one time or another, in particular Dave Nellist. If, on the other hand, Patten argued, the reason for the move against Fields was his support for Militant's left-wing policies, then Kinnock was bound to take action against the entire Campaign Group of Labour MPs, which shared most of those policies.[23]

Joyce Gould had been given five working days to prepare her report on Terry Fields for the full NEC. Somehow in that time she was able to prepare a 120-page dossier, consisting almost entirely of *Militant* clippings going back to the early 1980s. Some of the clippings did not even refer to Fields. The speed with which the dossier was assembled strengthened suspicions that Walworth Road had been compiling computer databanks on Labour left-wingers for some time. The NEC predictably decided to investigate Nellist as well as Fields, and referred another one hundred Liverpool members to the national constitutional committee for expulsion while again suspending the Liverpool Broadgreen CLP. Fields and Nellist were to be "invited" to the September NEC to be interviewed.

Chris Patten then sent Kinnock the names of twenty-five more Labour MPs (based on an out-of-date list of Campaign Group members) to be expelled. The press was also sent a copy. The *Evening Standard* observed that on Ireland and black sections most Campaign Group members were "even more extreme" than the Militant Tendency.

By any measure, Dave Nellist was one of the country's most effective and assiduous MPs. In the Commons, his ceaseless interventions on the Poll Tax provided rare moments of confidence and clarity in what passed for Labour's parliamentary struggle against Thatcher's flagship policy. His attendance in the House put him in the top 5 per cent of Labour MPs. For his efforts, Nellist was declared Backbencher of the Year by the *Spectator* in 1991.

In the otherwise grim world of Coventry Labour politics Nellist was a beacon. The 6 per cent swing to Labour in Coventry South East in 1987 was one of the best results for the Party anywhere in the country. By 1991 his constituency had made a clean sweep of all twelve local council seats, thanks in part to Nellist's high-profile efforts. "I do not mix with media stars at expensive restaurants," he explained in a letter to his constituents in August 1991. "I have no company directorships and I have never taken all-expenses paid trips overseas as the guest of foreign governments. I have maintained my pledge to take from my parliamentary salary only the same wage as the average skilled worker in a factory in Coventry. Both my home and my constituency office can be readily found in the phone book."

Nellist received hundreds of letters of support from local constituents and won the formal backing of local branches of the UCW, CPSA, NCU, COHSE, NUPE and the Inland Revenue Staff Federation as well as UCATT's Midland regional council and the joint shop stewards' committees of all Coventry's major factories. He was also backed by an amazing variety of local pressure groups and community organizations. Half the Coventry Labour Group signed a statement describing Nellist's reputation as "second to none with the people of Coventry". 6,500 of his constituents signed a petition against his expulsion. Even the right-wing Coventry *Evening Telegraph* came out in his defence.

> He admits that his views have not changed a jot since he was selected in 1982. That is the problem . . . we have criticised him many times but one thing is clear: he is a first-class hard-working MP. His conscientious approach to constituents' problems puts many other MPs to shame.

Matching the 112-page dossier compiled by Walworth Road against him (comprised mostly, again, of clippings from *Militant*), Nellist's supporters in Coventry submitted more than sixty endorsements from all quarters, including Neil Kinnock's own 1987 remark broadcast on West

Midlands local radio: "I think he has drawn widespread admiration for the performance he puts up."

None of this stopped the September NEC from suspending Nellist and Fields and referring them to the NCC. Fields was on holiday with his wife, who had been ill, and saw no reason, after sixty days in prison, to allow the Party leadership to disrupt his life any more than it had done already. At the NEC Nellist put up a fierce defence. Clare Short and David Blunkett pressed him on his links with Militant, demanding that he answer the basic question: are you or are you not a member of the Militant Tendency? They were apparently oblivious to the McCarthyite echoes in their questioning. Nellist explained that he had severed his formal ties to Militant some time ago and that he was prepared to abide by the rules of the Labour Party. The one thing he would not do was make an explicit denunciation of his comrades.

The NEC ruled that since they were under suspension, the two MPs would not be allowed to attend the upcoming annual conference in Brighton. Because the suspended Liverpool Broadgreen CLP had been unable to elect a delegate to conference, regional office had appointed a long-time Fields adversary, Barry Navarro. During the Sunday-night conference debate on the emergency resolution to overthrow the suspension of Fields and Nellist, Tom Sawyer in the chair called an unnamed delegate from the back of the hall. It was Navarro, who proceeded to deliver his scripted denunciation of Fields, omitting to mention that he was not an elected delegate and indeed had failed in several attempts to get himself voted into constituency office.

The conference decided to uphold the suspension and exclusion of Fields and Nellist by 4,630,000 votes to 523,000. The NUM and some of the smaller left-wing unions backed the emergency resolution, as did about half the constituency parties, but the large MSF delegation, which had been mandated to support Fields and Nellist, refused to do so. Nellist had been nominated for the constituency section of the NEC and was one of seven candidates on the Campaign Group slate. But when delegates arrived at the conference, they found his name Tippexed off the ballot papers.

In December Nellist defended himself at a marathon session of the national constitutional committee held in West Bromwich. He had written in advance to the NCC with a list of forty witnesses he wished to call on his behalf, including MPs, trade union officials and local Party activists. He was allowed only six. The Walworth Road dossier on him had now swelled to 142 pages. Among the clippings from *Militant* were 16 duplicate photocopies and 57 interviews with Nellist (the interviews he had given to other newspapers over the years were not included). Most of the evidence dated from the mid 1980s. There were photographs

of him on a Youth Trade Union Rights Campaign demonstration, photographs which had first appeared in the *Morning Star* and were only later
reproduced in *Militant*. Nellist pointed out that shadow cabinet members
Jo Richardson and Michael Meacher had been on the same demonstration and that in the last twenty years forty Labour MPs had made some
kind of contribution to *Militant* or one of its associated organizations. He
also reminded the NCC panel that Labour had been 7 per cent ahead in
the polls when the attack on him had started in July but was now only 1
per cent ahead.

But, it seemed, the panel were simply going through the motions.
Clare Short spent six hours waiting in a nearby hotel room for the
predetermined verdict. When Nellist's expulsion was announced she
appeared instantly before the television cameras to insist that justice had
been done and that there was no other way to deal with Militant. Soon
after, the NEC suspended Coventry South East Constituency Labour
Party for the crime of backing their MP.

Nellist, with support from local Labour Party members, decided to
stand in the general election against the imposed Labour candidate,
Coventry Council leader Jim Cunningham. Fields, deselected MPs Ron
Brown in Edinburgh and John Hughes in Coventry, as well as expelled
Militant supporter Tommy Sheridan, a leader of the Scottish campaign
against the Poll Tax, also stood against official Labour Party candidates.

Unlike the "independent" campaigns mounted by so many deselected
MPs, the Nellist campaign was no forlorn last-ditch stand. In order to
beat him the Labour leadership appointed a regional organizer for
Coventry and had to draft in hundreds of workers from other constituencies, including numerous full-time officials. In the end they only just
pipped Nellist, who captured 28.8 per cent of the vote, by a thousand
votes in a tight three-way race. A by-product was Labour's failure to win
the adjacent marginal constituency of Coventry South West, largely
because it had been stripped of Party workers pressganged into campaigning against Nellist. In Liverpool Broadgreen Terry Fields attracted
5,900 votes, 14 per cent of the total. After the election, the NEC referred
127 Coventry Labour Party members (including several who had already
resigned and some who were dead) to the national constitutional committee for their alleged part in the Nellist and Hughes campaigns.

The expulsions of Fields and Nellist reeked of double standards. In
Small Heath Roger Godsiff had fiddled union affiliations to secure
selection as a Labour candidate but no action was ever taken against him.
In Birkenhead Frank Field could urge people not to vote for official
Labour candidates with impunity. Scores of Labour MPs fail to do their
duties in Parliament or in their constituencies while the NEC turns a
blind eye. When the ostensibly Labour-supporting Robert Maxwell
brought the Party into genuine disrepute by his behaviour as a union-

busting employer at Pergamon Press, the NCC refused even to hear the case presented by his local Party. And the leadership never moved against any of the numerous Labour MPs who maintained extra-parliamentary links with outfits far more unsavoury than the Militant, including Freemasons, multinational companies and Washington-funded pro-NATO pressure groups.

The Culture of the Witch-hunt

A detailed history of the purge of the late 1980s and early 1990s would fill a volume in itself. Its effects were felt at all levels of the Labour Party. It must be remembered that for every member disciplined or even threatened with discipline there are a dozen others who know him or her and are affected.

The purge was also a major drain on the Party's meagre resources, preoccupying full-time officials, many of whom seemed to revel in their role as political police. The Southwark Bermondsey Constituency Party in London, for example, was suspended by the NEC in 1988 on the basis of a secret report. This had been compiled by London regional officers who had met with sympathetic activists the year before and agreed to build up a political profile of the Bermondsey Party. A breakdown of the "political associations" of the general committee was compiled in which delegates were categorized as either "MT" (Militant Tendency), "FT" (fellow traveller), "NA" (non-attender) or "OK" (supporters of the leadership). Jim Mortimer, a trade union delegate to the Bermondsey general committee and general secretary of the Labour Party in 1982–85, was classified as a "fellow traveller" of the Militant!

The standard of justice inside the Labour Party ought to be superior to that on offer in the British courts. Under Kinnock, it was frequently inferior. Violations of natural justice were legion. The presumption of innocence was hopelessly subverted. Guilt by association became commonplace. Smears, innuendo and catch-all charges proliferated. Hearsay and other forms of uncorroborated evidence were uncritically accepted. Judgements were made on the basis of secret dossiers compiled by anonymous figures whom the accused could never confront. Sentences were based exclusively on subjective political considerations.

The attack on Dave Nellist and Terry Fields was the culmination of a process which saw scores of Party members and sitting councillors removed from council selection panels; manifestos and candidates were imposed, constituency parties were closed down, parliamentary by-election panels were rigged and hundreds were expelled from the Party. In 1991–92 Walworth Road, at the behest of the NEC, conducted investigations into Birkenhead, Liverpool (several times), Nottingham East, St

Helens, Tower Hamlets, Brighton, Coventry and Lambeth. In a general election year, the waste of time and money was unforgivable.

In this period the real "intimidators" in Kinnock's Labour Party proved to be those who threatened outspoken activists with a drubbing in the media followed by a humiliating appearance in the dock and the loss of their Party card. They succeeded only in spreading fear, frustration and distrust within the Party and nurtured the many seeds of doubt already planted in the public mind about Labour's fitness to govern. In the end it was not Dave Nellist, or Terry Fields, or the Lambeth councillors, or any of the hundreds of other activists caught up in the purge, but the Kinnock leadership which, in pursuing its left-wing enemies without regard to democracy or justice, was guilty of a "sustained course of conduct prejudicial to the Party".

Notes

1. *Labour Party Annual Conference Report* 1986.
2. "Disciplinary Procedures: Proposals for an NCC", NEC report 1986.
3. ibid.
4. *Labour Party Annual Report* 1986.
5. *Guardian* 16 May 1989.
6. *Daily Mail* 19 May 1989.
7. ibid.
8. *Tribune* 5 June 1987.
9. *Guardian* 19 December 1990.
10. *Guardian* 24 June 1991.
11. *Guardian* 5 October 1990.
12. ibid.
13. *Guardian* 14 December 1990.
14. *Tribune* 21 February 1992.
15. Report to the NEC on the Lambeth Labour Group, March 1991.
16. ibid.
17. Report to the NEC on named Lambeth councillors, July 1991.
18. *Guardian* 5 July 1991.
19. *Socialist Organiser* 18 July 1991.
20. *Guardian* 5 July 1991.
21. *Observer* 7 July 1991.
22. *Guardian* 12 July 1991.
23. *Guardian* 16 July 1991.

11

Defeat from the Jaws of Victory:
Who Lost the 1992 General Election?

Oh Captain! My Captain! our fearful trip is done,
The ship has weathered every rack, the prize we sought is won,
The port is near, the bells I hear, the people all exulting.
Walt Whitman

Elections are not won in the three weeks of the campaign; they are
won in years of hard work and preparation.
Neil Kinnock, writing at the outset of the
1992 general election campaign

Labour's failure to win the 1992 general election, in the midst of the most
severe economic recession since the 1930s and against a party that had
been in government for thirteen years, mystified many people, not least
the pollsters, whose predictions had been grossly awry. Tired sociological explanations were trotted out, as in 1987, and the Labour hierarchy
grasped eagerly at these comforting substitutes for hard self-
examination. But the clues to the mystery of Labour's 1992 defeat lie not
in psephology, sociology or even the inadequacies of campaign management, but in politics. It was the political direction pursued by the Labour
Party in the preceding years that in the end made it unelectable, even in
such apparently favourable conditions.

Between 1987 and 1990 Labour had targeted Prime Minister Margaret
Thatcher as the weak spot in the government's armoury. By portraying
her as a callous extremist and ideologue, and contrasting her record on
the National Health Service and the Poll Tax with Kinnock's promise of
social consensus and pragmatic "competence", Labour hoped to exploit
the growing public disillusionment with the Prime Minister.

The strategy of narrowing the appeal of Labour and its leader to *not*
being the Tory government or Thatcher met with some success during
1989 when Labour won the Vale of Glamorgan by-election and emerged
from the elections to the European Parliament as the single largest party.

The following year, with the onset of recession and the emergence of mass hatred of the Poll Tax, Labour crushed the Tories in the Mid-Staffordshire by-election and at last opened up a substantial lead in the opinion polls, a lead that at times soared to a seemingly unassailable 17 per cent. Thatcher's personal popularity and the standing of her government plummeted.

The Tory coup against Thatcher in November 1990 changed the balance of forces dramatically and revealed just how much of Labour's apparent support was simply a protest against the existing government rather than a positive move towards its policies. Like Churchill, Eden, Macmillan, Home and Heath before her, Thatcher found the Conservative Party unwilling to risk electoral defeat for the sake of loyalty to a leader beloved within its ranks but detested outside. Having worked so hard for so long to identify Thatcher as the cause of all Britain's ills, Labour suddenly found itself without a target. By ditching Margaret Thatcher the Conservative Party had carried out the only specific task that the Labour Party seemed to have set itself.

Thus, it was John Major and not Neil Kinnock who reaped the benefits of Margaret Thatcher's removal. Major's shift of emphasis on Europe and, even more, his abandonment of the Poll Tax, established the necessary distance between himself and his predecessor precisely because the Labour Party offered no other yardstick by which to judge a Tory government.

In the autumn 1990 issue of *Labour Party News* Jack Cunningham reported on the Party's general election preparations:

> The Tories are already planning a rough, dirty election . . . our credibility is going to be the key issue in the election. We shouldn't promise more than we can deliver, we shouldn't raise hopes, we shouldn't build up people's expectations only to dash them.[1]

Though Cunningham was right in stressing that Labour's "credibility" would be the key election issue, his assertion that it could be secured by promising little, by raising no hopes, contradicted all Labour's previous electoral experience. Unwilling to commit itself to anything that might antagonize key "opinion formers" in the City and the media, Labour had to fall back on making a negative attack on the government's record and on John Major's competence as a manager of the economy.

Briefly, this seemed to bear fruit. Once the novelty of the new Tory leader had worn off and Gulf War fervour had ebbed, the abiding unpopularity of the government once more became apparent. Heavy Tory defeats in by-elections in Monmouth (by Labour) and in Ribble Valley and Kincardine and Deeside (by the Liberal Democrats) confirmed that the legacy of the Poll Tax, the deepening economic recession and rising anxiety about the NHS and other public services were fuelling a popular rejection of far more than just Margaret Thatcher's particularly brutal brand of Toryism. Unfortunately, they also indicated that this anti-government sentiment was not coalescing solidly behind Labour but simply decamping to whatever party was handy for a protest vote. There was little positive enthusiasm for either Labour or its leader.

The presentation of the fourth instalment of the Policy Review, "Opportunity Britain", in April 1991 attracted much less media interest than had its predecessors. At least the early stages of the review had had a clear purpose: to rid the Party of embarrassing socialist commitments. This gave the press launches the merits of drama, if nothing else. But by 1991, there was no drama left. Not a single solid commitment or clear priority emerged from "Opportunity Britain", making it easy for Paddy Ashdown and others to deride its launch as "the fourth time Labour has repackaged the same policies in as many years". However, the ridicule was not quite justified. The versions of the Policy Review issued in 1988–1990 had been predicated on the permanence of the Lawson boom and the concomitant need for a new consumerist approach to both economic and social policy. Now, in the light of deepening recession, Labour seemed to undergo yet another conversion, this time back to the tried and tested West German corporatist model in which government and industry worked together to promote economic development. "Opportunity Britain" made great play of government's responsibility to nurture private business. It implied that by dint of superior economic management, Labour would engineer a recovery without spending taxpayers' money or interfering in any way with existing patterns of industrial ownership.

Three months later John Major announced his "Citizen's Charter", which used much of the rhetoric of "Opportunity Britain" and made many of the same promises of improved public services and increased consumer rights. Labour accused the Tories of "plagiarism" and Kinnock promised to "tear it to pieces, paragraph by paragraph".[2] This proved impossible because the differences between the two parties' approaches were minimal. The upshot of the Policy Review had been to leave Labour with a programme so vague and innocuous that the Tories could steal from it with impunity. By autumn 1991 both Labour and Conservatives stood at around 40 per cent in the polls.

In September a MORI poll indicated that while 85 per cent of Tory supporters were satisfied with John Major only 57 per cent of Labour supporters were happy with Neil Kinnock. One in three Labour supporters were positively dissatisfied with him. The poll also indicated that if John Smith were to replace Kinnock as Labour leader, Labour would enjoy a 10 per cent lead over the Tories. That same month a Harris poll for the *Observer* demonstrated that dislike of the leader was quoted by nearly two in five non-Labour supporters as the main reason they would not vote for the Party. In response to sustained tabloid pressure Kinnock denied that he had any intention of resigning: "I have been, and am, a very good captain of the team. And you certainly don't drop winning captains."[3]

Some kind of internal challenge to the Labour leadership might have been expected, but despite occasional flurries of press speculation (in which John Smith was usually presented as a potential saviour of Labour's cause) none emerged. Since Labour's key strategists were intimately linked to Kinnock's personal power base and all other potential centres of decision-making had been destroyed in previous years, it is perhaps not surprising that the leadership's only response to this crisis was yet another attempt to use the annual conference to sell the leader to a sceptical public.

Contentious debates were kept to an absolute minimum at the 1991 Brighton conference. The delegates were treated not as makers of policy but as onlookers, hired extras in a carefully staged television political broadcast in which Kinnock starred as the Prime-Minister-in-waiting. During the debate priority was given to parliamentary candidates, who were called to the rostrum again and again, to the exclusion of elected delegates. With few exceptions they used their brief moment in the national spotlight not to argue the merits of any particular policy but to heap praise upon the leader and his front-bench team.

In Kinnock's conference speech he insisted that Labour would win the coming election because "it is time for a change", "time for a new direction", "time for a government with a real sense of national purpose", "time for Labour". Delegates dutifully rose to their feet to give the leader the pre-planned standing ovation and to join in an impromptu singalong. Under the headline "Kinnock's winning vision", the following day's Labour Co-ordinating Committee conference bulletin lavished praise on this not very memorable performance: "We wanted a good speech, we got a brilliant one . . . a speech that has Prime Minister written all over it."[4]

Kinnock's spin-doctors too set about praising the leader's speech; it was put to Peter Jenkins of the *Independent* that Kinnock "had regained his confidence and nerve" and that he "next intends to go out in the country to meet the people in open question-and-answer session". Kinnock would, "when it comes to it, out-campaign the Prime Minister and show the country who was the real man of the people".[5] Contrary to these predictions, Kinnock spent the next few months in his Westminster bunker, entering television studios only on rare occasions and keeping a safe distance from all members of the public.

The conference, which began with the ritual exclusions of Labour MPsTerry Fields and Dave Nellist (then under investigation for links with Militant), ended with the art of political stage management elevated to new heights. To the obvious embarrassment of some and the delight of others, the shadow cabinet was paraded before the remaining delegates (most of whom had gone home; the seats were filled with paid employees of the Party, the trade unions and Labour MPs and prospective candidates). In a foretaste of the coming election campaign, premature triumphalism reached dizzying heights as the roll call of the putative next government was read out to ecstatic applause. Party chair Tom Sawyer, Neil Kinnock himself and some of the less buttoned-up members of the shadow cabinet hugged and slapped one another's backs. Following the singing of "The Red Flag" and "Jerusalem" the proceedings were brought to a close with the Queen song "We Are The Champions", to the all too obvious discomfort of Roy Hattersley, Gordon Brown and some others on the platform. Party officials handed out Union Jacks and specially designed red dusters to the audience to be waved in time to the music as Labour celebrated the victory that was never to come.

In January 1992, "Made in Britain", a last repackaging of Labour's Policy Review, was unveiled amid the now predictable glitz, this time augmented by a patriotic appeal. At the launch, John Smith emphasized the prudence of Labour's budgetary proposals: "The first responsibility of government is to create a stable economic framework so that business can plan and invest for the future." Setting out Labour's priorities as "low inflation, competitive interest rates and a stable exchange rate", Smith and Gordon Brown stressed that "industrial policy" would be the dividing line between Labour and the Conservatives at the general election.[6]

A Harris poll for the *Observer* in January 1992 demonstrated Labour's difficulties. When asked who was responsible for rising unemployment, 43 per cent named Thatcher; 28 per cent cited the international slump and only 9 per cent blamed John Major. None the less, blaming the Tory government for creating economic recession became the main theme of Kinnock's twice-weekly attempts to discomfit Major during Prime Minister's Questions in the Commons. "This is a Major recession" was the slogan propagated by Labour. Ironically, while Labour blamed the recession on managerial mistakes made by the British government, it was left to the Tories to point to the world crisis of capitalism as the real cause. Labour's failure to offer any critique of the system let the Tories off the hook. Public discontent at the state of the economy was high but, in the absence of any serious Labour attempt to answer difficult economic questions, it was Margaret Thatcher and Nigel Lawson, not John Major and Norman Lamont, who were held to blame.

Labour's vulnerability on basic policy issues was exposed when the Tories launched a New Year offensive against the Party's tax plans, highlighting proposals to abolish the upper limit on National Insurance Contributions. Kinnock panicked. At an informal dinner with leading political correspondents in an Italian restaurant in central London he hinted that Labour would "phase in" the National Insurance changes so that no one would feel the pinch right away. This was no accidental indiscretion but a calculated tactical move which the leader had already discussed with his personal advisers. The problem was that he had not discussed it with either John Smith or Margaret Beckett. The next day's *Times* headline, "Labour doubts over speedy tax changes", with similar headlines in other papers, caught Labour's front-bench economic affairs team off guard. The upper limit on National Insurance Contributions would have to go immediately if Labour was to honour its pledges to increase child benefit and pensions. John Smith and Margaret Beckett moved quickly to contain the damage, insisting that their original proposals stood. In so doing they refrained from any criticisms of the leader, which was more than he did in regard to them. In the following week Charles Clarke briefed Westminster correspondents on the alleged foibles of John Smith, who was accused of disloyalty and was said by the usual unnamed sources to be "less clever than he thinks but less busy than he ought to be".[7]

A MORI poll in early March showed the government leading Labour by 11 per cent on the question of economic competence; 47 per cent considered John Major best equipped to handle the economy compared to only 31 per cent who considered Kinnock best equipped. Clearly, Labour's attempt to pin the blame for recession on the Tories was failing. Worse yet, its core argument – that it could manage the British economy better than the Tories – was widely disbelieved. None the less, Labour strategists, ignoring mounting evidence, entered the election campaign believing that all they had to do was stick to their game plan and they would win. Larry Whitty refused to acknowledge any problems. "Neil Kinnock's the best campaigning politician we've seen for decades in this country," he rashly told *Tribune*. "When the campaign starts he will thrive and Major will be exposed."[8]

It was widely assumed that Chancellor Norman Lamont's 1992 budget would propose tax cuts that would form the basis of the Conservatives' appeal to the electorate. Labour prepared itself to respond to this challenge, confident that the public would regard such a move as an irresponsible election bribe. But Lamont surprised everyone by proposing a new 20 per cent income tax band for the least well-off taxpayers. This wrong-footed Labour, which was itself committed to the introduction of a 20 per cent band. Both Kinnock and Smith attacked the Tory budget as fiscally irresponsible because of the high level of public borrowing it required. In Labour adverts appearing in newspapers the day after the budget, the Tories were attacked for "cutting taxes" while children died because the NHS was short of cash. Clearly, the advertisement had been placed before the actual content of the budget was known. An additional problem was that to the extent that the Tories had cut taxes they had done so in a manner that at least appeared to benefit the low-waged. This undermined Labour's already fragile support among its core voters in low-income groups. It also enabled the Tories to turn the election argument into one about general levels of taxation, rather than about relative tax burdens among rich and poor.

On March 11th, the day after Lamont's budget, John Major at last declared his intention to dissolve Parliament and go to the country on April 9th. Opening Labour's campaign the following morning, Neil Kinnock, "sober, serious and self-confident", predicted that Labour would secure a twenty-seat majority.[9] In the Commons, he challenged Major to a televised debate. Major justified his refusal by quoting Shakespeare: "He draweth out the thread of his verbosity finer than the staple of his argument." It was a good sally, long researched, but it should not have stopped Kinnock and his team from pressing home the challenge. Instead, they dropped the idea, allowing Major to emerge later in the campaign as a dogged political street-fighter in contrast to the increasingly Olympian Kinnock.

As in 1987, the joint meeting of the shadow cabinet and the NEC to agree the manifesto was a mere formality. The draft prepared by Kinnock's office was endorsed, virtually without debate, by the overwhelming majority of members present (including several, such as John Prescott and Roy Hattersley, who were later to rail bitterly against the campaign's failure to promote clear political commitments). Conference policy on reducing defence expenditure was rejected. Only Tony Benn and Dennis Skinner dissented. They proposed twenty separate amendments, which were all defeated, and voted against the final document as a whole.

The manifesto, entitled *It's Time To Get Britain Working Again*, was launched on March 18th. It promised "a fresh start for Britain" and placed the need for "national recovery and a competitive economy" at the heart of Labour's strategy. With its cover swathed in a Union Jack and the four flags of the United Kingdom, the 1992 manifesto was the first in Labour's history not to mention the word "socialism" once. Kinnock told the press that it offered "down-to-earth aims" and promised "no quick fix" to the economic problems the country faced.[10]

From the outset of the Policy Review process Kinnock and his advisers had been adamant that at the next general election they would not allow the Tories to portray Labour as a high-tax party. Not only did John Smith and Margaret Beckett excise every Labour Party commitment that might add to the tax burden (except, of course, its commitment to inordinate defence spending), they did so amidst orchestrated publicity specifically designed to counter this key component of the Tory attack. Labour's hedging on resources became a household joke. Paddy Ashdown caught the mood: "If Labour had written the New Testament I suspect that it would have said: 'the meek will inherit the earth, but only as resources allow'."[11]

Despite all this, the Tories still succeeded in stirring up fears that a Labour government would tax people blind. Already, in January, they had rocked the Party on its heels with a media blitz on the theme. In their budget, they had tried to shoot at least one of Labour's foxes. Now they began their drive to stick the "tax bombshell" label on Labour.

Labour's counterattack rested on John Smith's alternative budget, unveiled to the press on the first Monday of the campaign. He proposed an increase in personal tax allowances that would relieve 740,000 low-paid workers of all income tax burden. He maintained the Party's previously announced commitments on National Insurance Contributions, pensions and child benefits. He also pledged limited but at least specified extra resources for health and education. There would be no increase in public sector borrowing. Smith's budget was carefully balanced and his claim that eight out of ten families would benefit from it was well researched and documented. More important to the Labour strategists, however, than the actual details of the package was its presentation. They already enjoyed an advantage in the fact that John Smith was more widely trusted than Norman Lamont. His alternative budget was bound in red, like real budgets, and his speech introducing it was concise and managerial. However, the mood of sombre respectability was somewhat tarnished by the wild applause that broke out from the massed ranks of Party researchers and press officers. One observer noted Kinnock's press officer, Julie Hall, leading the clapping like a cheerleader.

Although after the first week of the campaign, Smith slipped from sight, the tax issue did not. Walworth Road answered anxious queries from the constituencies by explaining that tax had been dealt with; the Party had now moved on to other themes. The Kinnock strategists believed not only that Smith had served his purpose but that excessive media exposure of the shadow Chancellor might upstage and expose the limitations of the leader himself. But what had started as stuttering Tory sniper fire developed in the final ten days into a no-holds-barred scare campaign, with the tabloids promoting the idea that Labour would tax honest working people into oblivion.

In a Harris exit poll 49 per cent cited taxation as the decisive issue in the election campaign. During the last week of the campaign, the Tories' lead on the tax issue grew from 8 per cent to 21 per cent. Their lead on the issue of overall competence to run the economy leapt up even more, by a total of 18 per cent. An unpublished MORI exit poll for the BBC gave the Tories a massive 20 per cent lead over Labour as the party most trusted by the electorate to take the right decisions to improve the economy, the very issue that Labour had chosen to fight the election on. The same poll found that 62 per cent of the electorate believed that the basic rate of tax would be increased if Labour formed the government.

Exit polls also showed that 60 per cent favoured redistribution of income from rich to poor, confirming numerous previous polls that had shown that most people were willing to pay more tax for better public services and a fairer society. Contrary to what both Bryan Gould and Ken Livingstone argued after the election, the problem with Smith's budget was not the particular level at which tax increases began. In London and the south-east, voters who would have been hurt by the Smith budget backed Labour in sufficiently large numbers to help it win marginal constituencies in Lewisham and Ilford. Conversely, in the north-west, where a clear majority would benefit from Labour's budget, target marginals were lost by the dozen. The problem with the budget, rather, was one of credibility. Labour had spent the last few years proclaiming to voters that under no conditions would it so much as tinker with the workings of the market. It had set about a highly public drive – dubbed the "prawn cocktail offensive" by the *Financial Times* – to cultivate the business and financial communities. Indeed, it often appeared as if the mythical constituency of the City of London was number one on the list of Labour's target seats. Although in the end Labour did win the endorsement of the *Financial Times*, on the whole its efforts to entice Britain's corporate elite proved futile. The publication of a survey of finance directors of the top 200 quoted companies revealed that 86 per cent believed that a Labour government would be bad for the economy and 63 per cent believed it would be bad for their businesses.[12]

Worse yet, the appeal to the City and big business did little to assuage the fears of voters on average or below average incomes that they would have to foot the bill for Labour's programme. Labour made it abundantly clear that it would *not* tax the rich, but in doing so it left it unclear just whom it would tax. The elements in the equation that Smith offered the public seemed to be restricted to personal income tax, National Insurance, benefits and pensions. Little was said about other possible sources of revenue: about taxing profits, dividends, inheritances, transfers or cutting the defence budget. Once again, many ordinary voters were concerned that Labour would rob Peter to pay Paul. Smith's relatively progressive tax and benefits package was not enough to compensate for an economic policy that promised, above all else, to maintain the status quo.

Labour's economic conservatism left the Party vulnerable not only on the tax question, but on other issues, including what was supposed to be Labour's trump card, the National Health Service. Ever since the nurses' industrial action in the winter of 1987–88, the Tories had been on the defensive over health. Their NHS reforms had aroused a storm of protest from the medical profession and were deeply distrusted by the electorate.

Labour had won the Monmouth by-election in mid 1991 by turning it into a referendum on a proposed opt-out of the local hospital. Labour's health spokesperson, Robin Cook, had been one of Labour's few effective shadow cabinet ministers and had scored direct hits against the Tories time and again. But he was repeatedly embarrassed by the Party's refusal to commit specific resources to rebuilding the NHS. In early 1992, he told reporters inquiring about Labour's cash commitment to the NHS to ask John Smith.

After considerable pressure from Cook, who knew Labour was in danger of throwing away the health issue, the Smith alternative budget included £1.1 billion extra resources for the NHS to be provided over a twenty-two-month period. This was not nearly what was required to undo the damage done by the Tories, much less to modernize the NHS as Cook claimed, but at least it was an unequivocal cash pledge and as such allowed Labour campaigners on the ground something to work with.

After the heavy pressure on taxation, Labour sought relief by attempting to turn the campaign to the NHS. A party election broadcast on the NHS was shown on March 24th. The broadcast, directed by Mike Newell (who had made the film *Dance With a Stranger*), skilfully and succinctly told the tale of a child with a painful ear complaint forced to wait for an operation on the NHS because of government underfunding. Her experience was contrasted with that of another child with the same disability who was operated on immediately because her parents were able to pay for private treatment. Reflecting as it did the experience of millions across the country, and drawing on the deep personal anxieties of many more, this hard-hitting and, for once, unambiguous denunciation of the Tories' two-tier health service struck home. It was one of the few occasions in the campaign when Labour seized with gusto on the root question of class.

Precisely because the broadcast was effective, hitting the government in its weakest spot, the Tory counterattack was swift and ruthless. Labour was variously denounced as being "sleazy and contemptible", accused of "shroud-waving" and peddling "scurrilous lies". Labour spokespersons were upbraided at press conferences and Neil Kinnock was singled out for increased attacks. The *Daily Express* recalled its Moscow correspondent, Peter Hitchens, to harry Kinnock as he had during the miners' strike and the 1987 general election.

The hysterical Tory reaction seemed to surprise Labour strategists. They soon became bogged down in trying to justify the film as if it was a documentary. In London, first Robin Cook, then John Cunningham briefed the press to the effect that the film was based on a particular case. The press demanded to know the identity of the child concerned. At a second briefing held in Manchester, Julie Hall inadvertently revealed that the girl's name was Jennifer and read out letters from her father and the hospital consultant involved.

Actual documentation to back up the claim made in the broadcast was only produced twenty-four hours later. Further research proved that the letters from the girl's father and her consultant told only part of the story. Other evidence indicated that the long wait for Jennifer's ear operation might have been due not to underfunding but to administrative error.

When the identity of the girl involved was revealed in the *Independent* an unseemly row broke out between the Labour and Conservative camps over who had leaked her name to the press. When it further transpired that the youngster's parents were divided in their party loyalties and that her grandfather was an outraged Tory councillor and ex-mayor, the story behind Labour's broadcast became much bigger than the political issue it had sought to highlight. The media furore lasted over two full days. The debate over the NHS, which Labour badly needed to push to the top of the public agenda, was forgotten in the welter of claims and counter-claims about the accuracy and propriety of the broadcast and politicians' and newspapers' responses to it.

The *Sun* claimed the girl's name had been leaked by Julie Hall; Hall insisted on making a personal statement to the press denying any responsibility. It was an emotional performance complete with a declaration of her personal commitment to the NHS. When a *Sunday Express* reporter tried to question Hall, an enraged Kinnock intervened to protect her. BBC correspondent Nicholas Jones recalled the episode in his account of the election:

> There could hardly have been a moment when a political leader was upstaged so comprehensively by a press officer. Nor could I recall an occasion when the sight of Mr Kinnock losing his cool had been immortalised so clearly on television. Miss Hall certainly threw caution to the wind as she stepped forward to make her statement. So great was her emotion in the heat of the moment that she seemed oblivious of the impact she was having on Mr Kinnock.[13]

Throughout the fracas, dubbed by the press "the war of Jennifer's ear", Labour's media managers were constantly on the defensive, unable to get on top of the story. The broadcast had elicited a flood of letters from members of the public recording their own experiences with the underfunded NHS. Labour, keen to prove its case history was representative, released a dossier of two hundred case studies – without checking with the people named beforehand. This led to further embarrassment and the dossier had to be withdrawn.

In his post-election report to the NEC, Larry Whitty explained, "The initial impact of the [broadcast] was positive, but the briefing surrounding and following it diverted attention from our strategic aim . . . the implication was that it was based on the one single case (which it never was) and that case proved highly vulnerable."[14]

Why had the briefing and the media follow-up gone so wrong? First, Labour was so wedded to its pre-determined campaign plan and so inflexible in its tactics that it was unable to respond coherently to an attack that it should, in any case, have seen coming. Second, career competition among various Labour campaigners was now so ingrained that the immediate response of many to errors was to ensure that someone else got the blame. Third, Labour's leaders were themselves scared of the message in the broadcast, nervous of what one insider called its "class war propaganda", and they therefore tried to defend it solely on factual, not political grounds.

The whole affair led to a loss of nerve on Labour's part over the NHS. A second broadcast on the subject was cancelled. An unpublished NOP exit poll commissioned by the BBC found that on election day Labour had only an 8-point lead over the Tories on the health issue.

A similar fate befell other social concerns on which Labour might have been expected to score heavily. In many cases local parties built their entire campaigns around Labour's minimal pledges on child benefit and pensions. Candidates on the ground had no alternative; they knew the electorate was impatient of the waffle served up every night on television and demanded positive reasons for voting Labour. Yet pensions and benefits were hardly mentioned by Kinnock or the Party's other leading campaigners, even though they were issues over which the Tories were deeply vulnerable. In its quest for fiscal respectability the leadership had come to view spending plans of any kind as anathema, a concession to a hopelessly sentimental rank and file. Although local candidates made endless visits to old people's homes, nationally no attempt was made to link up with the vigorous and increasingly militant pensioners' movement, not least because many of the Party's campaign strategists thought identification with the elderly would compromise Labour's stress on "modernization" and "a fresh start". On polling day the elderly, an increasing proportion of the population, disproportionately favoured the Tories, despite the direct incentive for them to vote Labour.

During the campaign the minimum wage, a policy commitment extracted from Labour over a ten-year struggle by NUPE, USDAW, GMB and other unions representing low-paid workers, was mentioned far more often by the Tories, who claimed that it would cost jobs and inhibit recovery, than by Labour, despite the fact that Labour's policy could be shown to benefit some 4.5 million workers, 20 per cent of the country's workforce. Homelessness, the most visible totem of Tory failure and the cruelty of market forces, was a powerful motivating issue for many who worked for Labour, but it hardly featured at all in the campaign. In years past, no Labour leadership would have contemplated going to the electorate without at least a token commitment to a house building and refurbishment programme. But over the previous two years Kinnock had vetoed all such proposals. Any serious response to Britain's housing crisis would require the release of substantial sums from the public purse – and that was ruled out by the leadership's cautious budgetary approach. In the run-up to the campaign, Clive Soley, Labour's housing spokesperson, had suggested that the Public Sector Borrowing Requirement could be juggled to make funds available to local authorities to initiate new building. In a flash, Kinnock's office denounced the idea as "monstrous" and "entirely false" and Soley vanished for the duration of the campaign, as did the housing issue. Interestingly, in the final ten days, Kinnock, Gordon Brown and Tony Blair all made references to the plight of the homeless and juxtaposed it with the spectacle of hundreds of thousands of building workers on the dole. This old left-wing chestnut had been contemptuously rejected in recent years by the Labour leadership, but it was dusted off in the heat of the campaign for the simple reason that it was the only weapon to hand with which to bash the Tories.

Indeed, although Labour made great play of rising unemployment, it singularly failed to galvanize support around the issue. Tony Blair, the Party's employment spokesperson, failed to sound the note of outrage demanded by the tragedy of mass joblessness. His rhetoric about "training" and "skills" replaced a frontal attack on the Tories' use of mass unemployment to regulate the economy. It offered no answer to the obvious question: where would the jobs come from for which British workers were to be "trained" and "skilled"? Unlike in 1983 and 1987, there was no target figure for the reduction of unemployment and no job creation scheme, despite the last-minute insertion into John Smith's shadow budget of plans for a small-scale "emergency" work programme for the unemployed.

Gordon Brown's "Made in Britain" initiative, subtitled Labour's "Manufacturing Manifesto", was supposed to "play a crucial role in our campaign", according to Walworth Road's official "General Election Briefing" to candidates and agents. Party activists were urged thus:

> . . . get the following key points across – in every speech, in every interview, in every discussion on the doorstep: Labour will back Britain's industry, not back away from British industry; "Made in Britain" used to be the guarantee of quality, right across the world. But today it's getting harder and harder to buy British; Made in Britain must become the basis of economic success again; Labour is the only party with the determination to get Britain out of recession and lay the foundations for prosperity that lasts.

Such advice only confirmed fears that on the central issue of unemployment, the issue that should have been Labour's by right, the Party simply had too little of substance to say.

The single most unpopular measure of the outgoing Tory administration was the Poll Tax, and Labour's biggest opinion poll leads over the

Tories had been recorded at the height of the agitation against the Poll Tax in spring 1990. But after John Major declared a year later that it would be abolished, Labour's leaders appeared to lose what interest in the campaign against it they had ever had, even though the tax remained very much alive and kicking. As the government had always intended, Labour authorities struggled, in setting their 1991–92 budgets, to balance the evils of a high Poll Tax against the evils of huge cuts in services. Poll Tax capping proved far more immediately damaging to local services than ratecapping but went largely unopposed by Labour, which did not want to be seen to be the party of high local taxes. Instead, the Party's leaders in national and local government aimed their fire at the Poll Tax non-payment movement, launching high-profile campaigns against their own left-wing members who had refused to pay and taking drastic steps to recover money from people in arrears.

By the beginning of 1992, 10.5 million summonses had been issued for non-payment of the tax in England, Scotland and Wales. In February 1992, Bryan Gould had issued statistics to prove that Labour local authorities had made more strenuous efforts than their Conservative counterparts to collect the Poll Tax. Earlier that month, the High Court had ruled that computer evidence was inadmissible in the prosecution of people in Poll Tax arrears. Gould argued that Poll Tax defaulters were being let off the hook by a "lazy and incompetent government". He offered Labour's parliamentary support for a short government bill to remedy the defect and thus enable local authorities to recontinue committal proceedings.[15]

Almost every Labour council in the country made cuts in services in the six months running up to the general election of 1992. Although on average only 7 per cent of local authority budgets derived from Poll Tax revenue, Labour council leaders blamed non-payment, oblivious to the dangers of the backlash they were stirring up. By the general election, two-thirds of all jailings for Poll Tax non-payment had been instituted by Labour councils. The strategy of blaming non-payers for the catastrophe in local government only succeeded in letting the Tories off the Poll Tax hook.

Transport policy, which should have been yet another formidable weapon in Labour's electoral armoury, was also given short shrift by the Party's campaign managers. John Prescott, the Party's transport spokesperson and one of the most widely recognized and popular shadow cabinet members, was written out of the script. Frustrated at the refusal of the Party's media managers to promote him, Prescott arranged to have himself invited onto the BBC's *Election Call* programme. He also arranged to have local Labour Party members in his own constituency bombard Walworth Road with complaints about his non-appearance in the Labour campaign. Officials of the train drivers' union ASLEF worked to set up rallies on the transport issue in Newcastle, Birmingham and Leeds, but all were cancelled on orders from above – despite the fact that eight hundred tickets for the Leeds rally had already been sold.

Transport was a potential vote-winner for Labour. It was a perfect example of Tory destruction of an essential public service, which directly affected huge numbers of voters, especially in marginal suburban seats. Kinnock cast the issue aside not simply because of his long-term grudge against John Prescott, but because Labour had no transport policy worth the name. The one concrete promise in the manifesto was to secure private finance to improve the North Kent railway line.

The absence of major policy differences with the Tories inflected every stage and aspect of the campaign, which was run with strict control from the top down. As in 1987, a campaign management team, fronted by the campaign co-ordinator, John Cunningham, and his deputy, Bryan Gould, assumed command. Mid-way through the campaign Cunningham, whose aggressive behaviour towards reporters at press conferences was becoming an embarrassment, retreated to his marginal Copeland constituency, leaving Gould as the Party's undisputed front man.

Under the umbrella of the campaign management team were assembled all the resources of the Party. The committee was composed of sixteen members, only two of whom – Cunningham and Gould – were elected politicians. Throughout the campaigns, its deliberations were controlled by an even smaller clique made up of representatives of Kinnock's office and the Shadow Communications Agency. Unlike in 1987, Kinnock no longer felt the need even to appear to consult the Party's democratically elected bodies about policy options, election strategy or organization.

As in 1987, presentation was thought to be the key to success and once more the spin-doctors were placed in command. Of the five sub-committees of the campaign management team the largest was that termed Projection, covering all publicity and political matters, which had 140 people working under its umbrella. This included the small but powerful campaign assessment unit, headed by Patricia Hewitt, which was the key organizing body throughout the campaign. Within the Projection Sub-committee the Shadow Communications Agency called the shots, with Hewitt taking on the task of translating its tactical decisions into day-to-day realities. Labour's director of campaigns and communications, David Hill, served mainly as a bridge between the inner sanctum and the outside world. The GMB seconded its head of communications, ex-NUS president Phil Woolas, to Walworth Road. His job was to dream up photo-opportunities and other one-off campaign gimmicks.

On March 24th, the Labour Party's "General Election Briefing" urged Labour campaigners to "repeat the key themes" and "the core message".

This was deemed to be: "If the Tories can't get it right after thirteen years, they never will. It is time to get Britain working again. It is time for change. It is time for Labour." This facile attempt to dragoon popular sentiment without producing the substantive policies to merit it had little effect on an electorate impatient with vacuous electioneering. The "time to change" slogan, which was supposed to capitalize on the anti-government mood, became instead a constant reminder of the political emptiness of Labour's own campaign.

Labour's evasive approach to political realities was also evident in its first election broadcast, in which director Hugh Hudson's camera swooped over sparkling lakes and green, sun-filled mountains and valleys in what some viewers may have mistaken for a tourist plug for Britain designed for US television. The patriotic theme was blended with heavy promotion of the personal virtues of selected members of the shadow cabinet (John Smith, Gordon Brown and Tony Blair, but not Gerald Kaufman, John Prescott, Jo Richardson or Michael Meacher). The arrogance of the Shadow Communications Agency in picking and choosing among official Party spokespersons offended many of those not favoured. But the real flaw in the broadcast was its transparent huckster-ism. Voters who are bombarded by advertising appeals throughout their waking lives have become increasingly aware of the techniques of manipulation. The apolitical blandishments of Labour's hyper-smooth salesmanship simply made these voters more sceptical about the political product on offer. MORI's Robert Worcester observed that for Labour the "medium was the message".[16] Kinnock's own campaign was, in the words of one Labour official, one "giant photo-opportunity",[17] in which every school, factory or hospital he visited was treated as a stage set for that evening's television news bulletins. David Hill and the Shadow Communications Agency went to great lengths to design the campaign for the convenience of television journalists.

Much was made of the allegedly high level of organization at Walworth Road. But staff there, including Larry Whitty, the general secretary (in charge of "monitoring" for the duration of the campaign) and the organization director, Joyce Gould, were reduced during the election to putting into effect instructions received from Patricia Hewitt, Charles Clarke and members of the Shadow Communications Agency led by Philip Gould. In a message to full-time Labour organizers Kinnock had claimed, "The Labour Party enters the coming election in better organiza-tional shape and better spirit than at any time in living memory."[18] But in many constituencies there was a last-minute rush to assemble vital election paraphernalia. Fewer constituencies had a full-time agent than in 1983. Worse yet, while much time and effort had gone into training candidates to deal with the media, little had been done to train the dwindling band of rank-and-file members in canvassing and other basic electoral skills.

The despatch of materials from Walworth Road was reasonably brisk, but what was sent out was of little use to campaigners on the ground. Daily briefings for candidates and agents consisted almost entirely of the media soundbites to be repeated that day by national Party spokespersons, and of advice on which tricky issues to avoid. Ideas for practical activity were few and far between. Making a giant Mother's Day card and displaying it on a street stall was the principal proposal for capturing women's votes. The leaflets and election addresses that were produced centrally consisted of a few, spare sentences printed in very large type and spread generously across large amounts of glossy paper, profusely illustrated with full-colour pictures of the leader, his wife and selected members of the shadow cabinet. In the end, the Party lost money because few constituencies placed orders for the centrally printed material. Desktop publishing technology had made the production of high-quality leaflets possible for most local activists, who felt that they could dream up more resonant and relevant campaign copy than the hamstrung professionals at Walworth Road.

The precipitate drop in both Labour's paid and its active membership over the previous three years meant that there were few people willing or able to distribute campaign literature and even fewer who were prepared to canvass. Despite reliance on the mass media, on direct mail, on the photo-opportunity and on the soundbite, Labour found that it still needed troops on the ground to win elections. For years the Party leadership had sent out a clear message to activists that their contribution was not wanted or needed. Now, in the midst of a general election, it was too late to enthuse and mobilize them in the numbers needed to make an impact on a television-satiated electorate.

In defiance of all the evidence, Labour's strategists persisted in believing that Neil Kinnock himself was the Party's electoral trump card. Hence the presidential style of the Kinnock versus Major campaign, in which, as in 1987, the leader's image was placed at the centre of Labour's appeal to the voters. At the beginning of the election John Major's personal rating was 18 per cent ahead of Kinnock's, according to MORI. Twenty per cent of Labour supporters claimed to be dissatisfied with Kinnock's personal performance, as did 54 per cent of trade union members.

At the outset of the campaign, Kinnock described himself as Labour's winning factor, "a man who has demonstrated over the years the ability to lead, to set sensible objectives, to plan, to involve people in a talented team and to fulfil objectives".[19] Early in the campaign a MORI poll conducted for the *Sunday Times* and published on March 15th asked floating votes why they disliked Labour. Some 18 per cent replied that Labour would increase taxation; 19 per cent replied that Labour would give too much power to trade unions; and 47 per cent replied that Neil Kinnock would not make a good Prime Minister. In the same poll only 10 per cent of floating voters said they disliked the Tories because of John Major. An ICM poll published a few days later gave Labour a 5-point lead over the Tories, enough for a Commons majority of twenty seats. But when electors in the same poll were asked to name the Party leader they preferred as Prime Minister, 39 per cent chose Major, 23 per cent Ashdown and 22 per cent Kinnock.

But throughout the election Kinnock was elaborately shielded from media interrogation. Television crews and press photographers were encouraged, but journalists were kept at bay by Julie Hall. The set-piece television interviews on BBC's *Panorama* and LWT's *Walden* were harder to manage and were anticipated with trepidation among Labour ranks. A cautious Kinnock picked his way carefully through the questions but failed to communicate any specific reason why people should vote Labour. In his quest for office Kinnock pulled out all the stops. He travelled in excess of 7,000 miles during the campaign, touring the country by helicopter, chartered jet, first-class rail and chauffeur-driven Daimler. Walkabouts were planned like military manoeuvres in a foreign battlefield. In addition to official and impromptu press conferences, Kinnock delivered six speeches at ticket-only rallies, gave three formal lectures and visited nine factories, five hospitals, eight schools and colleges, three training centres and two old people's homes.

In contrast with John Major's "soapbox" style, in which the Prime Minister was seen to brave hostile crowds, Kinnock appeared remote and inaccessible. Talking to the media on March 20th, David Hill seemed to think this a good thing. "Major is already looking like a man out on the stump, trying to win votes. He is looking like a leader of the opposition and Neil is coming over as the Prime Minister."[20] Hill was oblivious to the significance of the paradox unfolding before his eyes. The Tories' "Citizen John Major" was emerging as a "man of the people" in comparison with Labour's Daimler-driven Neil Kinnock. Indeed, the very day Major first mounted his soapbox was also the day of a £10,000 private (except for the presence of press photographers and television crews) party to celebrate the Kinnocks' silver wedding anniversary.

The vainglorious Sheffield rally has become synonymous with all that was wrong with Labour's campaign. Walworth Road sources briefed the press to the effect that "Labour's greatest-ever political rally" would bring together music, video, speeches from the leadership and endorsements from celebrities in unprecedented fashion. Appropriately, it was held in the Sheffield Arena – a monument to the Kinnockite Labour council which had spent a fortune building the arena and other facilities to host the World Student Games.

The two and a half hour extravaganza, the brainchild of Philip Gould, had been in preparation for over eighteen months. It was attended by the entire shadow cabinet and NEC, with the exceptions of Tony Benn and

Dennis Skinner, as well as 10,000 Party supporters bussed in at great expense. Estimates placed the cost of the event to the financially strapped Party at over £100,000.

The Labour leadership, for so long mesmerized by defeat, now seemed mesmerized in equally mindless fashion by the prospect of victory. Neil Kinnock, arriving at the rally by helicopter, his procession into the hall relayed to the faithful on a giant video screen, was in ebullient form. Punching the air, clasping hands and slapping backs, he was greeted as a conquering messiah. Like a US television evangelist, the leader leapt on stage to bask in the crowd's adulation. Carried away, he cast aside eight years of self-imposed gravitas to disport himself before the adoring throng in the manner of a pop star or a boxing champion. His wife Glenys was seen to step forward to advise him to calm down. All this was conducted under a Union Jack supplemented by the separate flags of England, Scotland, Wales and the European Community, all fluttering in the artificial breeze generated by an offstage wind machine. The back-drop was dominated by the giant video screen which enlarged the platform speakers to gigantic dimensions and inadvertently invoked the spectre of an Orwellian Big Brother. One Party wag concluded that Hugh Hudson had been replaced by Leni Riefenstahl.

Sheffield proved a public relations disaster. Far from instilling confidence among the voters in an incoming Labour administration, it convinced many that Kinnock's Labour Party was indeed the massive confidence trick the Tory tabloids said it was. Dennis Skinner argued that the Sheffield rally was like a football team throwing a party to celebrate a half-time lead. In his union journal, Derrick Fullick, ASLEF general secretary, was even more scathing: "Where I come from there's a moral to that sort of tale – you don't belch before you've had the meal."

The day following the Sheffield rally had been dubbed Democracy Day by the pressure group Charter 88, which was organizing local meetings on constitutional reform in a number of constituencies. Patricia Hewitt was a leading supporter of Charter 88 and many of its emphases were shared by the Institute for Public Policy Research, the Labour-associated think-tank for which she worked. In particular, the group's support for proportional representation was shared by many in the media world, including volunteers in the Shadow Commmunications Agency. Despite the fact that agency members knew from their own polling data that voters wanted to avoid a hung Parliament, they decided to raise the issue of proportional representation – and by implication a post-election pact with the Liberal Democrats following a hung Parliament – only a week before polling day.

The preoccupations of Charter 88 were a minority concern notoriously confined to the chattering classes. Constitutional reform of the minimalist type propounded by Charter 88 could never be expected to supplant tax or unemployment or education as a salient issue in the majority of voters' minds, certainly not at this juncture of the campaign. None the less, Labour allowed this tiny clique to influence the Party's general election agenda – while ignoring "special interest" groups concerned with poverty, housing, racism, pensioners, trade union rights or disarmament, all of whom could fairly claim to speak for larger national constituencies than Charter 88.

On April 2nd, the morning of "Democracy Day", Kinnock publicly offered to lead a government of "broad consensus" in which Labour would serve "all the people". At the same time, he made a subtle but significant shift on proportional representation. Under pressure from advocates of Charter 88, the leader had indicated earlier in the year that Labour would consider the possibility of a referendum on the electoral system. It had also been announced that under a Labour government, the Party's inquiry into electoral reform, headed by Raymond Plant, would be given the status of a Royal Commission; now Kinnock added that its membership would include "people from other political parties".

It was well known that the Party remained divided and undecided on proportional representation. Kinnock insisted all along that it was inappropriate for him to make known his private views on the matter, but by raising the issue as he did he ensured that the questions surrounding proportional representation – questions for which Labour had no agreed answers – dominated the news. Kinnock was hopelessly cornered on April 3rd when the presenter of BBC Radio's The World at One, James Naughtie, asked him about a deal with the Liberal Democrats in the event of an inconclusive election result. In a tortuous reply Kinnock avoided the question by claiming that it was based on "a hypothesis" that at this stage in the "electoral calendar" he was not prepared to discuss.[21] Yet it was Kinnock himself who had set up the hypothesis and opened the discussion only the day before.

Labour thus promoted electoral reform, a non-issue in the minds of many of the electorate, to the top of the political agenda. Inevitably the media plunged into a whirlpool of speculation about possible coalition deals between Labour and the Liberal Democrats. For at least four crucial days at the end of the campaign, Labour strategists chose to fight on political terrain on which the Party was unable to play its strongest suits: health, employment and public services.

Kinnock's move was a long-calculated pitch for the Liberal Democrat vote and for that section of middle-class voters perpetually uncomfortable with the Tory–Labour two-party squeeze. On April 5th Kinnock stressed the point by arguing that "Labour would lead the consensus by promising a listening, non-confrontational government that will heed the advice of the professionals, such as doctors, engineers and educationalists".[22] David Hill admitted to journalists that the Democracy Day initiative was an attempt to squeeze the Liberal Democrats' vote by stealing their political agenda.

This was a major and avoidable tactical error. The idea of wooing Liberal Democrat voters over Paddy Ashdown's head was predicated on the assumption that people voted Liberal Democrat because of the Party's policies and, in particular, because of its support for electoral reform. In fact, the Liberal Democrat vote is far from homogeneous. In the cities and suburbs it is predominantly an anti-Labour vote. A BBC exit poll conducted by MORI showed that 44 per cent of Liberal Democrat voters thought their party should support the Conservatives in the event of a hung Parliament and only 33 per cent supported a deal with Labour. In the final days of the campaign Liberal Democrat supporters swung to the Tories precisely because they feared a Labour-dominated government of any kind, even one which offered the prospect of proportional representation.

From the start, the Tories greeted Kinnock's Democracy Day initiative as good news. It allowed them to offer themselves to the electorate as a stable, decisive and strong government prepared to lead from the front. Unlike Labour, they knew what they stood for and they expressed no interest in any result that did not give them a clearcut parliamentary majority. John Major hammered away gleefully at the issue, warning that electoral reform would mean weak leadership, unstable government and a perpetually hung Parliament. He also showed that he knew, if Kinnock did not, just where most Liberal Democrat supporters' hearts really lay. "People have a choice," he told ITN's *News at Ten*. "If they want Mr Kinnock in Downing Street they can vote for the Labour Party or they can vote for the Liberal Democrats. If they do not they must vote Conservative." Compared to Labour's vacuities and vacillations, this seemed a clarion call.

The onslaught from the Tory press in the final week left Labour spokespersons nearly speechless with anger. Yet for months Labour's strategists had warned of a last-minute tabloid smear campaign. Activists were warned that shadow cabinet ministers might be singled out for scandal-sheet treatment. In the end, though, the tabloids largely refrained from this type of coverage. Instead, they went for the political jugular. They lambasted the Party's tax plans, ridiculed its lack of coherent policies and devoted pages to its leader's long record of incompetence and inconsistency. While the Party's press apparatus was all set up to respond to personal smears or allegations of sexual misconduct, the one thing it appeared not to anticipate and which left it floundering was an all-out attack exploiting the central weakness of the Party's policy: its lack of a coherent strategy for economic recovery.

Labour's own polls indicated that there was a crumbling of the Labour vote in the last week of the campaign. From the beginning, there had been a large number of "undecideds" showing up in every poll; Labour canvassers noticed the same phenomenon on the doorstep. Retrospectively, it is clear that many of the undecided voters backed the government reluctantly simply to keep out Labour, which had failed to win their trust. In the last week, the Party had no fresh appeal to make to them. It had loosed off its best shots to little avail earlier in the campaign. All it had left was the constant refrain that it was "time for change" and therefore "time for Labour". Exit polls conducted for the Labour Party showed that nearly all the undecideds went to the Tories in the last forty-eight hours. Larry Whitty reported to the NEC: "It is difficult to escape the conclusion that at the very end of the campaign the electorate just felt unable to risk voting for the Labour Party." In his view, the reasons for not voting Labour "relate to the general perceptions of the Party and its leadership, rather than specifically to fears of tax increases".[23]

Labour was shattered by its fourth successive defeat. Nothing had prepared members for this blow. True, Labour had cut the Tory majority in the Commons to twenty-one; if a few thousand voters had switched in twenty-odd marginal constituencies Major might have been denied a majority altogether. But there was no way to disguise the abject failure represented by Labour's 35 per cent share of votes cast, an increase of only 3 per cent on 1987 and 6 per cent on the electoral disaster of 1983. Worse yet, the Party had been unable to undermine the Tory popular vote, which since 1987 had dropped by only a single point to 42 per cent. Despite strong swings to Labour throughout the south at the expense of the Liberal Democrats, the Party captured only ten of its twenty-three Tory-held target seats in London. The critical West Midlands area, which at one point during the campaign looked to be moving heavily in Labour's favour, proved another disappointment, yielding in the end a swing below the national average. In the north-west, home to the largest number of target marginals, the results were poor. In Scotland, Labour's vote receded under the combined impact of the nationalist challenge and a Tory revival that had been predicted by no one.

Exit polls indicated that Labour underperformed among three crucial groups: older women, young men (traditionally a bastion of Labour strength) and, most telling of all, its own "core vote". Labour won a smaller proportion of the votes of the unemployed than in 1987. It also lost support among council tenants and people on low incomes. Whitty identified this failure to mobilize maximum support among the "core vote" as "extremely worrying".[24] It was, however, part of a long-term trend. Since 1966 Labour had gained 4 per cent among managerial groups but lost 5 per cent among clerical workers, 15 per cent among unskilled manual workers and 18 per cent among skilled workers.[25]

The public rejection of Neil Kinnock and everything he stood for, along with the poor result for the Liberal Democrats, made a nonsense of the predictions of pollsters, media pundits and the public relations industry. The argument that electoral success could come only from an appeal to the middle ground – and the middle class – collapsed in the face of electoral reality. But any hopes that the people who had sold the Party this poor-quality merchandise would, in the wake of defeat, spare it the benefit of further advice were quickly dashed. Echoing Roy Hattersley in 1979 and Neil Kinnock in 1987, Labour's strategists declared that there should be "no postmortems" and urged the Party to get on with the job it had started under Kinnock. The same newspaper columnists and leader writers who had applauded Kinnock's policy and constitutional changes now called for still more of the same. They posed the same self-serving question they had posed after the 1983 and 1987 defeats: can Labour ever win again? Yet only weeks before they were convinced that Kinnock's new model party not only could but would win. After the election, the Party's campaign slogan, "if they can't get it right after thirteen years they never will", appeared to apply more to these people than it did to the Tories.

The painful fact is that the Kinnock leadership threw away an election that was there for the taking. It did so not only in the five weeks of the campaign but in the five years preceding it. The leadership strategy of appeasing the establishment, capping working-class aspirations and taming the membership left Labour hopelessly vulnerable to the Tories on polling day. The tactic of giving no hostages to fortune in the form of clearcut policy commitments was simply an attempt to evade political realities and responsibilities – and was seen as such by the public. A Labour opposition offering fiscal rectitude, economic respectability and little else can never hope to overturn a Tory government. In the end, Labour's safety-first approach was predicated on an assumption that the political pendulum would swing back in the Party's favour of its own accord, so long as the Party dissociated itself from past "extremism".

The election result was, above all, a disaster for those whose political and economic interests the Labour Party exists to represent. On the morning of April 10th 1992, not a few Labour activists bitterly recalled Neil Kinnock's speech to Party conference in 1983: "Do not ever forget how you felt on June 9th, 1983 – and say to yourself that that will never, ever happen again."[26] But it did happen again and it will go on happening until the Party rediscovers its radicalism and its popular roots. What has to be faced is that, in this country, a general election is ultimately a test of strength between the labour movement and its party and the establishment and its party, a test whose outcome is determined by comparative strength of leadership, organization and ideology. On April 9th 1992 Labour lost, fundamentally, because on balance nine years of the Kinnock leadership had made it the weaker side in all respects.

Notes

1. *Labour Party News* autumn 1991.
2. *Guardian* 17 July 1991.
3. *Sunday Times* 22 September 1991.
4. *Labour Activist* conference special edition October 1991.
5. *Independent* 2 October 1991.
6. *Tribune* 10 January 1992.
7. *Independent on Sunday* 23 February 1992.
8. *Tribune* 21 February 1992.
9. *Guardian* 13 March 1992.
10. *Independent* 19 March 1992.
11. *Guardian* 13 March 1992.
12. *Sunday Times* 8 March 1992.
13. Nicholas Jones, *Election 92*, London 1992.
14. "Preliminary Report on the General Election by the Secretary to the NEC", May 1992.
15. *Guardian* 5 February 1992.
16. *Guardian* 16 March 1992.
17. *Sunday Times* 22 March 1992.
18. *Labour Organiser* 1992 general election special edition.
19. *Guardian* 11 March 1992.
20. Nicholas Jones, *Election 92*, London 1992.
21. *Guardian* 4 April 1992.
22. *Guardian* 6 April 1992.
23. "Preliminary Report of the General Secretary on the General Election to the NEC", May 1992.
24. ibid.
25. *Tribune* 29 May 1992.
26. *Labour Party Annual Conference Report* 1983.

APPENDIX
Running on Empty:
the "Mass Membership" Debacle

As the Labour machine geared up for the 1992 general election, nine years after Neil Kinnock was elected leader, the Party was heading for a deficit on its 1991 general account of over £700,000. Its overdraft at the Co-op Bank was about to hit £2.5 million. Costs of the Party's new National Membership System had over-run by £400,000 and the scheme itself had resulted in the loss of one third of the Party's existing membership, placing it at an all-time low. Bundles of unopened envelopes containing membership applications and subscriptions were heaped on the desks of full-time staff of all grades at Walworth Road. In a belated effort to rein in expenditure, staff were told to use second-class postage; Party organizers – hard pressed already to prepare Labour for election battles in key seats – were ordered not to work evenings or weekends. Political education was also at an all-time low, with a budget in 1990 of a mere £1,000 and fewer political education officers in the constituencies and wards than at any time in the Party's post-1945 history. Attendance at Party meetings of all kinds was sparser than anyone could remember. Achieving a quorum had become a major problem. And finding volunteers to take on the wide variety of tasks needed to maintain an effective local political machine was nearly impossible.

This crisis of activism was acknowledged, at least in private, by nearly everyone with direct experience of the Party. Although members of the parliamentary elite and senior officers at Walworth Road claimed that Labour was humming with activity and was in great shape for the general election battle, the failure of the mass membership drive to remedy the Party's long-standing deficiencies at the grass roots was an open secret.

For decades Labour Party membership figures had been bogus, based on a wildly unrealistic assumption of 1,000 members per constituency. In 1979, when a new, more genuine system of counting the members was instituted, it became apparent that real membership was no more than 300,000. Membership calculated on this basis rose during the early 1980s and hit a peak during the 1984–85 miners' strike when it passed 323,000. Since then, despite repeated proclamations by the leadership of its intention to "double the membership" or recruit "a million members" – and despite fiddling of the membership records at Walworth Road – Labour's membership has declined steadily.

During the 1983 general election Labour's membership rose by 21,000, but in 1987 it declined by 8,500. Clearly, something had to be done. Labour's leaders pledged to recruit a "mass membership". For the left, mass membership and mass participation in the Party – and especially in policy formation – have always gone hand in hand. It wanted an active rank and file that could exercise real control over the leadership. For Neil Kinnock and his supporters, mass membership was a different matter altogether. What they wanted was a sufficient number of "ordinary" Labour voters to drown out the allegedly unrepresentative, left-wing activists. This influx of "moderates" would be enfranchised through a system of postal voting by which council and parliamentary candidates as well as members of the NEC would be chosen – a system of one member, one very occasional consultative vote.

In 1987, the Tribune Group of Labour MPs, fronted by the rising star Gordon Brown, launched its own proposals for a mass membership. The key, Brown argued, was to focus on the millions of trade unionists who were already paying their union's political levy, but were not individual members of the Party. The trick would be to offer them a specially reduced membership fee of £1–2.

A year later, after much negotiation, the 1988 conference approved a special trade union rate of £5. Writing in the conference bulletin of the Fabian Society, Brown claimed to make clear the import of the scheme as far as the leadership was concerned: "In our battle plan for winning the next general election no issue is more important than securing a mass membership . . . guaranteeing that Labour's policies are rooted in the aspirations of millions of working people." In other words, the existing membership could not be relied upon to support the politics of the leadership.

This trade union rate was introduced for a three-year trial period as part of the new National Membership System package, but it bore no fruit. Over three years, fewer than 15,000 of the 4.5 million eligible levy-paying trade unionists bothered to take up the offer.

In the autumn of 1988, Labour Party general secretary Larry Whitty described the leadership's plans for a new National Membership System in a *Labour Party News* article entitled "Operation Mass Membership". Presenting this as part and parcel of a transformation of the Party's internal life, he called for "far-reaching changes, not only in the way we recruit people, but also in the way we treat one another".[1] Introducing the proposed rule changes to the Party's conference, Whitty expressed confidence that it would lead to a membership of 500,000 by the mid 1990s and then rapidly build towards a membership of one million by the end of the century.

The document put to the conference was prepared by an NEC membership development working group chaired by Eddie Haigh but really run by John Evans; other members included Gordon Colling, Diana Jeuda of USDAW, Larry Whitty, Joyce Gould and regional official John Braggins. They made much of a new procedure for endorsing membership applicants centrally at Walworth Road (instead of locally, through constituency parties) which, it was claimed, would speed up the recruitment process. In the end, the response time from Walworth Road was much longer than the delays created by local mismanagement.

The National Membership System was instituted in three phases. The first phase in 1989 allowed people for the first time to apply directly to head office at Walworth Road for membership. This was coupled with encouragement for members to pay by direct debit to Walworth Road, which would later send the constituency party its share of the fee. In the second phase, in 1990, constituencies would have to submit details of all their members to Walworth Road, which would reconcile these with its lists of direct debits and existing national members so that by the end of 1990 all members would be on a single national membership list. This would form the basis for phase three, beginning in January 1991, when all membership cards would be issued and all subscriptions would be collected centrally by Walworth Road. All this was approved by the 1988 conference despite the fact that notice of the necessary rule changes had only been published two weeks previously.

In January 1989 the campaign for a mass membership was launched by Neil Kinnock and Gordon Brown with a blitz of publicity, a party political broadcast, press advertisements, a promotional video and a host of glossy leaflets with the slogan "It's never been more important to join Labour. And it's never been easier." The leaflets depicted carefully chosen friendly faces saying things like "I'd hardly call myself a fanatic or an extremist. But I would call myself angry." Another more puzzlingly opined, "If this government refuses to take skills seriously, we can forget the future. Or join Labour."

After the initial fanfare, actual returns from the 1989 membership drive were disappointing. A report to the NEC Finance and General Purposes Sub-committee in May admitted that the scheme was not a success.[2] Generalized drives to recruit new members, apart from periodic adverts in the *Guardian*, were virtually abandoned. Instead, concentrated recruitment campaigns were organized in a handful of politically targeted constituencies, among them John Cunningham's Copeland, Tony Blair's

Sedgefield and the Newcastle East seat held by Nick Brown, a former GMB full-time official and now one of Labour's front-bench Treasury team.

The leadership recognized that it was vital to sustain the fiction of a successful membership campaign. It was announced in the summer of 1990 that the previous year had seen a 27,796 increase in membership, which was wrongly declared to be the first real increase since genuine membership records began in 1979 (in fact, there were increases in both 1983 and 1984). In the preceding two years the leadership's idea of a mass membership appeared to have changed. First a target of 1,000,000 members had been declared; then a doubling of the existing membership was promised; finally an increase of 10 per cent was hailed as a triumph.

In 1991 an increase in membership of just under 6 per cent was claimed. However, the figures used by Walworth Road to claim these increases in membership were based on the total number of names in its computer records, which included duplicates (people who had died or had changed addresses). They were not based on paid fees. If the Party really had the paying members it claimed, the income from their fees in 1990 should have been £1,127,000 instead of the £957,000 listed in the Party's accounts. A comparison of the published figures for membership in the various categories (full-rate, reduced, trade union) with the audited accounts indicates a gap between claimed and paid membership of at least 22,000 in 1989 and 42,000 in 1990. This gap has always existed, but the introduction of a national computer system should have closed, not opened it. Elsewhere in the 1990 NEC report to Labour's annual conference there is a reference to the names of "250,000 existing members" having to be fed into the computer. Given that the national advertising campaigns and the nationally organized local recruitment drives did succeed in bringing in 26,000 new members in 1990, this implied that some 30,000 existing members failed to renew their subscriptions in 1990. Two years later, after Kinnock's departure, it was announced by Walworth Road that the 1990 membership figure as previously published was indeed wildly inaccurate – but no explanation was offered.

Poor planning and technical problems dogged the new system from the start. Walworth Road issued an application form containing fifteen separate questions and clearly aimed at the credit-card-wielding classes. The previous year, before conference had even approved the scheme, the NEC authorized purchase of a computer system developed by Miller Technology to handle it. The Miller system had already been adopted by the steelworkers' union and the GMB. Since the trade unions were footing the bill, the unions' preference carried weight, but Computing for Labour, a mainly voluntary group of Labour-supporting computer experts, was critical of the Miller system, which it believed was neither

the cheapest not the most efficient available. In its opinion the membership project could better be carried through, at half the cost, using the
equipment the Party already owned.

Computing for Labour wrote to the NEC expressing its reservations
about the proposed purchase, and when the matter was raised at the July
1988 NEC Larry Whitty assured members that he would look into it.
Whitty then wrote an angry letter to Computing for Labour telling the
experts they should refrain from further interference in this matter. The
trade unions then forked out £250,000 for the Miller system.

Between 1988 and the introduction of the full National Membership
System in January 1991, the Labour Party, with the aid of the unions,
spent at least £840,000 on membership development and processing. All
this was before the system finally came on stream, with disastrous
consequences and even greater costs. First, the lists of existing members
submitted by constituency parties came in a welter of forms from card
indexes through notebooks to computer discs of varying formats. Less
than half the CLPs had submitted their records to Walworth Road by the
January 1st deadline and only a further 25 per cent had submitted them
two months later. Walworth Road blamed this on the constituencies.
However, when the new system had first been presented to the conference, increased back-up for hard-pressed local membership secretaries –
all volunteers, most operating without any computer aid – had been part
of the package. This back-up had never materialized. In its absence, it
was no surprise, given the number of constituencies no longer functioning with a full complement of officers, that membership returns to
Walworth Road were slow and incomplete.

The NEC admitted that Party officials had underestimated the amount
of work involved in inputting members' details into the computer
system, not to mention dealing with the supplementary additions and
corrections that came in from constituency parties. Walworth Road
argued that hardware and software were working well but that sheer
volume was creating problems. Since all long-standing members had
been arbitrarily assigned a subscription renewal date of January 1st a
system designed to issue reminders and collect subs on an even, year-
round basis became seriously overloaded at the very start. As a result it
took from January to March 1991 to deal with the first week's renewals.

Apparently no one had bothered to work out that correspondence
regarding membership would be received in large but irregular amounts
and that it would have to be answered in some systematic manner.
Instead it was allowed to pile up randomly so that an early payment or
simple query was often not rewarded with an answer for months on end.

Meanwhile, constituencies were waiting for Walworth Road to pay
them their share of the nationally collected subscriptions. They had no
idea which of their members had paid and which had not. When they did

receive the computer print-outs from Walworth Road many of the individuals listed as unpaid insisted that they had paid. Some CLPs had to borrow money to keep functioning and general election preparations were affected. Walworth Road was inundated with complaints. A letter was sent out in May 1991 apologizing for the mess. "It's not the system, it's the backlog," the letter claimed, pleading for activists' patience.

The administrative staff immediately responsible for operating the National Membership System cannot be blamed. They worked long hours of drudgery to try to correct faults for which they were not responsible. This, however, meant that the cost of the system escalated well beyond its original budget, nullifying any of the cash flow gains from the direct payment of subscriptions. Such was the chaos at Walworth Road that a large sum of money listed in 1991 Party accounts as donations was in fact received as membership fees the details of which had been lost.

Only a handful of 1991 membership cards were sent out in the first half of the year. In September, Walworth Road had to instruct constituencies that the previous year's membership cards would have to be used to determine eligibility to participate in the ballots for the 1991–92 NEC, conducted for the first time on a "one member one vote" basis. Indeed, tens of thousands of 1991 cards were still being sent out in early 1992, weeks and months after their expiry date. Many people who had paid their £10 in January 1991 were still receiving reminders to pay in November. Not surprisingly, there was considerable confusion at Party meetings about who was and who was not a member. In late 1991, Walworth Road, now panicked about the number of lapsed members, decided to extend the deadline for payment of 1991 subscriptions to the end of March 1992, thereby creating yet more confusion.

One small story will have to stand for thousands. In December 1990 a young man in south London decided that it was about time he joined the Labour Party. He filled in an application form and posted it off to Walworth Road before the New Year. For nine months he heard nothing and his local constituency remained in ignorance of his desire to join the Party. At last, in September, he was told how to get in touch with his local Party and received a membership card. He scrutinized the card – only to find that it gave the date of his first joining the Party as July 1968 – when he was two years old.

As the NEC acknowledged, the delays and inaccuracies "seriously undermined the credibility of the system". At the 1991 conference in Brighton, John Evans gave the Finance and General Purposes Sub-committee report immediately following the leader's speech. The media were outside the hall giving Labour celebrities their chance to laud Kinnock. The revealing scene inside the hall was not broadcast and barely reported in the press. From the platform, Evans claimed that all membership applications were now being dealt with within three weeks. This assertion was greeted by the same delegates who only moments before had dutifully cheered and applauded the leader with hoots of derision and cries of rage. Evans was accused of being "a liar" by one constituency membership secretary who had spent months trying to get Walworth Road to acknowledge his updated membership lists.

One after another delegates mounting the rostrum bore witness to the failures of the new system. Evans replied by accusing critics of being unfair to overworked and underpaid staff at Walworth Road. As several hecklers made plain, it was Evans himself and his "membership development working group" which was the object of their anger, not the clerical workers. Several delegates pointed out that the fundamental flaw in the system was that it had been built on mistrust – on a belief that local activists had to be by-passed, not consulted and included.

Shortly after the conference, Fraser Kemp, West Midlands regional organizer, sent a letter to all the CLP secretaries in his area thanking them for coping with the increased workload caused by the new membership scheme and asking them to take action to increase the level of payments. He enclosed data on the state of collection in the region, which revealed that with three-quarters of the year gone paid membership was only 53 per cent of what it had been the previous year. Only four of the region's fifty-eight CLPs had collected 70 per cent or more of last year's membership fees; only fifteen had reached 60 per cent or more and eighteen (mostly CLPs with Labour MPs) had collected less than 50 per cent. The long-term financial plans presented to the NEC in early 1992 by Larry Whitty were predicated on the basis of a much-reduced membership projection. The leadership seemed now to have resigned itself to a party with an ever-dwindling grass roots, kept afloat by state subsidies – to be introduced by an incoming Labour government.

Why did the National Membership System fail? And why has Labour still not built the mass base it so desperately needs? On the technical side, the leadership, unversed in computer technology, assumed that state-of-the-art hardware and software would solve all problems. They never grasped that the human element remains paramount. As a result, their plans were unrealistic and they failed to allocate the necessary resources. The ballyhoo surrounding the launch of the system made it difficult for full-time officers to admit to problems until it was too late.

The system was sold to the Party on the basis of a series of myths that fell apart when reality intruded: that people did not join because the existing membership did not want them or was uninviting; that it had been technically difficult to join or that local bureaucracy discouraged applicants; that the politics of local constituency Labour parties was too left-wing or too preoccupied with special interests or single issues of little interest to most Labour supporters; that a national appeal would inevitably be more attractive than a local one.

There was a grain of truth in some of these assertions, but the argument as a whole was disproved by the upshot of the leadership's efforts to by-pass local activists. The system's failure was due not merely to poor organization and lack of foresight, but to the politics that led to it being foisted upon the Party in the first place.

Traditionally people have joined the Labour Party as a result of contact with local campaigns on issues as diverse as traffic schemes and nuclear disarmament. They join the Party when they feel they can influence the local council through it or when it has helped to fight for a local library, school or swimming baths, when it has been part of a strike or anti-racist campaign. But it was precisely this kind of activity that was frowned upon by the Kinnock leadership and that in the two years prior to the introduction of the National Membership System had virtually ground to a halt. People who wanted to play an active, critical part in local or national politics or who wanted the benefits of unrestricted political debate decided they had better things to do with their time and money than give them to the Labour Party. Those who sympathized with Kinnock were happy to leave the job to him and could see no reason to join a Party whose members had been painted in such lurid colours by their own leadership. Others, including thousands who considered themselves socialists, were made to feel that their contribution was decidedly unwelcome.

Even among the remaining members, many gave up attending meetings or taking part in Party activities. This left the few who still came to meetings in one of two camps: either on the right, committed to the leadership and prepared to defend its every move, or on the left, hostile to the leadership and bitter at what it had done to the Party, but still hanging on out of deep political commitment and often sheer bloody-minded determination not to abandon the fight. As a result, in many areas local meetings, divided between these bitter opposing armies, became increasingly ugly and acrimonious, with a few undecided members ready to be swayed by arguments from either side.

In 1989, regional organizers took turns appearing before the NEC organization sub-committee to report on the state of the Party in their domains. They tried to make the best of a dismal show, but few could disguise the diminishing level of activism. In January a report from the eastern region, whose twenty-one full-time organizers (plus clerical and support staff) made it by far the best-serviced region in the country, noted:

> Morale at the grass roots remains poor and is having a marked effect . . . attendance at Party meetings has fallen since the general election with many constituencies now considering changing quorums to enable business to

continue . . . contributory causes include a lack of belief in our ability to win . . . uncertainty about policy.

Kinnock moved successfully that the report not be circulated and it was summarized in the official NEC minutes as "a good record of Party activity" despite "problems relating to morale and participation".[3]

Even after the opinion polls turned towards Labour in mid 1989, morale failed to pick up. By the following year reports were coming in from all over Britain of inquorate meetings at all levels, of defunct wards and of a dearth of volunteers to perform Party chores. In huge areas the local Labour Party had disappeared from public view. The newsletters, street stalls and meetings that had proliferated in the early and mid 1980s had vanished. Finding candidates to stand in local elections became difficult and the quality of Labour councillors declined precipitately. The Young Socialist groups and women's sections that had blossomed in the previous decade closed down.

The new, widened franchise for the selection of parliamentary candidates did not result in participation by greater numbers of Party members. Turnouts for the individual members' part of the electoral college were often below 20 per cent, even in safe Labour seats like Birmingham Hodge Hill and Erdington, where parliamentary selections were hotly contested. Participation in the NEC "one member one vote" ballots in the autumn of 1991 was abysmal. Many CLPs failed to register a vote at all and in hundreds of others fewer individual members cast votes than under the old system, where voting had been left to General Committee members. Even by the most generous estimate it is unlikely that more than 15 per cent of the membership took part in the election.

The geographical distribution of the Party's membership is highly uneven. Wales, with twenty-five Labour MPs, had only 20,000 members in 1990 while the south-west, with just one Labour MP and a smaller total population, had 18,000. The northern region, one of Labour's heartlands, also had 18,000 members, whereas the eastern region, with one Labour MP, had 25,000, about the same number as Scotland, Yorkshire and the West Midlands. The heavier the grip of the right-wing bureaucracy, the lower the proportional membership. The two regions with the largest membership were those where the left has been strongest, London and the north-west, with 55,000 and 38,000 respectively.

An increasing proportion of Party members pay the reduced rate for pensioners and unwaged people – up from 40 per cent in 1982 to 48 per cent just before the implementation of phase three of the National Membership System. In part, this reflects the relatively high membership fee the Party is now charging. When the £10 full rate was first mooted, traditionalist Labour MPs saw it as a proposal to price the working class out of the Labour Party. The move to increase that fee yet again to £15 from

1992 was greeted with even more dismay; it would add to the existing difficulties in recruiting and retaining members and make Labour membership even more middle class. Partly because of the increased fee, the working-class membership of the Party has become largely a mixture of the elderly, the unemployed, part-time workers and full-time parents.

Between December 1989 and April 1990 Patrick Seyd, of Sheffield University, and a group of researchers carried out a survey of the Party membership in co-operation with Walworth Road. They scrutinized over 5,000 completed postal questionnaires coming from all the Party's regions. An edited version of their findings was published in *Labour Party News* in autumn 1990. This revealed that the Party was by no means dominated by middle-class yuppies: while 14 per cent of the membership had household incomes of above £30,000 a year, 16 per cent had incomes of below £5,000 per year. The authors of the study concluded that there was a stark social divide among the membership.

But the version of the survey published in *Labour Party News* left out a number of revealing findings, which were also withheld from Labour's NEC. Among the facts that officials at Walworth Road decided to keep hidden from the membership and its elected representatives were the following:

- 65 per cent of members agreed that "the central question of British politics is the class struggle between labour and capital"
- 60 per cent thought "the Labour Party should always stand by its principles even if this should lose an election"
- 81 per cent thought "the public enterprises privatized by the Tory government should be returned to the public sector"
- 72 per cent thought "workers should be prepared to strike in support of other workers, even if they don't work in the same place"
- 80 per cent thought a future Labour government should cut defence expenditure
- 68 per cent favoured a non-nuclear defence policy (non-attenders at Party meetings were even keener on this than activists).

In answer to the question "Do you think Neil Kinnock will stick to his principles?" the majority said no; support for non-nuclear defence was 13 per cent higher among women than among men and support for withdrawal from Ireland was 30 per cent higher; women were also proportionally more critical of Neil Kinnock and more supportive of Tony Benn.

Perhaps, then, it really is true, as the Kinnock leadership liked to claim, that the activists are "unrepresentative" of the members; if so, it is just that they are "unrepresentative" in a different way: they hold positions, or at least vote for resolutions, somewhat to the right of those preferred by the members at large.

Of course, there can be no doubt that much of Labour's membership despaired of left politics as the Thatcherite decade wore on. And many of the activists who had identified with the left became suspicious and even hostile to it as they sought desperately for an electoral solution to the grim daily problems of Labour supporters. The leadership's attacks on the left did have resonance, which was why they were successful. And yet if you ask Party members not what they think the public wants to hear, not what they believe will win elections, not what policy they think is judicious for the Party to adopt, but what they themselves believe in their hearts, they still give socialist answers.

The Kinnock leadership presided over the virtual collapse of the Party organization in many localities and left the Party with the lowest individual Labour membership in decades. Yet in two critical respects the bedrock of the Labour Party has not been altered. First, it remains financially and organizationally dependent on a huge but passive trade union affiliated membership. Second, the bulk of its members remain to the left of the parliamentary leadership and, however demoralized by successive defeats or mesmerized by the quick fixes offered by the leadership, committed to socialist ideals. These twin pillars of the Labour Party – the unions and the constituency activists – also remain its two principal resources. It is not until these two forces are fused and activated that the Party will be able to recruit a real mass membership and through it begin to solve its organizational, financial and political weaknesses.

Notes

1. *Labour Party News* September–October 1988.
2. NEC Finance and General Purposes Sub-committee minutes May 1989.
3. NEC Organization Sub-committee minutes January 1989.

Index

Gilbert, John 243
Gilby, Bill 68, 184
Gillespie, Bob 104
Gladwin, Derek 7, 152, 158, 213
Glasgow Govan by-election 103-4
Godman, Norman 187, 190, 197
Godsiff, Roger 75, 153-5, 298
Golding, John 26, 38, 46; and 1983
    campaign 28, 29, 34, 149; and TULV 149,
    150
Gorbachev, Mikhail 70, 242, 245, 252
Gordon, Mildred 125
Goss, Sue 181
Gould, Bryan 127-30; and Gulf War 197;
    and Kinnock 110, 115; and left
    realignment 68; and LCC 183; and media
    strategy 215, 216; and 1987 campaign 78,
    80-81, 83, 94-5, 96-7, 242, 244; and 1992
    campaign 309, 315; and poll tax 314; in
    shadow cabinet 126, 137; and Tribune
    125; and unilateralism 251-2, 253, 254,
    256; mentioned 114
Gould, Joyce: and Kinnock 117; and
    Lambeth Council 283-90 passim; and
    Liverpool party 291, 294, 295; and
    membership campaign 327; and 1983
    campaign 28; and 1987 campaign 80;
    and 1992 campaign 316; and selection
    disputes 153-4, 265, 267, 274, 275; and
    Socialist Organiser 277-9
Gould, Philip: and Kinnock 117, 118; and
    media strategy 84, 210; and 1992
    campaign 316, 318
Grant, Bernie 76, 125, 266
Grant, Nick 30-31
Grantham, Roy 24, 150, 160, 161
Greater London Council 29
Green, Roy 114
Greenwich by-election 71-4
Grice, Andrew 212, 219
Guardian 41, 60, 65, 72, 111, 115, 116, 117,
    182, 183, 190, 206, 212, 230-31, 242, 243,
    256, 267, 268, 280, 285, 287, 291, 327; and
    Mandelson 219, 221

Hadden, Alan 57, 60, 161
Haigh, Eddie; and membership campaign
    327; and selection disputes 267, 268, 274,
    276; and unilateralism 252, 253, 254
Hain, Peter 62, 169; and LCC 166, 171-2,
    176, 181
Haines, Joe 110, 219, 221
Hall, Julie 118, 228, 229; and 1992 campaign
    308, 310, 311, 318
Hall, Stuart 64; (with Martin Jacques) The
    Politics of Thatcherism 63
Hammond, Eric 55, 60
Hammond, Lesley 287
Hanna, Vincent 73

Hanson, Keith 152-3
Harman, Harriet 68, 118, 127, 256
Hart, Judith 24, 28
Hattersley, Roy: and Black Sections 76;
    and Capstick 107; challenge to, and LCC
    176-7; Choose Freedom 101; on defence
    policy 237, 242, 250; and deputy
    leadership, contest for 40-42, 132, 133;
    and Kinnock 137-8; and Labour
    leadership, contest for 36, 37, 39-40, 42,
    47; and left 72, 170; and media 206, 231;
    and miners' strike 50, 54; at 1980
    conference 15; in 1983 campaign 26, 28,
    31, 34; in 1987 campaign 78, 79-80, 81-2;
    in 1992 campaign 305, 307; and Policy
    Review 216; and purges 294; and
    selection disputes 267, 268, 274, 281; in
    shadow cabinet 48, 126, 142; mentioned
    323
Hatton, Derek 82
Havers, Michael 241
Hayter, Diane 75
Hayward, Ron 16, 19, 117
Heal, Sylvia 255
Healey, Denis: election of, to deputy
    leadership 16, 17-24, 37, 40, 41, 143; and
    Gulf War 189; at 1980 conference 9; in
    1983 campaign 26-34 passim; in 1987
    campaign 80; in shadow cabinet 48; and
    unilateralism 26, 234, 236, 238, 244, 249;
    mentioned 171
Healy, Gerry 118
Heath, Ted 188, 193, 302
Heathfield, Peter 62, 106
Heffer, Eric: challenge for deputy
    leadership 102, 133, 144, 160; death of
    292; and Gulf War 186, 187; and Kinnock
    22, 23; and Labour leadership 38, 39; and
    LCC 172, 176, 177; and miners' strike 49,
    52, 54, 55, 57; on NEC 42, 119; and 1983
    campaign 28; in shadow cabinet 48; and
    soft left 67; and Tribune Group 21
Heller, Richard 243
Heseltine, Michael 7
Hewitt, Patricia 112-13; and Kinnock 7, 45,
    110, 112-13, 118, 124; and left
    realignment 65; and LCC 169; and
    "loony left" 74, 76; and media 208; and
    miners' strike 56; at 1980 conference 7,
    13; and 1987 campaign 80-81, 82, 83-4;
    and 1992 campaign 315, 316, 319; and
    policy 114
Hill, David 132; and media strategy 225,
    230, 231; and 1992 campaign 315, 316,
    318, 320
Hill, Keith 155, 286, 290
Hitchens, Peter 310
Hobsbawm, Eric 34, 64